D1556972

THE OCTAVIUS OF
MARCUS MINUCIUS FELIX

Ancient Christian

Writers

THE WORKS OF THE FATHERS IN TRANSLATION

EDITED BY

JOHANNES QUASTEN   WALTER J. BURGHARDT

THOMAS COMERFORD LAWLER

No. 39

THE OCTAVIUS OF
MARCUS MINUCIUS FELIX

TRANSLATED AND ANNOTATED

BY

G. W. CLARKE

Professor of Classical Studies
University of Melbourne

NEWMAN PRESS

New York, N.Y./Ramsey, N.J.

BR
65
.M523
O2513
1974
c.1

COPYRIGHT 1974
BY
REV. JOHANNES QUASTEN
AND
REV. WALTER J. BURGHART, S.J.
AND
THOMAS COMERFORD LAWLER

Library of Congress
Catalog Card Number: 74-75994

ISBN: 0-8091-0189-0

PUBLISHED BY PAULIST PRESS
Editorial Office: 1865 Broadway, New York, N.Y. 10023
Business Office: 545 Island Road, Ramsey, N.J. 07446

PRINTED AND BOUND IN THE UNITED STATES OF AMERICA

CONTENTS

THE OCTAVIUS OF
MARCUS MINUCIUS FELIX

INTRODUCTION

TESTIMONIA

T.1. Minucius Felix, in his book entitled the *Octavius*, argued that Saturn, on his arrival in Italy after he had been expelled by his son, was said to be a son of Heaven (Caelus). This was so because it is our custom to say that those who have arrived unexpectedly or whose qualities we admire "have fallen from heaven." On the other hand, he was also said to be a son of earth because "sons of earth" is a name we give to those whose parentage is unknown.
    Lact. *Div. inst.* 1.11.55 (ML 6.180); cf. *Oct.* 23.12.

T.2. It so happens that wisdom and truth demand suitable spokesmen—and of those men of letters who have devoted themselves to this cause not one has proved to be perfect for its defense. 22. Of those writers that I know Minucius Felix was an advocate of no mean standing. His book, entitled the *Octavius*, testifies what a suitable champion of the truth he would have been had he devoted himself entirely to this task. 23. Septimius Tertullian, too, was skilled in every type of literature, but his pen was too facile, he wrote with inadequate attention to style, and he was highly obscure. And so, not even he became sufficiently well known. 24. Accordingly, the one outstanding famous name has been that of Cyprian; he had earned for himself a considerable reputation in his profession of the orator's art and he composed a very large volume of works notable of their kind.

Lact. *Div. inst.* 5.1.21 ff. (ML 6.551).

T.3. Minucius Felix, an outstanding advocate of Rome, wrote a dialogue entitled the *Octavius,* in which a Christian and a pagan debate. There is also in circulation under his name another work entitled *The Problem of Fate* or *The Case against Astrology;* although it, too, is the work of an able writer, it does not seem to me to harmonize in style with the former book. Lactantius also mentions this Minucius in his writings.

Jerome *De viris illust.* 58 (ML 23.706); cf. *Oct.* 36.2.

T.4. I will not mention the Latin writers—Tertullian, Cyprian, Minucius, Victorinus, Lactantius, Hilary; otherwise I may appear not so much to be defending myself as to be attacking others.

Jerome *Ep.* 49.13 (ML 22.502).

T.5. (Nepotian) was held to be very learned: that nostrum, he would say, was Tertullian's, this one Cyprian's; another saying came from Lactantius, a further from Hilary; this was a phrase to be found in Minucius Felix, in Victorinus, that was a quotation from Arnobius.

Jerome *Ep.* 60.10 (ML 22.595).

T.6. I shall now deal with the Latin authors. Could you find anything more learned than Tertullian, more to the point? His *Apology* and his *Books against the Pagans* include all the learning of this world. And consider Minucius Felix, an advocate of the Roman courts. In his book en-

titled the *Octavius* and in his other one called *The Case against Astrology* (if, indeed, the authorship ascribed is correct) did he leave any of the pagan writings untouched?
Jerome *Ep.* 70.5 (ML 22.668).

T.7. Let it be clear that we are writing for serious inquirers who are anxious to know their holy Scripture; we are not writing for the highbrows who are squeamish about points of detail—if they want the stream of eloquence, if they want elegant compositions, let them read Cicero, Quintilian, Gallio, Gabinianus, and to cite from our own writers, Tertullian, Cyprian, Minucius, Arnobius, Lactantius, Hilary.
Jerome *Comm. in Isaiam proph.* 8 praef. (ML 24.281).

T.8. And when am I going to enumerate those authors widely acclaimed for their eloquence—Lactantius, Minucius, Cyprian, Hilary, John, Ambrose—from that roll call of multitudinous writers?
Eucherius *Ep. paraenetica ad Valer.* (ML 50.719).

PREFATORY

The *Octavius* of Marcus Minucius Felix is a document that has survived from antiquity by lucky chance. In the sixteenth century the superintendent of the Vatican Library got possession somehow of a finely written ninth-century manuscript of Arnobius' *Adversus nationes;* it appeared to be in eight books and was first published as such in 1543.[1] It was not till some seventeen years later that a French lawyer and scholar, Baudouin, in a very able dissertation, proved beyond doubt that the eighth book was not by Arnobius at all.[2] Instead of the title being *Octavus* (eighth), it should have been *Octavius*, and it was then shown from the ancient *testimonia* to be a lost work by Minucius Felix. The only other surviving manuscript is an eleventh-century copy, similarly of Arnobius and the *Octavius* together, which is demonstrably directly descended from the ninth-century manuscript.[3]

The ancient *testimonia* are indeed few in number; they are, however, sufficiently detailed to settle the question of authorship. Writing in the early fourth century, Lactantius begins the fifth book of the *Divine Institutes* (*De iustitia*) with an apologia for his undertaking the work; previous Latin writers have not been perfectly equal to the task. Among these figures is Minucius Felix, described as an advocate of some standing; his book, entitled the *Octavius*, he snidely observes, shows what a suitable champion of the truth he might have been, had he devoted himself entirely to the task (T.2). Elsewhere in the same work (T.1) Lactantius has occasion to give an account of various legends attached to Jupiter and to Saturn, and in the course of this account paraphrases, with acknowledgment, the story given in the *Octavius* of Minucius Felix. This refers to chapter 23.12 of the dialogue. The two passages close the question of attribution.

Writing almost a century later, St. Jerome mentions the writings of Minucius Felix on five occasions (T.3-7), on four of which, it will be readily observed, the name of Minucius Felix occurs in enumerations of those Latin writers belonging to the Christian following who could rival in literary merit the stylistic and rhetorical models of paganism. But Minucius Felix' work is not merely a literary tour de force; Jerome also goes on to tell us (T.5) that assiduous reading of his writings and those of other Latin authors (including Jerome's own!), together with long periods of contemplation, helped to make the heart of Nepotian a veritable *bibliotheca Christi* ("a library of Christ").

The *Octavius* appears to have been the only genuine work of Minucius Felix; a treatise *De fato vel Contra mathematicos* attributed to him, Jerome considered spurious on stylistic grounds (T.3, T.6).[4] It does not survive. Jewish and Christian antiquity is rich in pseudepigraphic production; so an unauthentic piece would not be altogether a surprise, though one does wonder whether Minucius Felix was sufficiently well known to provide suitable authorship for a spurious work.[5] St. Augustine, for example, appears to be unaware of his existence.[6] On the other hand, St. Eucherius, bishop of Lyons in the second quarter of the fifth century, did know of him; he is mentioned in a literary catalogue (T.8)[7] of Christian *clarissimi facundia*, similar to those in Jerome and very possibly borrowed from him. But despite the ability, rather grudgingly acknowledged by Lactantius, and the literary polish and spiritual value, freely admitted by Jerome, the *Octavius* appears to have been little noticed from the fifth century until the sixteenth-century publication.[8] Some explanation for this is suggested below.

So much for the *oeuvre*. Now for its author.

The Author and His Time of Writing

On the testimony of Lactantius (T.2) and Jerome (T.3, T.6), Minucius Felix had been a prominent advocate who had practiced at the Roman bar. According to the prologue of the *Octavius* itself, Minucius Felix had availed himself of the traditional autumn legal vacation to journey from Rome with his two friends, a fellow convert to Christianity, Octavius Januarius, and the hitherto unconverted Caecilius Natalis, to the seaside resort and port of Rome at Ostia on the Tiber's mouth. There, on the shore near open sea-baths, after a leisurely debate (it lasted from dawn till dusk) the erstwhile pagan Caecilius finally declared himself convinced and converted.[9]

The sceptical may suspect that Lactantius and Jerome (who, as he avers, had read the notices of Lactantius) may have culled some, if not all, of their information about Minucius' profession and provenance ultimately from the text of the *Octavius* itself, but it still remains clear that if the details of the dialogue can be taken as autobiographical —and there is really nothing else to go on—the domicile of Minucius Felix was Rome, his professional milieu the Roman legal Forum. The same can, accordingly, be said of Caecilius Natalis, for he is described as being constantly at the side of Minucius Felix, both at home and in public;[10] whatever his origins or family associations,[11] he was at the time clearly resident at Rome and accompanied Minucius in his forensic activities there. Octavius, though living away from Rome,[12] and being merely on a visit to the Capital, had had a professional legal career[13] as well, and he had spent, whether at Rome or elsewhere we are not told, a great deal of his life in the company of Minucius.[14]

Such is the legal—and Christian—company Minucius Felix describes himself as keeping in Rome. The question to what extent this setting and description, and this company, represent literary fiction or historical fact is a difficult one to answer briefly.

As for the setting, there are some suggestions or allusions in the text which might imply special knowledge of, or interest in, not so much Rome, where Minucius describes himself as being resident, as Africa; but such references cannot be decisive alone for establishing an African environment for Minucius Felix.[15] Many of the allusions could, however, readily be derived from other authorities possessed of such knowledge or interest (e.g., Tertullian).[16] But certainly, an *ultimately* African provenance for a writer composing in the Latin tongue would make sound literary sense in the context of Rome's cultural history of the late second and third centuries A.D.; generally speaking, Greek was the favored medium of expression elsewhere (and even Tertullian wrote in Greek also). The existence of North African inscriptions of Minucii Felices should not, however, be overstressed for this question of provenance; they signify little.[17]

But the *Octavius* is composed in clear and direct imitation of Cicero.[18] Ciceronian practice ought, therefore, to be relevant. And while Cicero might openly compose speeches in his dialogues *honoris causa*, the characters to whom he assigned them were undeniably historical.[19] The proper course is, therefore, to conclude that while the debate at Ostia in the *Octavius* is, in all probability, pure literary contrivance, the protagonists of that debate and the few biographical facts assigned to those protagonists are not. Minucius Felix, we should assume, though very possibly possessing an African background or at least connections, practiced law at Rome.

We can thus trace some elements to suggest—but really we have no more than that—that Minucius Felix may have gravitated from his native province of (say) Africa Proconsularis (where Christianity was rather unusually strong) to the centre of Rome, with the intention of making his fortune in the Roman Forum, like many another rhetorically trained provincial. That at least makes a credible picture consonant with our data, though it is not one precisely established by them.

When was Minucius Felix so practicing law in Rome? This is a perplexing problem which has excited an unending debate.[20] Much of this debate has been needlessly vituperative and repetitious, and many scholars have insisted on adhering to patently perverse doctrines,[21] but even so, the terms of the debate are clear enough:

1) Are there any internal indications in the text which openly allude to, or imply a reference to, contemporary or near contemporary writings or historical events?

2) Failing a conclusive answer to (1), was the work composed before or after Tertullian's *Apology* (and *Ad nationes*), i.e., c. 197 A.D.?[22]

3) If after, before or after Cyprian (d. 258 A.D.)?

4) If after, how long before Lactantius (and possibly Arnobius[23]), the first authority to refer directly to the *Octavius* in the early fourth century?

Categorical answers to many of these questions are inappropriate when the solution to them so frequently lies in the detailed, and often necessarily subjective, examination and comparison of parallel texts. But one can allow oneself the luxury of being categorical on the first question. Internal evidence merely indicates that the work was composed after that speech of Fronto which included an attack on Christian mores (9.6): Fronto died perhaps as late as the second half of the 170's. And the most reasonable judgment on the other questions is that the *Octavius* was composed after 197 A.D. (the approximate date of Tertullian's compositions) and before Cyprian began his career as a patristic writer (c. 248 A.D.). That is to say, the *Octavius* is a document of Severan Rome. The basis on which these judgments are made is as follows.

Concerning the first question, some have attempted to find certain allusions to contemporary history in the *Octavius* at 2.3,[24] 2.4 and 22.1,[25] 7.4[26] and 18.6.[27] However, none of these attempts can be made to bear any weight at all. On the literary side, others have purported to trace dependence of Minucius Felix on Aulus Gellius' *Noctes Atticae* (and have proposed a publication date as late as c. 180 A.D. for that work). Neither the late publication date[28] nor the dependence[29] is an established proposition. A similar agnostic conclusion, both as to dependence and certainly as to date, could obtain for the *Oration* of Tatian equally well,[30] and the endeavor to claim Clement of Alexandria as a direct source must be likewise abandoned.[31] There remains, therefore, by elimination, the allusion to Fronto, which merely establishes a *terminus a quo* of c. 140 A.D.–c. 175 A.D. (the approximate span of Fronto's prominence in public life). The actual date of composition might be appreciably later.

And so we must address ourselves to the second question, viz., the relationship of the *Octavius* to Tertullian's *Apology* and *Ad nationes* (c. 197 A.D.), for there are many closely parallel phrases, clauses, and arguments in Tertullian's two early works of apologetics and the *Octavius:* direct interdependence between these works is, therefore, on any reasonable count,[32] certain. In many passages it is proper to admit—though many scholars are reluctant to appear to be so uncommitted—that either author might have phrased the prior version,[33] but there is a sufficient number of instances where considerations of logic and inherent probability argue strongly for the priority of Tertullian's text.[34] It should, however, be observed that no supporting chronological indication can be safely drawn from the (variable) order in which Minucius Felix, Tertullian, Cyprian, etc. are listed by Lactantius and Jerome.[35] Jerome's order appears to be frankly erratic[36] and Lactantius' (T.2) can be reasonably construed as that of merit and importance. And the paucity of other contemporary metrical Latin prose, as well as the vagaries of an author's own taste and difference in models, should make one sceptical about supporting arguments drawn from the rhythmical *clausulae* of the *Octavius* vis-à-vis those of Tertullian; these arguments have also been invoked in the context of the priority question,[37] but their force is rather nugatory. However, a *terminus post* c. 197 A.D. for the *floruit* of Minucius Felix and for the composition of the *Octavius* still seems to be a reasonable conclusion.

But how long after 197 A.D.? That brings us to our third question, for one *terminus ante* that has been not infrequently advocated is that of Cyprian.[38] In this regard the antipagan tractate *Quod idola dii non sint*, attributed on the authority of Jerome and Augustine[39] to the hand of Cyprian, is perhaps best eliminated from the discussion; it certainly manifests a close literal imitation of certain sections of the *Octavius*, but its attribution to Cyprian has been thought to be of weak foundation (it does not, for example, figure in the catalogue of Cyprian's *opera* drawn up by his biographer Pontius[40]) and a good case can be argued—if not proven—for a post-Lactantian date for its composition.[41] There is, therefore, at least room for doubt that it is authentically Cyprianic. There are, however, in addition, a scatter of possible echoes that might be traced in some certainly genuine opuscules of Cyprian: in, for example, *Ad Donatum, Ad Demetrianum, De lapsis, De habit. virg., De bono patient.*, and in two of his epistles.[42] Many of these purported reminiscences are in fact very faint, if indeed they are not to be termed fanciful, and the extent of rhetorical clichés on a common theme ought not to be underestimated, as in these matters it often is, especially for this period of Latin literature;[43] but there is at least one reminiscence that, in the light of our surviving evidence, appears to be probant, viz., *De bono patient.* 3 (ML 4.623) and *Oct.* 38.6 (see n. 664 *ad loc.*), and there are others where imitation seems highly plausible, e.g., *Ad Donat.* 1 (ML 4.193 ff.) and *Oct.* 2.3 f. As the scatter of probable reminiscences is so widely spread over a number of Cyprian's writings, it is much more feasible to presume that Cyprian recalled, on odd occasions, his reading of Minucius Felix rather than vice versa (the attempts by Beaujeu, Intro. lxx ff., to find internal support for this thesis—claiming priority for the phraseology of Minucius Felix—are somewhat strained and indecisive). One may conclude, therefore, that a date before Cyprian began his career as a patristic writer (and composed the *Ad Donatum*) is not without plausibility, though the nature of the evidence does not allow one to be categorical on the issue.[44] Such a conclusion would certainly be consonant with the markedly nonbelligerent tone of the *Octavius.* It was composed, it would seem, in a period of comparative peace for the Church—which the Church did enjoy for most of the first half of the third century.[45] We will not be far wrong, therefore, in placing the *floruit* of Minucius

Felix as a practicing advocate at Rome, and as the writer of the *Octavius*, within the first third of the third century.

The Literary Setting

Now some words about the literary background of this period which may help to explain the composition of the *Octavius*.

If, in the early third century of our era or thereabouts, a man of culture and education were to try to purchase a copy of the Sacred Scriptures at the regular bookstalls in Rome, he would pretty surely have found them unobtainable.[46] There was no supply because the general reading-public of the day created no demand for them. The question to pose is, why should this have been the case?

At this time the cultivated man of letters admired classical models; he read them, enjoying with sensitivity their verbal felicity, their elegant rhetorical flourishes, their neat format, the cunning elaboration of the rules of their genres. As a person trained in the arts of rhetoric, he was excessively interested in the techniques of fine writing. And Aulus Gellius, writing about the mid-second century,[47] admirably shows what intense interest might be devoted to questions of linguistics, especially etymology, to grammatical niceties, and to antiquarian vocabulary (though Aulus Gellius was not himself above innovating vocabulary, in careful proportion, also; there was a certain taste for novelty as well as for rarity[48]). And Aulus Gellius' contemporary, Cornelius Fronto, was especially renowned for his heavy insistence on the search for the *mot juste*, the special (and the often archaic) word.[49]

As for the content, too, the reader was happy if it reflected past reading and not necessarily contemporary reality; he preferred the material to be familiar, traditional; great enjoyment was derived from the literary game of recognizing allusions, echoes, cross references, arguments deftly rephrased from classical authorities of the past, or from their Greek predecessors. To be well versed in quotable quotations was part of the education, and hence of the literature, of an age flourishing in miscellanies, florilegia, and doxographical collections. Aulus Gellius actually lists some thirty titles given to such collections already in use in his day, and he tells us that there were more titles to consider when he was searching for a name for his own assortment.[50] (The Christian writers were, of course, of this mind as well. They clearly employed not only general *aides-mémoire* of this sort;[51] they also used handbooks of biblical quotations for their purposes.[52] Thus Irenaeus and Justin, in the second century, both erroneously attribute a biblical passage to Isaiah instead of to Numbers: it may have been the fault of an inaccurate compilation which they both used.[53])

This general attitude of mind towards both the form and the content of literature is neatly illustrated by Fronto when he lists the homework activities of a pupil being trained in rhetoric. Apart from composition, they are (1) the delivery of set speeches from memory, (2) the search for special words, (3) the elaboration of synonymous phrases, and (4) the turning of Greek models into Latin.[54]

Now the Christian Scriptures failed to provide enjoyment for men of such tastes, as regards both material and style. The material lacked the authority and the appeal of antiquity—as A. D. Nock observes, "at the time a most damaging criticism of Christianity—namely, that it was a

14 INTRODUCTION

new thing followed in contravention of good old customs.
The Jewish writer said in weariness of spirit, 'There is
nothing new under the sun.' Most thinking citizens of the
Empire would have resented this suggestion that there
could be."[55] Earlier, in the Republic, Cicero in the *De
natura deorum*[56] had presented the classical case for the
validity of Roman religion based simply and explicitly on
the authority of its antiquity, the *auctoritas maiorum*.
Characteristically, the Emperor Augustus is reported
(Suet. *Aug.* 93) as having treated "with great respect such
foreign rites as were ancient and well established, but held
the rest in contempt,"[57] and later Tacitus,[58] who obviously
disliked Jews, was quite prepared to admit in mitigation
that their religious practices were justified by their antiquity (*antiquitate defenduntur*). Hence Jewish apologetic
literature displays an anxiety to establish beyond question
the antiquity, and indeed the priority, of the religious
views and rites of the Jewish people. For example, there
are preserved in the fragments of Alexander Polyhistor
the attempts of various Hellenized Jews to show that the
Jewish culture was the oldest in the world and that the
Jews had, therefore, really taught other people.[59] Another
example is to be found in the late first century[60] when
Josephus wrote two apologetic books, nowadays entitled
the *Contra Apionem;* their original and more informative
title was *On the Antiquity of the Jews.*[61] Their main purpose is simply to refute charges of the modernity of the
Jewish religion (esp. 1.58 ff.) and to establish the existence
of the Jewish race prior to the age of Homer, who is emphasized as being the most ancient surviving work of
Greek literature (1.12). This deficiency in the authority

and the appeal of antiquity explains why the Christian apologists go to such extraordinarily desperate, and unconvincing, lengths to establish the antiquity of their religious beliefs. Justin, Tatian, Theophilus, all Greek Christian apologists of the second century, are quite preoccupied with this task. Thus Plato—and Homer, and the Sophists generally—are soberly and painstakingly made out to be nothing but Atticized Moses,[62] a theory, if not a formulation, of Jewish provenance.[63] This is proved by establishing the priority of Moses (in Tatian and Theophilus by rather outlandish chronological tables[64]); Plato and company, then, must either be receivers of the Spermatic Word[65] or be derivative from Moses via Egyptian sources,[66] Plato traditionally having visited Egypt;[67] it was only fear of the hemlock cup which prevented Plato from acknowledging his debt.[68] Later, even Augustine at one stage (*De doct. christ.* 2.28) actually ventured the belief that Plato had seen Jeremiah in Egypt and had read the Septuagint— a theory of derivation which he prudently was to abandon subsequently on sound chronological grounds (*De civ. Dei* 8.11).

There were other somewhat parallel lines of approach towards this same end. The testimony of the "Sibyl," for example, who was credited with having foretold the coming of Christ, is frequently exploited; she is carefully declared to be "most ancient and extremely old."[69] And there is the remarkable passage in Arnobius (*Adv. nat.* 1.38) where Christ is virtually represented as another Epicurus; following closely the eulogy of Epicurus by Lucretius, Arnobius gives Him a teaching programme which basically consists of cosmogony and cosmology, of physics and metaphysics. Christ thus appears as the father of a school who devoted His life largely to giving lectures to His disciples.[70]

The point of importance is that these writers are all desperately striving to establish the authority and the appeal of the biblical message. It had to have a respectably antique pedigree.

The importance they attached to this point is probably best exemplified by Theophilus. The programme which he announces at the beginning of his third book of apology is this (c. 4): to refute charges made against Christianity. And the charges are (1) promiscuous immorality, (2) incest, (3) cannibalism, (4) modernity of doctrine.

The pagans were clearly unconvinced by their arguments. In his polemic against Christianity (written probably towards the close of the second century[71]) Celsus makes a great deal of the opposite point of view—the Christians lack the authority of antiquity; and those teachings of theirs which happen to resemble traditional religious or eschatological beliefs have been plagiarized from the non-Christian cultural tradition,[72] and distorted in the plagiarism at that. For Celsus, it is axiomatic that nothing can be both new and true (*C. Cels.* 4.14). Later, Arnobius' pagans were to assert the corollary, that their literature carried credence and truth *because* it was the more ancient.[73]

If the material of the Sacred Scriptures was thus an obstacle to pleasurable reading because of what was considered to be its novelty and its untraditional character, the style in which they were couched was an insuperable barrier. The holy books to a man of education were plainly uncouth and barbaric, written (by this time) in a Latin

which grated on the sensibilities of a person bred on
Ennius and Cato, or Cicero and Vergil.[74] Good examples
of the sort of translation available are to be found in the
quotations of Scripture embedded in the Latin version of
Clement's *Letter to the Corinthians*.[75] The quotations are
perhaps to be dated to the mid-second century.[76] The
vocabulary would have been quite offensive to one con-
versant with polite letters in the Latin world: calques,
foreignisms (Greek and, occasionally, Hebrew), theological neologisms, vulgarisms clearly pockmarked the
pages of the biblical text available at the time. Not only
that, morphology reveals extreme vulgarity and, further,
the translator(s) scrupulously and respectfully endeavored
to keep very close to the sacred word; perhaps they were
in this under Jewish influence.[77] The result of all this is an
extreme literalism, an almost interlinear version, many
Grecisms, and altogether a very bizarre and exotic Latin
syntax (*Quäker-Latein*, to use a phrase of A. A. T. Ehrhardt), quite unacceptable to the sophisticated and conservative Latinist.[78]

The reader of such a Latin biblical translation would
have found, in vocabulary, ugly neologisms devised to
match the original Greek, e.g., *propter maletractationem*
(16.7) to parallel διὰ τὸ κεκακῶσθαι; in morphology, incorrect forms, tainted by false analogies, e.g., *perient*
(12.6) and *doceam* (57.4). And there are, in syntax, puz-
zling and anomalous Latin constructions; e.g., *os tuum abun-
davit maliciam* (35.8) and *quod non possunt sibi adiuvare*
(39.5); they are to be explained by reference to the Greek
original (ἐπλεόνασεν κακίαν and ἑαυτοῖς βοηθῆσαι). And so
on. No wonder Tertullian, at the very end of the second
century, could exclaim: "Men are so far from accepting

our Scriptures, no one approaches them unless he is already a Christian."[79]

A century later the situation appears to be unaltered. Early in the fourth century or thereabouts,[80] Arnobius wrote the seven books of his *Adversus nationes* to answer all the objections that could be urged against Christianity. Among many other things (he reports), the opponents of Christianity assert that the Evangelists do not deserve ready credence because they are ignorant, simple folk;[81] their language is crude and vulgar;[82] the Christian writings are filled with barbarisms and solecisms, and are marred and disfigured with faults.[83] Arnobius proceeds quite seriously to undertake the refutation of these and other charges: for example, errors in number, case, preposition, participle, conjunction;[84] and he goes to some length to defend the confusion of grammatical genders to be found in Christian letters.[85] The point of importance is that men were serious in making such objections and in meeting them. For this passage in the *Adversus nationes* cannot be merely due to Arnobius' professional interests as a teacher of rhetoric.[86] It is no isolated example, and parallel passages of this sort of refutation might be cited from, *inter alios*, Clement of Alexandria,[87] Tertullian,[88] and Pseudo-Justin.[89]

This impression is also confirmed by the witness of Arnobius' pupil, Lactantius. The burden of his complaint is twofold. Firstly, his audience. Among the *sapientes*, *docti*, and *principes huius saeculi* nothing is read unless it is polished and fluent; such people are impressed by words only if they charm with sweet sounds; they will believe nothing to be true unless it is pleasant to hear, gives enjoyment, and is artificially adorned.[90] In the sacred books, however, the prophets use common and unsophisticated speech[91] as if addressing the ordinary people; the books, therefore, are considered by the *sapientes* etc. to be *anilia, inepta, vulgaria* because of their inelegance (*sordida videntur*). And then there are the Christian writers. Biblical exegetes fail to carry weight on the grounds that they are *aut omnino rudes, aut certe parum docti.*[92] And the Latin apologists, he goes on to say, despite notable exceptions (especially Cyprian), have generally failed to bring to the defense of the cause of truth the necessary battery of literary flourish and adornment, persuasiveness and subtlety of argument, learning and the verve of enthusiastic polemic.[93]

Lactantius has also at times a counterattack to this criticism of the biblical crudity of style: God, he declares, expressly caused the Scriptures to be plain and unadorned in style so that all men, without regard to education, might understand them (*Div. inst.* 6.21; ML 6.713 f.). Origen had earlier attempted to make similar virtue out of a *fait accompli* (*C. Cels.* 1.62), with the variant argument that God had used ill-educated speakers so that the truth of their teaching *must* be due to self-evidence and not to any persuasiveness of style and composition.[94] The stylistic deficiencies of the Bible, despite the defense, are, however, clearly acknowledged.

This point, the literary inacceptability of the Sacred Scriptures for the rhetorically cultivated Roman, is worth laboring. It helps to explain the social distribution of Christianity especially in the Roman West during the early centuries of our era; it may also go far to explain the *Octavius* of Minucius Felix as a literary phenomenon. It means an unsympathetic, if not hostile, attitude towards the central Christian writings, the Bible—an attitude which, indeed, continues throughout the course of the fourth century, and beyond.

In 362, for example, Julian the Apostate issued his edict and his rescript on Christian teachers[95]—what has been called "the first academic persecution inflicted on the Christians."[96] By these, *inter alia*, he forbade Christians to teach the classics—or apostatize—and challenged Christian professors to defend Matthew and Luke against the authority of the pagan classics.[97] Only two professors, father and son Apollinaris in Laodicea, are known to have taken up the challenge; even they felt that the Christian Scriptures were, in their crude form, impossible as a vehicle of education; they composed a grammar book "with a Christian character" and they proceeded to rewrite the Bible in classical genres. Apollinaris the Elder rewrote the Pentateuch in Homeric epic, the Historical Books of the Old Testament as Attic tragedies and poems in dactylic metre, and the rest of the Old Testament in the remaining poetic forms including Pindaric odes and Menandrian comedies; and then the New Testament was rewritten (by the Younger) as a series of Platonic dialogues.[98] Such was the mental climate in the East towards the Scriptures as literature. (The Christians had, of course, predecessors in this movement; Hellenized Jews had already translated Jewish history into more acceptable literary modes.[99])

In the West similar attempts had been made by this time:[100] hexameter verses survive, retelling the Old Testament stories of Jonah and the Whale (*De Iona*), and of Sodom and Lot (*De Sodoma*);[101] centos, mosaics of Vergilian elements, were composed on various subjects taken from both Old and New Testaments;[102] and the mysteries of the Christian faith were even cast into Vergilian ec-

logue, with Tityrus instructing Meliboeus in the shade of
a spreading beech tree, swapping dogmas instead of amorous adventures.[103] The Maccabees, a favorite topic with the
early Church militant, was the subject of hexameters by
Victorinus, embellished with highly elaborate and rhetorical speeches,[104] in the by now long-prevailing style. But
the most significant figure is Iuvencus, a Spaniard of high
birth, writing in the reign of Constantine.[105] He was
moved to harmonize and remodel the four Gospels as a
Vergilian epic, in thoroughly Vergilian style (save in
beauty of cadence), thereby "showing that the Church
had her own heroic story, her own epic of the Incarnation, the wonderful life, death, and resurrection of the
Saviour."[106]

The prose writers of this period reveal a similar
attitude, though not in quite so striking a manner. Ambrosiaster, in the late fourth century, feels constrained to
meet once more the objection which Arnobius had already
faced: Christian teachings are a novelty, a counterfeit of
older beliefs, and, therefore, they are inferior to paganism[107] because (they said) what is earlier cannot be false.
No wonder, then, Christian poets had attempted to give the
teachings of their religion an air of antiquity and respectability by couching them in forms hallowed by literary tradition and favored by the educated circles of the time. All
the more reason because the style of the Bible continued
to give offense. For example, Jerome, the contemporary of
Ambrosiaster, tells us in his famous dream passage that the
Prophet (i.e., Latin Scriptures?) was quite unpalatable, so
rough and uncouth, after a self-indulgent diet of Plautus;[108]
again he mentions the simpleness and the vulgar diction
and the confusion of grammatical genders in the sacred

books.[109] Similarly with Augustine; in his *Confessions* there is the instructive and famous incident. As a young student of eighteen, he became fired with the pursuit of philosophy; in this quest he decided to look into the Holy Scriptures, and there he was quite repelled by their simplicity, their puerile characteristics; he found nothing to be compared with the stateliness of Cicero, and so he turned elsewhere in his search, for philosophic literature more to his taste.[110] He did not return to the Bible until some twelve years later. It is clear that Christians were judged by their Book. Later, Augustine reports that opponents to Christianity could slyly inquire: *Magnus vir, bonus vir, litteratus, doctus, sed quare christianus?*[111] and, still according to the testimony of Augustine, bishops and priests continued to use solecisms and barbarisms and faulty pronunciations in their prayers,[112] even failing to comprehend the words they used.[113] Catechumens who came from rhetorical schools had to be taught how to read the Bible without being offended by its *solidum eloquium*.[114]

There has been thus traced a consistent reaction towards the Bible, over some two and a half centuries, by the (admittedly somewhat narrow) elite interested in pure literature:[115] the pagans were frankly repelled, and literary-minded Christians were constrained either to defend and explain, or to take the more positive action of re-presenting the data of Christianity in a form that would be received with sympathy and understanding. This latter step was more drastic for poetry, with its strongly entrenched conventions, than it was for prose,[116] but even in that medium there was need of much work. The *Octavius* of Minucius Felix forms part of this re-presentation movement in Latin

prose, with attempts at defense as well in a hostile environment.[117]

It must be borne in mind also, concerning this question
of the literary context of Minucius Felix, that the reactions
against the Scriptures, and the corresponding attitudes of
the Christians to this reaction, were much more marked in
the Roman West, where we have seen Minucius Felix
lived, than in the Greek East. General distinctions between
East and West are very apt to be misleading, particularly
in literary matters and at a season where bilingualism, a
marked feature of the Roman educated, appears to have
been common among the littérateurs of the Roman world.[118]
But a fair case can be maintained that it was in the East,
and especially in the Hellenized East, that Christianity
spread the more deeply and the more quickly through the
levels of society.[119] By the course of the third century its
intellectual stature can be gauged not only by the achieve-
ments of men of the calibre of Clement of Alexandria and
of Origen, but also by the polemical attacks leveled against
the Christians by men such as the Neoplatonic Porphyry,
the favorite pupil of Plotinus, who comes a century after
Celsus (of Alexandria?), to whom Origen made his famous
reply.[120] (But, in balance, one perhaps ought to underline
the fact that these men tend to be somewhat isolated figures; Origen, in particular, was acutely aware of the gulf
which separated the intellectual few from the many.) This
general permeation can be traced to a number of causes;
one point only need be stressed here, that in the East
Christianity spoke and wrote in largely contemporary
idiom;[121] it had a reasonable degree of homogeneity with
its environment. And its literary exponents even en-

deavored to keep abreast of current trends in linguistic
sophistication.[121a]

It would be incautious to cite as evidence the passage in
"Longinus" where the author quotes a Greek version of
Genesis as an example of sublimity attained by a proper
appreciation of the divine. The questions of dating and of
later interpolation are highly controversial.[122] Better evidence comes from the Greek apologists of the second century: Aristides, Justin, Tatian, Athenagoras, Theophilus.
They give, or we are given, accounts of their conversions;[123]
they are admittedly rather standardized and idealized accounts; however, we are told that they all owed their conversion to a perusal of the Greek Bible, and they are quite
prepared to urge their audience to go and read the Scriptures for themselves.[124] The unadorned simplicity of the
Bible as a literary work, which they confess,[125] though an
obstacle, was not an insurmountable one.

Not so in the West. Scarcely a mention of the Bible in
the formal *Apology* of the Latin Minucius Felix, only a
casual and oblique reference to the "writings of the
Jews,"[126] and even the echoes of the New Testament are
but slight and philosophically respectable.[127] Only, too, in
passing, in Arnobius[128] and slightly at greater length in Tertullian.[129] And in the West Christianity seems to have been
very much more thinly spread, especially in the more sophisticated and aristocratic levels of Roman society. Its intellectual tone was lowbrow and low-class. In Rome particularly, where the "old-family" tradition was to remain strong
for some centuries to come, it was, generally speaking,
socially and culturally unattractive and politically unin-
viting.

Among other things, Christianity still bore the marks

of its foreign origins, both in language and in social distribution. Greek betrayed the Eastern provenance of many of its leaders and writers: Clement of Rome, Irenaeus,[130] Hippolytus. The hegemony of that language in the liturgy and in the official sepulchral inscriptions of a Church *tenax antiquitatis* is well known and documented. That continued into the fourth century. Thus, late in that century, Ambrosiaster can voice a familiar-sounding complaint: the singers of the Greek liturgical chants in Rome do not understand the words they are singing; they are merely delighted by the sounds of the words (*oblectati sono verborum*[131]).

And as for the social distribution, the cumulative evidence suggests that for the last quarter of the second century and for the first half of the third, the Church in Rome was composed largely, though by no means entirely, of foreign groups[132] (as was, perhaps, Rome itself); it had a marked tendency to form its own πολίτευμα or social ghetto, and its general tenor was that of an "ungentlemanly popular religion."[133]

Into this context, at last, enters Minucius Felix. As a practitioner of the Roman bar he must often have been confronted with the question how he was to defend his Christianity before the critical and unappreciative audience he encountered in Rome, an audience, moreover, whose habit of mind was such that if they wanted, for example, information about the Jews, they would be inclined to go to an established or reputable classical authority, perhaps Tacitus, rather than to an up-to-date and accurate handbook which had no literary pretensions.[134]

What was Minucius Felix to do?

To have recourse to the Greek apologists would be of

little avail; they were, in the main, unacceptable both in form and in content. As for form, with one or two notable exceptions (Athenagoras, the *Ad Diognetum*—if it was written by this date[135]), they were untidy, ramshackle, inelegant documents, in the case of Justin Martyr even positively slipshod in organization. In addition, the predominant cast was the form of the *libellus*, a petition to the legal authorities to put a stop to persecution. As the tone of the *Octavius* is noticeably nonbelligerent, we might legitimately assume that the *libellus* format was inappropriate; for we have observed that Minucius Felix is very possibly writing in a time of relative peace for the Church.

The content of the Greek apologies, too, was largely out of the question. Apologists like Aristides and Theophilus were heavily reliant on such relatively unclassical sources as Jewish apologies; they even quoted non-Hellenic writings like the Bible *in extenso* (as in the case of Theophilus[136]) or attacked traditional Hellenic culture itself (as in the case of Tatian[137]). That would not do.

To win sympathetic attention, he would have to renovate the by now fairly canonical form, and content, of the Christian apology as elaborated by his Greek predecessors in the field.

For form he decided to exploit the possibilities of the philosophical dialogue, with its highly respectable pedigree, traceable to Plato and familiar in Latin letters since the time of Cicero. Indeed, Cicero's *De natura deorum* was carefully chosen to be his model in style as well as in form. It possessed a rich array of arguments on chance and providence all ready to be quarried and used to show that Christians could philosophize about God as impeccably, as respectably, and precisely in the same terms as any

Roman of the time of Cicero. *Optimus quisque* could, therefore, give the religion his full approbation.[138]

Minucius Felix was, of course, not alone in this exploitation of the *De natura deorum*. Later, Arnobius reports pagan zealots as declaring that the *De natura deorum* ought to be burnt, the work being there described as *haec scripta quibus christiana religio comprobetur* (*Adv. nat.* 3.7). And Arnobius' pupil, Lactantius, is so imbued with the spirit of Cicero that the atmosphere of the *Divine Institutes* is such that one would imagine that little has changed since the scene at Cotta's house in the last century of the Republic, despite the intervening period of Neoplatonism.[139]

Both dialogues, the *Octavius* and the *De natura deorum*, open with the usual prologue to establish the setting of the debate. In the *Octavius* this *mise-en-scène* is a promenade along the seashore of Ostia. To suggest, as does G. Charlier,[140] that this spot is chosen because the sea in the background symbolizes the infinity which is the subject of discussion is to ignore the literary history of such prologues. The literary evidence of similar dialogues overwhelmingly suggests that the setting is probably intended to be merely traditional;[141] it is indeed possible to find parallels for almost every point in the design of the prologue from other literary works.[142]

In one important respect, however, the *Octavius* is dissimilar in structure to the *De natura deorum*. In Cicero there are three main protagonists and each has a philosophical line to defend: Academic, Epicurean, Stoic. In the *Octavius* there are but two: the pagan, Caecilius, has a set speech giving his case; Octavius then presents the Christian reply. At the end of this speech the pagan rather per-

functorily declares himself converted, and that is the end
of it. Minucius Felix merely plays the adjudicator, with
some hardy commonplaces on sincerity versus subtle oratory.[143] His role is, in fact, pretty otiose.

The main explanation—beside the obvious ease and simplicity of presentation—is that, while strongly influenced
by the *De natura deorum,* Minucius Felix is also drawing
from another source. As is well known, in the rhetorical
curriculum current at this time figured the *controversia*
designed to train a student in deliberative and forensic
oratory. The student was given a case and told to plead in
its defense or for its contrary, or both. These cases were
not only about legal issues; they were also on historical
propositions and general philosophical points. Technically,
an exercise on controversial material of a speculative kind
was classified as a *thesis,* the Academy, with its scepticism,
having particularly encouraged this form of discourse *in
utramque partem.* Quintilian[144] tells us specifically that one
such *thesis* was *an providentia mundus regatur* ("whether
the world is governed by providence"). Later, Greek rhetoricians of the second century, Aelius Theon[145] and
Hermogenes,[146] in their rhetorical handbooks mention the
same topic, and Aelius Theon actually gives elaborate and
detailed instructions for dealing with this particular thesis.

Minucius Felix is a trained advocate; he would have
written such theses, and so would his contemporaries. Not
only that; the *controversia* was a reasonably respectable
literary form—the Elder Seneca published samples, so did
Calpurnius Flaccus, and a number have survived in the
manuscript tradition of Quintilian. So Minucius Felix, to
some extent, transforms his defense for Christianity; he
turns his Ciceronian material partly into a copybook exer-

cise, *pro* and *contra*, with an *actio*, a *responsio*, and an *arbiter*, on the traditional thesis *an providentia mundus regatur* and along the lines sketched by Aelius Theon. In this form there is, of course, need for only two major speakers. And by this form Christians can not only be seen to deal with material established by tradition; they can also be seen to deal with it in a fashionable and rhetorical manner, and moreover, to judge from the number of tractates *De providentia* we know of from this period, on a theme that was not only traditional but currently fashionable.[147]

Obviously Minucius Felix was highly pleased with his piece of salon epideixis; he could not refrain from giving himself a rather delightful verbal pat on the back at the conclusion of the speech which he had worked up for the Christian. He writes (39): "Thus Octavius completed his oration. For some time afterwards we were so stunned that we could say nothing but kept our eyes fixed on him. So far as I was concerned, I was completely lost in profound amazement at the wealth of proofs, examples, and authoritative quotations he had used to illustrate matter easier to feel than to express; by parrying spiteful critics with their own weapons, the arms of philosophers, he had shown the truth to be so simple as well as so attractive." The aims of Minucius Felix' composition are here neatly illustrated by the points he singles out for self-praise.

One of the most remarkable literary features of the dialogue is the abundance of verbal echoes, and occasionally quotations, from authors of the past. The list of credits in so brief a work is, indeed, lengthy (though many references, both Greek and Latin, that commentators have professed to discover could be put down equally well to rhetorical commonplace or to the choice rhetorical phrases that formed the *supellex* of an educated mind[148]). Such virtuosity in literary allusion was to the taste of the time; it was meant to win admiration and applause. Christians were erudite with the best of them.

Another remarkable feature of the *Octavius* is that at first reading it appears to be a curious apology for Christianity. Scarcely a mention of the Bible, no Christology; nothing of the Word, the Holy Spirit, the Trinity, the Redemption (Christ is only mentioned by a paraphrase[149]); no ecclesiology; nothing of the apostles, the ministry, the sacraments. What is given is largely about providence, and also eschatology: the end of the world, the immortality of the soul, the resurrection, the eternity of rewards and punishments after death.

Various explanations for this parsimony of Christian doctrine have been offered. Minucius Felix was only a neophyte,[150] he knew no better; or he was actually a member of a heretical sect like the Theodotians.[151] The former hypothesis fits ill with information supplied in the dialogue;[152] the latter hypothesis seems fairly untenable when a character of the robust orthodoxy of Jerome could declare that assiduous reading of the *Octavius*, with other works, helped to make a soul into a veritable *bibliotheca Christi*, a library of Christ.

In explanation, one could make out a case that Minucius Felix is noticeably less persuasive and informative when he touches on more or less specifically Christian beliefs and practices (e.g., inhumation, the humanity of Christ, the bodily resurrection[153]) just because they had no classically standardized attack and defense. By contrast, he is much more fluent, and credible, when he deals with questions which had a long philosophical pedigree in the pagan tra-

dition (e.g., idolatry, demonology, mythological fancies[154]);
for these topics arguments were to be found already fully
assembled, if not well worn, in the arsenals of the great
philosophical schools. It is therefore possible that many
sections of the *Octavius*, as indeed in Christian apology
generally, including even parts of Origen's great *Contra
Celsum*, can be legitimately classified as being of this rather
academic (versus realistic) debating-school sort.

But there is another, and more obvious, explanation:
Minucius Felix wishes to avoid the irritation which a discussion of the more esoteric matters exclusive to Christianity might rouse. He will discuss only those aspects which
are also of current interest for his pagan audience, which
are also in the Roman philosophical tradition. And he
wants to show that a Christian can deal with them in an
elegant and refined way, with scholarly dignity and grace.
Christians are true philosophers.

An excellent illustration of this point is to be found in
chapters 19 and 20 of the dialogue. Following the *De
natura deorum*, Minucius Felix cites the opinions of pagan
philosophers concerning the governing power of the Universe. He quotes Thales, Anaximenes, Diogenes of Apollonia, Anaxagoras, Pythagoras, Xenophanes, Antisthenes,
Speusippus, Democritus, Straton, Epicurus, Aristotle,
Theophrastus, Heraclides of Pontus, Zeno, Chrysippus,
Cleanthes, Diogenes of Babylon, Xenophon, Aristo, and
finally Plato. And then he concludes: "These opinions
are pretty well identical with ours; we recognize a God
and we also call Him father of all. . . . I have disclosed
the views of almost all philosophers of any outstanding
distinction; though under a multiplicity of names they
have defined God as unique. So it is open to anyone to

suppose that either present-day Christians are philosophers or philosophers of the past were already Christians." (This appears to be but a more subtle variation on the "Atticized Moses" theme.[154a])

Of course, current topics of interest change, and the *Octavius* was perhaps relatively soon out of date. Hence the paucity of the *testimonia* referring to him and the tenuous manuscript tradition. From a literary point of view, the *Octavius* is a marginal opuscule in the corpus of classical literature; it is of importance, however, for the reconstruction of the intellectual and literary life of Christians in the early Roman Empire.

The Historical Setting

It is also of importance for the reconstruction of the social life of early Christians in the Roman Empire. The next question to ask is, therefore, how far were Minucius Felix and his friends isolated figures as Christians among the educated and professional classes in Rome at this period?

There can be no doubt that in general the Church had been increasing in numbers (and spreading to new areas) throughout the course of the preceding century; that expansion should apply to Rome, as it did elsewhere, and there are many texts which strongly support such a conclusion.[155] Minucius Felix, for example, has the pagan say (9.1): "Evil weeds grow apace and so, day by day, this depraved way of life now creeps further over all the face of the globe and the foul religious shrines of this abominable congregation are getting a stronger hold." To this the Christian replies in contradiction (31.7): "You say our numbers grow daily. This does not convict us of error; it provides evidence for our credit. It is a fact that if you have an honorable way of life, adherents persist and persevere in it, and outsiders augment its ranks." Texts might be multiplied, for this "proof from expansion" (often incautiously phrased) was by now popular and well established with formulations ready-made to cater for its lengthy history to follow.[156]

Some texts, however, have been exploited somewhat injudiciously to illustrate this expansion for Rome specifically. One such is the so-called *Second Letter of Clement to the Corinthians* 2.3, where it is asserted that Christians outnumber Jews.[157] This has been taken as evidence that a considerable body of Christians must have been living in Rome. This assumes that the author's environment is Roman and that he is estimating from his own environment—which are possible but by no means certain hypotheses; the remark, like many similar ones, is meant to be general. And the exaggeration of the enthusiast is always a danger in this field; this is especially true in a context where the rival claims of Judaism are being considered.[158] The passage, therefore, should be weighed against the other evidence.

Tertullian was never loath to wield the tools of the enthusiastic controversialist or to be carried away by the impulse of his own rhetoric; in his celebrated encomium of the progress of Christianity, written at the close of the second century,[159] he is happy to claim: "We are only of yesterday and we have filled everything you have: cities, apartment blocks, forts, towns, market places, even the military camps, tribes, town councils, the palace, the senate, the forum. We have left you the temples only" (*Implevimus . . . palatium, senatum, forum; Apol.* 37.4).

Caution is demanded, though it is not always given, in using this passage as historical testimony. Tertullian's heavy penchant for forensic hyperbole must be borne in mind; in the very next chapter (38.3) he is equally happy to exclaim: "We [Christians] shrink from all burning desires for renown and position. . . . There is nothing more foreign to us than affairs of state"; or, as he said again later, "I owe no obligation to the forum, assembly place, or senate" (De pallio 5.4).

A third passage frequently quoted as evidence for this period in Rome is from Eusebius' Church History (5.21.1). He tells us that in the reign of Commodus (180–192) "the word of salvation began to lead every soul of every race of men to the pious worship of the God of the universe, so that now many of those who at Rome were famous for wealth and family turned to their own salvation with all their house and with all their kin."[160] One initially suspects that Eusebius speaks perhaps both anachronistically and with details of his native East, rather than those of Rome, in mind; and he gives no illustrations, save the case of Apollonius, and there the value of his testimony has been doubted.[161]

These general remarks clearly ought not to be overplayed, but they should imply at least that there were not inconsiderable numbers of Christians in Rome; such observations would be difficult to make unless there was some modicum of truth in them. But given the strongly entrenched conservatism of the Roman upper classes, with their deep respect for ancestral and cultural traditions (and that would include religiones traditae[162]), one cannot at all assume that in their expansion Christians permeated the higher echelons of Roman society in due proportion. Can one substantiate, therefore, from other sources Tertullian's *implevimus . . . palatium, senatum, forum?*

As for the senate, specific candidates seem to be singularly lacking.[163] Apollonius (mart. c. 185) is a remote possibility, but his status largely depends on Jerome, who appears to have garbled his sources.[164] There are some catacomb inscriptions which may, or may not, provide information, but their dates are either dubious or clearly fall beyond our period, and nomenclature alone, here almost our only guide, is a very imprecise informant: very many of the texts could just as readily concern people not of senatorial status at all.[165] And certainly, inscriptional candidates from Phrygia, sometimes canvassed for the Senate of the second or third centuries, can be safely eliminated; they were members of local senates or town councils.[166] A few specific candidates remain. There is a Christian epitaph of a consul and martyr, Liberalis, but identification and dating are highly conjectural;[167] another Christian consul, Aemilian, though frequently cited for the mid-third century,[168] depends for his religious adherence on the very doubtful validity of the *Acta* of Parthenius and Calocerus, documents which certainly cannot be relied upon for such detail.[169] A third, Antonius Severianus, rests on the (again) doubtful identification of an undated Christian epitaph—it sounds later—with an inscription of a *clarissimus vir* of similar name, possibly but not certainly of the third century.[170] The claims of Tertullian himself have been advocated on the evidence of Euseb. *H.E.* 2.2.4, but such a deduction is highly dubious (see below). A final candidate, of the mid-third century, is the most certain of all: he is Astyrius (= M. Bassaeus Astur?[171]), proudly described by Eusebius (*H.E.* 7.16.1) as "a member of the

Roman senate, a favorite of emperors and well known to all both for noble birth and wealth." Others have attempted to find senators or at least provincial governors (who might in some areas be of equestrian status also) later in the century from Eusebius' general remarks in *H.E.* 8.1.2, but the examples Eusebius gives are of imperial functionaries (e.g., Dorotheus and Gorgonius, *H.E.* 8.1.4 f., 8.6.5;[172] Adauctus, *H.E.* 8.11.2) or local officials (e.g., Philoromus, *H.E.* 8.9.7), and his language seems studiously vague ("he entrusted to them the government of the people"). The third century was one of rapid growth for the Church, especially in its second half,[173] and Eusebius is unwilling to forgo any opportunity to emphasize the status or cultural attainments of Christians. If, therefore, as seems a reasonable inference, there were in fact few prominent Christian officials at the end of that century,[174] the period for which Eusebius supplies us with the few names, one might reasonably conjecture that some 75 years earlier the numbers of such candidates, regrettably anonymous, were meagre.

Some control over this conjecture comes from two sources. At the end of the first half of the third century came the persecution of Valerian. Cyprian reports[175] that the emperor's second rescript (258 A.D.) was directed against the clergy, senators, prominent men, Roman knights, matrons, members of the imperial staff. A precious piece of information, Cyprian's letter is written to warn Bishop Successus (of Abbir Germaniciana) of the coming of the new rescript and of its terms. It is a contemporary document. This was a time of severe economic crisis; the attack on prominent, and moneyed, adherents of the Church specifically may possibly have been aimed, in part, at securing additional revenue.[176] It should have at least been worth all the trouble involved. And the persecution, at any rate, was certainly not idle. It is highly likely, therefore, that there were Christians in all the classes mentioned in the rescript (though legal completeness might have also dictated that such social categories be covered). If there were a number of senators in 258, at least a handful (out of a full tally of perhaps 600 or more senators[177]) could be conjectured for c. 200. The testimony of Origen,[178] writing about a decade before the rescript, could perhaps lend some support: Christian teachers are received by men who are wealthy, men in high station, women of noble birth. Caution is demanded, however; he has probably predominantly in mind his own Eastern conditions and the defense of his own activities, that is to say, his relationship with the members and courtiers of the ruling Severan house.[179]

A second source of control is to be found in the repeated charge that Christians do not take part in the public offices of Roman government and the equally repeated defense by Christians of such an abstention. The abstention is not denied. Thus in the *Octavius* the pagan states that Christians "scorn the purple robes of public office, though they go about in rags themselves" (8.4): that is to say, they did not wear the ceremonial toga, purple-edged or otherwise, characteristic of Roman official life. The Christian replies (31.6): "If we refuse your purple robes of public office, it does not follow that our ranks are composed of the very dregs of the rabble." This abstention from office-holding, here testified as elsewhere,[180] certainly was not absolute at this period, but such statements could be made so openly and so repeatedly only if such Christian officials were neither plentiful nor prominent, and only if there were in fact potential office-bearers, possessing the necessary income and family connections or patronage, who notoriously refrained from such secular advancement on religious grounds. This general attitude towards public life must to some extent have had the practical effect of dissuading actual senators from conversion to Christianity, and potential senators from canvassing for at least the quaestorship, an appointment which *ex officio* gave them a seat in the senate house. Had attitudes been otherwise, for all we know there may very well have been stronger representation of the Christian community in the *curia;* to find such scant trace of actual senators is, therefore, probably misleading. Even so, the state of our present knowledge does not allow us to believe that had such possible Christian senators actually entered on senatorial careers as they might normally have done, they would have swamped the senate house (*implevimus . . . senatum*), as Tertullian claimed they did in fact.

From the evidence there would appear to have been a greater number of women of high rank who were Christians than of men, a situation which one might have inferred from probability in any case, though the emphasis which the critics of Christianity placed on proselytism among gullible women should not be taken too solemnly; that is a literary *topos*.[181] Tertullian mentions the Christian wife of a governor of Cappadocia, Hippolytus that of a governor of Syria;[182] these ladies are reasonably conjectured to be of some standing. *Clarissimae*, as well as *clarissimi*, are rescued by the emperor Septimius from the angry mob; they were Christians.[183] And Pope Callistus, in the early third century, was bold enough to give ecclesiastical approval to unions between women of free birth and men who were of servile class or origin, contrary to the regulations of Roman civil law.[184] The implication, at least, is that women outnumbered men in the Christian fold, so far as the freeborn classes were concerned (the alternative, a mixed marriage, was at this time considered sinful[185]). This should apply to the higher ranks of society as elsewhere. But the number of such highborn women appears to be altogether not very large;[186] the number of men, therefore, is not considerable and the lack of names suggests they were not particularly prominent (though it would not have been to their advantage to advertise their religious persuasion); we might infer, however, that they were growing in numbers and influence.[187] Hence, both men and women of this class are singled out by Valerian.

This much we can divine of the senatorial company Minucius Felix and his friends might have kept within the Christian community at Rome.

There is better documentation for Tertullian's *palatium*. Writing about the year 186, Irenaeus makes a general remark concerning "the faithful in the royal palace"; they appear to be servants and minor officials.[188] Among men of such class we know of Carpophorus,[189] who was wealthy enough to own the future Pope Callistus as his slave and to lend him a considerable sum of money to invest;[190] the former "procurator" Proculus, favored by Septimius and close friend of the future emperor Caracalla (as a child?); and, of course, the nurse of Caracalla (he was reared on Christian milk—*lacte christiano educatus*[191]). They are all pretty small beer. Tertullian could find for his urgent plea to the governor Scapula only Proculus and the nurse, in Septimius' court. Prosenes, who rose to the rank of imperial chamberlain, would be of much greater

significance, but his Christianity depends on the phrase
receptus ad Deum, inscribed in 217 by his freedman
Ampelius on the side of his large sarcophagus. The main
inscription, set up by his freedmen collectively, has no
such phrase. His may have been a cryptic adherence to
Christianity; it was not exploited by Tertullian.[192]

There are some possible traces of other named palatine
officials towards the end of the first half of the third century, but the evidence for them is either doubtful or controversial.[193]

Court influence for Christians, however, did go so far as
the powerful mistress of Commodus (180–192), Marcia,[194]
described by Hippolytus as "god-loving" (φιλόθεος), but
not specifically as a Christian (the epithet is a conventional
one of praise in a religious context).[195] She had, so Hyacinthus asserted, been reared by him, a Christian presbyter;[196]
and she was at least favorably disposed towards Christians,
securing the release of Christians condemned to a mine in
Sardinia.[197] That is to say, there was sympathetic influence
c. 190 within the palace.

That imperial ladies should be concerned with matters
religious was no novelty; Nero's mistress and later consort, Poppaea Sabina, had been surrounded by a troop of
astrologers and had evinced some interest in Judaism.[198]
The women of the Severi, the dynasty that followed the
death of Commodus, were no exception. Christianity fell
within the wide purview of their religious interests
whether mystical, esoteric, or philosophical—and especially as it was of Eastern provenance like the Severan
ladies themselves.[199] They thus seem to have continued
this sympathy of Marcia's towards the Christians. Specifically, we know that Julia Mamaea, mother of Alexander

Severus (222–235), summoned Origen to Antioch and discussed religious topics with him there; the significance of this event for a religious movement that had suffered a long history of persecution and contempt cannot be over-emphasized.[200] The role of the Christian chronographer Julius Africanus is also instructive; friendly with the son of Julia Mamaea, the emperor Alexander Severus, he designed for him a library in the Pantheon at Rome.[201] That is to say, he enjoyed a position of some patronage and favour. Origen's friend, convert, and patron, Ambrosius, appears to have been influential in these court circles also; he possessed great wealth and nobility of birth, according to Jerome.[202] Hence Eusebius can talk of the court of Alexander Severus—himself credited, on the authority of later and highly debatable evidence, with strong interests in Judaism and Christianity[203]—as composed of many Christians.[204] This sympathetic hearing at court accorded to Christianity seems not to have been entirely lost after the collapse of the Severan dynasty (March 235). Origen addressed a letter to a later emperor Philip (244–249), and one to his wife;[205] the latter was perhaps the dedicant of a treatise on the resurrection by Hippolytus.[206] And Christian tradition was noticeably favorable to this emperor; it soon claimed him as an adherent. That should mean, at the least, that he had been sympathetic to the Christian cause.[207]

It seems fair to conclude, therefore, that the number of Christian *Caesariani* (despite the paucity of precise evidence[208]) and correspondingly, the influence commanded by Christians within the *palatium*, was increasing steadily during the period of Minucius Felix' *floruit*. Hence when Valerian began his reign (253), he found his court so filled with Christians that it could be described—by a Christian—as a "Church of God."[209] The tone of the *Octavius,* with its heavy stress on the philosophical pedigree of Christian tenets and its noticeable lack of nervous urgency, readily fits into the philosophically inclined atmosphere and the largely tolerant context of Severan Rome.

This analysis would accord with the gradually, but perceptibly, changing attitude towards the Christians generally. In the preceding century the notice of Marcus Aurelius is cold and critical;[210] whereas Galen, court physician and philosopher under Marcus Aurelius and then his son Commodus, displays much more sympathetic appreciation and understanding; but he still has doubts about the intellectual integrity of the sect.[211] And then there follows what appears to be the more favorable regard of the Severi.[212] Not only was this a dynasty noted for its wide religious interests,[213] but it is also possible that favor resulted in part from support Christians rendered to Septimius Severus in his fight for power. This is one of the hypotheses which would make sense of the remark said to have been uttered by Caecilius Capella when Byzantium eventually fell to the Severan forces: "Christians, rejoice!"[214]

Persecutions follow roughly the same pattern.[215] They are sporadic and unsystematic, and after the difficulties of Marcus Aurelius at Lyons and Vienne (177 A.D.),[216] they recur but locally and probably for special reasons of pressure of circumstances or of personal bias on the part of local authorities. Generally speaking, they take place in the large urban centres where popular feeling had most effect (Christianity being, besides, predominantly an urban religion) and not wholesale throughout a province.[217] There had been outbreaks elsewhere[218] about the same time as those in Southern Gaul (also briefly in Africa[219] and perhaps in Egypt[220] and Cappadocia[221]). And then there were but isolated cases of persecution until the beginning of the third century, when Africa Proconsularis and Egypt were the main centres of trouble.[222] This may have been in large part, but not entirely, due to disciplinary measures against fanatical Montanist extremists in those areas. But from the accession of Caracalla to that of Decius, 211–249, there are some thirty-seven years of religious peace largely unbroken save for trouble under the short-lived emperor Maximinus Thrax (235–238); Eusebius suggests that this persecution was due to reaction against the tolerant policy of the previous emperor Alexander Severus.[223] Thus the rhythm of the persecutions would fit with the analysis of the growing influence which the evidence suggests Christians were commanding in court circles; likewise, in the *Octavius* (28), persecutions figure as a memory of the recent past rather than as an actuality of the immediate present.[224]

As for Tertullian's third category, the *forum*, it is a little difficult to divine the precise meaning. In the context it is a rhetorically vague word that would cover the particular usage of the legal profession[225] and the wider extension of business life generally (especially banking). Evidence to support Tertullian's contention for the precise sense is, curiously, rather scarce for the Roman scene.

Tertullian himself, it is claimed on the testimony of Eusebius, was a learned and distinguished Roman advocate (though there is little independent evidence to support this description[226]). Similarly for Cyprian in Carthage a generation later: the available evidence suggests his secular career had been that of rhetorician rather than of practicing advocate.[227] At the end of the third century Arnobius, himself a rhetorician from Africa and teacher of the African rhetorician Lactantius,[228] noted the effect of Christianity on "talented orators, schoolteachers and rhetoricians, jurists and doctors, and even those engaged in delving into the mysteries of philosophy."[229] Christians should at least be moving into these professional circles, at Rome as elsewhere,[230] half a century or so earlier. But we should perhaps not be too openhanded in conjecturing anonymous professional colleagues for Minucius Felix and his friends for two reasons.

Firstly, many Christians still avoided, so far as possible, contact with the law courts and litigation generally, as places and occasions of unchristian violence and unchristian revenge (though acting as an impeached defendant was allowable). Hence many Christians avoided as well the offices of judge, magistrate, and advocate associated with such unchristian activities in the Forum.[231] Secondly, the charge, at this period, is still constantly repeated that Christians are unlettered, unlearned, and uncultured. This is certainly standard rhetorical abuse of one's opponents, but the charge is leveled so frequently and attempts to rebut it are made so solemnly that the accusation cannot have been entirely idle. In the *Octavius*, for example, the pagan calls Christians "untrained in education, outcasts from humane studies, ignorant of even the meanest skills" (5.4); they are "utter boors and yokels, ungraced by any manners or culture" (12.7).[232] The Christian rather lamely replies that all men, illiterate and untrained as they may be, and irrespective of age and station, can still philosophize about God and discover the truth—and lack of rhetorical flourish even makes the discourse of such amateurs more lucid (16.5 f.).[233] We should probably conclude from such a passage that the charge did, in fact, apply to a large proportion of the Christian community. Cultured and educated Christians there certainly were,[234] but the majority of Roman Christians may still not have received an education at the rhetor's school to qualify them for a career at the bar in the Forum; and even if they had received such an education, conscience might have precluded them from such a forensic career.

As for the general significance of *forum* (including commercial activities generally), there is abundant evidence to suggest that Christians were wealthy enough to engage in the transactions of the Forum.[235] The author of the *Shepherd* of Hermas, whose environment was very probably Roman, was writing some generation or more before the beginning of the third century;[236] he is constantly[237] directing remarks at the money-making preoccupations of Christians; he complains, for example, about those Christians "who have never investigated the truth nor made inquiries about the Godhead; they merely have the faith and are absorbed in business affairs, wealth, friendship with pagans, and many other occupations of this world."[238] This should be even more true a generation or so later. Confirmatory evidence comes from various sources. About 170 A.D. Dionysius of Corinth wrote to Pope Soter of Rome: "This has been your custom from the beginning, to do good in manifold ways to all Christians and to send contributions to the many churches in every city, in some places relieving the poverty of the needy and ministering to the Christians in the mines, by the contributions which you have sent from the beginning, preserving the ancestral custom of the Romans, true Romans as you are" (Euseb. *H.E.* 4.23.10, trans. Kirsopp Lake).[239] In other words, the Roman Church was proverbial for its generous wealth. Eighty years later the situation is even more precisely known: the Church in Rome in 251 A.D. is wealthy enough to be supporting 154 full-time clergy in various orders and over 1,500 widows and indigent.[240] And this is the period of the acquisition of Church property and Church building as well. The papal crypt, for example, in the cemetery of Callistus was first used for the burial of Pope Pontian (d. 235), and "both in its architecture and in its inscriptions the papal crypt plainly manifests a certain wealth and elegance which does not suffer in comparison with the best classical work of the kind";[241] and, of course, there was the construction of the *Memoria apostolorum ad catacumbas* by the Via Appia.[242] Payment for such schemes would come not merely from widows' mites; there would be the contributions of the business classes as well (like the merchant Marcion, who could contribute to the Church in Rome no less than 200,000 sesterces, Tert. *De praescr. haer.* 30.2).[243]

Elsewhere in the Roman Empire there certainly were Christians among the ranks of the wealthy, the educated, and the propertied.[244] We can safely suppose that as bankers, traders, etc. naturally tended to come from the provinces to the legal and commercial centre of Rome, such travelers would have included their due proportion of men of the Christian following as well.[245] Thus Pope Soter, as we know from the testimony of Dionysius of Corinth, increased the charitable funds of the Roman Church "by exhorting with his blessed words the brethren

who come to Rome, as a loving father would his children"
(Euseb. *H.E.* 4.23.10, trans. Kirsopp Lake).

One should not exaggerate, however, the presence of
this business class in Rome. The Church in the West continued to emphasize that to preserve one's wealth was to
prefer mammon to Christ, whereas in the more sophisticated East a man of property could be more readily accepted and justified.[246] The Western Church does not
sound, at this time, like a predominantly rich man's religion. The *Octavius* confirms this impression. The pagan
is made to claim (12.2): "Some of you Christians, the
greater half (the better half, you say), go in need, suffer
from cold, from hunger and toil." The Christian studiously,
and significantly, does not deny the claim. Instead he
speaks the praises of poverty: poverty not only allows a
man to see more clearly celestial matters (16.5) but it
provides suitable training for strengthening the soul (36.
3–7). It is, besides, he goes on to say, a relative concept:
if one is free from want, one cannot be poor; that the
majority of Christians are said to be poor is therefore a
cause not for disgrace but for pride.[247] Clearly the moneyed
classes did not predominate in the Roman Christian community.

We should conclude, therefore, that the Roman Forum
was not without some Christian brethren for Minucius and
his friends, but our scanty and partial records certainly do
not allow us to assert that they swamped it (*Implevimus
. . . forum*), as Tertullian claimed they did.

Generally speaking, the evidence for the spread of
Christianity in Rome during the period under discussion
is manifestly erratic and fragmentary; much has survived
merely at the hazard of chance. The picture that we are

able to form of the social circles in which Minucius Felix
and his Christian associates may have moved must, therefore, be partial and fugitive; and arguments *e silentio* must
remain of dubious value when the light of information is
so fitful. But so far as we *can* judge, there do appear to be
the elements of a slowly maturing Church both socially
and intellectually. The *Octavius* forms a valuable literary
addition to that historical picture of gradual sophistication,
of a Church starting on that long, and indeed never-end-
ing, task of coming to terms with its secular milieu.

EDITIONS AND TRANSLATIONS

Now a few points about the commentary, editions and
translations, and bibliographical aids. In the commentary,
as a general rule, I have confined the citation of parallels
to ante-Nicene writers unless illustration from these
sources appeared to be incomplete or inadequate. Should
illustration be sought from outside these texts, a generous
collection of post-Nicene parallels will be found in the
commentary of M. Pellegrino (Turin 1947); the many
reminiscences and parallels in Lactantius, given sparingly
in this commentary, are adequately listed in M. Pellegrino,
Studi su l'antica apologetica (Rome 1947) 151–207.
Neither have Cyprian and Tertullian been completely
culled for the ideas which they hold in common with the
Octavius; it seemed more pertinent to cite instead illustration rather from the earlier Christian apologists and such
classical writers as Cicero, for it is directly in the traditions
of Cicero and the literary genre of the apology that the
Octavius was composed.

Most editions have been consulted, particular profit

being gained from the *variorum* edition of Gronovius (Leiden 1709) and those of Holden (Cambridge 1853), Waltzing (Louvain 1903), Pellegrino (Turin 1947), and Beaujeu (Paris 1964; this work appeared when a large portion of my notes was already complete). I have similarly read through, and profited by, earlier translations into English: those of James (Oxford 1636), Combe (London 1703), Reeves (London 1709), Dalrymple (Edinburgh 1781), Wallis (Edinburgh 1880), Freese (London 1919), Rendall (London–Cambridge, Mass. 1931), and Arbesmann (New York 1950). The text followed is that which, it is assumed, would be most readily accessible to the reader, namely, the Budé edition of J. Beaujeu (Paris 1964). The very few places where I have diverged from this generally well-chosen text have been noted in the Commentary *ad loca*.

Students of the *Octavius* are generously served with bibliographical aids, so well served, in fact, that to repeat here the labors of others would be otiose. A complete bibliography up to 1901 will be found in the edition of J.-P. Waltzing (Louvain 1903) 5–49. Thereafter, J. Quasten, *Patrology* 2 (Westminster, Md.–Utrecht–Antwerp 1953) 159–63, provides invaluable assistance up to the date of that publication. The pages of the annual *L'Année philologique* afford the most reliable, and the most readily accessible, guidance for the literature that has appeared subsequently.[248]

* * *

I should like to express my gratitude for the many kindnesses, so generously given, of Russell Meiggs and Gordon

Williams (who suggested this task and gave my script the inestimable benefit of much of his valuable time and his searching criticism). To the Nuffield Foundation I am endebted for a fellowship which made possible a year spent, away from the demands and distractions of teaching, in the British Museum and the Institute of Classical Studies, London. To the library staffs of the School of General Studies, Australian National University, Canberra, and of the University of Western Australia, Perth, I am grateful for endeavoring to meet my many demands for books and microfilms; and the editors of the *Journal of Religious History* have kindly permitted me to reproduce some of the substance of two articles that appeared in that periodical. To my wife I owe tireless encouragement to complete and indefatigable typing to prepare this work for publication.

THE PROLOGUE

CHAPTER I

1. I was thinking and turning over in my mind my memories of Octavius.[1] He had been a good friend, a most constant companion. And such warmth of feeling[2] for him possessed me that I seemed not to be invoking remembrance of what was finished and done but actually to be transported right back into the past; 2. for the further Octavius has been physically removed from my eyes, the more vivid has his picture grown in the depths of my heart.[3] 3. It was only to be expected that when this man of exceptional integrity departed from us[4] I should have regretted his loss so deeply; this was so because for his part he, too, had been at all times very warmly disposed towards me. We had been, as a result, in complete harmony together, in our moments of gaiety as well as gravity, with but a single will; one mind, you might say, had been shared between the two of us.[5] 4. In him alone I had confided my personal feelings;[6] he, too, had been my ally in error.[7] And he did not reject my companionship when I was beginning to rise out of the dispersing mists and the abyss of darkness into the light of true wisdom;[8] but to his greater credit, he rushed on ahead.

5. This explains why, as I turned over in my mind all the period of our close friendship and life together, my attention became fixed on one particular conversation of

51

his. It was by this conversation that he had converted to the true religion Caecilius,[9] who was at that time still clinging to superstitious folly.[10] It was a most profound debate.[11]

CHAPTER 2

1. Octavius had journeyed to Rome to attend to some business and to pay me a visit. He had left behind his home, his wife, and his children—the children were still young and innocent, and still at that particularly attractive stage when the words they attempted were only half-formed:[12] this manner of speech is made all the more endearing because the tongue is clumsy and the words are broken.[13] 2. I cannot express in words how highly excited and delighted I was to see him;[14] my joy was the greater simply because I had not expected a visit from my good friend. 3. Two successive days we spent constantly together; by that time we had sated our eager longing to see each other, we had exchanged our news and had found out what each did not know, through separation, of the other. And so we agreed to go to Ostia. It is a very pleasant town and there are sea-baths which would provide an agreeable and suitable treatment for drying the humors of my body.[15] Besides it was also harvest time. The holidays had eased my judicial responsibilities,[16] and at that season, with the summer over, autumn was beginning to bring milder weather. 4. And so at dawn we started off towards the sea. Our object was to stroll along the shore,[17] so that the gently blowing breeze could refresh our limbs and that we might have the delightful pleasure of feeling the yielding sand

sink away beneath our footsteps.[18] As we went, Caecilius noticed a statue of Serapis[19] and following the custom of the superstitious masses, he moved his hand to his lips and formed a kiss.[20]

CHAPTER 3

1. Thereupon Octavius said: "Marcus, my brother,[21] it is not right for you to forsake in such blindness and crass ignorance[22] one who is constantly at your side, in private as well as in public;[23] you should not allow him, in such broad daylight, to dash himself against stones,[24] even though they may be carved, anointed, and garlanded.[25] You are well aware that the shame of this error brings as much discredit on you as it does on him."

2. As he talked, we had crossed the centre of the town; and we now found ourselves on the open shore. 3. There the gently flooding waters were smoothing the edge of the sand as if spreading it for a promenade. The sea is always restless even if the winds have dropped,[26] though on this occasion when it reached land the waves were not white or foaming. We were, all the same, thoroughly delighted with its curling, winding, irregular course; when we dipped our feet in the very edge of the sea, it would surge forward and play its waves against our feet; then it would slip away, and as it receded, try to suck our feet back with it.

4. In this way, gradually, peacefully, we made our way along the softly curving shoreline, whiling away the time with pleasant stories. These were from Octavius, who talked about sailing.[27]

5. When we had gone far enough, talking as we walked,

we turned around and retraced our steps. And we came to a spot where some small boats had been drawn up and were resting on oak supports off the ground to prevent rot.[28] There we saw some small boys eagerly competing with one another in a game of throwing shells into the sea. 6. In this game[29] you choose from the shore a shell that has been rubbed smooth by the action of the waves; this you hold horizontally in your fingers, and stooping at an angle and low to the ground you hurl it with all your might over the water.[30] The object is that as it spins, it should sheer and skim the surface of the sea, gliding smoothly all the while; or it can shave the tops off the waves, constantly springing up again in a series of leaps and bounds. Among the boys, the one whose shell had gone farther and skipped more times considered himself to be the winner.

CHAPTER 4

1. We were all[31] then watching this scene, entranced. But Caecilius, unamused by the contest, refused to give it any attention; he stood aside, silent and preoccupied, his face showing that he was troubled about something. 2. "What is the matter?" I said to him. "Where is your usual enthusiasm, Caecilius? What has become of the cheerful look you usually have in your eyes even in serious moments?" 3. "For some time," came his reply, "I have been acutely nettled by what our friend Octavius said; it has been preying on my mind. He attacked you, reproaching you with neglect; but this was intended only as a cover for the more serious charge of ignorance against me. 4. I will come right into the open; I will argue out the whole question with Octavius, at full length. If he agrees, I will

debate with him, though I do not belong to his school.[32]
He will promptly realize that one can more readily debate among fellow believers than enter into a direct philosophical engagement. 5. Do you see over there that stone
breakwater which has been built out into the water to
protect the baths? Let us now sit down there.[33] We can
then rest from our walk and debate with deeper concentration."

6. At his suggestion we sat down, myself in the middle
with the other two flanking me on either side.[34] This was
not intended as a mark of deference either to rank or office
—friendship always either finds or makes equals[35]—but I
was to act as arbiter;[36] I could thus give a hearing sitting
next to each and by my position could keep the two dis-
putants apart.

CHAPTER 5

The pagan's case: Is the world ruled by providence?

1. Caecilius then began as follows: "Marcus, my brother,
it is true that there is no doubt in your own mind about
the central issue of our inquiry. You have lived conscien-
tiously according to both ways of life: one you have rejected, the other you have adopted. But for the time being
you must be so minded as to hold the scales of justice
exactly balanced. You must not lean or incline to either
side, otherwise you run the risk of passing your verdict
based not on our debate but on your own personal feelings. 2. Therefore, would you please take the chair as if
you were a perfect stranger, unacquainted with either
point of view.

"In that case it will be no effort to demonstrate that in human affairs everything is doubtful, uncertain, and unsettled, everything is a matter of probability rather than of certainty.[37] 3. And so one is all the more surprised that some weary of the task of probing into the depths of reality; they do not pursue this quest with relentless persistence but, instead, they make a random surrender to any opinion that may chance their way. 4. Since this is so, we should all surely find it outrageous and deplorable that there are people who have the insolence to pronounce a dogmatic judgment on the awesome nature of the universe—and these are people who are untrained in education, outcasts from humane studies, ignorant of even the meanest skills.[38] And they are legislating on a problem which even today philosophy herself is still pondering, despite the multiplicity of philosophical schools of all the preceding centuries.[39]

5. "And this state of philosophy is as we might expect, for the mediocre abilities of man are quite inadequate for exploring divine matters. And we are, therefore, not privileged to know nor are we permitted to pry into what has been raised aloft, poised in the sky above our heads, or what has been plunged into the depths of the earth beneath our feet. These things it is sacrilegious for us to violate.[40] Surely we are to be considered wise enough, happy enough, if we follow the old maxim of the Sage and get to know ourselves more intimately.[41]

6. "But we still insist on wandering far beyond the bounds which our lowly condition imposes, indulging in extravagant schemes outside our abilities;[42] though we have been cast down onto this earth, with reckless ambition we soar above the sky itself, the very stars. This is a mistaken

enterprise and we should at least avoid making it worse by combining with it baseless opinions derived from fear.[43]

7. "For we can suppose that in the beginning, by spontaneous generation of nature,[44] the seeds of everything were begotten in a condensed mass. In this case what god was their creator? We can suppose that by the chance collisions of atoms[45] the limbs of the entire universe were composed, arranged, and shaped. What god was their architect? We can posit that fire set the stars alight, that the very nature of its own substance lifted the sky aloft, that by its weight the earth was set down on firm foundations, that the liquid element flooded in to form the sea.[46] What reason is there, then, for this religious dread, this superstition?

8. "Man and every creature that is born, given breath and reared, is a spontaneous conglomeration of atoms. Into these atoms, in turn, man and every creature is divided, parted, and dispersed.[47] Thus, in cycles, all things revert to themselves, flowing back, as it were, to their source. There is no need for any designer, any judge, any creator.[48]

9. "This could explain how, through the concentration of seeds of fire, new suns are always shining in constant succession;[49] and this explains, in turn, why the earth exhales its warm vapors and thus mists are always developing; when these mists have become condensed in a packed mass, they rise high up into the air as clouds; and in their turn as they collapse, rains flood down, the winds blow,[50] there is the clatter of hail, or if storm clouds collide, there is the roar of thunder, the glow of lightning, the flash of the thunderbolt. And note that their blows are without aim, crashing onto mountains,[51] dashing against trees; without distinction they strike places sacred and profane,[52] the unjust they smite and often the righteous.

10. "But I have no need to discourse on the capriciousness and variability of storms in which everything is whirled about without any order or arrangement. In a shipwreck are not the fates of good and bad intermingled, irrespective of deserts? In a fire do not innocent and guilty alike meet their death? Do not all perish without discrimination when pestilence and plague taint some region of the air? When there is a fierce war raging, is it not rather the good men who are the first to fall?[53] 11. In time of peace, too, the wicked are not simply on an equal footing with the good; wickedness is in fact revered to the point that in a large number of cases you are undecided whether to abhor people's depravity or to covet their prosperity. 12. But if the world were ruled by divine providence[54] and by the will of some deity, Phalaris[55] and Dionysius[56] would never have been given their kingdoms, nor Rutilius[57] and Camillus[58] their exile, nor Socrates[59] his poison. 13. Look, the trees are laden with fruit, the harvest is already white, the grapes are full to bursting; yet they are spoiled by rain, they are beaten down by hail.[60]

"So you can see, you have a choice: either it is the case that the truth is uncertain, being hidden and concealed from our gaze, or, as is the more probable conclusion, it is Fortune who is the ascendant power, completely unrestrained in her use of the variability and unpredictability of chance.[61]

CHAPTER 6

The traditions and value of Roman religion

1. "Thus we have either Fortune, whose character we know, or Nature, whose character we do not know.[62] In

that case, you hierophants of truth[63] would surely show greater reverence—and hence be better advised—if you embraced the system taught by your ancestors,[64] if you worshiped according to traditional practice, if the gods you adored were those whom your parents trained you as children first to fear—only later might you get to know them more intimately.[65] You would be better advised if you did not pronounce any opinion of your own on deities; you should, rather, trust your forbears who in a still uncultured age at the very infancy of the world were blessed with gods who were propitious—or their kings.[66]

"And this is precisely the explanation why right throughout all empires, provinces, and towns, we observe that individual groups have their native rites and rituals and worship their local gods.[67] For example, the Eleusinians have Ceres,[68] the Phrygians the Great Mother Goddess,[69] the Epidaurians Aesculapius,[70] the Chaldaeans Baal,[71] the Syrians Astarte,[72] the Taurians Diana,[73] the Gauls Mercury,[74] and the Romans have them all.[75] 2. As a result, the power and sway of the Romans has encompassed the entire circuit of the globe, it has spread its domain beyond the paths of the sun, the very bounds of Ocean.[76] And this is so because they have been plying arms with religious valor, fortifying their city with religious rituals, with the chastity of their virgins,[77] and with the many dignities and titles they grant their priests. When, for example,[78] they had been taken by siege and captured all but for the Capitol, they still worshiped their gods—and gods whom anyone else would by that time have rejected as angered with them; the Romans astounded the Gauls with their intrepid piety—they moved through their battle ranks unprotected

by weapons save for the arms of their religious obser-
vances.

"Even though the Romans have stood on the enemies'
ramparts which they have captured, still flushed with victory, they have persisted in respecting the divinities they
conquered; from every quarter they have continued to
seek gods to be their guests, to make them their own,[79] to
erect altars even to unknown deities[80] and to the shades of
the dead.[81] 3. By adopting the rites of all nations in this
way, they have won their empires as well.[82] And to this
day there has been no pause in the unending reverence
they show; indeed, it has been strengthened rather than
impaired with the long passage of time; for, as a general
rule, the greater the age that ceremonies and shrines ac-
cumulate, the more hallowed these institutions become
with their accruing years.[83]

CHAPTER 7

Further proofs for the value of Roman paganism

1. "At this stage I might venture myself to concede a
point—and to err in better company.[84] It was not, I would
claim, without sound reasons that our forbears zealously
strove to watch auguries, consult entrails,[85] establish rituals,
and dedicate sanctuaries. 2. Consider what you read in our
chronicles. You readily discover why they introduced
every manner of religious ritual; it was to repay divine
favor, to avert impending wrath, or to placate the actual
rage and fury of the gods.[86]

3. "One example is the Mother Goddess from Mount

Ida; by her arrival she vindicated the chastity of a matron and in addition she set Rome free from fear of her enemies.[87] There is another example in the equestrian statues which have been erected in honor of the two brothers in the lake; these represent them just as they appeared with panting breath and with their horses foaming and steaming, announcing their victory, the very day they had won it, over Perseus.[88] Another instance is the repetition of the games in honor of Jupiter, who had been offended; this was prompted by the dream of a man from the lower orders;[89] and one could also cite the self-dedication vowed by the Decii which the gods ratified.[90] Curtius provides yet a further example: when there yawned a deep chasm, he closed the opening with the honorific sacrifice of the bulk of his horse and its rider.[91] 4. Besides, only too often have the scorning of auspices given us clear evidence of the powerful presence of the gods. Hence there is the cursed name of Allia;[92] hence there was no battle between Claudius and Junius, and the Carthaginians —there was fatal shipwreck.[93]

"Flaminius spurned the auguries, and the Trasimene was swollen and dyed with Roman blood.[94] Crassus incurred, and mocked, ill omens and imprecations, and we seek back our military standards from Parthia.[95] 5. I am leaving aside the many illustrations that could be drawn from antiquity, not to mention the poems that have been written about the genealogies of the gods and the gifts and benefits they bestow; nor will I dwell on destinies foretold in oracles.[96] I suspect you may imagine that being so ancient they are merely folk myth. Turn your attention, then, to the temples and the sanctuaries of the gods, which protect and adorn the Roman state. Their sanctity, which

is to be ascribed to the presence of the deities who inhabit
and occupy them, far outweighs their richness of offering,[97]
ornament, and decoration. 6. And that is precisely why it
is in them that our seers, in communion with god, and
filled with his presence, have a foretaste of the future;
warning they furnish for danger, remedy for disease, hope
for suffering, help for affliction, comfort for disaster, relief
for hardship.[98] Why, even in sleep we see, hear, and recognize the gods whom, blasphemously, we deny, disown,
and forswear in daylight.[99]

CHAPTER 8

Attacks on the behavior of atheists and Christians

1. "And so the conclusion I draw is that while the origin
and nature of the immortal gods may still remain obscure,
there nevertheless continues to be unhesitating agreement
from all nations about their existence.[100] This religious
belief is so venerable, so beneficial, and so salutary; and I
cannot therefore tolerate that anyone in the arrogance of
his irreligious 'enlightenment' should have the effrontery
to try to weaken or destroy it. 2. I do not care whether he
is the famous Theodorus of Cyrene or his predecessor
Diagoras of Melos (surnamed in antiquity the atheist);[101]
both asserted that there were no gods, thereby completely
removing all the piety and all the awe by which human
actions are governed.[102] (And yet, for all their systematized
impiety, the fame and authority of their sham philosophy
will never grow strong.) 3. Neither do I care if he is
Protagoras of Abdera; he was one time disputing about
divinity in a spirit of inquiry rather than of disrespect.

Nevertheless, he was expelled by the Athenians from their land and his writings were burnt in a public assembly.[103]

"In view of this, is it not an absolute scandal—you will allow me, I hope, to be rather forthright about the strong feelings I have for my case—is it not scandalous that the gods should be mobbed by a gang of outlawed and reckless desperadoes?[104] 4. They have collected from the lowest possible dregs of society the more ignorant fools together with gullible women (readily persuaded, as is their weak sex[105]); they have thus formed a rabble of blasphemous conspirators,[106] who with nocturnal assemblies, periodic fasts, and inhuman feasts[107] seal their pact not with some religious ritual but with desecrating profanation; they are a crowd that furtively lurks in hiding places, shunning the light; they are speechless in public but gabble away in corners.[108]

"They despise our temples as being no more than sepulchres,[109] they spit after our gods,[110] they sneer at our rites, and, fantastic though it is, our priests they pity—pitiable themselves; they scorn the purple robes of public office, though they go about in rags themselves.[111]

5. "How amazingly stupid, unbelievably insolent they are. Tortures of the present they scoff at, but they live in dread of the uncertain tortures of the future; they are afraid to die after they are dead, but meantime they have no fear of death.[112] So effectively are they beguiled of alarm by the comforting expectation of a renewal of life hereafter.

CHAPTER 9

Further attacks on the rites and morals of Christians

1. "Evil weeds grow apace and so, day by day, this depraved way of life now creeps further over all the face of the globe and the foul religious shrines[113] of this abominable congregation are getting a stronger hold.[114] This confederacy must be torn out, it must be sworn to perdition.

2. "They recognize each other by secret marks and signs;[115] hardly have they met when they love each other, throughout the world uniting in the practice of a veritable religion of lusts. Indiscriminately they call each other brother and sister, thus turning even ordinary fornication into incest by the intervention of these hallowed names. Such a pride does this foolish, deranged superstition take in its wickedness.[116]

3. "Unless there were some underlying truth, such a wide variety of charges, and very serious ones, would not be made about them; they can hardly be repeated in polite company. Rumor is a shrewd informant.[117] I hear, for example, that they do reverence to the head of that most degraded of beasts, an ass; I cannot imagine what absurdity has persuaded them to consecrate it, but it is indeed a cult born of such morals and well suited for them.[118] 4. It is also reported that they worship the genitals of their pontiff and priest, adoring, it appears, the sex of their 'father.'[119] Perhaps this is incorrect but it certainly is a suspicion that befits their clandestine and nocturnal ceremonies. There are also stories about the objects of their veneration: they are said to be a man who was punished with death as a criminal and the fell wood of his cross,[120] thus providing

suitable liturgy for the depraved fiends: they worship what they deserve.

5. "To turn to another point. The notoriety of the stories told of the initiation of new recruits is matched by their ghastly horror. A young baby is covered over with flour, the object being to deceive the unwary. It is then served before the person to be admitted into their rites. The recruit is urged to inflict blows onto it—they appear to be harmless because of the covering of flour. Thus the baby is killed with wounds that remain unseen and concealed. It is the blood of this infant—I shudder to mention it—it is this blood that they lick with thirsty lips; these are the limbs they distribute eagerly; this is the victim by which they seal their covenant; it is by complicity in this crime that they are pledged to mutual silence; these are their rites, more foul than all sacrileges combined.[121]

6. "We all know, too, about their banquets; they are on everyone's lips, everywhere[122] as the speech of our Cirtensian testifies.[123] On a special day they gather for a feast with all their children, sisters, mothers—all sexes and all ages. There, flushed with the banquet after such feasting and drinking, they begin to burn with incestuous passions. They provoke a dog tied to the lampstand[124] to leap and bound towards a scrap of food which they have tossed outside the reach of his chain. 7. By this means the light is overturned and extinguished, and with it common knowledge of their actions;[125] in the shameless dark with unspeakable lust they copulate in random unions, all equally being guilty of incest, some by deed, but everyone by complicity. For whatever may happen in individual cases is the general aspiration and desire of them all.

CHAPTER 10

Attacks against the secrecy and absurdity of Christian monotheism

1. "I am deliberately passing over a number of points—those that I have already given are more than enough; and that all of them, or practically all, are true is revealed by the very obscurity which shrouds this perverted religion. 2. Why else should they go to such pains to hide and conceal whatever it is they worship? One is always happy for honorable actions to be made public; crimes are kept secret.[126] Why do they have no altars,[127] no temples,[128] no publicly-known images?[129] Why do they never speak in the open,[130] why do they always assemble in stealth? It must be that whatever it is they worship—and suppress—is deserving either of punishment or of shame. 3. Furthermore, who is this unique god of theirs,[131] what is his origin, where does he live, so solitary, so totally forlorn that no free nation has knowledge of him, nor any empire—not even the religious fanatics of Rome?[132] 4. The only other group to have worshiped one god is the wretched tribe of the Jews, but they did so in the open, with temples and altars, with sacrifice and ceremonial.[133] But you can see that this god has neither power nor strength; he and his very own people are captives of the Romans, who are but men.[134]

5. "Besides, look at the fantastic, unnatural creature that these Christians have devised!

"They make that god of theirs—whom they are unable to show to others or see for themselves[135]—they make him pry with scrupulous care into the morals and actions of all men, even down to their words and hidden thoughts; he has to rush to and fro, he has to be present everywhere! They make him out to be a restless troublemaker, and shamelessly inquisitive, as he has to be too, if he is to witness everything that happens and wander in and out of every place. Of course it is impossible for him either to devote himself to particular details if his attention is distracted in every direction or to deal adequately with everything if he is concentrating on particular details.[136]

CHAPTER 11

Further Christian absurdities: their beliefs about the end of the world and an afterlife

1. "And that is not all. The entire world they threaten with conflagration[137]—the firmament itself, constellations and all—thus conspiring its utter ruin. To imagine that the eternal order established by the divine laws of nature could be thrown into chaos! Or that the bonds that bind all elements together could be torn asunder, that the framework of the heavens could be severed, that the vast structure which girds and holds in place the universe could thus be undermined![138] 2. And they are not just satisfied with this lunatic notion; they embellish and embroider it with old wives' tales.[139] After death, ashes, and cinders,[140] they tell us, they are born again.[141] They all believe their own lies with such unaccountable confidence you might take them to have already come to life again! 3. Look at their double delirium, their twofold madness: they solemnly herald that the heavens and constellations will perish, though we leave them just as we find them; and they firmly pledge themselves eternity when they are dead and

destroyed, though we perish just as once we were born.[142]
4. I presume this is supposed to explain why they abominate funeral pyres and condemn cremation.[143] But of course every body, withdrawn from the flames or not, is eventually reduced to earth in the course of the passing years; it makes no difference if it is torn apart by wild beasts or swallowed up by the seas or covered over with earth or taken away by the flames.[144] If corpses have sensation, any kind of interment causes them suffering; if they have none, speedy dispatch is the most salutary treatment.[145]
5. Led astray by this ridiculous idea, they promise themselves, being the just, an everlasting life of blessedness[146] after death, and the rest, being the wicked, perpetual punishment.

"If I had leisure to expatiate at length, I could adduce many supporting arguments for what I have just said. But that it is rather they who are the wicked I need not go to further pains to establish; I have already demonstrated it. But yet, let me disregard this point. The verdict of the majority is that the responsibility for blame and innocence belongs to Fate; and with this view you all concur.[147] 6. Others say that all our actions are due to fate; you say, similarly, that they are due to god. This entails that it is not of their own free will that men desire to join your school;[148] they have been chosen. Therefore, the judge that you fashion is unjust: he punishes men not for their intentions but for their lot in life.

7. "Here I should like to make an inquiry on another point: When we rise again, do we have bodies? And if so, what bodies, the same or renewed? No body? So far as I know, that means no intelligence, no soul, no life.[149] The same body? But it has already decomposed. Another body?

In that case a new man is born, not the former one re-stored. 8. Countless centuries have slipped by, but in all these bygone ages I know of not one man who has left to come back from the underworld—even on the conditions of Protesilaus, granted a visit of but a few hours—if only to make this notion credible by his example.[150]

"Really, you are so gullible—you have refashioned all these figments of morbid imaginations, the absurd consolations, the frivolities invented by poets to give beguiling charm to their verse,[151] and you have applied them to your god, and to your discredit.

CHAPTER 12

The miserable life and antisocial behavior of Christians

1. "But you draw no lesson, none at all, from your present situation; you do not see how misled you are by empty aspirations and baseless promises. You pitiable fools, you ought to calculate while you still have life left in you what is likely to befall you after your death. 2. Look: some of you, the greater half (the better half, you say[152]), go in need, suffer from cold, from hunger and toil. And yet your god allows it, he connives at it; he will not or he cannot assist his own followers. This proves how weak he is—or wicked.[153]

3. "You have dreams of posthumous immortality, but when you quake in the face of danger,[154] when you burn with fever or are racked by pain, are you still unaware of your real condition? Do you still not recognize your human frailty? Poor wretch, whether you like it or not, you have proof of your own infirmity, and still you will

not admit it! 4. But these evils, common to us all, I omit. Look: you Christians are menaced with threats, torments and tortures, with crosses—meant not this time to be adored but endured[155]—and with fire as well, just as you foretell and fear.[156] And where is that god of yours who can help those who come to life again, but cannot help those who are alive? 5. Is it not true that without the help of your god Rome has her dominions and empire, she has the whole world to enjoy, and she has you as well beneath her sway?[157]

"But in the meantime, in your anxious state of expectation, you refrain from honest pleasures: you do not go to our shows, you take no part in our processions, you are not present at our public banquets, you shrink in horror from our sacred games,[158] from food ritually dedicated by our priests, from drink hallowed by libation poured upon our altars.[159] Such is your dread of the very gods you deny. 6. You do not bind your head with flowers, you do not honor your body with perfumes; ointments you reserve for funerals,[160] but even to your tombs you deny garlands;[161] you anemic, neurotic creatures, you indeed deserve to be pitied—but by our gods. The result is, you pitiable fools, that you have no enjoyment of life while you wait for the new life which you will never have.

7. "And so, if you do have any trace of sense or shame, stop prying into the tracks of heaven, the destinies and the mysteries of the universe. Keep your eyes fixed on where you walk[162]—that's employment enough for utter boors and yokels, ungraced by any manners or culture.[163] If you have not been privileged to understand the concerns of a citizen, you most surely have been denied discussion of the affairs of heaven.[164]

CHAPTER 13

The virtues of a sceptical attitude

1. "But should any of you simply have to philosophize, I urge him, if he is so audacious, to imitate, if he can, that prince of wisdom, Socrates.[165] Whenever he was asked a question about the heavens, he made his famous reply: 'What is above us is no concern of us.'[166] 2. That is why he thoroughly deserved the confirmation which the oracle gave of his unique sagacity. The significance of the oracle he realized clearly himself: the reason why he had been ranked before all others was not because he had discovered everything, but because he had learnt that he knew nothing.[167] Truly the admission of ignorance is the height of sagacity. 3. This is the source from which has sprung the prudent scepticism, on fundamental questions, of Arcesilaus and, considerably later, of Carneades and of the numerous philosophers of the Academic school.[168] This is the method in which the uneducated are able to philosophize with prudence, and the educated with distinction.

4. "You must agree that we should all admire and emulate the hesitancy of the lyric poet Simonides.[169] When Hiero the tyrant inquired of him what he thought the gods were and what they were like, he first of all asked for a day's adjournment so he could deliberate the question. On the following day he got a two-day extension, and then, after a reminder, he added a further two days. Finally, when the tyrant inquired the reasons for this lengthy delay, he replied that the truth seemed to increase in obscurity the longer he went on with his inquiry.[170] 5. These are exactly my feelings on the matter: what is doubtful should

be left just as it is. When so many great minds continue to deliberate a question, it is arrogant and irresponsible to presume to pass judgment in favor of either side. Otherwise there is the danger that we may promote some doting superstition, or that we may destroy all true religion."[171]

Chapter 14

Interlude: the dangers of clever speaking

1. Such was Caecilius' speech; he was beaming and relaxed, for in his speech he had poured out without restraint his pent-up feelings of indignation. "Does Octavius dare," he said, "to have anything to say in reply, scion of Plautine pedigree that he is, being the best of bakers and therefore the poorest of philosophers?"[172] 2. "You must not jeer at him," I said, "nor is it proper for you to vaunt the elegance of your discourse until the very last word has been spoken on both sides, particularly as the object of the dispute is the truth, not applause. 3. It's true that the subtlety and variety in your speech did give me much pleasure; but what concerns me more deeply is not so much the present proceedings as the general question of the nature of debating. Very frequently the truth may be limpidly clear; but even so it tends to become obscured, according to the strength and effectiveness of a speaker's oratory. 4. And why? The notorious explanation is that it so happens that an audience is easily swayed by the charm of words; thus distracted from attending to the facts, they agree without reservation with everything that is said, failing to separate correct from incorrect and unaware that falsehood may lie in what seems likely and truth is what sounds improbable.[173]

5. And so, the stronger their habit grows of believing whatever they hear confidently asserted, the more often they are outwitted by experienced speakers. They are constantly misled by their own impetuosity.[174] But instead of putting the blame on their own powers of judgment,[175] they complain about the uncertainty of things; they prefer to condemn everyone and to be completely sceptical[176] rather than to judge for themselves on subjects where they may be deceived. 6. And so we must be on the lookout that we do not become victims ourselves of this abhorrence for every form of discussion in the manner of the simple-minded masses; they become so exasperated that they rage against their fellow men with hatred and abuse.[177] What happens is that, being gullible and unsuspecting, they are cheated by those who they thought were honest men; and then, by repeating their mistake, they grow suspicious of everyone—even men whose excellence they might have appreciated they fear, supposing they must be wicked.

7. "This, then, is what I am concerned about—both sides may take great pains in presenting their cases:[178] on the one side may lie the truth, though by and large hard to see, while on the other hand there may be a brilliant display of subtlety, and this, combined with verbal amplitude, quite often creates the semblance of a reliable and conclusive proof. We must be on our guard, therefore, to weigh every point with the utmost care. We will then be in a position not only to give praise to nicety of argument, but we will also be able to select, approve, and adopt what is right."

CHAPTER 15

1. "You are deserting the duties of a conscientious[179] judge," Caecilius said. "It is flagrantly unjust that you should impair the force of my pleading by intervening in this very serious debate.[180] Octavius has to refute, if he can, every single argument of mine whole and entire."

2. "Unless I am mistaken," I said, "what you are objecting to I advanced for the common profit: our verdict must be the result of scrupulous balancing not of inflated eloquence but of hard facts. But, as you complain, our concentration must not be distracted any further. Our friend Januarius is dying to speak, and we can now listen to his reply in unbroken silence."

CHAPTER 16

The Christian's reply. Christians are well qualified to speak about divine matters

1. And Octavius began: "I shall speak to the best of my ability. But you[181] must lend me a helping hand to wash away such bitter stains of censure in the stream of words of truth.[182] And at the outset, I must honestly say that the views of my friend Natalis meandered and wandered along paths so devious and so slippery[183] that I hesitate to decide whether the chaos was due to deliberate cunning or the vacillation was the result of error. 2. For example, he wavered so much that at one point he believed in the gods, at another he was still pondering the question; consequently, the case he put forward was equivocal[184] and, therefore, even more equivocal must be the basis and di-

rection of our reply. But I will not impute my friend Natalis with chicanery; I refuse to believe it—there is a world of difference between Natalis' ingenuous candor and sophisticated subtlety.[185] 3. What, then, is the solution? Natalis is like a man at an intersection when, as is often the case, one road branches into several, and he does not know the right road. In his ignorance he hesitates perplexed, not daring to select any particular road nor to decide that all will do equally well.[186] The case is similar if a man does not have a steadfast appraisal of the truth; the wider the range over which he spreads his ill-founded suspicions, the more nebulous become his already indecisive views.

4. "So you can see that it comes as no great surprise to find that Caecilius is ceaselessly driven about, heaving and tossing to and fro before contrary winds and currents. To prevent this happening further, I shall refute and counter the arguments he made (inconsistent though they were) by the tried and tested, the one and only Truth.[187] He then will have no further cause for doubt or perplexity.

5. "In an angry storm of outraged indignation my brother[188] has complained that it is intolerable that men lacking in education, in money, and in skill should debate about the heavens.[189]

"I would have him be aware, however, that all men, regardless of age, sex, and class, have been born with the capacity for reason and with the power of understanding; wisdom is not acquired by the accidents of fortune, it is implanted by nature.[190] Why, he should not forget that even philosophers themselves, as well as those who are remembered in history as the discoverers of arts, were considered to be born common men, ignorant and half-clad,[191] before their intelligence won them an illustrious name.

"And moreover, he should remember that wealthy men, attached to their own riches, are more in the habit of contemplating their gold than the heavens; whereas it was our followers, poor as they were, who carefully thought out the meaning of true wisdom and handed down their teaching to others.[192] The obvious inference is that genius is not bestowed through riches nor acquired through studies, but is engendered within us when the mind itself is fashioned. 6. There is no need, therefore, to feel indignant or to complain if anyone, of any rank, makes inquiries, holds views, or advances theories on divine matters. After all, the object of your research is not the status of the one who argues but the truth of his actual argument.[193]

"And there is the further point that reasoning gains in lucidity the more one's speech is lacking in skill;[194] it is not dressed up in a parade of stylish oratory but stands on its own merits, supported only by the standard of truth.[195]

CHAPTER 17

The beauty, order, and variety of the universe, and of its produce and its inhabitants, prove the existence of God

1. "And I do not deny the point that Caecilius endeavored to establish as one of his main principles, that man ought to know himself[196] and to examine from every angle what he is, where he is from, why he is alive—whether he is a compound of elements or a harmonious arrangement of atoms,[197] or whether it is rather God who has made, shaped, and quickened him. 2. But these very prob-

lems we cannot explore and delve into without holding an investigation of the whole of the universe as well.[198] The explanation is that all things are so closely linked, bound, and chained together that unless you have taken great care to unravel what is the nature of God, you cannot know what is the nature of man; just as you cannot properly devote yourself to the duties of a citizen unless you have some knowledge of this city-state that is common to all men, the world.[199] This is especially true because the point of difference between us and brute beasts is this: animals naturally bend and stoop towards the ground, with no other purpose in life than to look out for food, whereas we walk with head erect, with gaze directed towards the heavens,[200] gifted with the power of speech and reason[201] which enable us to recognize, perceive, and imitate God. Therefore, we ought not and we may not remain in ignorance of the celestial radiance which impinges on our eyes and senses. It is tantamount to an act of sacrilege to seek on the ground what you ought to discover on high.[202]

3. "And so I am all the more convinced that men are possessed of neither reason nor any sense, not even eyesight, when they refuse to regard the whole of this beautiful universe as the finished work of a divine intelligence, but rather consider it as a random collection and conglomeration of bits and pieces.[203] 4. Lift your eyes heavenwards and survey what is beneath and about you: there can be nothing more evident, more undeniable, more obvious than that there does exist some divine being,[204] endowed with transcendent intelligence, who sustains the whole of nature with breath and with movement, with guidance and with nourishment.

5. "Consider the sky itself: see how far it extends, how

swiftly it revolves; observe that by night it is spangled with stars, and by day it is lit with sunlight.[205] This will quickly make you realize how wonderful, how marvelous is the balance maintained by that supreme guiding hand. Consider, too, how the year is caused by the sun's revolution and how each month is brought round by the moon's waxing, waning, and eclipse. 6. There is little point in describing the recurrent changes of darkness and light which provide us with an alternating restoration of work and rest, and lengthier discussion of the stars—how they guide the course of ships or how they bring on the season for plough and harvest—is best left to the astronomers.[206] The creation, the production, and the arrangement of each one of these phenomena demanded a supreme artisan and perfect reason; but one can go further and say that to perceive, discern, and comprehend them one also needs to have supreme intelligence and reason.[207]

7. "Let me further illustrate my point. There is a regular variety which distinguishes the seasons and their produce, in due order (Is this not evidence that they have a creator, a father?): spring with its flowers, summer with its harvests, glad autumn with its maturing fruits, winter with its essential olive crop. But this order could easily be turned into chaos, were it not dependent on the greatest intelligence. 8. Mighty indeed must be the providence which interposes the temperate means of autumn and spring to prevent an incessant winter from searing with its icy cold or an incessant summer from scorching with its blazing heat; instead the year gently retraces its footsteps[208] in harmless and imperceptible stages.

9. "And consider the sea, kept in bounds by the law of the shore. Look at all the trees, drawing life from the

bowels of the earth. Observe the Ocean, flowing back and forth with alternating tides. Look at the springs, gushing from inexhaustible sources. Gaze upon the rivers, moving down their never-resting courses.[209] 10. It is unnecessary to describe the happy arrangement of mountain peaks, rounded hills, and expansive plains; similarly with the many different ways living creatures protect themselves against each other—some have horns for weapons, others a barricade of teeth; they stand firm on hooves, they are spiked with stings, or they fly free on swift feet or soaring wings.[210] 11. Above all, it is the very beauty of our own body which declares that there is a God who designed it: upright posture, head erect, eyes stationed on high as in a watchtower, and all the other senses deployed as in a fortress.[211]

CHAPTER 18

The providence of God is revealed in the detailed workings of nature, and the uniqueness of God in the speech of the common man

1. "It would take too long to deal with this question in detail. There is no member of man's body which beauty and necessity do not justify; and, what is more remarkable, though we all have the same general figure, each of us has some features which are different. The result is that while taken together we all seem alike, yet individually we are found to be unalike.[212] 2. And do you not find a convincing proof in the process of birth? The desire for begetting children must surely be a gift from God; so too the fact that as the time of birth draws near, the breasts begin to

fill with milk, and that the weak offspring grows strong on the fulness of this milky dew.[213]

3. "And it is not only the universe as a whole that is God's concern; He attends also to its particular parts. Britain, for example, is lacking in sunshine, but it is refreshed by the warmth of the sea which surrounds it. The waters of the Nile regularly moderate Egypt's drought, the Euphrates compensates Mesopotamia for its lack of rainfall, the river Indus, it is said, both sows and waters the Orient.[214] 4. Now if you went into a house and saw that everything in it was splendidly cared for, arranged, and appointed, you would think that there must be a master in charge of it and that he must be far superior to all those fine possessions. Likewise in this house of the world: when you discern in heaven and on earth order, law, providence, you must believe that there is a master, a father of the universe, and that He actually surpasses in beauty the constellations and the separate parts of the whole world.[215]

5. "It may possibly occur to you that since the question of providence admits of no doubt, we ought to investigate whether the heavenly kingdom is governed by the command of one or by the will of many. To clarify this particular point will be no great trouble if you consider earthly empires, for they are surely modeled on those of heaven.[216] 6. When did a joint monarchy ever begin with mutual trust or break up without bloodshed?[217] I need not dwell on the story of the Persians who found the omen for selecting their new emperor in the neighing of horses,[218] nor will I mention the obsolete legend of the Theban pair.[219] We all know the old story of the twins who fought for a kingdom of shepherds and a cottage.[220] Father- and son-in-law spread wars over the entire globe; the fortunes

of an empire so vast could not contain the two.[221] 7. Consider other illustrations: bees have but one king, flocks have but one leader, herds have but one head.[222] As for heaven, could you believe that there the supreme power is shared, that the absolute majesty of that real and divine realm is sundered, in face of the plain fact that there does exist a God who is father of all, who has neither beginning nor end, who blesses all with birth and Himself with eternity, who before the world was, was to Himself the world? He it is who by His word orders, by His reason disposes, and by His might perfects each and every thing that exists.[223]

8. "This God cannot be seen; He is too bright for sight. He cannot be grasped; He is too pure for touch. He cannot be measured; He is too great for our senses—a boundless infinity, sharing with Himself alone the knowledge of His vastness. But the understanding we have is too limited to comprehend Him and that is why we measure Him worthily when we say that He is immeasurable.[224] 9. In my honest opinion, if a man thinks that he knows the magnitude of God, he diminishes it; if he does not want to diminish it, he does not pretend to know it. 10. Nor should you seek a name for God: God is His name. We have need of titles in cases where we want to separate individuals from a large group; we use, then, the distinguishing mark of personal names. But God is unique; all He has for title is God.[225] Should I call Him father, you would consider that He is earthly; should I call Him king, you would suspect that He is made of flesh;[226] should I call Him lord,[227] you would certainly understand that He is mortal. Remove the aggregate of names and you will see clearly His splendor.

11. "And I have on this point universal agreement; is it not so? I hear the common people as they stretch forth their hands towards heaven. They say simply 'God,' and 'God is great,' and 'God is true,' and 'if God grants it.' Is that the natural speech of the common people or the prayer of an avowed Christian?[228] Those who would have Jupiter to be sovereign are misled in name but are in agreement about his unique power.[229]

Chapter 19

The poets and philosophers bear witness to the existence of a unique God

1. "The poets too[230] I hear proclaiming that there is a unique father of gods and men,[231] and that the thoughts of mortals are no more than the daylight produced by the father of all.[232] 2. Is it not so that Maro of Mantua[233] speaks with great distinctness, accuracy, and truth when he says 'in the beginning heaven and earth' (and the other limbs of the world) 'are nourished by a spirit within' and 'are stirred by an indwelling mind . . . and hence come the race of men and flocks' (and all the other living creatures)? Elsewhere this same poet calls this mind and spirit God. Here are his words: '. . . for God moves through all lands and the expanses of ocean and the abyss of sky . . . whence men and flocks, whence rain and fire.'[234]

"Do not we, too, proclaim that God is nothing but mind and reason and spirit?[235]

3. "If you like, let us pass in review the teaching of philosophers. You will discover that while they may use

different expressions, in essence they all concur and accord with this very same opinion.[236]

4. "I will leave out those uncouth philosophers of old, whose sayings won them the title of sages.[237] Let Thales of Miletus, then, be the first on the list; he was the first of them all to discuss the heavens. This Thales of Miletus said that the primary element of things was water and that God is the mind which fashioned all things from water;[238]† we must confess that it is a theory of water and spirit at once too profound and too lofty for human discovery; it was taught by God.[239]† You see that the view of this pioneer of philosophers is in perfect harmony with ours. 5. After him, Anaximenes,[240] and later Diogenes of Apollonia,[241] set up air as God, infinite, measureless. We are in similar agreement with these philosophers, too, on the question of divinity.

6. "Anaxagoras declared God to be the disposition and movement of infinite mind;[242] Pythagoras that He is soul, permeating and diffused throughout the entire universe of nature, and the source of life for every living creature.[243] 7. Xenophanes, as is well known, taught that God is the infinite whole endowed with mind;[244] Antisthenes that while among the common people there are many gods, in nature there is but one pre-eminent God.[245] Speusippus recognized as God the life force which governs all things.[246] 8. Furthermore, is it not true that Democritus, though the first to invent atoms, frequently speaks of nature (the source of images) and intelligence as God?[247] Likewise Straton, too, calls nature God.[248] Even the great Epicurus, who supposes the gods to be either idle or nonexistent, nevertheless sets nature over and above them.[249]

9. "Aristotle's theory varies, but there is, however, a unique power which he assigns: sometimes it is mind, other times the universe, or again it is the ruler of the universe that he declares to be God.[250] Theophrastus likewise varies, in some places attributing the divine sovereignty to the universe, in others to mind;[251] Heraclides of Pontus (though with variations) also ascribes a divine mind to the universe.[252] 10. Zeno, Chrysippus, and Cleanthes, too, hold diverse opinions but they all come back to the unity of providence. Cleanthes argued sometimes that God is mind and soul, sometimes that He is ether, and frequently that He is reason.[253] Zeno, his teacher, asserted that the first principle of all things is natural, and divine, law, or sometimes it is ether, occasionally reason. He was also the philosopher who interpreted Juno as air, Jupiter as sky, Neptune as sea, and Vulcan as fire, and demonstrated, in a similar fashion, that all the other gods of the common people were elements, thus launching a vigorous attack on, and refuting, these popular misconceptions.[254]

11. "Chrysippus' views are pretty well identical: he believed that the divine, rational energy, that nature and the universe, and sometimes the necessity of Fate, are God; he imitated Zeno as well in the naturalistic interpretation which he applied to the poems of Hesiod, Homer, and Orpheus.[255]

12. "In his teaching Diogenes of Babylon also expounded and argued that 'the childbearing of Jupiter' and 'the birth of Minerva' etc. were expressions that applied to physical realities, not to gods.[256]

13. "Xenophon, the follower of Socrates, said that the figure of the true God cannot be seen and that, therefore, we ought not to search for it;[257] the Stoic Ariston said that

He cannot be comprehended in any way.[258] Both realized the majesty of God when they despaired of understanding Him.

14. "Plato's discourse about God is more lucid both in content and in style; it would be altogether divine were its beauty not sullied by the occasional intrusion of popular prejudices.[259] Now for Plato, in the *Timaeus*, God is in His own name father of the universe, architect of the soul, engineer of all things in heaven and on earth; and he declared the difficulty of discovering Him—so extraordinary is His might and so beyond our powers of belief—and the impossibility, when you have discovered Him, of describing Him to the general public.[260]

15. "These opinions are pretty well identical with ours: we recognize a God, and we also call Him father of all, and unless we are cross-examined, we never proclaim Him in public.[261]

CHAPTER 20

Our gullible ancestors do not merit credence about the gods; the gods were, in fact, merely honored mortals

1. "I have disclosed the views of almost all philosophers of any outstanding distinction: though under a multiplicity of names, they have defined God as unique. So it is open to anyone to suppose that either present-day Christians are philosophers or philosophers of the past were already Christians.[262]

2. "Now if the world is ruled by providence and guided by the will of a unique God, the ignorant generations of the past, charmed, or rather captivated, by their own

fables, have no right to dragoon us into the mistake of agreeing with them; in fact, they are refuted by the opinions of their own philosophers, supported as they are by the authority of reason and ancient tradition.[263] 3. And indeed, such was the credulity of our ancestors[264] towards lies that they even gave unquestioning acceptance to such preternatural and weird marvels[265] as Scylla with her many shapes,[266] the Chimera with her many bodies,[267] the Hydra coming to life again from prolific wounds,[268] the Centaurs, horses and riders all in one;[269] all the fictions of folklore— these they would gladly hear. 4. And let us not forget those old wives' tales of men transformed into birds and beasts, and into trees and flowers.[270] If such wonders did happen, they would happen; as they cannot happen, then they did not happen.[271]

5. "In a similar fashion our ancestors believed in their gods, too—uncritical, gullible, naive, simple-minded.[272] They would pay court to their kings with pious reverence; after their death they would desire to see their likeness in effigies, and be anxious to preserve their memory in statues. Thus what they adopted as a means of consolation became objects of worship.[273] 6. And, as a matter of fact, there was a time when the world was not yet opened up to trade, when peoples had still not exchanged their native rituals and manners; each individual nation[274] used to revere as a citizen of happy memory their founder or a renowned general or a chaste queen, unusually valiant for her sex, or the discoverer of some benefit or skill. In this way they gave tribute to the dead and example to the future.

Chapter 21

Proofs that the gods were merely men

1. "Read the writings of historians as well as those of philosophers.[275] You will come to the same conclusions as I have.

"Euhemerus lists those who have been treated as gods in recompense for benefaction or valour;[276] he enumerates their parentage, their native land, their tombs, and illustrates his case from different districts: Jupiter of Dicte,[277] Apollo of Delphi,[278] Isis of Pharos,[279] Ceres of Eleusis.[280]

2. "Prodicus states that there were assumed into the ranks of the gods[281] those who advanced man's progress by their discovery of new fruits of the soil in the course of their wanderings. The philosopher Persaeus argues for the same thesis, linking by the same names the fruits discovered and those who discovered them,[282] as in the line from Comedy, 'Venus stays cold in the absence of Liber and Ceres.'[283] 3. The famous Alexander the Great of Macedon in a remarkable work wrote to his mother that a priest, overawed by his power, betrayed to him this secret about these human gods.[284] In it he represents Vulcan as the very first god of all;[285] after him came the line of Jupiter;[286] and then he passed down the list from the ears of corn of Isis to her swallow and timbrel,[287] and the scattered limbs and empty tomb of your Serapis (or Osiris).[288]

CHAPTER 22

Absurdities and inconsistencies in pagan mythology

1. "And furthermore,[289] consider the actual rites and mysteries of these gods. You will find tragic departures, disasters, and deaths, weeping and wailing among these wretched gods.

"Isis weeps and wails for her lost son[290] as she searches for him with her Cynocephalus[291] and her bald priests;[292] her wretched votaries beat their breasts and imitate the anguish of that woebegone mother. Later, when the little boy has been found again, Isis rejoices, her priests revel, Cynocephalus who found him exults. Year in, year out there is no end to their losing what they find or finding what they lose. Is it not absurd to bewail what you worship or worship what you bewail?[293] Nevertheless these rites, once Egyptian, are now practiced even in Rome.[294] 2. Ceres, amid a blaze of torches and her serpent, wanders careworn and anxious trying to trace the footsteps of her Libera, victim of abduction and rape. Such are the mysteries of Eleusis.[295]

3. "And as for the rites sacred to Jupiter, he has a she-goat for nurse as a baby; he is stolen away from his father greedy to devour him; and to prevent that father hearing his wails, the Corybantes make their cymbals clash and reverberate.[296]

4. "I am embarrassed to mention Dindymus sacred to Cybele;[297] ugly old crone that she was (as well she might be, being after all the mother of a large number of gods), she failed in her efforts to seduce her own paramour, whom, unluckily for him, she found attractive.[298] And so she

castrated him—her object must have been to make a
eunuch-god! Because of this legend her Galli go so far as
to sacrifice the virility of their own bodies in their worship of her.[299] These are no longer sacred rites; they are
tortures.

5. "Why, you must admit that the very form and features of your gods confirm that they are a laughingstock
and a scandal.[300] Vulcan is a lame and crippled god,[301]
Apollo still has smooth cheeks after all these years,[302]
Aesculapius has a splendid beard though he is the son of
the ever-youthful Apollo,[303] Neptune's eyes are watery-
green,[304] Minerva's are bluish-grey,[305] Juno's cowlike,[306]
Mercury's feet are winged,[307] Pan's hooved, Saturn's
shackled.[308] Janus is double-faced, as if he could walk for-
wards as well as backwards.[309] On occasion Diana is a
huntress in short tunic; as goddess at Ephesus she is en-
cumbered with many distended breasts; as goddess of the
Crossroads she is a terrifying sight with triple head and
many hands.[310]

6. "And what is more, statues of your Jupiter himself
are erected, sometimes without a beard, at other times they
are set up with a beard.[311] Bearing the title of Hammon, he
has horns;[312] of Capitolinus, he carries thunderbolts;[313] of
Latiaris, he is bespattered with gore;[314] of Feretrius† and
he is not heard†.[315] I shall not bore you with a long catalogue of Jupiters; his monstrous shapes are as numerous as
his titles. 7. Erigone hung from a noose so she could be
marked out among the stars as Virgo;[316] Castor and his
brother take it in turns to die in order that they may
live.[317] Aesculapius was struck by the thunderbolt that he
might rise up and join the gods;[318] Hercules, to rid himself
of his mortal frame, was consumed in the Oetaean flames.[319]

CHAPTER 23

*Further absurdities and indignities of the pagan gods, who
were once men*

1. "Such are the delusive fables that we learn not only
on the knees of our parents who know no better;[320] what is
more serious, we take great pains to acquire knowledge of
them by study and education, particularly from the works
of poets—it is they who have done unrivaled harm to the
truth by the weight of their authority.[321] 2. And this is
why Plato very properly ejected the great and famous
Homer (though duly praised and crowned) from the city-
state he was constructing in his dialogue.[322] 3. For it was
particularly Homer, in his Trojan War, who, while making fun of your gods,[323] mingled them in among the deeds
and doings of men; he it was who arranged them to fight
like pairs of gladiators,[324] wounded Venus,[325] cast Mars into
chains, caused him to be hurt, and put him to flight.[326] 4.
He tells the story that Jupiter was freed by Briareus to save
him from being bound by the rest of the gods;[327] that
being unable to rescue his son Sarpedon from death,
Jupiter wept showers of blood for him;[328] that enticed by
Venus' girdle he lay with Juno, his wife, with more ardor
than he usually showed in his acts of adultery.[329]

5. "Elsewhere in poetry Hercules removes the dung,[330]
and Apollo pastures the flocks for Admetus.[331] Neptune
constructed the walls for Laomedon but the unlucky
builder received no payment for his work.[332] 6. In poetry,
too, we hear tell of Jupiter's thunderbolt being forged on
an anvil at the same time as Aeneas' armor—and this despite the fact that the heavens and thunderbolts existed

long before the birth of Jupiter on Crete and that a Cy-
clops could no more have copied the flames of a genuine
thunderbolt than Jupiter himself could have helped being
terrified of them.[333]

7. "I shall not bother to mention Mars and Venus caught
in adultery nor the unnatural lust of Jupiter for Ganymede, a passion hallowed in heaven.[334] All these things have
been published for just this purpose, to furnish some sort
of sanction for the vices of men.[335]

8. "The minds of boys are corrupted by these and similar beguiling lies and fabrications; they grow up to full
manhood with these fables still deeply fixed in their minds;
they grow old, poor wretches, in these same beliefs. And
yet the truth is there before their eyes if only they look
for it.[336]

9. "Saturn, the head of this swarming race, was a man
according to all the writers of antiquity, Greek and
Roman.[337] In their historical works, Nepos[338] and Cassius[339]
are aware of this fact. Thallus[340] and Diodorus mention it
also.[341] 10. Now this Saturn, in fear of his son's rage, fled
from Crete and made for Italy; there, welcomed as a guest
by Janus, he taught many things to those uncouth and
boorish people[342]—as you might expect from a smart and
refined little Greek;[343] he taught them how to write letters,
to stamp coins, to make tools.[344] 11. And so he chose that
his place of hiding (*latebra*) should be called Latium because he had lain in hiding (*latuisset*) there. And to the
memory of posterity he left the city of Saturnia, named
after him, and similarly Janus the Janiculum.[345] 12. He
was certainly, therefore, a man: he fled, he lay in hiding,
he was the father of a man, the son of a man himself; he
was reputed to be the Son of Earth or of Heaven because

his parentage was unknown among the people of Italy, and
even to this day those whom we see unexpectedly we call
heaven-sent; Sons of Earth are those whose origins are
disreputable or unknown.[346] 13. Saturn's son, Jupiter, ruled
over Crete after the expulsion of his father; there he died,
there he had sons. Today people visit Jupiter's cave and
are shown his tomb.[347] The very places sacred to him
verify that he was human.

Chapter 24

*Why are there no new gods, except kings? The stupidities
of idolatry and of pagan ceremonials*

1. "But it would be a waste of time to set out the entire
lineage of this race, going through the pedigree one by
one; the first parents have been proved to be mortal and,
therefore, so are the rest, being direct descendants, by the
transmission of heredity.[348] The only possible escape is for
you to imagine that men became gods after their death:
that Romulus is a god by the perjury of Proculus,[349] Juba
by the will of the Mauretanians,[350] and likewise the rest of
the kings, consecrated not to testify to their divinity but
to pay homage to the office they once held. 2. And what
is more, it is against their own will that they are enrolled
among the gods. They want to continue as men, they are
afraid and unwilling to become gods, in spite of their old
age.[351]

3. "It follows that there are no gods from among those
who are dead—a god cannot die; nor are there any from
those who are born—everything that is born dies. That is
divine which has neither beginning nor ending.[352] And I

should like to ask why, if they were ever born, they are
not born today as well. I suppose it is that Jupiter is now
too old, that Juno is past childbearing, that Minerva's hair
turned white before she bore children. The explanation is
surely rather that this supposed procreation has ceased
because people no longer place any credence in tales of this
kind. 4. Besides, if the gods were capable of propagating
but incapable of perishing, we would have a larger number
of gods than all of mankind put together; by this time
heaven could not contain nor the air accommodate nor the
earth support their numbers. The obvious conclusion is
that they who we read were born and those who we know
died were but men.[353]

5. "There is no room for doubt, then, that when the
common masses say prayers and render public worship to
their consecrated images,[354] their simple minds and thoughts
are being deluded by the elegance of art, dazzled by the
radiance of gold, and dulled by the lustre of silver and the
whiteness of ivory.[355] 6. Picture to yourself the instruments
of torture,[356] the devices that men use in fashioning every
statue, and you will become ashamed of any dread you
have for matter abused according to a craftsman's fancy
in order to create a god. A god of wood—a remnant, perhaps, from a funeral pyre or a gallows tree[357]—is hoist up,
hewn, hacked, and planed. 7. A god of bronze or silver—
frequently made from a filthy vessel, as for the king of
Egypt[358]—is cast into the melting pot, beaten with ham-
mers, shaped on anvils. A god of stone is cut, carved, and
polished by some lewd workman;[359] the god is just as unaware of the indignities that attend his birth as he is later
of the homage you pay him in your veneration.

8. "Possibly the stone, wood, or silver is not yet a god.

Well, when does he come into being? He is being cast,
forged, filed; he is not yet a god. He is being soldered,
assembled, erected; he is still not a god. He is being
adorned,[360] consecrated,[361] supplicated; at long last he is a
god, just when man wills him to be and so dedicates him.[362]

9. "By sheer instinct, dumb animals have a much more
accurate estimate of your gods: mice, swallows, kites are
perfectly well aware that they have no feelings. They
trample over them, settle on them, and unless you drive
them off, they build their nests even in your god's mouth.
Spiders weave their webs over his face and hang their
threads even from his head.[363] 10. And it is left to you to
wipe, clean, and scour them, protecting, and dreading,
gods you have made yourselves.[364] All this time not one of
you has reflected that he ought to get to know his god first
and then to worship him. Instead, anxious to give blind
obedience to your parents, you prefer to be party to
another's error than to rely on your own judgment;[365] in
short, you are in total ignorance of the things which you
fear.

"This is how covetousness has become enshrined in gold
and silver; this is how empty statues have become hallowed
forms; this is how Roman superstition has come into
being.[366]

11. "In a survey of Roman rituals you would find so
many practices that are laughable if not pitiable. Some devotees run about naked in the depths of winter;[367] others
move in procession wearing felt caps and parading old
shields;[368] or they beat drums of hides and go begging from
quarter to quarter, dragging their gods with them.[369] Some
sanctuaries they allow you to approach once a year,[370]
others it is totally anathema to visit.[371] There is a ritual

where a man may not be present,[372] there are several rites forbidden to women,[373] there are certain ceremonies where the mere presence of a slave constitutes an outrage that requires expiation.[374] Some sacred objects are garlanded by a matron married once,[375] others by one married several times; zealous and devout search is made for a woman who has a large tally of adulteries.[376]

12. "And you must admit that if a man pours a libation of his own blood and if he offers supplication with his own wounds, he would be better off as an outcast from religion than as adherent in this fashion;[377] or that if a man shear off his genitals with a sherd,[378] he cannot possibly insult his god if this is the way to appease him.[379] Surely if god wanted eunuchs, he would create them such, not make them so afterwards.[380]

13. "It is universally realized that people who indulge in these aberrations are of unsound mind; that in fact they are deluded and deranged and in their divagation from the truth they provide themselves with mutual protection by sheer numbers. For the way to defend a widespread madness is to have a multitude of madmen.[381]

CHAPTER 25

Rome's greatness is due not to piety but to unpunished impiety

1. "Now all the same, your theory is that it is just this superstition which gave the Romans their empire, and increased and consolidated it; their might lay not so much in valor as in the conscientious practice of their religion. There can be no shadow of doubt, of course, that the

illustrious and celebrated Roman justice made its auspicious appearance at the very infancy of the Empire![382] 2. You must admit that at its beginning what gathered the people together was crime, what protected them was the terror of their barbarities. That is how they grew in numbers. What happened was that the original lower orders assembled at Asylum—a conglomeration of the scum and dregs of society, profligates, gangsters, traitors—and to surpass his own people in crime Romulus, their guide and mentor, himself murdered his own brother.[383] These were the original auspices of this devoutly religious state!

3. "And then, contrary to all custom, they abducted, violated, and abused young women from another state, though they were already promised in marriage and betrothed, and in some cases had even been recently married; and they stirred up war with the parents of these girls, their own parents-in-law, shedding the blood of their kindred. Where would one find less religious devotion, greater outrage, stronger protection than in this barefaced wickedness?[384] 4. Thereafter, to drive neighbors from their lands, to overthrow adjoining states, together with their altars and temples, to herd their inhabitants into captivity, to grow fat on others' losses and their own misdeeds—this was the way of life taught both by Romulus and the other kings, and by the generals who succeeded them.[385]

5. "The consequence is that whatever the Romans hold, occupy, and possess is the booty of outrage. All their temples come from the plunder of war, and that means the destruction of cities, the pillaging of gods, the slaughter of priests.[386]

6. "It is downright insult and mockery to be subservient to gods you have conquered, to adore them after their

capture and your victory. To adore what you have seized by force is to consecrate sacrilege, not deities.[387] And so the number of Roman triumphs means an equal number of desecrations; the victorious trophies won over other nations mean an equal number of robberies of their gods.[388]

7. "It follows that Rome is so great not because she has been devoutly religious but because she has been sacrilegious and gone unpunished. And it cannot be true that in their actual wars they could have had others' gods to help them; it was against those gods that they had seized their arms, it was they whom they challenged to surrender;[389] and it was not until they had triumphed over them that they started to worship them. Besides, what assistance can these gods give to the Roman cause when they could do nothing for their own people against the arms of Rome?

8. "And as for the indigenous gods of Rome, we know them well.[390] There's Romulus,[391] Picus,[392] Tiberinus,[393] Consus,[394] Pilumnus,[395] and Volumnus.[396] Tatius discovered and worshiped the goddess Sewer,[397] Hostilius Panic and Pallor;[398] later someone consecrated Fever.[399] These are the superstitions which have nursed this fine city of yours—diseases and distempers. Of course, the scandalous prostitutes, Acca Larentia and Flora, must also be reckoned among the diseases, and the divinities, of Rome.[400] 9. Apparently we are to believe that it was these gods who advanced Rome's empire against the rest of the gods worshiped among other nations. But surely, Mars of Thrace did not help the Romans against his own adherents nor did Jupiter of Crete[401] nor Juno, whether of Argos, Samos, or Carthage,[402] nor Diana of Taurus, nor the Mother of Ida, nor those ominous monsters—I could not call them deities —of Egypt.[403]

10. "Possibly it may have been the case that with the Romans of those days there was greater chastity among their virgins and deeper religious devotion among their priests. Even so, the majority of the virgins have been avenged for the violation of their sacred vows, having somewhat indiscreetly given themselves to men—presumably without the connivance of Vesta; and the remainder of the Vestals have won exemption from punishment not by a better guarded chastity but by a more fortunate impurity.[404] 11. And as for your priests, where, I should like to ask, is prostitution traded, procuring transacted, adultery contrived more frequently than by them amid their altars and shrines? In fact, burning lust is assuaged more often in sacristans' cells than in actual bordellos.[405] 12. And yet, before the Roman era, by the dispensation of God, the Assyrians, the Medes, the Persians, the Greeks also, and the Egyptians enjoyed long-flourishing empires,[406] and this despite the fact that they had no college of Pontifices, no Arval Brethren,[407] no Salii,[408] no Vestals, no Augurs, nor any chickens cooped in a cage, by whose appetite or distaste for food the supreme destinies of the state were directed.[409]

CHAPTER 26

Demons are the cause for any truth in pagan divination and oracles

1. "This brings me to those Roman auspices and auguries which you took great pains to collect together; on your evidence, to neglect them means remorse, to observe them success.[410] 2. Clodius, it would appear, and Flaminius, and

Junius did lose their armies simply because they thought they need not wait for the chickens' most favorable omen: to feed voraciously.[411] 3. But Regulus did observe the auguries, did he not?—and he was taken prisoner.[412] Mancinus faithfully adhered to his religion, and he was sent beneath the yoke and delivered up to the enemy;[413] Paulus, too, had hungry chickens, yet he, and the greater part of the state besides, was crushed at Cannae.[414] 4. Caius Caesar, on the other hand, scorned the auguries and auspices which opposed his fleet's sailing across to Africa before the winter solstice. He sailed, and conquered all the more easily.[415]

5. "As for oracles, I am uncertain how long a treatment I should give to them and what points I should deal with.[416] Amphiaraus gave oracular responses about the future after he had died, though he did not know that he was to be betrayed by his wife for a necklace.[417] The blind Tiresias used to see what was going to happen, though he could not see what was happening at the time.[418] 6. Ennius forged the replies of Pythian Apollo about Pyrrhus, for Apollo had ceased to produce verses by that stage.[419] That wary and ambiguous oracle failed just when men started to become more sophisticated and less gullible.[420] And Demosthenes, knowing that the replies were fabricated, used to complain that the Pythian priestess was 'Philippizing.'[421]

7. "You retort that on occasion, however, auspices or oracles have hit upon the truth. Of course, one could argue that in the midst of a host of falsehoods, mere chance can masquerade as design. But what I propose to do is to go deeper and unearth and expose more clearly to view the actual source of error and wickedness, the origin of all this widespread obscurantism.[422]

8. "There exist unclean spirits who wander abroad de-

prived of their heavenly vigor, being weighed down by
the heavy burden of earthly stains and desires. These
spirits ruined the purity of their substance by becoming
laden and steeped in vice;[423] accordingly, they never cease
in their efforts to alleviate their own catastrophe by ruin-
ing others, being ruined themselves, by instilling in others
their perverse error, being perverted themselves, and being
themselves estranged from God, by alienating others from
God with the introduction of perverted cults.[424] 9. These
spirits are demons; the poets are acquainted with them,
they are discussed by philosophers,[425] Socrates knew them
—he would shun or seek undertakings according to the will
and judgment of the demon who was always at his side.[426]
10. The Magi, too, are acquainted with demons; but more
than that, all their magical tricks they perform through
demons; it is filled with their inspiration that they produce
their feats of legerdemain, making appear things that do
not exist and disappear things that do.[427] 11. The foremost
of these Magi, both in eloquence and performance, is Hostanes, and he describes the true God with fitting majesty;[428]
he knows that there are angels, that is to say, servants and
messengers,[429] who protect His throne and stand by His
side to render Him homage, so that, at a mere nod or
glance from the Lord, they begin to quake in terror.[430] He
also recorded that there are demons, earthly beings who
wander abroad hostile to mankind.

12. "Plato, you will recall, believed that it was a difficult task to discover God;[431] but he talks of angels and demons without any difficulty at all, does he not?[432] And in
his *Symposium* he actually endeavors to define the nature
of demons. He would have it that there is a substance
halfway between mortal and immortal, that is, between

body and spirit, a composite of earthly heaviness and heavenly lightness. Of this substance, he also warns us, Love† meaning Lust† is formed; it thus penetrates into the hearts of men, stirring our senses, moulding our passions, and instilling within us the flames of desire.[433]

CHAPTER 27

Demons (that is to say, pagan gods) are the cause, too, of many other evils, and the persecution of Christians

1. "And so it is, these impure spirits—demons, as the Magi, philosophers, and Plato have demonstrated them to be—lurk in hiding beneath consecrated statues and images[434] and by their spiritual influence they gain authority equal to that of a deity who is actually present. Sometimes, as they haunt their shrines, they suggest prophecies[435] to soothsayers; at other times they animate the fibres of entrails, direct the flight of birds, manage the drawing of lots, and produce oracles enveloped in a multitude of lies.[436] 2. For they deceive themselves as well as others;[437] the simple truth they know not, and what truth they do know they will not acknowledge, to their own ruin.

"It is in this way that they drag down men's souls, away from heaven, alluring them from the true God towards material things; they throw disorder into our lives, they bring disquiet to our sleep; being subtle spirits, they secretly creep into our bodies, contriving diseases, terrifying our minds, and wrenching our limbs.[438] Their object is to force us to worship them; they will then be in a position, when they are gorged with the reek of altars and the sacrifice of beasts, to appear to cure us merely by relaxing their stranglehold.[439]

3. "They are the cause, too, of those maniacs you see dashing into the streets: these are soothsayers, too, though they are in no temple. They rave and whirl about in the same frantic way as temple prophets; they are victims of the same demonic possession, though they manifest their frenzy differently.[440] 4. The demons are the source, too, of those phenomena which you spoke of earlier: Jupiter in a dream asking for the repetition of his games, Castor and his brother appearing with their horses, the boat following a matron's girdle.[441]

5. "All these things, as the majority of you are well aware, the demons themselves acknowledge as their own doing, whenever we drive them out of bodies by the torment of our words and the fire of our prayers.[442] 6. Saturn himself, Serapis, Jupiter, all the demons you worship are overcome by the pain and speak out what they are;[443] we can be well assured that they would not tell lies that bring disgrace upon themselves, especially when any of you are present. 7. You must believe, therefore, their evidence; they admit the truth about themselves: they are demons. And when they are adjured in the name of the one true God,[444] the poor wretches shudder in the bodies they possess in spite of themselves;[445] either they leap forth instantly or they fade away by degrees—it all depends on the support given by the faith of the sufferer and the influence of the grace of the healer.[446] They thus at close quarters take to flight from Christians whose assemblies from afar they used to assail through you.[447]

8. "What happens is that they slip into the minds of the ignorant;[448] there they secretly implant hatred against us

by means of fear; for it is only natural to hate and, if you can, to molest one who makes you afraid and terrified.[449] This is how they take hold of men's thoughts and stop up their hearts, so that they begin to hate us even before they know us.[450] For if men investigated us,[451] they might then either be able to imitate us or be unable to condemn us.

CHAPTER 28

Persecutions are unjustified, the trial of Christians unfair, and pagan slanders against Christians apply rather to paganism

1. "It is thoroughly unjust to pass judgment without investigation and inquiry; that is what you are doing. Take our word for it, our word of regret. 2. We, too, were once just like you, we thought just as you do; we were still blind and obtuse.[452] We fancied that the Christians worshiped monsters,[453] devoured infants, joined in incestuous banquets. We still did not realize that it is these demons who are constantly circulating such tales, and that the tales themselves are never investigated or verified. We did not see that all this time not one person had come forward to betray the Christians,[454] though he would gain pardon for his actions and recompense for his information; nor did we see that the evil is so far illusory that Christians were neither ashamed nor afraid to be brought to trial; their only cause for regret was that they had not been Christians earlier.[455] 3. "Despite all this, time was when we actually used to undertake the defense and protection of men guilty of sacrilege, incest, even parricide,[456] whereas Christians we

thought need not be given any hearing at all;[457] sometimes we even showed pity towards them to the point of acting with greater ruthlessness and cruelty—we tortured those who confessed to make them deny; of course, we only wanted to save their lives. It was a perverted court of inquiry: the object was not to draw out the truth but to force out lies.[458] 4. And should a weaker member, crushed and overwhelmed by our torments, deny that he was a Christian, we would regard him with favor, supposing that by his denial and his repudiation of the Name he was exonerated of all that he had done.[459]

5. "You now recognize that we felt and acted just as you feel and act? Whereas, if our judgment had been swayed by reason, and not by the incitement of a demon, Christians ought rather to have been pressed not to disown their Christianity but to own up to incestuous debauches, sacrilegious rites, and the immolation of infants.

6. "These are the sorts of tale which these demons have used to cram the ears of the ignorant masses,[460] thus rousing against us horror and detestation. It comes as no great surprise, of course: common gossip always grows fat on scattered lies and withers away in the light of truth; it is likewise a work of the demons: they are the ones who broadcast and husband lying rumors.[461]

7. "This is the origin of the story you have on hearsay, that the head of an ass is for us a divine object. Is there anyone stupid enough to worship such an object? Is there anyone even more stupid as to believe that such an object is worshiped? Unless, of course, you suppose this because *you* dedicate complete asses in your stables in the company, for example, of your Epona;[462] asses, too, you devour ceremonially, in the company of Isis;[463] likewise you sacri-

fice, as well as worship, the heads of oxen and of rams,[464] and you enshrine gods half-goat, half-man, and lion- and dog-headed deities.[465] 8. You adore and feed, do you not, with the people of Egypt, the ox Apis?[466] And the rites they have established you do not condemn—in honor of snakes, crocodiles, and all the other beasts, birds, and fishes.[467] To kill any of these gods is actually a capital offense.[468] 9. And yet these Egyptians, like a great many of you, dread the pungency of onions just as much as Isis; they quake at the loud sound of broken wind no less than at Serapis.[469]

10. "And as for the man who spreads the rumor against us that we adore the genitals of our priest, he is trying to foist on to us his own misdeeds.[470] It may well be that such indecencies are sacred rites among men and women who offer for public use their sex and indeed every part of their body,[471] and among whom completely uninhibited obscenity is termed sophistication. They are envious of the license of prostitutes, they perform acts of unmentionable bestiality[472]—men whose tongues would be evil even if they were silent and who begin to grow weary of their obscenities before they become ashamed of them. 11. How abominable! They commit against each other such offenses which no youth of tender years can endure nor even hardened slaves can be compelled to tolerate.[473]

CHAPTER 29

The alleged worship of crosses

1. "These and similar acts of indecency we are not at liberty to hear described; it is improper for us to refute

them at any further length.[474] It is about people who are modest and decent that you invent things which we would not believe possible, did you not exemplify them in your own behavior.

2. "Now, you ascribe to our religion a criminal and his cross.[475] You are not even remotely correct in supposing that either a criminal could have merited or an earthly creature been able to be thought a god.[476] 3. He indeed is to be pitied whose every hope is reliant on a mortal man; his support is completely removed when that man is destroyed.[477] 4. And I know for a fact that people in Egypt choose a man for their worship; him alone they propitiate, him they consult on all questions, to him they slay sacrificial victims. But he, though a god in the eyes of the others, is without doubt in his own eyes a man, whether he likes it or not; if he dupes the minds of others, he still does not delude his own.[478]

5. "The same applies to emperors and kings; they are not honored, as would be right, as great and extraordinary men, but they are flattered and fawned upon as gods, disgracefully and falsely. (And yet there would be a more truthful tribute to a man of outstanding quality in honor, a more agreeable one to a man of excellence in affection.[479]) This is how they come to invoke the godhead of such men, to make supplication before their effigies, to beseech their Genius, that is to say, their demon;[480] it is safer for them to swear falsely by the Genius of Jupiter than by that of their king.[481]

6. "Besides, crosses are not objects that we worship or desire,[482] and yet, clearly, it is very possible that as you consecrate gods of wood, you adore crosses of wood because they form part of your gods.[483] 7. And, surely, your

military ensigns, standards, and banners, what are they but gilded and decorated crosses?[484] Your trophies of victory copy not merely the appearance of a simple cross but that of a man fastened to it as well.[485]

8. "And as for the sign of the cross, there is no doubt that we see it in the world of nature about us:[486] when you see a ship sailing with canvas swelling or gliding with oars extended;[487] or when you set a yoke in place you form the sign of the cross;[488] or when a man pays homage to God with purity of heart, stretching out his hands.[489]

"In this way you can see either that the sign of the cross is fundamental to the order of nature or that it forms the framework of your own religion.

CHAPTER 30

The slander of infanticide is more appropriate to pagan rites and practices

1. "There is a man I should now like to address, and that is the one who claims, or believes, that our initiations take place by means of the slaughter and blood of a baby.[490] Do you think it possible to inflict fatal wounds on a baby so tender and so tiny? That there could be anyone who would butcher a newborn babe, hardly yet a human being, shed forth and drain down its young blood?[491] The only person capable of believing this is one who is capable of actually perpetrating it.[492] 2. And, in fact, it is a practice of yours, I observe, to expose your very own children to birds and wild beasts, or at times to smother and strangle them—a pitiful way to die; and there are women who swallow drugs to stifle in their own womb the beginnings

of a man to be—committing infanticide before they give birth to their infant.[493]

3. "And these practices, of course, derive from the examples set by your own gods.[494] Saturn, indeed, forbore to expose his own children; he devoured them.[495] Parents used to do right, therefore, in some parts of Africa, to sacrifice their babies to him, suppressing with endearments and kisses their wailing for fear they should sacrifice tearful victims.[496] 4. Furthermore, it was a religious custom of the Pontic Taurians[497] and of the Egyptian Busiris[498] to sacrifice travelers who were their guests;[499] Gauls would slay in honor of Mercury human, or rather inhuman, victims;[500] it was part of a Roman sacrifice to bury alive a Greek man and woman and a Gallic man and woman.[501] Even today the Romans worship Jupiter Latiaris with manslaughter, and as befits the son of Saturn, he is glutted with the gore of a wicked criminal.[502] 5. It was this god, I believe, who instructed Catiline to seal his conspiracy with a covenant of blood,[503] and Bellona to steep her own ritual in draughts of human blood,[504] and who taught men how to cure epilepsy by man's blood, that is, by a remedy worse than the disease.[505]

6. "There is little to distinguish between such men and those who devour wild beasts from the amphitheatre all smeared and stained with man's blood and glutted with his flesh and limbs.[506] But for us it is not right either to look at or to hear of acts of manslaughter;[507] in fact, we are so careful to avoid human blood that in our meals we do not allow even the blood of edible animals.[508]

CHAPTER 31

The calumnies of incest, immorality, and secret signs

1. "I now come to the 'incestuous banquets.'[509] This is a monstrous lie which the demons have conspired together to spread about us. They intended to sully our glorious purity of life by bespattering it with repulsive disrepute and to drive men away from us, before they might investigate the truth, by the horror of such abominable ideas.[510] 2. Your Fronto is one example: he did not produce evidence on this point as a claimant but bespattered us with abuse as a pleader at the bar.[511]

"As a matter of fact, one can trace the origin of these slanders rather to your pagan nations. 3. In Persia, for example, union with your mother is lawful,[512] in Egypt and Athens you can legally marry your sister.[513] Incest is a cause for pride in your traditions and your tragedies,[514] which you take pleasure in reading and hearing. Likewise, the gods you worship are incestuous, guilty of intercourse with mother, with daughter, with sister.[515]

4. "It is, therefore, only to be expected that among you incest is frequently detected and constantly practiced. Even unwittingly, you pitiable fools, you may plunge into unlawful liaisons. By indulging in promiscuous lust, by fathering children hither and thither, by frequently exposing even those born in your own home to the pity of others,[516] you must inevitably come across your own relations again and chance upon your own children. Hence you are creating a tale of incest even though you are unaware of it.[517]

5. "But with us modesty is paraded not in our appear-

ance but in our hearts: it is our pleasure to abide by the bond of a single marriage; in our desires for begetting children, we know one woman or none at all.[518] In our banquets we have regard not for modesty alone but for temperance as well: we do not indulge in sumptuous feasting nor do we prolong the banquet with unmixed wine. Rather we temper gaiety with gravity, chaste in our conversation, even more chaste in our persons. Very many of us preserve (rather than take pride in) the perpetual virginity of our undefiled bodies;[519] and indeed, desires of incest are so far removed from our minds that even modest intercourse causes not a few of us to blush.

6. "If we refuse your purple robes of public office,[520] it does not follow that our ranks are composed of the very dregs of the rabble, neither does it follow that we constitute a conspiracy if we are united in our acknowledgment of the one and the same good[521] (rather, in our assemblies we are just as peaceable as we are by ourselves[522]). It also does not follow that we prattle in corners, if you are ashamed, or afraid, to give us a public hearing.[523]

7. "You say our numbers grow daily.[524] This does not convict us of error; it provides evidence for our credit. It is a fact that if you have an honorable way of life, adherents persist and persevere in it, and outsiders augment its ranks.[525]

8. "And there is another point to make here: we do have an easy way of distinguishing our followers, but it is not, as you suggest, by a small mark on our bodies. It is by the signs of innocence and sobriety![526] Hence it is true that we do love one another—a fact which you deplore—since we do not know how to hate.[527] Hence it is true that we

do call one another brother—a fact which rouses your spleen—because we are men with the one and same God for father,[528] copartners in faith, coheirs in hope.[529] But you have no such signs of recognition among yourselves; instead, what you have in common is wild hatred for each other, and you acknowledge one another as brothers only, of course, if it is for the purposes of fratricide.[530]

CHAPTER 32

The proper worship of the invisible and omniscient God

1. "Now you think that if we have neither temples nor altars we are concealing the object of our worship?[531] But what image would I fashion for God, seeing that man can be rightly considered as himself the image of God?[532] What temple would I erect to Him, seeing that this entire universe, the work of His hands, cannot contain Him?[533] Would I enclose the might of such majesty within the confines of a single chapel, while I, a man, may lodge more spaciously?[534] 2. It is a better course, you must agree, that He should be dedicated in our minds, or rather consecrated in our hearts.[535] Would I offer to God victims and sacrifices which He has produced for my benefit, casting back at Him His own gifts?[536] That would show ingratitude, seeing that an honest heart, a pure mind, and a clear conscience make acceptable offerings.[537] 3. And, therefore, to cherish innocence is to make supplication to God; to practice justice is to pour libation to God; to refrain from wickedness is to offer propitiation to God; to rescue another from peril is to slay a perfect victim. These are

our sacrifices, these are our acts of homage to God. This explains why, with us, a man is counted devout according as he is just.

4. "Now you say that we neither show nor see the God we worship.[538] The truth is that this is just the reason why we believe in Him. Though we are not able to see Him, we are able to perceive Him; for His ever-present power we discern in His works and in all the movements of the universe: in thunder, lightning, in the thunderbolt, in the clear sky.[539] 5. And there should be no cause for surprise if you fail to see God. The winds and breezes may stir, shake, and toss everything about, and yet neither wind nor breeze comes before our view. There is another example in the sun. To it we all owe our ability to look at things, but upon it we cannot look: its rays dazzle our eyes; if you contemplate it directly, your sight becomes dimmed, and if you gaze on it too long, you lose your powers of vision altogether.[540]

6. "Now would you be able to tolerate the creator of the sun Himself, the very source of light, when you turn away from the flash of His lightning and hide from the bolts of His thunder?[541] Do you want to see God with your eyes of flesh,[542] when your very own soul, on which you depend for speech and life,[543] you can neither behold nor grasp?

7. "But your claim is that God is ignorant of the actions of men; ensconced in the sky, He is able neither to confront us all nor to know us individually.[544] You are deceived, my mortal friend, and mistaken. Can God be far distant from any point when all things in heaven and on earth and beyond this district of the world are known to God and filled with His presence?[545] He is not merely

very close to us; He is deep within us.[546] 8. Indeed, consider the sun once more; though fixed to the sky, it is shed
over all the earth. It is equally present everywhere, inter-
mingling with everything, but at no point is its brilliance
impaired.[547] 9. How much more truly must God, the
author of everything, the observer of everything, He from
whom no secret can be hidden, how much more truly
must He be present in the darkness, in that second darkness of our thoughts.[548] We not only act beneath His gaze;
but in a manner of speaking, with Him we share our life.[549]

CHAPTER 33

Why the Jews have enjoyed prosperity and adversity

1. "And let us not be deluded by our large numbers. To
us we appear to be many, but to God we are very few
indeed.[550] We men draw distinctions between nations and
peoples, but to God this entire universe is but a single
household.[551] Kings are acquainted with all the details of
their realms, but through the offices of their servants; God
is in need of no such information:[552] we live our lives not
merely in His sight but in His bosom.[553]

2. "Now you assert that it has brought no profit to the
Jews that they too have worshiped a unique God—and
with altars and temples, and with meticulous scrupulous-
ness.[554] Here your mistake is due to ignorance in that you
recall only their later history but forget or are unaware of
earlier events. They, too, to be sure, [once worshiped[555]]
our God; He is the God of all. 3. While they continued to
do this with hearts pure, innocent, and devout, while they
continued to be obedient to His salutary commandments,

they who were once small in number became countless,
once needy they became rich, once slaves they became
kings; even as they fled from their pursuers, though not
numerous themselves they overwhelmed a multitude,
though without arms themselves they overwhelmed armed
troops, by the command of God and the support of His
elements.[556] 4. Peruse their writings;[557] get hold of the
works of Flavius Josephus on the Jews (I am omitting
ancient authors) or, if you would rather Roman writers,
those of Antonius Julianus on the same subject.[558] You will
soon find out that their present lot they have deserved
through their own wickedness and that not one thing has
befallen them which was not foretold to them, should they
persist in their stiff-necked arrogance. 5. You will realize
that they deserted before they were deserted, that they
were not, as you blasphemously put it,[559] taken captive
along with their God, but that they were delivered up by
their God as deserters from His law.[560]

CHAPTER 34

*A defense of the Christian doctrine about the end of the
world and the resurrection of the body*

1. "As for the conflagration of the world,[561] it is an
error common among the masses to refuse to believe in the
exhaustion of moisture and a sudden precipitation of
fire.[562] 2. What philosopher has a moment's doubt or is
unaware that what has a beginning must have an end, what
has been made must perish?[563] And the Stoics have never
wavered in their view[564] that the heavens, along with
everything enclosed by the heavens, just as they had a

beginning, will resolve into the substance of fire once the
fountains of sweet water and the seas have ceased to
nourish the firmament.[565] They consider that when the
supplies of moisture have been exhausted, this entire universe will catch fire. 3. What the Epicureans believe about
the conflagration of the elements and the collapse of the
universe is identical.[566] 4. Plato mentions that parts of the
world are, in turns, at one time under water, at another on
fire;[567] though he does say that the world itself was made
everlasting and indestructible, he still adds that it is perish-
ible and destructible but only for its maker, God Him-
elf.[568] It would not cause any surprise, then, should this
'ast structure be destroyed by the one who constructed
t.[569]

5. "You observe that the philosophers discuss the very
deas which we hold. The explanation is not that we have
:ollowed after their footsteps but that they have made a
shadowy, though distorted, imitation of the truth found in
the inspired proclamations of the prophets.[570]

6. "The case is similar with the conditions for rebirth
taught by your outstanding philosophers, in the first place
Pythagoras and in the foremost rank Plato;[571] their transmission is corrupt and only partially accurate. They hold
that our souls alone, after the dissolution of our bodies,
remain forever and that they are constantly migrating
from one body into other new ones. 7. To these ideas they
add another perversion of the truth, that the souls of men
return into cattle, birds, and beasts.[572] This is a viewpoint
more suitable to comic ribaldry than to the researches of
a philosopher.[573] 8. But for our purposes it is sufficient if
even on a point like this your philosophers are in a certain
measure of agreement with us.[574]

9. "Is there anyone so senseless and stupid as to dare to object to the claim that man can be reshaped by God anew, just as he could have been fashioned by Him in the first place? That he is nothing after death, just as before birth he was nothing? That it is, therefore, equally possible for him to be restored from nothing as it was for him to be born from nothing? Besides, it is a much more difficult task to begin something that does not exist than to repeat something that once existed.[575] 10. Something may be removed from our feeble eyes; do you believe it therefore is lost to God as well? A corpse may dry into dust or dissolve into liquid or reduce into ashes or fade into smoke; however it is, every corpse is withdrawn from us but its elements are preserved in the safekeeping of God.[576] And it is not true, as you believe, that we fear to suffer any harm from cremation, but our practice is to adhere to the old, and therefore the preferable, custom of inhumation.[577]

11. "Furthermore, notice how the whole of nature brings us comfort by rehearsing our future resurrection.[578] The sun sinks down and is reborn, the stars slip away and return, flowers fall and come to life again, shrubs decay and then burst into leaf, seeds must rot in order to sprout into new growth. As trees are in winter, so are our bodies in this world; they keep their verdure concealed beneath deceptive barrenness.[579] 12. Why be impatient for the body to come to life again and to return when it is still the depths of winter? We, too, must await the springtime —the springtime of the body.[580]

"And it is obvious to me that being conscious of their deserts, many people desire (rather than believe) that after death they are nothing;[581] their preference is to be totally annihilated rather than to be restored, for punishment. In

their error they are led further astray both by the un-
fettered freedom allowed to them in this world[582] and by
the supreme patience of God, whose judgment is all the
more just because it is slow.[583]

CHAPTER 35

The fires of hell, which pagans deserve

1. "And yet, in the books of the erudite and the verses
of the poets,[584] men are warned of that river of fire whose
burning heat, issuing from the Stygian marsh, traces its
many encircling courses;[585] this, as is the tradition they
report (discovered from the evidence of demons[586] and the
oracles of prophets[587]), has been prepared for everlasting
torments.[588] 2. And that explains why, in their writings,
even King Jupiter himself swears his most solemn oath by
its blazing banks and black abyss,[589] shuddering in his foreknowledge at the punishment destined for himself and for
his worshipers.[590] 3. And these tortures are without measure and without end. There the fire of wisdom[591] at once
scorches and restores men's limbs, gnaws and nourishes
them.[592] It is as when bodies are blasted by the fires of
thunderbolts and are left unconsumed,[593] or when the fires
of Mount Aetna and Mount Vesuvius, indeed of volcanic
lands everywhere, blaze on with flames unspent;[594] so, too,
with these flames of punishment—as they feed they do not
destroy those they burn[595] but they find nourishment in
rending their undevoured bodies.[596]

4. "They who do not know God are rightly tortured for
their impiety and wickedness; nobody is undecided on this
point save the irreligious; to be ignorant of the father of

all, the lord of all, is no less a crime than to do Him in-
jury.[597] 5. It is a fact that ignorance of God is sufficient
reason for punishment, just as knowledge of Him helps to
win His pardon; yet, all the same, if we Christians are
compared with you, we will be found to be far superior
to you, even though some Christians may fail to measure
up to the full standard of our teaching.[598] 6. You prohibit
adultery and practice it, we are born men for our wives
and our wives alone;[599] you punish crimes once perpe-
trated, for us the mere thought of crime is sinful.[600] You
are afraid that others should be conscious of your actions,
we are afraid only of conscience itself—it is inseparable
from our existence.[601] In a word, the prisons seethe with
hordes from your ranks; but no Christian is there unless
he has been arraigned for his religion or is a renegade from
it.[602]

CHAPTER 36

*Christians are not victims of Fate; they, in fact, reap
benefit from their hardships and tribulations*

1. "As for Fate, no one should clutch at it for comfort
or find excuse in it for what has happened.[603] It may be
true that our material fortunes are due to chance; even so,
our minds are free;[604] and therefore it is the actions of men,
not their social rank, that are judged. 2. And, after all,
Fate (*fatum*) is simply and solely what God has 'fated'
(*fatus* = spoken) about us individually.[605] As He is in a
position to know beforehand our basic characters, He can
also determine the decrees of fate to suit our individual
deserts and traits.[606] It is, therefore, not the stars attendant

on our birth that are chastised; it is our natural dispositions
which are punished.[607] That is possibly a brief, but sufficient, statement on the subject of Fate for the time being;
I intend to discuss this question more amply and more fully
elsewhere.[608]

3. "I now come to the accusation that most of us are
said to be poor;[609] that is not to our shame, it is to our great
credit. Men's characters are strengthened by stringent circumstances, just as they are dissipated by luxurious living.
4. Besides, can a man be poor if he is free from want, if he
does not covet the belongings of others, if he is rich in the
possession of God?[610] Rather, he is poor who possesses
much but still craves for more.[611] 5. It is my honest opinion
that nobody can be poorer than the day he is born.[612] Birds
live on though they have no patrimony, cattle are fed day
after day; and yet these have been produced for our benefit;[613] desiring nothing, we own all things.[614]

6. "And so it is that when a man walks along a road, the
lighter he travels, the happier he is; equally, on this journey
of life, a man is more blessed if he does not pant beneath
a burden of riches but lightens his load by poverty.[615] 7.
Nevertheless, we would ask God for material goods if we
considered them to be of use; without a doubt, He to
whom the whole belongs would be able to concede us a
portion. But we prefer to hold possessions in contempt
than to hoard them; it is rather innocence that is our aspiration, it is rather patience that is our entreaty; our preference is goodness, not extravagance.

8. "Now you say that we experience and suffer the
defects of the human body.[616] That is part of our training
as soldiers;[617] it is no punishment. Bravery gains in strength
by infirmities, calamity is more often than not a lesson in

courage. And moreover, one's vigor of mind and of body
needs hard training, otherwise it grows slack. In fact, all
your brave heroes, whom you extol as models, owe their
enduring fame to their ordeals. 9. And so it is with us, too;
God is neither unable to come to our aid nor does He dis-
dain to help us. He is, after all, the one who governs all
things and loves His own. But in adversities He is investi-
gating and examining each of us, in dangers He is weighing
our individual characters; assured that nothing can be lost
to Him, He continues to search into a man's disposition
right up to the point of his death.[618] As gold is tested in
fire, so we are tested by tribulation.[619]

CHAPTER 37

*The nobility of the Christian martyr, the vanity of
worldly aspirations, the squalor of the pagan spectacles*

1. "What a noble sight it is for God when a Christian
comes to grips with suffering,[620] when he confronts threats,
tortures, and torments, when without a trace of fear he
spurns beneath his heel the din of death and the dread
executioner, when he raises aloft the banner of his liberty
in defiance of princes and kings, yielding submission to
God alone, to whom he belongs, when, triumphant and
victorious, he vaunts over the very man who pronounced
sentence against him. He wins the victory who gains the
prize he sought.[621] 2. What soldier would not display
greater daring in challenging danger were he beneath the
gaze of his general?[622] No one receives rewards unless he
proves himself.[623] But the general does not give what he
does not have; he cannot prolong life, although he can en-

noble the soldier's service. 3. Now you must remember that the soldier of God is neither forsaken in his suffering nor destroyed by death. A Christian can thus give the appearance of being wretched, but he cannot be found to be so in fact.[624] You yourselves laud to the skies men who were victims of catastrophe, like Mucius Scaevola, who went astray in his attack on the king and would have perished amid his enemies had he not lost his right hand.[625] 4. And how many of our followers have endured with not one cry throughout, that not merely their right hands but their entire bodies be burnt and reduced to ashes—though, mark you, they had it in their power to be released. 5. Do I compare our *men* with Mucius or Aquilius or Regulus?[626] Why, our children and weak women are inspired with such powers of enduring suffering[627] that they scoff at crosses and tortures, at wild beasts and all your terrifying array of torments.

6. "Poor wretches, you do not realize that there is no one who is willing to undergo punishment without good reason or who can endure torments without the aid of God.

7. "It is possible, I suppose, that you are misled by the sight of men who are ignorant of God, and yet enjoy a superabundance of wealth, splendid honors, and far-reaching powers. The poor wretches are being raised the higher only that their downfall may be the greater.[628] They are like victims being fattened for execution, like sacrificial animals being garlanded[629] for punishment. Moreover, the very reason why they are lifted to such heights of dominion and empire is that they may be free to barter their talents for the price of absolute power and the corruption of their souls.[630]

8. "Since there is the fact of death, what solid happiness can there be divorced from the knowledge of God? Happiness is like a dream: it slips from your grasp before you can lay hold of it.[631] 9. Maybe you are a king.[632] You still feel fear just as much as you are feared;[633] however large be the retinue which crowds round you, you are alone when you face danger. Maybe you are rich. There is no secure reliance to be placed in your fortunes; abundant traveling-provisions do not equip the brief journey of life, they encumber it.[634] 10. Maybe your boast is in the rods[635] and purple robes of office. It is a foolish error of mankind, a worthless cult of social prestige, to be resplendent in purple and to be squalid in soul. Maybe you are of high and noble birth. You give praise to your parentage. Yet we are all born of the same condition,[636] it is virtue alone that distinguishes us.

11. "And, therefore, we who are ranked by our morals and modesty, we have good cause for abstaining from your wicked pleasures, from your processions and your spectacles;[637] we are well aware that they originated in religious rites[638] and we condemn their pernicious attractions. Who would fail to be horrified to see at the chariot races the frenzied brawling of the mob,[639] to see at the gladiatorial contests a school in murder?[640] 12. At the theatre, too, this raving madness is undiminished, and the display of indecencies is greater;[641] at one time an actor of farce may describe or represent acts of adultery, at another an effeminate pantomime[642] may stimulate lust by simulating it—he even dishonors your gods by investing them with lovers' sighs, discords, and debauchery; he even induces your tears by feigning suffering with senseless gestures and signs. We

can only conclude that murder is what you demand in fact and what you weep at in fiction.[643]

CHAPTER 38

Final reply to various attacks made against Christian practices, and Octavius' peroration

1. "Now you claim that we reject food left over from sacrifices and cups from which libations have been poured.[644] This is no admission of fear;[645] it is a declaration of real independence. It is not that anything that comes into existence can possibly be spoiled—it is, after all, the inviolable gift of God;[646] nevertheless we do abstain, for fear it might be thought that we make submission to the demons to whom libation has been poured or that we are ashamed of our own religion.[647]

2. "And I should like to know who is the person who doubts that we find delight in spring flowers,[648] seeing that we gather the rose of spring, the lily, and all the other flowers with attractive colors and fragrance. These tender blossoms we use, untied, for strewing, and bound together for entwining our necks. If you would be so kind, forgive us for not garlanding our heads; it is usual for us to inhale the pleasant scent of flowers with our noses, not to breathe it in with our hair or the backs of our heads.[649] 3. Neither do we place garlands on our dead. To my mind, it is you who are the cause for wonderment here: how you can apply torches[650] to the deceased (if they have sensation) or garlands (if they have none); if their state is blessed they have no need of flowers, if it is wretched they derive

no joy from them. 4. To our funerals the adornment we give is the same composure we show in our lives; neither do we bind a garland that withers, but from God we await a garland of flowers that blossom forever.[651] Tranquil, moderate, confident in the generosity of our God,[652] we enliven our hopes for happiness in the future[653] by our faith in the majesty He manifests at present. And so, blessed is the state to which we rise again, blessed is the state in which we now live, by meditating on that future.[654]

5. "And so, for all I care, that buffoon of Athens, Socrates,[655] can go on looking,[656] admitting his complete ignorance, and boasting of the testimony of an archdeceiving demon;[657] Arcesilaus, too, and Carneades,[658] Pyrrhon,[659] and the whole crowd of the Academics can go on pondering, Simonides also can go on postponing for ever and ever.[660] We hold the arrogance of philosophers[661] in scorn, we know that they corrupt, that they are adulterous, that they rule as despots,[662] that they are ceaselessly declaiming against vices—which they have themselves.[663]

6. "Philosophical wisdom *we* parade not in our dress but in our hearts, grandeur we show not in our speech but in our lives.[664] Our boast is that we have won what they made supreme efforts to seek and failed to find. 7. What grounds have we to grumble or be dissatisfied, seeing that the fulness of the divine truth has come in the days of our lifetime?[665] Let us enjoy our blessing,[666] and let us modify your verdict on what is right.[667] The prayer I make is that superstition may be curbed, that impiety may be expiated, and that the true religion may be preserved."[668]

Chapter 39

Epilogue

1. Thus Octavius completed his oration. For some time afterwards we were so stunned that we could say nothing but kept our eyes fixed on him.[669] So far as I was concerned, I was completely lost in profound amazement at the wealth of proofs, examples, and authoritative quotations[670] he had used to illustrate matter easier to feel than to express;[671] by parrying spiteful critics with their own weapons, the arms of philosophers,[672] he had shown the truth to be so simple as well as so attractive.

Chapter 40

1. I was silently turning these thoughts over in my mind[673] when Caecilius burst out with the words: "Heartiest congratulations, Octavius, my friend; and I congratulate myself as well. I need not wait for the verdict. We have both won in a sense: it may sound outrageous, but I claim victory too, for while Octavius is victorious over me, I am triumphant over error.

2. "And so, regarding the central issues of our inquiry,[674] I admit your case on the subject of providence, on the question of God I concede defeat, on the integrity of the sect (now my own) I am in agreement with you. There are, however, some points still remaining; they do not drown the voice of truth, but they ought to be dealt with to complete my instruction.[675] The sun is now sinking down in the west, so we will investigate them tomorrow,[676]

and it will not be too slow a task, as we are now of one mind on the subject as a whole."[677]

3. And I said: "I, too, am very glad for us all, and not least because by his victory Octavius has also done me a service: he has relieved me of the singularly invidious task of passing judgment. Words fail me, however, in paying due praise to his achievement: the testimony of man, and of one man at that, is a paltry thing. But incomparable reward he has from God: it was God who inspired him in his plea and aided him in his victory." 4. Thereupon we departed, lighthearted and cheerful,[678] Caecilius rejoicing because he had come to believe, Octavius because he had been victorious, and I because the one had come to believe and the other had been victorious.[679]

NOTES

LIST OF ABBREVIATIONS

AC	Antike und Christentum (Münster 1929–50)
ACW	Ancient Christian Writers (Westminster, Md.-London-New York, N.Y.-Paramus, N.J. 1946–)
AJP	American Journal of Philology (Baltimore 1880–)
AnalBoll	Analecta Bollandiana (Brussels 1882–)
Axelson	B. Axelson, *Das Prioritätsproblem Tertullian–Minucius Felix* (Lund 1941)
Bailey on *Lucr.*	C. Bailey, *T. Lucretius Carus* (3 vols. Oxford 1947)
Baylis	H. J. Baylis, *Minucius Felix and His Place among the Early Fathers of the Latin Church* (London 1928)
Beaujeu	J. Beaujeu, *Minucius Felix: Octavius* (Paris 1964)
Beutler	R. Beutler, *Philosophie und Apologie bei Minucius Felix* (diss. Königsberg 1936)
CAH	Cambridge Ancient History (London-New York 1923–39; rev. ed. Cambridge, Eng. 1961–)
CCSL	Corpus christianorum, series latina (Turnhout-Paris 1953–)
CIL	Corpus inscriptionum latinarum (Berlin 1863–)
Cook, *Zeus*	A. B. Cook, *Zeus* (3 vols. Cambridge, Eng. 1914–40)
CP	Classical Philology (Chicago 1906–)

CQ	Classical Quarterly (London 1907–)
CR	Classical review (London 1887–)
CSEL	Corpus scriptorum ecclesiasticorum latinorum (Vienna 1866–)
DACL	Dictionnaire d'archéologie chrétienne et de liturgie (Paris 1907–53)
DTC	Dictionnaire de théologie catholique (Paris 1903–50)
Fahy	T. Fahy, *M. Minucii Felicis Octavius* (Dublin-Belfast 1919)
FF	Forschungen und Fortschritte (Berlin 1925–)
FHG	Fragmenta historicorum graecorum, ed. C. Müller (5 vols. Paris 1841–70)
Frazer on Ovid *Fasti*	J. G. Frazer, *The Fasti of Ovid* (5 vols. London 1929)
Frazer on Pausanias	J. G. Frazer, *Pausanias' Description of Greece* (6 vols. London 1898)
GCS	Die griechischen christlichen Schriftsteller der ersten Jahrhunderte (Leipzig 1897–)
GIF	*Giornale italiano di filologia* (Naples 1948–)
Gronovius	J. Gronovius, *M. Minucii Felicis Octavius* (Leiden 1709)
Hirzel *Dialog*	R. Hirzel, *Der Dialog* (2 vols. Leipzig 1895; repr. Hildesheim 1963)
Holden	H. A. Holden, *M. Minucii Felicis Octavius* (Cambridge 1853)
HSCP	Harvard Studies in Classical Philology (Cambridge, Mass. 1890–)
HTR	Harvard Theological Review (Cambridge, Mass. 1908–)
ILCV	E. Diehl, *Inscriptiones latinae christianae veteres* (3 vols. Berlin 1925–31)
ILS	H. Dessau, *Inscriptiones latinae selectae* (3 vols. in 5. Berlin 1892–

	1916; 2nd ed. 1954–55 with supplement)
JAC	Jahrbuch für Antike und Christentum (Münster 1958–)
James *Apoc.N.T.*	M. R. James, *The Apocryphal New Testament* (Oxford 1924)
JEH	Journal of Ecclesiastical History (London 1950–)
JHS	Journal of Hellenic Studies (London 1880–)
JRS	Journal of Roman Studies (London 1911–)
JTS	Journal of Theological Studies (London 1899–1949; n.s. 1950–)
Mayor on Juv.	J. E. B. Mayor, *Juvenal* (2 vols. 1900–1901)
MG	J. P. Migne, *Patrologia graeca* (Paris 1857–66)
ML	J. P. Migne, *Patrologia latina* (Paris 1844–55)
Mohrmann *Études*	Chr. Mohrmann, *Études sur le latin des chrétiens* (3 vols. Rome 1961–65)
Naber	S. A. Naber, *M. Cornelii Frontonis et M. Aurelii imperatoris epistulae* (Leipzig 1867)
OCD	Oxford Classical Dictionary (Oxford 1949)
Ogilvie on Livy	R. M. Ogilvie, *A Commentary on Livy Books 1–5* (Oxford 1965)
Otto *Sprichwörter*	A. Otto, *Die Sprichwörter und sprichwörtlichen Redensarten der Römer* (Leipzig 1890; repr. Hildesheim 1962)
Pease on *De divin.*	A. S. Pease, *M. Tulli Ciceronis De divinatione* (2 vols. Urbana, Ill. 1920–23; repr. Darmstadt 1963)
Pease on *De nat. deor.*	A. S. Pease, *M. Tulli Ciceronis De natura deorum* (2 vols. Cambridge, Mass. 1955–58)

Pellegrino	M. Pellegrino, *M. Minucii Felicis Octavius* (Turin 1947)
PhW	Philologische Wochenschrift (Berlin-Leipzig 1881–1944)
PIR	*Prosopographia imperii romani* (edd. E. Klebs, P. de Rohden, H. Dessau, 3 vols. Berlin 1897–8; 2nd ed., edd. E. Groag, A. Stein, et al., Berlin 1933–)
Platner-Ashby	S. B. Platner and T. Ashby, *A Topographical Dictionary of Ancient Rome* (Oxford 1929)
Pohlenz	M. Pohlenz, *Die Stoa* (2 vols. Göttingen 1948–49)
PW	Pauly-Wissowa-Kroll, *Realencyclopädie der classischen Altertumswissenschaft* (Stuttgart 1893–)
Quispel	G. Quispel, *M. Minucii Felicis Octavius* (Leiden 1949)
RAC	Reallexikon für Antike und Christentum (Stuttgart 1941 [1950]–)
RB	Revue bénédictine (Maredsous 1884–)
RechAug	Recherches augustiniennes (Paris 1958–)
REA	Revue des études anciennes (Bordeaux 1899–)
REL	Revue des études latines (Paris 1923–)
RFIC	Rivista di filologia e d'istruzione classica (Turin 1873–)
RhM	Rheinisches Museum für Philologie (Bonn 1833–)
Roscher	W. H. Roscher, *Ausführliches Lexikon der griechischen und römischen Mythologie* (Leipzig 1884–1937; suppl. 1893, 1902, 1921)
Ruinart	*Acta martyrum sincera* (Ratisbon 1859)
SC	Scuola cattolica (Milan 1873–)

SE	Sacris erudiri (Bruges 1948–)
S.H.A.	Scriptores Historiae Augustae
Spanneut	M. Spanneut, *Le stoïcisme des pères de l'église* (Paris 1947)
SVF	J. von Arnim, *Stoicorum veterum fragmenta* (4 vols. 1921–24; repr. Stuttgart 1964)
SymbOslo	Symbolae Osloenses (Oslo 1922–)
TAPA	Transactions and Proceedings of the American Philological Association (Hartford 1871–)
ThGl	Theologie und Glaube (Paderborn 1909–)
TLL	Thesaurus linguae latinae (Leipzig 1900–)
TU	Texte und Untersuchungen zur Geschichte der altchristlichen Literatur (Berlin 1882–)
VC	Vigiliae christianae (Amsterdam 1947–)
Waltzing	J.-P. Waltzing, *M. Minucii Felicis Octavius* (Louvain 1903)
Waszink on Tert. *De an.*	J. H. Waszink, *Tertullianus, De anima* (Amsterdam 1947)
WSt	Wiener Studien (Vienna 1879–)
YCS	Yale Classical Studies (New Haven 1928–)
ZkTh	Zeitschrift für katholische Theologie (Vienna 1877–)
ZNTW	Zeitschrift für die neutestamentliche Wissenschaft und die Kunde der älteren Kirche (Giessen-Berlin 1900–)

INTRODUCTION

Where a reference is given to another note, this will be to the notes of the commentary unless it is stated otherwise.

[1] The superintendent was Faustus Sabaeus; he is rather dubiously cautious over the provenance (Bohemia?) of the MS: *iure enim belli meus est Arnobius, quem e media barbarie non sine dispendio et discrimine eripuerim* (from his Preface, quoted by J.-P. Waltzing in his edition of 1903, Louvain, 9 n. 2). I am grateful to the Nuffield Foundation for a special grant in order to be able to examine this MS now in Paris (Bibliothèque Nationale 1661). The date on the colophon of the *editio princeps* is 1542, in the preface, 1543: George E. McCracken, *Arnobius of Sicca, The Case against the Pagans* 1 (ACW 7; Westminster, Md. 1949) 54.

[2] This dissertation is most easily accessible in ML 3.207 ff., or in Holden's edition (Cambridge 1853). At least four earlier editions also reprint it; cf. Waltzing, *op. cit.* 6 item 3, 7 item 11.

[3] The characteristics of this MS (Brussels 10847) are conveniently described by Beaujeu in his edition (Paris 1964) xcix ff. I have seen this MS only in microfilm (an unsatisfactory medium for the clear observation of correcting hands).

[4] Might difference in model and source (e.g., Seneca as opposed to Cicero for the *Octavius*) account for difference in style?

[5] In *Oct.* 36.2 the perennial problem of God's prescience and man's free will is briefly mentioned, only to be dismissed with the words *ac de fato satis, vel si pauca, pro tempore, disputaturi alias et uberius et plenius*. This may be an example of the common enough literary device for making a convenient end to a laborious topic. It could have easily been exploited by a later author writing on the very traditional theme *De fato*. See further n. 608 *ad Oct.* 36.2.

[6] For Augustine's doxographical lists, see J. Doignon, " 'Nos bons hommes de foi': Cyprien, Lactance, Victorin, Optat, Hilaire

(Augustin, de doctrina christiana iv, 60,61)," *Latomus* 22 (1963) 795 ff.

[7] On Eucherius see N. K. Chadwick, *Poetry and Letters in Early Christian Gaul* (London 1955) 151 ff.

[8] For an (unconvincing) attempt to trace the influence of Minucius Felix beyond these writers (to Gregory Illiberitanus), see V. Bulhart, "Ignis Sapiens," SE 13 (1962) 60 f. (and see n. 591 *ad Oct.* 35.3).

[9] The placing of a debate on a leisurely holiday, the *mise en scène* by the seashore, the discussion broken by the onset of evening (often, as in the *Octavius*, without pause for lunch or siesta!), are all not uncommon procedures in literary dialogues. For details see nn. 16, 17, 676 *ad Oct.* 2.3, 2.4, 40.2.

[10] For a suggestion that Caecilius was a *sectator* of Minucius Felix, a young man who lived in the home of the more experienced advocate and accompanied him to the law courts to learn his skills, see 3.1 and n. 23 for parallels.

[11] In 9.6 Caecilius invokes the testimony of Fronto by the oblique title *Cirtensis noster* (Cirta, in Numidian Africa, being Fronto's home town). H. Dessau, "Über einige Inschriften aus Cirta," *Hermes* 15 (1880) 471 ff., with further discussion in Minucius Felix und Caecilius Natalis, *Hermes* 40 (1905) 373 ff., attempted *inter alia* to identify this Caecilius with the Caecilius Natalis of CIL 8.6996 (210 A.D.), 7094-98 (211-217 A.D.) (Cirta). Such direct identification is without warrant, but there is a strong suggestion that Caecilius had at least family connections in that town (see further n. 123 *ad. Oct.* 9.6, and n. 9 *ad Oct.* 1.5).

[12] 2.1. Contra Beaujeu in ed. *ad* 3.4 and xxix, one cannot safely deduce from the phrase *Octavi disserentis de navigatione narratio* that Octavius had traveled by sea from Africa. See my note "Minucius Felix *Octavius* 4.6," CP 61 (1966) 252 f., at 253 n. 4.

[13] 28.1 ff. (repentant words for having once participated in the trial and condemnation of Christians). If Octavius, as is often surmised, is speaking about activities in Africa, he cannot be referring to events before 180 A.D. (the date of Africa's proto-martyrs).

[14] 1.3 ff. For further discussion on Octavius, see n. 1 *ad. Oct.* 1.1.

[15] W. H. C. Frend, *The Donatist Church* (Oxford 1952) 91, seems to assume that conditions reflected in the *Octavius* are those of the African Church.

[16] Notable allusions are 9.6 (see n. 11 above) and 24.1, where

the deification of the Mauretanian king, Juba II, is instanced. That is an almost unique literary notice (confirmed by CIL 8.20627). Tertullian *Apol.* 24.8 has a general statement on the Mauretanians' custom of deifying their chieftains. Note, however, Isid. *Etym.* 8.11.1 with the same example of Juba; Minucius and Isidore may, therefore, have both culled their information from an ultimately common literary source; see further n. 350 *ad. Oct.* 24.1.

[17] Viz., CIL 8.1964, 12449, 19600, 25584. But for Italian Minucii Felices, see CIL 6.9208, 22547 (Rome), 14.1359, 5028 (Ostia). "Felix" was a cognomen particularly frequent in African provinces; see I. Kajanto, "Peculiarities of Latin Nomenclature in North Africa," *Philologus* 108 (1964) 310 ff. (35% of the total 3,540 examples). That fact also signifies little.

[18] Notably the *De natura deorum* and *De divinatione*. One suspects that the *Hortensius* (surviving only in fragments) was a further model. See n. 1 *ad. Oct.* 1.1, and consult E. Behr, *Der Octavius des Minucius Felix in seinem Verhältnis zu Ciceros Büchern "De natura deorum"* (diss. Jena 1870); W. Krause, *Die Stellung der frühchristlichen Autoren zur heidnischen Literatur* (Vienna 1958) 142 ff.; I. Opelt, "Ciceros Schrift De natura deorum bei den lateinischen Kirchenvätern," *Ant. und Abendland* 12 (1966) 141 ff., esp. 147 f. For (an exaggerated) collection of references, J.-P. Waltzing, ed. *Octavius* (Louvain 1903) 209 ff.

[19] For documentation see n. 1 *ad. Oct.* 1.1.

[20] The bibliography for the question is voluminous. As so much has been said on the subject, a complete treatment of the chronology problem, giving due consideration to previous scholars' arguments and theories, would be impossible here. At the obvious risk of being dogmatic, I have, therefore, aimed at brevity on this question. The best single treatment on it remains that of B. Axelson, *Das Prioritätsproblem Tertullian–Minucius Felix* (Lund 1941). Since that time the discussion has nevertheless continued vigorously. For a well-balanced recent summary, consult the introduction of J. Beaujeu, *Minucius Felix: Octavius* (Paris 1964) xliv ff.

[21] E.g., S. Rossi, "L' 'Octavius' fu scritto prima del 161," GIF 12 (1959) 289 ff., at 292 ff., insists that 7.4 *ut Parthos signa repetamus* has a contemporary (Antonine) reference. That notion was refuted long ago by F. di Capua, "Minucio Felice, Octavius 7.4," *Didaskaleion* 2 (1913) 175 ff.; cf. A. della Casa, "Le due

date dell' '*Octavius*,' " *Maia* 14 (1962) 26 ff., at 30 f. There can be no doubt that the reference is to the three military standards lost at Carrhae in 53 B.C. and recovered in 20 B.C. See n. 95 *ad. Oct.* 7.4.

²² The *Ad nationes*, an earlier draft (it would seem) of the more expansive *Apology*, on occasion bears closer resemblance to the *Octavius* than the *Apology* does (e.g., *Ad nat.* 1.11.6 is closer to *Oct.* 28.7 than *Apol.* 16.5 [on Epona]; cf. *Ad nat.* 1.12.15 f., *Apol.* 16.8, and *Oct.* 29.7; *Ad nat.* 1.12.7 and *Oct.* 29.8). For doubts (by no means compelling) about the usually accepted date (based on allusions in the texts) of c. 197 for the *Apology*, see M. Sordi, *Il christianesimo e Roma* (Bologna 1965) 474 ff.

²³ The case for Arnobius' imitation of the *Octavius* is argued by McCracken, *op. cit.* 1.44 f. Such imitations are possible but not indubitable. Arnobius was writing c. 300 A.D.

²⁴ See nn. 15 and 16 *ad loc.*

²⁵ See nn. 19 and 294 *ad loc.*

²⁶ Cf. n. 21 above.

²⁷ See n. 217 *ad loc.*

²⁸ Proposed by E. Castorina, "Gellio e la data di publicazione delle "Noctes," GIF 3 (1950) 137–45, and accepted by Beaujeu liii. The passage adduced (*Noctes Atticae* 19.12.1) is simply not conclusive for a date after Herodes Atticus' death; cf. R. Marache, *Lustrum* 10 (1965) 229.

²⁹ See n. 17 *ad Oct.* 2.4 for disbelief in the theory of dependence: the points of similarity are paralleled elsewhere. The attempt by E. Griset, "Un cristiano di Sabrata," *Riv. di stud. class.* 5 (1957) 35 ff., to establish an Antonine date by reference to Apuleius *Apol.* 16, 56 equally does not convince.

³⁰ For the passage *Or.* 6.2, see n. 516 *ad Oct.* 34.10; on the date see my note "The Date of the *Oration* of Tatian," HTR 60 (1967) 123 ff., against R. M. Grant, "The Date of Tatian's Oration," HTR 46 (1953) 99 ff. See further L. W. Barnard, "The Heresy of Tatian—Once Again," JEH 19 (1968) 1 ff.

³¹ See W. den Boer, "Clémente d'Alexandrie et Minucius Félix, *Mnemosyne* 11 (1943) 161 ff., contra A. Beltrami, "Clemente Alessandrino nell'*Ottavio* di M. Minucio Felice," RFIC, 1919, 366 ff., 1920, 239 ff., and *idem*, "Minucio (Octavius)–Cicerone (De natura deorum)–Clemente Alessandrino (Opere)," *Atti della Reale Accademia delle Scienze di Torino* 55 (1919/20) 179 ff. The prudent might ascribe parallels in other apologists (see J.-P.

Waltzing, ed. 1903, 37 ff.) in like manner not so much to direct borrowing (on Just. *Apol.* 1.55 and *Oct.* 29.8, see n. 488) as to "common sources" (and in an ecclesiastical tradition of homilectics, need these be exclusively *literary* sources, as is the usual assumption?).

[32] The appeal to a purely hypothetical common source for the two authors, though it has occasionally been made, is not only poor methodologically but wholly unwarranted. For a convenient table of parallels, see M. Pellegrino, in ed. 1947, 9 f.

[33] It strains credulity, e.g., to establish any certitude from *Oct.* 18.9 and Tert. *Apol.* 34 (see n. 227 *ad.* 18.9), *Oct.* 18.11 and Tert. *Apol.* 17.5 ff. (see n. 228 *ad* 18.11), etc. Passages that have been thus exploited are remarked in the commentary.

[34] Among the most impressive instances are *Oct.* 34.7 and *Apol.* 48.1 (see n. 573), *Oct.* 38.5 and *Apol.* 46.10 ff. (see n. 662), *Oct.* 27.3 and *Apol.* 23.3 (see n. 440), *Oct.* 37.1 and *Apol.* 50.2 (see n. 621). Other examples are also noted in the commentary.

[35] Contra, e.g., F. Ramorino, "Minucio Felice e Tertulliano: nota biografico-cronologica," *Didaskaleion* 1 (1912) 125 ff.

[36] See T.4–T.7. In the *De viris illustribus* (T.3) Minucius appears as no. 58, Tertullian as no. 53. Tertullian is there described as *primus Latinorum ponitur post Victorem;* that might suggest Jerome at least thought Tertullian came before Minucius Felix (so PW 15.2 (1932) 1818 *s.v.* Minucius 12 [A. G. Opitz]).

[37] The basic studies on this question are those of H. Bornecque, "Les clausules métriques dans Minucius Félix," *Musée belge* 7 (1903) 247–65, and F. di Capua, "L'evoluzione della prosa metrica latina nei primi tre secoli e la data dell'Ottavio di Minucio," *Didaskaleion* 2 (1913) 1–41.

[38] This case is most clearly argued (if somewhat overstated) by Beaujeu, intro. lxvii ff.

[39] Jerome *Ep.* 70.4; Aug. *De bapt. contr. Donat.* 6.44.87.

[40] Cyp. *Vit.* 7 (ML 3.1547). It also does not figure in the "Cheltenham List" of c. 359 A.D.

[41] So B. Axelson, "Quod idola und Laktanz," *Eranos* 39 (1941) 67–74 (but see contra, M. Simonetti, "Sulla paternità del 'Quod idola dii non sint,'" *Maia* 3 (1950) 265–88, and cf. H. Koch, *Cyprianische Untersuchungen* (Bonn 1926) 1–78.

[42] For a table of eight "emprunts sûrs" and thirteen "emprunts probables," see Beaujeu, intro. lxix. See also S. Colombo, "Osser-

vazioni sui rapporti fra l'Octavius di M. Minucio Felice e alcuni opuscoli di Cipriano," *Didaskaleion*, 1915, 215 ff., and M. Pellegrino, *Studi su l'antica apologetica* (Rome 1947) 107 ff.

[43] E.g., *Ad Demetr.* 25 (ML 4.562) *ad verae religionis candidam lucem de profundo tenebrosae superstitionis emergere* is claimed (by Beaujeu) as an "emprunt sûr" from *Oct.* 1.4 *cum discussa caligine de tenebrarum profundo in lucem sapientiae et veritatis emergerem;* one need but compare Pont. *Vit. Cyp.* 2 *mundi nube discussa in lucem sapientiae spiritalis emersit* and see n. 8 *ad Oct.* 1.4 for this widely employed metaphorical language. Similarly *Ad Demetr.* 16 (ML 4.556) can scarcely win credence as an "emprunt sûr" from *Oct.* 17.2; the point there made is a commonplace of the hardiest variety and the phrasing is rhetorically standard (see n. 200 *ad Oct.* 17.2). Neither is it safe to catalogue *De habit. virg.* 14 (ML 4.453) and *De lapsis* 12 (ML 4.475) as "emprunts sûrs" from *Oct.* 26.8; this description of the earth-laden and the fallen angels was manifestly common (see n. 423 *ad Oct.* 26.8).

[44] A post-Cyprianic date (not a complete impossibility) has had some supporters, but they have won little general acceptance for their viewpoint. Recently J.-G. Préaux has advocated at least a post Origenic date, but his case is by no means decisive ("A propos du 'De fato' (?) de Minucius Felix," *Latomus* 9 (1950) 395 ff. See commentary n. 606). The tenses used and the tone adopted by Lactantius (T.2) are suggestive that Minucius Felix lived at least a good generation before Lactantius' own day.

[45] Note, however, the memory of trial (28), imprisonment (35.6), and martyrdom (37.1 ff.) One could scarcely pen an apology without some mention of them.

[46] Though Tertullian does claim, rather vaguely, that *plerique casus* do bring the Scriptures into the hands of outsiders (*Apol.* 31.1). The essentially "private" method of distributing books in antiquity—the demand, literally, creating the supply—is rightly emphasized by V. Tcherikover, "Jewish Apologetic Literature Reconsidered," *Eos* 48 (1956) fasc. 3, 169 ff. at 171 ff.

[47] For the date see n. 28 above and Henry Nettleship, "The Noctes Atticae of Aulus Gellius," AJP 4 (1884) 391 ff.; P. K. Marshall, "The Date of Birth of Aulus Gellius," CP 58 (1963) 143 ff.

[48] For examples of contemporary interest in verbal niceties, see

Noctes Atticae 2.26; 13.29; 19.8,10,13. Discussion in R. Marache, *Mots nouveaux et mots archaïques chez Fronton et Aulu Gell* (Paris 1957) esp. 97 ff., 263 ff.

⁴⁹ E.g., Naber 139 ff.

⁵⁰ *Noctes Atticae*, praef. 6–10; cf. Augustine on his own education some two centuries later: *multa philosophorum legeram memoriaeque mandata retinebam*" (*Conf.* 5.3.3; on this passage see A. Solignac, "Doxographies et manuels dans la formation philosophique de saint Augustin," RechAug 1 [1958] 113 ff.).

⁵¹ Tatian mentions the collection of Laitos (*Or.* 37); for Irenaeus' use of such works, R. M. Grant, "Irenaeus and Hellenistic Culture," HTR 42 (1949) 41 ff.; Athenagoras consulted them (*Leg.* 6).

⁵² E.g., Melito of Sardis drew up biblical *eclogai*, Euseb. *H.E.* 4.26.13 f.; for later collections, R. Harris, *Testimonies* (Cambridge 1916–20). Manuals of anti-Jewish *testimonia* were especially common; for the New Testament evidence, B. Lindars, *New Testament Apologetic: The Doctrinal Significance of the Old Testament Quotations* (London 1961) esp. 251 ff. See also L. W. Barnard, "The Use of Testimonies in the Early Church and in the Epistle of Barnabas," in *Studies in the Apostolic Fathers and Their Background* (Oxford 1966) 109 ff.

⁵³ So B. Hemmerdinger, "Les Hexaples et saint Irénée," VC 16 (1962) 19 f. See also J. S. Sibinga, *The Old Testament Text of Justin Martyr* (Leiden 1963) 49 f.

⁵⁴ Ed. C. R. Haines (Loeb Classical Library) 2 (London 1920) 82.

⁵⁵ *Conversion* (Oxford repr. 1961) 251; cf. Celsus *ap.* Orig. *C.Cels.* 5.33: "I will ask them where they have come from, or who is the author of their traditional laws. Nobody, they will say."

⁵⁶ 3.5–9. A useful discussion of this point is to be found in G. Bardy, *La conversion au christianisme durant les premiers siècles* (Paris 1949) 211 ff.; and cf. n. 64 *ad* Oct. 6.1.

⁵⁷ Cf. n. 83 *ad* Oct. 6.3.

⁵⁸ *Hist.* 5.5. Josephus *C.Ap.* 2.73 ff. emphasizes that the antiquity of the Jewish cultus was a cogent factor in winning toleration from the Roman government for the exercise of Jewish rites and laws.

⁵⁹ FHG (Müller) 3.206 ff. A précis of the contents will be found in W. W. Tarn, *Hellenistic Civilisation* (3rd. rev. ed. Lon-

don 1952) 233 f. Celsus counterclaimed that the Jews were in fact relative newcomers (Origen, *C.Cels.* 1.14).

[60] For the date see T. Reinach, *Flavius Josèphe Contra Apionem* (Paris 1930) xv, and R. J. H. Shutt, *Studies in Josephus* (London 1961) 15.

[61] For the title, Orig. *C.Cels.* 1.16, 3.11.

[62] E.g., Just. *Apol.* 1.60–64. For these chronological arguments, see A. Puech, *Recherches sur le Discours aux grecs de Tatien* (Paris 1903) 82 ff.; H. Chadwick, *Early Christian Thought and the Classical Tradition* (Oxford 1966) 13 ff.; B. Z. Wacholder, "Biblical Chronology in the Hellenistic World Chronicles," HTR 61 (1968) 451 ff., esp. 463 ff.; RAC *s.v.* Erfinder ii (K. Raede). For a discussion of Clement of Alexandria's (somewhat more sophisticated) arguments on the "Atticized Moses" line, E. Molland, "Clement of Alexandria on the Origin of Greek Philosophy," *Symb. Oslo.* 15/16 (1937) 57 ff.

[63] This theory of derivation from Moses appears to be found first in Aristobulos (second century B.C.?), Eusebius *Praep. ev.* 13.12; Clem. *Strom.* 5.14.97. The formulation appears first in Numenius of Apamea: Clem. *Strom.* 1.150.4. See H. Ch. Puech, "Numénius d'Apamée et les théologies orientales au second siècle," *Mélanges Bidez* 2 (Brussels 1934) 745 ff., at 753 f.; J. Whittaker, "Moses Atticizing," *Phoenix* 21 (1967) 196 ff.

[64] Tatian *Or.* 31; Theophilus *Ad Autol.* 2.30 f. Cf. the activities of the early Christian chronographers; see, for a general account, R. L. P. Milburn, *Early Christian Interpretations of History* (London, 1954) 21 ff.

[65] Just. *Apol.* 2.13. On Justin and philosophy, see H. Chadwick, "Justin Martyr's Defence of Christianity," *Bull. John Rylands Lib.* 47 (1965) 275 ff.

[66] Just. *Apol.* 1.59 ff.; [Just.] *Cohort.* 9 ff.

[67] E.g., Orig. *C.Cels.* 4.39; Diog. Laer. 3.6, Philost. *Vit Apoll.* 1.2, etc.

[68] [Just.] *Cohort.* 25.

[69] [Just.] *Cohort.* 38. Theophilus makes much use of her. Consult DACL 12.2 *s.v.* Oracle at 2225 f. (H. Leclercq) for Jewish and Christian exploitation of the "Sibyl."

[70] Note the appearance, graphically, of Christ as a *Sapiens*: G. M. A. Hanfmann, "Socrates and Christ," HSCP 60 (1951) 205 ff.; H.-I. Marrou, Μουσικὸς Ἀνήρ (Grenoble 1938) 56 ff., 141 ff., 283 ff.

[71] For Celsus' origin and dates, see H. Chadwick, *Origen: Contra Celsum* (Cambridge, 1953) xxiv ff.; W. H. C. Frend, *Martyrdom and Persecution in the Early Church* (Oxford 1965) 297 n. 56.

[72] E.g., *C.Cels.* 5.65.

[73] *Adv. nat.* 1.57 *sed antiquiora . . . nostra* [sc. *scripta*] *sunt, ac per hoc fidei et veritatis plenissima.* Cf. the attitude of Arnobius' contemporary, the emperor Diocletian, in his edict against the Manicheans (*Gregorian Code* 14.4.1–2) to the effect that the providence of the gods has shown man what is right and true, and established religion ought not to be set aside for a new one; it is a very serious charge to tamper with what has been laid down by the ancients. Later, the credo of the pagan "circle" of Symmachus was enunciated by Rufius Albinus: *vetustas quidem nobis semper, si sapimus, adoranda est* (Macrob. *Sat.* 3.14.2). Tertullian complains (*Apol.* 19.1) that to make credit depend on the lapse of time was a pagan superstition (*apud vos quoque religionis est instar, fidem de temporibus adserere*).

[74] Cf. A. H. M. Jones, "The Social Background of the Struggle between Paganism and Christianity," in *The Conflict between Paganism and Christianity in the Fourth Century* (Oxford 1963) 20. For Cato and Ennius, cf. *Noctes Atticae* 17.5.7.

[75] Text (with the Greek original) provided by C. Th. Schaeffer, *S. Clementis Romani Epistula ad Corinthos quae vocatur prima* (Florilegium patristicum 44; Bonn 1941).

[76] For a discussion of the chronology, Christine Mohrmann, "Les origines de la latinité chrétienne à Rome," VC 3 (1949) 78 ff. Clemens Latinus is there dated to c. 180 (p. 86); the biblical quotations are more ancient than the body of the letter.

[77] Christine Mohrmann, "Linguistic Problems in the Early Christian Church," VC 11 (1957) 11 ff., at 27.

[78] On the question of the Latin Bible, H. F. D. Sparks, "The Latin Bible," in *The Bible in Its Ancient and English Versions* (ed. H. W. Robinson; Oxford 1940) 100–127; L. R. Palmer, *The Latin Language* (London 1954) 184–90; and the studies by Christine Mohrmann assembled in the three volumes of her *Études sur le latin des chrétiens* (Rome 1961 and 1965).

[79] *De test. anim.* 1 (ML 1.683).

[80] For a balanced discussion of Arnobius' date of writing, George E. McCracken, *op.cit.* (n. 23 above) 7 ff.

[81] *Sed ab indoctis hominibus et rudibus scripta sunt, et idcirco non sunt facili auditione credenda: Adv. nat.* 1.58 (ML 5.796).

[82] *Trivialis et sordidus sermo est (ibid.).*

[83] *Barbarismis, solecismis obsitae sunt, inquit, res vestrae, et vitiorum deformitate pollutae:* 1.59 (ML 5.797); cf. 2.6 for Christian illiteracy.

[84] *Aut minus id, quod dicitur, verum est, si in numero peccatur, aut casu, praepositione, participio, coniunctione? (ibid.).*

[85] *Quaenam est enim ratio naturalis, aut in mundi constitutionibus lex scripta, ut hic paries dicatur et haec sella? . . . Humana ista sunt placita et ad usum sermonis faciendi non sane omnibus facienda: nam et haec paries forsitan, et hic sella dici sine ulla reprehensione potuisset, si ab initio sic dici placuisset . . .* etc.: 1.59 (ML 5.798-800); cf. 2.66, 2.69, 2.72.

[86] Jerome *De viris illustribus* 79.

[87] *Protrep.* 8.99.1.

[88] *Apol.* 49 ff.

[89] *Cohort.* 35f.

[90] Lact. *Div. inst.* 5.1 (ML 6.550). For a fuller discussion, J. Stevenson, "Aspects of the Relations between Lactantius and the Classics," *Stud. patr.* 4 (1961) = TU 79, 497–503.

[91] Lact. *loc. cit.; Nam haec in primis causa est cur apud sapientes, et doctos, et principes huius saeculi Scriptura sancta fide careat, quod Prophetae communi ac simplici sermone, ut ad populum, sunt locuti.*

[92] Lact. *loc. cit.*

[93] Lact. *Div. inst.* 5.1 ad fin., 5.2 init. (ML 6.551 f.); cf. T.2.

[94] Cf. Euseb. *H.E.* 3.24.3; and for other formulations of the argument, see E. Auerbach, *Literary Language and Its Public in Late Latin Antiquity and in the Middle Ages* (Eng. trans. R. Manheim; London 1965) 47 ff. In view of all these passages, one wonders whether the tone of M. L. W. Laistner is correct (*Christianity and Pagan Culture* [Ithaca 1951] 27): "Pagan readers of these early Latin versions [sc., of the Bible] were repelled by what they *affected* to regard as their crudity" (italics mine).

[95] For the evidence, *Cod. Theod.* 13.3.5; Theodoret 3.4.2, 3.8; Socrates *H.E.* 3.12, 3.16 (MG 67.412, 417 ff.); Sozomen *H.E.* 5.18 (MG 67.1269 ff.); Julian *Ep.* 42 (Hertlein); Ammianus Marcellinus 25.4. For a discussion, T. R. Glover, *Life and Letters in the Fourth Century* (Cambridge 1901) 68–71.

[96] H.-I. Marrou, *A History of Education in Antiquity* (Eng. trans. George Lamb; London 1956) 323.

[97] Julian *loc. cit.* in n. 95 above.

[98] Socrates and Sozomen, *op. cit.*, in n. 95. For this point, A. H. M. Jones, *art. cit.* in n. 74 above, 20 f., and *idem, The Later Roman Empire 284–602* 2 (Oxford 1964) 1006. The elder Apollinaris was a *grammaticus* and presbyter; the younger was a *rhetor* and a reader. Sozomen comments on the speed with which the works were composed and gives them high praise. Socrates, however, drily remarks that their labors were reckoned as nugatory. Only the metrical paraphrases of the Psalms survive, and even the authenticity of these is disputed. For bibliography, J. Quasten, *Patrology* 3 (1960) 380 f.

[99] See W. W. Tarn, *op. cit.* in n. 59 above, 234, for the Greek tragedy of Ezechiel on the Exodus, and the Greek hexameters by Philo and Theodotus on Jewish history. On Philo's epic see also Y. Gutman, "Philo the Epic Poet," *Scripta hierosolymitana* 1 (1954) 36 ff.

[100] I have disregarded Lactantius' (?) "Phoenix" on the grounds that its claim to being a specifically Christian poem is weak: see J. Hubaux and M. Leroy, *Le mythe du Phénix dans les littératures grecque et latine* (Paris 1939) 56 ff.; and for text, translation, and commentary, M. C. Fitzpatrick, *De ave Phoenice* (diss. Univ. Penn., Philadelphia 1933).

[101] These poems are ascribed to Tertullian or Cyprian; they might be considerably later as the ascription is without warrant (CSEL 23.212–26).

[102] E.g., by Proba (whose antecedents and descendents were consulars, grandfather cos. 310, father 322, brother 341, sons 379 and 391), in CSEL 16.568–609; on her family, P. R. L. Brown, "Aspects of the Christianization of the Roman Aristocracy," JRS 51 (1961) 1 ff., at 9. There is another on the Incarnation in CSEL 16.515–620. On such centos, D. Comparetti, *Virgil in the Middle Ages* (trans. E. F. M. Benecke; London 1895) 53–55. Note the Vergilian cento of a Greek philosophical dialogue composed by a relative of Tertullian's, Tert. *De praescr. haer.* 39.4 (CCSL 1.219 f.): *meus quidem propinquus ex eodem poeta inter cetera stili sui otia Pinacem Cebetis explicuit;* the whole chapter is instructive on the subject.

[103] CSEL 16.609–15 (by "Pomponius").

[104] CSEL 23.255–269. On the dates of Victorinus, (c. 280–c.

363), A. H. Travis, "Marius Victorinus: A Biographical Note," HTR 36 (1943) 83–90.

[105] Jerome *Ep.* 70.5 (ML 22.668); text in CSEL 54.

[106] F. J. E. Raby, *A History of Christian Latin Poetry* (2nd ed. Oxford 1953) 18. I am heavily indebted to Raby for this paragraph (Raby 15–18). The Renaissance period evinced a very parallel tendency to retranslate the Bible into what was considered more acceptable classical Latin: see, e.g., the bibliographical note by W. Leonard Grant, "Neo-Latin Verse Translations of the Bible," HTR 52 (1959) 205 ff.

[107] *Quaest.* 84: *nec enim verum potest, inquiunt, aestimari quod postea est inventum.* See Pierre Courcelle, "Critiques exégétiques et arguments antichrétiens rapportés par Ambrosiaster," VC 13 (1959) 161–62; and *Quaest.* 114: *quod anterius est, inquiunt, falsum esse non potest.*

[108] *Ep.* 22.30.2 (ML 22.416): *si quanto in memet reversus prophetam legere coepissem sermo horrebat incultus. . . .* Chronology is uncertain, but Jerome may be talking of events c. 374; possibly he took up the study of Hebrew later, in c. 376 (*Ep.* 125.12). See James Duff, *The Letters of Saint Jerome* (Dublin 1942) 8–13. Therefore he probably read the Latin version of "the Prophet"; he may, however, have had the Greek. For further discussion, J. J. Thierry, "The Date of the Dream of Jerome," VC 17 (1963) 28–40. He dates the dream between 375 and 377 (p. 39).

[109] *Ep.* 53.9.1 (ML 22.549); *Comment. in Jonam prophetam* 3 (ML 25.1141 ff.); *Ad Ezech.* 40 (ML 25.376 ff.); and see H. Hagendahl, *Latin Fathers and the Classics* (Göteborg 1958) 309 ff.

[110] *Conf.* 3.4.5. Augustine's enthusiasm was stirred by reading the *Hortensius* of Cicero; the incident is mentioned again in *Conf.* 6.11.18, 8.7.17, and elsewhere in Augustine's writings. See John Hammond Taylor, S.J., "St. Augustine and the *Hortensius* of Cicero," *Studies in Philology* 60 (1963) 487–98. For a fuller discussion, Maurice Testard, *Saint Augustin et Cicéron* 1 (Paris 1958) cc. 1–2; John J. O'Meara, *The Young Augustine* (London 1954) 59 ff.; H.-I. Marrou, *Saint Augustin et la fin de la culture antique* (2nd ed. Paris 1949) 474.

[111] *Ennar. in Ps.* 39.26 (CCSL 38.443).

[112] *De catechizandis rudibus* 9.13 (ML 40.320): *ita enim non irridebunt si aliquos antistites et ministros Ecclesiae forte anim-*

adverterint vel cum barbaris et soloecismis Deum invocare, vel eadem verba quae pronuntiant non intelligere perturbateque distinguere. This example is exploited by Pierre Courcelle, "Propos antichrétiens rapportés par saint Augustin," *RechAug* 1 (1958) 176 f. See also *De doctrina christiana* 2.13.20, 2.14.21.

[113] Cf. Aug. *Ep.* 22.3.7: *rustica et minus instructa clericorum turba;* and see F. van der Meer, *Augustine the Bishop* (trans. Brian Battershaw and G. R. Lamb; London 1961) 225 ff.; and W. H. C. Frend, "The Gnostic-Manichean Tradition in North Africa," JEH 4 (1953) 23 ff.

[114] *De catechizandis rudibus* 8.12, 9.13 (ML 40.318–20). E.g., *maxime autem isti* [sc., *de scholis usitatissimis grammaticorum oratorumque venientes*] *docendi sunt Scripturas audire divinas, ne sordeat eis solidum eloquium, quia non est inflatum.* Significant also is the stylistic advice which the pagan Seneca is made to give to St. Paul in their (apocryphal) correspondence, *Epp.* 7 and 13 (ML Suppl. 1.676, 678).

[115] Orig. *C.Cels.* 6.1 declares that people educated in learning and scholarship form a very narrow and limited circle.

[116] See Chr. Mohrmann, "La langue et le style de la poésie chrétienne," REL 25 (1947) 280 ff.

[117] For this dual role of defence and exposition, cf. [Athenag.] *Resur.* 1.

[118] See F. A. Wright, *A History of Later Greek Literature* (London 1932) 278 ff. The portentous example is Aelian (*fl.* c. 200), who came from Praeneste and yet wrote his philosophical works in a Greek which enjoyed fame for its Attic purity. Earlier, Fronto composed in Greek as well as in Latin. Note the survival of the laudatory phrase *utriusque linguae peritus* in the hagiographic tradition; see M. Coens, "Utriusque linguae peritus," AnalBoll 76 (1958) 118 ff., esp. 131 ff. Note also T. Kotula, "*Utraque lingua peritus.* Une page relative à l'histoire de l'éducation dans l'Afrique romaine," *Hommages à Marcel Renard* 2 (= Collection Latomus 102, Brussels 1969) 386 ff.

[119] For remarks on the dichotomy between East and West, H. Grégoire, *Les persécutions dans l'empire romain* (Brussels 1950) 22 f.; A. H. M. Jones, *The Later Roman Empire 284–602* (Oxford 1964) 986 ff.

[120] For the attacks see P. de Labriolle, *La réactione païenne* (rev. ed. Paris 1942) Parts 2 and 3.

[121] Cf. Chr. Mohrmann, "Le latin commun et le latin des chrétiens," VC 1 (1947) 1 ff., at 9.

[121a] On the diglossy of the Second Sophistic period, see R. Browning, *Mediaeval and Modern Greek* (London 1969) 54 f.

[122] 9.9. Cf. *The Life of Apollonius of Tyana* by (Minucius Felix' contemporary?) Philostratus, which shows at least acquaintance with some of the Gospel stories; see P. de Labriolle, *op. cit.* in n. 120 above, 170 ff.

[123] Just. *Dial.* 2 ff.; Tat. *Or.* 29; Arist. *Apol.* 15 f. (Syr.); Theoph. *Ad Autol.* 1.14; for Athenagoras' conversion cf. Philip of Side (MG 6.182); on Commodian cf. Gennadius *De viris illust.* 15.

[124] E.g., Just. *Apol.* 1.62 f.; Athenag. *Leg.* 9; Arist. *Apol.* 15 f.; Theoph. *Ad Autol.* 1.14, 2.30, 2.34, 2.35, 3.15. On the influence of the Greek Bible on Hellenistic culture see C. H. Dodd, *The Bible and the Greeks* (London 1935) part ii, 99 ff.

[125] E.g., Tat. *Or.* 29; [Just.] *Cohort.* 35, 38.

[126] See *Oct.* 33.4 and n. 557 *ad loc.* There are also possible allusions to scriptural writings at *Oct.* 34.5 and 35.1, but the allusions, if they are such, are vague in the extreme; this can only be construed as deliberate. E. K. Rand, in CAH 12 (1939) 595, incorrectly paraphrases Octavius as appealing to the testimony of "pagan poets and philosophers no less than the Holy Scriptures."

[127] Notably 31.6 and 8; 32.1, 4, and 9, where see nn. *ad loc.* For a more generous list of possible veiled echoes, see Beaujeu, intro. xxxvii.

[128] *Adv. nat.* 1.58 ff., 4.36. J. E. B. Mayor, *Tertulliani Apologeticus* (Cambridge 1917) 279 exaggerates, therefore, when he claims "Arnobius, alone, of the early apologists neglects the argument from prophecy." Cf. McCracken, *op. cit.* 25.

[129] E.g., Tert. *Apol.* 18 ff., 32, 46 ff. Fundamentally, however, Tertullian bases his apology on revelation and hence, ultimately, the Bible.

[130] The thesis of J. Colin, *L'Empire des Antonins et les martyrs gaulois de 177* (Bonn 1964), against a Western setting for Irenaeus has (rightly) not found general acceptance; see, e.g., G. Jouassard, "Aux origines de l'église de Lyon," *Rev. étud. aug.* 11 (1965) 1 ff.

[131] *Comment. in ep. 1 ad Corinth.* 14 (ML 17.255B). For further discussion see Th. Klauser, "Die Übergang der römischen Kirche

von der griechischen zur lateinischen Liturgiesprache," *Misc. Giov. Mercati.* 1 (Vatican City 1946) 467 ff., esp. 475 n. 19.

[132] See the articles by George La Piana, "Foreign Groups in Rome during the First Centuries of the Empire," HTR 20 (1927) 183–403; "The Roman Church at the End of the Second Century," HTR 18 (1925) 201–77.

[133] A. D. Nock, *op.cit.* in n. 55 above, 203. Further discussion below.

[134] On this point (notoriously true of geographical and ethnological *data*) cf. A. Momigliano, "Pagan and Christian Historiography in the Fourth Century A.D.," in *The Conflict between Paganism and Christianity in the Fourth Century* (Oxford 1963) 82; E.J. Bickerman, "Origines Gentium," CP 47 (1952) 65 ff.

[135] For a discussion see H. G. Meecham, *Epistle to Diognetus* (Manchester 1949) 16–19.

[136] E.g., *Ad Autol.* 2 is virtually an extended commentary on the opening chapters of Genesis.

[137] *Or.* 26, 29–31.

[138] See n. 18 above for references on this point.

[139] Cf. J. Stevenson, "Aspects of the Relations between Lactantius and the Classics," *Stud. Patr.* 4 (1961) = TU 79, 497 ff., esp. 502 f.

[140] "Le dialogue dans l'*Octavius*," *Musée belge* 10 (1906) 75 ff., at 77.

[141] See n. 17 *ad Oct.* 2.4.

[142] See commentary on chaps. 1–4. Note, too, the artificial construction of the Épilogue (see commentary on chap. 40). On the *Octavius* qua dialogue, see also M. Hoffman, *Der Dialog bei den christlichen Schriftstellern der ersten vier Jahrhunderte* (Berlin 1966) = TU 96, 28 ff.

[143] See commentary nn. 173, 194. One can hardly conclude with G. L. Ellspermann, O.S.B., *The Attitude of the Early Christian Latin Writers towards Pagan Literature and Learning* (Washington 1949) 21–22, that Minucius Felix is making a vehement attack on the false rhetoricians of his day; the point is a rhetorical commonplace.

[144] *Inst. or.* 3.5.6, 5.7.35, 7.2.2, 12.2.21. For discussion on the educational system, see H.-I. Marrou, *A History of Education in Antiquity* (trans. George Lamb; London 1956) Part 3, chap. 6; D. L. Clarke, *Rhetoric in Greco-Roman Education* (New York

1957) chaps. 6 and 7; and E. P. Parks, *The Roman Rhetorical Schools as a Preparation for the Courts under the Early Empire* (Baltimore 1945) esp. 61 ff.

[145] *Progym.* 12, *Rhet. Gr.* ed. C. Walz, 1.242 ff.; cf., on the *thesis*, Aphthonius, *Progym.*, *Rhet. Gr.* ed. Spengel, 2.49 ff. For a discussion, G. Quispel, "Anima naturaliter christiana," *Latomus* 10 (1951) 163 ff.; R. Reitzenstein, "Zu Minucius Felix," *Hermes* 51 (1916) 609 ff.

[146] *Progym.* 11 cd. Rabe (Spengel, *Rhet. Gr.* 6.24 ff.)

[147] For a survey of the pagan literature on the theme, cf. D. Amand, *Fatalisme et liberté dans l'antiquité grecque* (Louvain/Paris 1945) 71 ff. (Roughly contemporary writers include Maximus of Tyre, Alexander of Aphrodisias, Oenomaos of Gadara, [Plutarch], and cf. Fronto's model elaboration on the question *si providentia res gubernantur*, Naber 232 ff.) The presence of the *arbiter* may be due to current literary fashion (see n. 36 *ad Oct.* 4.6) also.

[148] For exaggerated catalogues, J.-P. Waltzing, in ed. (Louvain 1903) 209 ff.; for corrective on such exaggerations, Harald Hagendahl, *Latin Fathers and the Classics* (Göteborg 1958) 79. And the odds are heavily against the inclusion of Juvenal: see G. Highet, *Juvenal the Satirist* (Oxford 1954) 296 f., A. D. E. Cameron, "Literary Allusions in the Historia Augusta," *Hermes* 92 (1964) 367 ff., at 368. The attempt by M. Galdi, "Quid Minucius Felix in Octavio conscribendo a Trogo seu Justino derivaverit," *Riv. grec.-ital. di filol., ling., antichità* (1932) 136 ff., to add Justin (Trogus) to the list does not persuade.

[149] 9.4 and 29.1 (and see nn. *ad loc.* for parallels in other apologists).

[150] So R. Kühn, *Der Octavius des Minucius Felix* (diss. Leipzig 1882) 30 ff.

[151] So A. Baehrens in ed. (Leipzig 1886) xiiff.; H. Dessau, "Minucius Felix und Caecilius Natalis," *Hermes* 40 (1905) 373 ff. Against this improbable theory, J.-P. Waltzing, "Le texte, l'oeuvre, et la vie de Minucius Felix depuis 1902," *Musée belge* 10 (1906) 245 ff., at 271 ff.

[152] Octavius had preceded his friend Minucius Felix into the Church (1.4); the friends had been parted some time (2.3) before the debate at Ostia; Octavius, it seems, had subsequently died (1.1).

[153] 34.10, 29.1, 34.6 ff.

[154] 32.1 ff., 26.8 ff., 20.3ff., 22.1ff., etc.

[154a] Cf. 34.5, 34.8.

[155] The most useful collection of evidence remains that of A. von Harnack, *The Expansion of Christianity in the First Three Centuries* 2 (trans. J. Moffatt; London and New York 1905) 147 ff.; note also (in translation) J. Stevenson, *A New Eusebius* (London 1963). For discussion see C. J. Cadoux, *The Early Church and the World* (Edinburgh 1925; repr. 1955) 202 ff.; G. La Piana, "The Roman Church at the End of the Second Century," HTR 18 (1925) 201–77; W. H. C. Frend, *Martyrdom and Persecution in the Early Church* (Oxford 1965) 303 ff. If the number of bishoprics can be safely taken as evidence, expansion was rapid in Italy during this period: c. 190 A.D., only three: Rome, Milan, Ravenna. Sixty years later, in 251, there assembled 60 Italian bishops at the Council of Rome convened by Pope Cornelius (Euseb. *H.E.* 6.43.2). The later Counc. Sard. *can.* 6 forbidding bishoprics in villages and small cities may act as a brake against exaggerating the force of the evidence: there may have been such bishoprics in Italy.

[156] Origen, *inter alios*, was much given to it; e.g., *C.Cels.* 1.47, *Hom. in Luc.* 7 (GCS Origen 9.46), and see H. Chadwick, "The Evidences of Christianity in the Apologetic of Origen," *Stud. Patr.* 2 (1957) = TU 64, 331 ff., at 335 ff. For a collection of texts from Tertullian, see J. E. B. Mayor's commentary on Tertullian's *Apology* (Cambridge 1917) 375–78.

[157] "We who believe now outnumber those who seemed to possess God."

[158] The Jews got a particularly bad press from most Christians: see n. 554 *ad Oct.* 33.2.

[159] For the date see n. 22 above.

[160] Trans. Kirsopp Lake (London 1959).

[161] PIR² A 931. For bibliography on this much debated question, see Quasten, *Patrology* 1.184, adding: DACL 4.2 (1921) *s.v.* Droit Persécuteur 1633 ff. (H. Leclercq); M. Sordi, "Un senatore cristiano dell'età di Commodo," *Epigraphica* 17 (1955) 104 ff.; *idem*, "L'Apologia del martire romano Apollonio, come fonte dell'Apologeticum di Tertulliano e i rapporti fra Tertulliano e Minucio," *Rivist. di storia della chiesa in Italia* 18 (1964) 169 ff. (against this latter article, see G. Tibiletti, "Gli Atti di Apollonio e Tertulliano," *Atti della Accad. delle Scienze di Torino* 99 [1964–65] 295 ff.). The Greek version of his *acta* is to be found

in AnalBoll 14 (1895) 281 ff. On Eusebius' historical terms of reference, see D. S. Wallace-Hadrill, *Eusebius of Caesarea* (London 1960) 165 ff.

[162] In *Oct.* 6.1 ff. Caecilius defends Roman paganism (*religiones traditas*) on these grounds.

[163] A convenient (but not complete) assembly of evidence in DACL 1.2 (1924) *s.v.* Aristocratiques (Classes), 2876 ff. (H. Leclercq).

[164] Jerome *De vir. illust.* 42 (ML 23.691). See n. 161 above. M. Sordi tentatively, but without real warrant, identifies him with a member of the family of Claudius Apollonius of Smyrna (PIR² C 1001); some of the family were at any rate clearly non-Christian later: G. Barbieri, *L'Albo senatorio da Settimio Severo a Carino (193–285)* (Rome 1952) 545.

[165] See DACL, *loc. cit.* in n. 163 above, 2886 ff. The Caecilii, Pomponii, etc. can be, and probably are, (remote) descendants of freed slaves etc. of these aristocratic families.

[166] W. M. Ramsay, *Cities and Bishoprics of Phrygia* 2 (London 1898) nos. 210, 219, 361, 364, and presumably also nos. 204, 359, 368, 371.

[167] E. Diehl, ILCV (2nd ed. Berlin 1961) 56, 57. Noted as "sec. 111?" by A. Degrassi, *I fasti consolari dell'impero romano* (Rome 1952) 128, neglected by G. Barbieri, *L'Albo senatorio da Settimio Severo a Carino (193–285)* (Rome 1952). The first two lines of his epitaph read *martyris hic s(an)c(t)i Liberalis membra quiescunt/qui quondam in terris consul honore fuit.*

[168] E.g., H. Daniel-Rops, *The Church of Apostles and Martyrs* (trans. A. Butler; London 1960) 334; J. Moreau, *La persécution du christianisme dans l'empire romain* (Paris, 1956) 92.

[169] For discussion of their rich (and variable) *acta* tradition, see B. de Gaiffier, "Palatins et eunuques dans quelques documents hagiographiques," AnalBoll 75 (1957) 17 ff., at 30 f.; DACL 13.2 (1938) 2244–50 (H.Leclercq). There certainly was a Fulvius Aemilianus, cos 11, 249 A.D., PIR² F529, Barbieri, *op.cit.* 1586.

[170] The epitaph ILCV 1583 has M.A.I. Severiani c(larissimi) v(iri). That could be M. Antonius Severianus of CIL 9.6083.17 (undated), who might, in turn, be identified with M. Antonius . . . anus of CIL 6.1984, dated to 210–25 A.D. The connections are flimsy and the Christian epitaph could be otherwise restored (e.g., *restituit titulum m[amoreum] a[nno] 1* etc. has been suggested). Cf. PIR² A876, Barbieri, *op. cit.* 37, 44; S. Gsell, *Les*

monuments antiques de l'Algérie 2 (Paris 1901) 398 f.; P. Monceaux, *Histoire littéraire de l'Afrique chrétienne* 2 (Paris 1902; repr. 1966) 125 ff.; L. Leschi, "Les vestiges du christianisme antique dans le département d'Alger," *L'Algérie catholique*, 1936, 13 ff., at 14. Note that Quadratus (Codratius)—if his Acts have a basis of authenticity—appears to have been a Christian senator of this period; see F. C. Conybeare, *The Armenian Apology and Acts of Apollonius and other Monuments of Early Christianity* (London 1896) 193 ff., at 197f.

[171] PIR² A1269, B67, Barbieri, *op.cit.* 1456, 1486. M. Bassaeus Astur was son of a *praeses Arabiae*. There was a tradition, unknown to Eusebius, and of confused and doubtful quality, that he and his two daughters, Rufina and Secunda, were martyrs; see H. Delehaye, *Les origines du culte des martyrs* (2nd. ed. Brussels 1933) 181 n. 9.

[172] Note the analysis of their *Acta* by B. de Gaiffier, *art. cit.* in n. 169 above.

[173] Emphasized by Frend, *op. cit.* in n. 155 above, 440 ff. ("The Triumph of Christianity," 260–303).

[174] The inference is strengthened by 1 *can.* 7 of the bishops of Arles (314 A.D.) concerning Christian *praesides* or governors of provinces *et de his qui rempublicam agere volunt*. The wording unmistakably implies that the situation was somewhat novel: the good behavior of such men is to be supervised by the local bishop. See A. H. M. Jones, *The Later Roman Empire 284–602* (Oxford 1964) 2.983, 3.329 f. n. 96.

[175] *Ep.* 80 (CSEL, ed. Hartel, 839 f.): *Rescripsisse Valerianum ad senatum ut episcopi et presbyteri et diacones in continenti animadvertantur, senatores vero et egregii viri et equites Romani, dignitate amissa, etiam bonis spolientur; et si ademptis facultatibus Christiani esse perseveraverint, capite quoque multentur; matronae ademptis bonis, in exilium relegentur; Caesariani autem quicumque vel prius confessi fuerint vel nunc confessi fuerint, confiscentur et vincti in Caesarianas possessiones descripti mittantur.* For details of this persecution, cf. P. J. Healy, *The Valerian Persecution* (London 1905) esp. chaps. 5–8, and see the commentary of J. Moreau, *Lactance: De la mort des persécuteurs* 2 (Sources chrétiennes 39; Paris 1954) 217 ff.; also my article, "Prosopgraphical notes on the Epistles of Cyprian—III: Rome in August, 258 A.D.," *Latomus* (forthcoming).

[176] Note the detail of St. Lawrence (m. Aug. 10), first deacon

of Pope Xystus, grilled to reveal the whereabouts of the funds of the Roman Church: see J. Gagé, "Le livre sacré et l'épreuve de feu," *Mullus: Festschrift Th. Klauser* (Münster 1964) 130 ff.; and cf. Prudent. *Peristeph.* 2 (CCSL 126.257 ff.) with colorful detail: the urban prefect demanding, before Caesar's effigy, Render to Caesar. . . . The point, based on legendary evidence, is not to be pressed.

[177] See M. Hammond, "Composition of the Senate A.D. 68–235," JRS 47 (1957) at 80 n. 22 (c. 800 or 900 members. Too high?).

[178] Orig. *C.Cels.* 3.9.

[179] On these see below.

[180] Celsus, e.g., ended his attack on Christianity with an appeal to Christians to hold public office, *ap.* Orig. *C.Cels.* 8.75; and see generally for this period C. J. Cadoux, *The Early Church and the World* (Edinburgh 1925) 358 ff., 393 ff.; cf. n. 111 *ad Oct.* 8.4.

[181] Thus Caecilius in *Oct.* 8.4: "collecting . . . gullible women (easily persuaded as is their sex)"; and see n. 105 *ad loc.* On the general point, see also J. G. Davies, "Deacons, Deaconesses and the Minor Orders in the Patristic Period," JEH 14 (1963) 4 ff.

[182] *Ad. Scap.* 3.4. Her husband was Claudius Lucius Hieronymianus, dated by PIR[2] C888 *sub finem II vel initio III saec.* And Hippoly. *Comm. in Dan.* 4.18 (GCS Hippolytus 1.232); cf. earlier Ign. *Ad Polyc.* 8.2: Ignatius sends greetings to the Christian wife and household of the Curator (*epitropos*) of Smyrna—or is it of Epitropos of Smyrna?

[183] Tert. *Ad Scap.* 4.6: *sed et clarissimas feminas et clarissimos viros, Severus huius sectae esse . . . populo furenti in nos palam restitit;* cf. *ibid.* 5.2: "What will Carthage herself suffer, decimated by you . . . seeing that everyone has observed in the Christian ranks possibly men and matrons of your class, all the prominent citizens, and either the relatives of your friends or your friends themselves" (*Quid ipsa Carthago passura est, decimata a te . . . cum* [sc., *unusquisque*] *viderit illic fortasse et tui ordinis viros et matronas, et principales quasque personas, et amicorum tuorum vel propinquos vel amicos?*). This should not be used without caution; it refers to African conditions, and it is the purpose of Tertullian to dissuade Scapula, governor of Africa Proconsularis, from persecution; gross exaggeration of the numbers and importance of Christians would be in point.—Harnack, *op. cit.* in n. 155 above, calls the woman convert of Just. *Apol.* 2.2 "a promi-

nent Roman lady" (186), "a distinguished Roman lady" (233). Such station has little warrant.

184 For a satirical account see Hipp. *Philos.* 9.12.24 f. (GCS Hippolytus 3.250). For discussion see J. J. I. von Döllinger, *Hippolytus und Kallistus* (Eng. trans. A. Plummer; Edinburgh, 1876) 147 ff.; J. Gaudemet, "La décision de Callixte en matière de mariage," *Studi in onore di Ugo Enrico Paoli* (Florence 1956) 333–44; and cf. Tert. *Ad uxor.* 2.8 on the theme *Christianam fidelem fideli re minori nubere piget?* ("Is a Christian lady reluctant to marry a Christian man of lesser means?")

185 See Harnack, *op. cit.* in n. 155 above, 236 ff., and note especially Tert. *Ad uxor.* 2.3; Cyp. *Test.* 3.62, *De lapsis* 6: *iungere cum infidelibus vinculum matrimonii, prostituere gentilibus membra Christi.*

186 Discussion is bedeviled by several factors, not always taken into account. Firstly, there is the selectiveness of our sources: no wide coverage is available, so that one cannot securely extrapolate from information about the part to inference about the whole. In addition, one must be wary of romantic or loose usages of words such as *matronae, clarissimae,* etc. with which the *Acta* are liberally embroidered. For example, this might apply to Caecilia, martyr of Rome, who is made to call herself *ingenua, nobilis, clarissima;* she has been canvassed as a *nobilis* for this period, but her *Acta* are of very doubtful value for such details and her martyrdom, besides, cannot be dated with any certainty—conjectures range from Marcus Aurelius to Julian the Apostate (e.g., La Piana, *art. cit.* in n. 155 above, 261). Similarly for Aurea *virgo sacratissima, nobili genere orta, imperatorum filia;* see R. Meiggs, *Roman Ostia* (Oxford 1960) Ap. 7, 518 ff. There is dubiety, too, for the date and significance of Pescennia Quodvultdeus (CIL 8.870 = ILCV 333: she is *bonis natalibus nata, matronaliter nupta*); Vibia Perpetua (m. Carthage 203) is described as *honeste nata, liberaliter instituta, matronaliter nupta;* her *Acta* are more reliable, however (by Tertullian?); Eugenia, again, often quoted as a *nobilis* of this period (daughter of a prefect of Egypt), is credited with having even converted Basilla *quae erat neptis Gallieni Augusti* (see B. de Gaiffier, *art. cit.* in n. 169 above, 38 ff.). Further, one cannot be sure that testimonies can be taken without hesitation to refer to society in the Capital; they may well really be concerned with local provincial conditions, and local worthies described loosely in terms which do not allow of exact analysis.

This might very well be the case with Tert. *De cult. femin.* 2.9.4: *si quas vel divitiarum vel natalium vel retro dignitatum ratio compellit ita pompaticas progredi ut . . .* ("if any women are compelled by considerations of wealth, birth, or station to so parade in ostentatious array that . . .").

[187] The influence and example of wives should mean conversions among the men of senatorial class. Hieronymianus, e.g., (see n. 182 above), barely escaped unconverted, *paene Christianus decessit*" (Tert. *Ad Scap.* 3.4); and cf. Libanius *Ep.* 1411.1 (ed. Foerster): "When a man gets home, his wife and her tears and the night plead otherwise and draw him away from the altars." Note aristocratic Christian ladies persecuted at this period, Palladius *Laus. Hist.* 65 (if Hippolytus is recounting a contemporary incident); Ambrose *De officiis* 1.41 (ML 16.84): Agnes, under Valerian?—and was she indubitably aristocratic? See Ruinat, *Acta Sincera* (Ratisbon 1859) 484 ff.; and see generally F. Augar, *Die Frau in römische Christenprocess* (TU 13.4 1905).

[188] *Adv. haer.* 4.30.1 (MG 7.1065). For a discussion see my note "Irenaeus *adv. Haer.* 4.30.1," HTR 59 (1966) 95 ff. Among their numbers perhaps figured "Alexamenos," blasphemously parodied for his religion in a graffito on the Palatine: see Michael Gough, *The Early Christians* (London 1961) 83 f. Note the earlier Euelpistus, a slave of Caesar, and companion of Justin in his martyrdom (*Acta Just.* 3; Ruinat, *op. cit.* in n. 187 above, 106).

[189] Hipp. *Philos.* 9.12 (GCS Hippolytus 3.246 ff.). He is described as being "of Caesar's household." He was, in fact, *Augg. lib.* (an imperial freedman), as we learn from the inscription on his *munimentum sive cepotafium*: CIL 6.13040 (Rome), omitted in ILCV.

[190] Hipp. *loc. cit.* Callistus' subsequent activities became almost a literary commonplace (voluntary martyrdom to avoid the consequences of embezzlement); see G. E. M. de Ste Croix, "Aspects of the 'Great' Persecution," HTR 47 (1954) 75 ff., at 83 n. 41.

[191] Tert. *Ad Scap.* 4.5: *Nam et Proculum Christianum qui Torpacion cognominabatur, Euhodeae procuratorem, qui eum per oleum aliquando curaverat, requisivit* [sc., *Septimius Severus*] *et in palatio suo habuit usque ad mortem eius: quem et Antoninus optime noverat lacte Christiano educatus.* Caracalla was born c. 186–88 (see Mason Hammond, "Septimius Severus, Roman Bureaucrat," *Harv. Stud. in Class. Phil.* 51 [1940] 160 and the

citations there). He, therefore, was a small child when his father took over the *palatium* in 193. Proculus is inaccurately called a slave by R. M. Grant, *The Sword and the Cross* (New York 1955) 102.

[192] PIR² A1588, ILS 1738, ILCV 3332: he had been *a cubiculo Aug., proc. thesaurorum, proc. patrimoni, proc. munerum, proc. vinorum, ordinato a divo Commodo in kastrense*. For further discussion see Ludwig Hertling and Engelbert Kirschbaum, *The Roman Catacombs and their Martyrs* (trans. M. Joseph Costelloe; London 1960) 189–91; H.-G. Pflaum, *Les carrières procuratoriennes équestres sous le haut-empire romain* 2 (Paris 1960) 670; DACL 3.1 (1948) *s.v.* Chambellan 146 ff. (H. Leclercq). The precise phrase *receptus ad Deum* is imperfectly attested for Christian inscriptions: see ILCV 107 *adn.* (*recep . . .*), 3332 *adn.* (*. . . eceptus . . .*), 3871 (*recep . . .*). The value of the evidence is somewhat doubtful, therefore. Tertullian's brief tractate *Ad Scapulam* was composed c. 212.

[193] Controversial are the *cubicularii* (?) Calocerus and Parthenius (see n. 169 above). Doubtful are Pupenius, Balbeinus, and several "Gordiani" (ILCV 3995, A.B.C.), though claimed as Christians (e.g., by P. W. Townsend, "The Revolution of A.D. 238," *Yale Class. Stud.* 14 [1955] 49 ff., at 87) and as members of the imperial household (e.g., by H. Chadwick, "St Peter and St Paul in Rome: The problem of the *Memoria apostolorum ad catacumbas*," JTS n.s. 8 [1957] 31 ff., at 33 n. 1, followed by Frend, *op. cit.* in n. 155 above, 436 n. 197). Both the ascription of religion (depending on a Christian graffito) and the interpretation of the names (were they simply burial-club names?) are dubious: see J. Toynbee and J. Ward Perkins, *The Shrine of St. Peter and the Vatican Excavations* (London 1956) 175, 178; and on burial-club names, H. Wuilleumier, "Étude historique sur l'emploi et la signification des signa," *Mém. présentés par divers savants à l'Acad. et de l'Inst. de France* 13.2 (1933) 559–696. See further my article "The *collegium funeraticium* of the *Innocentii*," *Antichthon* 1 (1967) 45 ff., and H.-I. Marrou, "Encore les 'Innocentii' de San Sebastiano," *Mélanges d'archéologie, d'épigraphie et d'histoire offerts à Jérôme Carcopino* (Paris 1966) 657 ff. For two further candidates, see my note "Two Christian *Caesariani* in the *Familia Caesaris*," HTR 64 (1971) 121 ff.

[194] PIR¹ M187. For a lurid account of her part in Commodus' death, see Herodian 1.16f., 2.1f. She is called by J. P. V. D. Bals-

don, *Roman Women* (London 1962) 149 "The first great con-
cubine in Roman history."

[195] Hippol. *Philos.* 9.12.10 ff. (GCS Hippolytus 3.247 f.); cf.
Dio-Xiph. 72.4.7. For the epithet see E. Mary Smallwood, "The
Alleged Jewish Tendencies of Poppaea Sabina," JTS n.s. 10
(1959) 329 ff., and cf. n. 200 below. She should not be called a
Christian *tout court*, as does H. Mattingly, *Christianity in the
Roman Empire* (Dunedin 1955) 42.

[196] Hippol. *loc. cit.* The Greek is possibly ambiguous Ὑακίνθῳ
τινὶ σπάδοντι πρεσβυτέρῳ (= "rather elderly" and not "presbyter"?). This and the article cited in n. 169 above might be
added to R. P. C. Hanson, "A Note on Origen's Self-Mutilation,"
VC 20 (1966) 81 f., on the topic of Christians and castration.

[197] Hippol. *loc. cit.* Cf. Poppaea Sabina, who used her influence
in Nero's court to secure the release of Jews from Judaea sent
under arrest to Rome, Joseph. *Vit.* 3.16.

[198] For her *mathematici* see Tac. *Hist.* 1.22. For her interest in
Judaism, see previous note and Joseph. *Ant. Jud.* 20.8.11.195. E.
Mary Smallwood, *art. cit.* in n. 195 above, is (rightly) sceptical
of her alleged influence in the Neronian persecution of the Christians; for the theory see J. Beaujeu, *L'incendie de Rome en 64 et
les chrétiens* (Coll. Lat. 49; Brussels 1960) 40.

[199] For these ladies (from Emesa in Syria), Julia Domna (wife
of Septimius Severus, 193–211, and mother of Caracalla, 211–17),
her sister Julia Maesa, and the two daughters of the latter, Julia
Soaemias (mother of Elagabalus, 218–22) and Julia Mamaea
(mother of Alexander Severus, 222–35), see J. P. V. D. Balsdon,
Roman Women (London 1962) 150 ff., and the literature cited
in the footnotes, 308 ff. J. Réville, *La réligion à Rome sous les
Sévères* (Paris 1886) is still useful on the (strongly syncretistic
and strongly supported) religious movements of Rome at this
period.

[200] Date c. 232 A.D., Euseb. *H.E.* 6.21.3. She is there described
as being "most god-loving" (εἰ καί τις ἄλλη θεοσεβεστάτη). Later
tradition claimed her as a Christian, falsely: see Mary Gilmore
Williams, "Studies in the Lives of Roman Empresses 11: Julia
Mamaea," *Univ. Mich. Stud.* 1 (1904) 99.

[201] Euseb. *H.E.* 1.6.2 describes him as "no ordinary historian";
see also *H.E.* 6.31; Jerome *De vir. illust.* 63 (ML 23.709 ff.); PIR[1]
J82 for other services for this emperor. For the library see *Oxy.
Pap.* 3 (1903) no. 412 ll. 63 ff., and cf. F. Granger, "Julius

Africanus and the Library of the Pantheon," JTS 34 (1933) 157-60.

²⁰² Epiph. *Adv. haer.* 64.3 (MG 41.1074): τῶν διαφανῶν ἐν αὐλαῖς βασιλικαῖς; Jerome *De vir. illust.* 56 (ML 23.703).

²⁰³ S.H.A. *Sev. Alex.* 22.4, 29.2, 31.4, 43.6 f., 45.7, 51.7 f. See A. Jardé, *Études critiques sur la vie et le règne de Sévère Alexandre* (Paris 1925) esp. 95 ff., and A. Momigliano, "An Unsolved Problem of Historical Forgery: The Scriptores Historiae Augustae," *Journ. Warb. Inst.* 17 (1954) 22 ff., esp. 40 f. Alexander's syncretistic shrine is best regarded (with most of this *vita*) as pure fiction; cf. R. Syme, *Emperors and Biography: Studies in the Historia Augusta* (Oxford 1971) 276.

²⁰⁴ *H.E.* 6.28.

²⁰⁵ Euseb. *H.E.* 6.36.3: "And there is extant also a letter of his to the Emperor Philip himself, and another to his wife Severa, and various other letters to various persons" (tr. J. E. L. Oulton). This does not constitute "a lengthy correspondence" with the emperor and his wife (contra Daniel-Rops, *op. cit.* in n. 168 above, 375).

²⁰⁶ The question is extremely complex. For the evidence and discussion, see J. B. Lightfoot, *The Apostolic Fathers* 1.2 (London 1890) 338 f., 397 f.; M. Sordi, *op. cit.* in n. 22 above, 434 f. Hippolytus may, however, have perished earlier, in the "persecution" of Maximinus Thrax. See my article "Some Victims of the Persecution of Maximinus Thrax," *Historia* 15 (1966) 445 ff., at 451 f.

²⁰⁷ Euseb. *H.E.* 6.34 for his purported Christianity.

²⁰⁸ Cyprian describes this period of lengthy religious peace as the time when many Christians forgot the duties of their state, even including a large number of bishops (*De lapsis* 5 f.): *episcopi plurimi . . . divina procuratione contempta, procuratores regum* (v.l. *rerum*) *saecularium fieri* ("very many bishops . . . despised their divine stewardship and became stewards of secular kings [affairs]"). Despite the uncertainty over the reading, this should provide corroborative evidence. Compare the later activities of Paul of Samosata, Euseb. *H.E.* 7.30.8 (he wished to be called *ducenarius* rather than bishop).

²⁰⁹ Diony. Alex. *ap.* Eusebius *H.E.* 7.10.3. This is a partisan description; Dionysius wishes to flatter Valerian's son and successor Gallienus; he assigns the blame for persecution to the machinations of Macrianus (*H.E.* 7.10.5, 7.23).

[210] *Med.* 11.3.2. Cf. the earlier Epict. 4.7.6. Christians figure as stock examples of theatrical obstinacy. Such passages are conveniently assembled by W. den Boer, *Scriptorum paganorum i-iv saec. de christianis testimonia* (London 1948). The supposed anti-Christian passages in Apuleius' *Golden Ass* are very dubious. For a discussion in favor, see L. Hermann, "L'âne d'or et le christianisme," *Latomus* 12 (1953) 188 ff.; also P. G. Walsh, "Lucius Madaurensis," *Phoenix* 22 (1968) 143 ff., at 151 ff. The remarks of Aelius Aristides (*Or.* 46, 2.399 ff. Dindorf) may not be about Christians at all. For discussion see A. Boulanger, *Aelius Aristides et la sophistique dans la province d'Asie au IIe siècle de notre ère* (Paris 1923) 249 ff., and P. de Labriolle, *La réaction païenne* (Paris 1934) 79 ff.

[211] R. Walzer, *Galen on Jews and Christians* (Oxford 1949) esp. 15, 37 ff.

[212] Some interpret the collection of rescripts against Christianity by the jurist Ulpian (Lact. *Div. inst.* 5.11.19) as an unfriendly move (so Frend, *op. cit.* in n. 155, 327), but such a collection was necessary if one was to codify *de officio proconsulis* ("on the duties of a proconsul [provincial governor]") as Ulpian was (c. 215 A.D.).

[213] See above n. 203. The story of Alexander Severus' personal shrine is instructive, if apocryphal (S.H.A. *Alex. Sev.* 29.2): it contained statues of, *inter alios*, select deified emperors, Apollonius of Tyana, Christ, Abraham, Orpheus, Alexander the Great, the emperor's ancestors. Compare the similar comprehensive cult of the Gnostic Carpocratians: they are said to have worshiped images of Homer, Pythagoras, Plato, Aristotle, Christ, and St. Paul (Iren. *Adv. haer.* 1.25.6 [MG 7.685]). For discussion see W. Schmid, "Bilderloser Kult und christliche Intoleranz: Wesen und Herkunft zweier Nachrichten bei Aelius Lampridius," *Mullus* (Festschrift Th. Klauser; Münster 1964) 198 ff.; E. R. Dodds, *Pagan and Christian in an Age of Anxiety* (Cambridge 1965) 107 f.

[214] Tert. *Ad Scap.* 3.4. Discussion in M. Sordi, *op. cit.* in n. 22 above, 225 f. For other passages in Tertullian relating to the events of Septimius' fight for power, see J.-P. Waltzing, "Les premiers écrits de Tertullien chrétien," *Musée belge* 2 (1898) 165 ff.

[215] For an up-to-date and readable account, see W. H. C.

Frend, *Martyrdom and Persecution in the Early Church* (Oxford 1965) with generous bibliography; but see the review of Fergus Millar, JRS 56 (1966) 231 ff.

²¹⁶ Euseb. *H.E.* 5.1 ff. See esp. Frend, *op. cit.*, 1 ff.; J. H. Oliver and R. E. A. Palmer, "Minutes of an Act of the Roman Senate," *Hesperia* 24 (1955) 320 ff., esp. 324 ff.; A. Birley, *Marcus Aurelius* (London 1966) 275 ff., 328 ff.; P. Keresztes, "Marcus Aurelius a Persecutor?" HTR 61 (1968) 321 ff.; W. O. Moeller, "The Trinci/Trinqui and the Martyrs of Lyons," *Historia* 21 (1972) 127. The thesis of J. Colin, *L'empire des Antonins et les martyrs gaulois de 177* (Bonn 1964), is unconvincing; see the criticisms of G. Jouassard, "Aux origines de l'église de Lyon," *Rev. étud. aug.* 11 (1965) 1 ff.

²¹⁷ Cf. Euseb. *H.E.* 3.33.2 (on persecutions after Trajan): "Sometimes the populace, sometimes even the local authorities contrived plots against us, so that with no open persecution partial attacks broke out in various provinces and many of the faithful endured martyrdom in various ways" (tr. Kirsopp Lake). *H.E.* 5 praef. 1: "Persecution in some parts of the world broke out against us more violently as the result of attacks by the populace in the cities. . . "; cf. Tert. *Apol.* 37.2, and see J. Colin, *Les villes libres de l'Orient et l'envoi au supplice par acclamations populaires* (Brussels 1965) 126 ff. for popular agitation against Christians.

²¹⁸ Euseb. *H.E.* 5 praef. 1 (persecution in some parts of the world c. 177). The activities of Arrius Antoninus in Asia (*Ad Scap.* 5.1) should be placed c. 184 (PIR² A1088). Some assign the martyrdom of Polycarp in Asia (so H. Grégoire, "La véritable date du martyre de saint Polycarpe (23 février 177)," AnalBoll 69 [1951] 1 ff.–a doubtful thesis) and those of Carpus, Papylus, and Agathonice in Pergamum (H. Delehaye, "Les actes des martyrs de Pergame," *ibid.* 58 [1940] 142 ff.) to this period.

²¹⁹ The evidence is to be found in the moving *Acta Scillitanorum* (180 A.D.). See also J. H. Baxter, "The Martyrs of Madaura, A.D. 180," JTS 26 (1924–25) 21 ff.

²²⁰ If Orig. *C.Cels.* 8.69 implies actual persecution at Celsus' time of writing (c. 178–"if anyone does still wander about in secret, yet he is sought out and condemned to death") and *if* Celsus' environment is Alexandrian (see Frend, *op. cit.* 297 n. 56, and the literature there cited).

²²¹ If the order in Tert. *Ad Scap.* 3.4 is strictly chronological:

Africa (180 A.D.), Cappadocia, Byzantium (c. 196; see CAH 12.11).

²²² For an analysis, and doubts about a general prohibition against proselytism (S.H.A. *Sept. Sev.* 17.1), see K. H. Schwarte, "Das angebliche Christengesetz des Septimius Severus," *Historia* 12 (1963) 185 ff.; also J. G. Davies, "Was the Devotion of Septimius Severus to Serapis the Cause of the Persecution of 202–203?" JTS n.s. 5 (1954) 73 ff.; R. Freudenberger, "Das angebliche Christenedikt des Septimius Severus," WSt 81 (1968) 206 ff.; T. D. Barnes, "Legislation against the Christians," JRS 58 (1968) 32 ff., at 40f.; *idem,* "Pre-Decian *Acta martyrum*," JTS 19 (1968) 509 ff., at 526 f. Perpetua and Felicity are the most celebrated victims. Persecution in Gaul about this time (with the martyrdom of Irenaeus) rests on doubtful tradition.

²²³ Euseb. *H.E.* 6.28; one might hold some suspicions of the alleged motivation–it is repeated for the persecution of Decius (*H.E.* 6.39.1); see also A. T. Olmstead, "The Mid-Third Century of the Christian Era, II," CP 37 (1942) 318. For an analysis of what is known of this persecution, see my article "Some Victims of the Persecution of Maximinus Thrax," *Historia* 15 (1966) 445 ff. The martyrdom of Pope Callistus in Rome (222) would also interrupt the peace, but the details suggest a mob pogrom (see Hertling and Kirschbaum, *op. cit.* in n. 192 above, 52).

²²⁴ See n. 45 above.

²²⁵ The best collection of evidence for Christian advocates that I know is in DACL 1.2 (1924) *s.v.* Avocats 3243 ff. (H. Leclercq). The legal studies of Gregory Thaumaturgus and his brother might be added (Greg. Thaum. *Panegy. Orig.* 5 f. [MG 10.1065 ff.]), and see the commentary of Lawlor and Oulton on Euseb. *H.E.* 6.30).

²²⁶ Euseb. *H.E.* 2.2.4: "Tertullian, who had an accurate knowledge of Roman law, a man especially famous among those most distinguished in Rome. . ." (Eusebius is preparing to quote Tertullian on the legal status of Christians, and cf. *H.E.* 1.5.3 [Josephus], 3.33.1 [Pliny], 4.7.6 [Agrippa Castor], 4.18.6 [Trypho], 5.21.2 [Apollonius], etc.). The vague words of eulogy do not make Tertullian of senatorial class (contra Lawlor and Oulton *ad loc.*) and there appears to be little ground for identifying him with a jurist namesake (*Dig.* 28.5.3.2; 29.2.30.6; 38.17.2.44). See J. Lortz, *Tertullian als Apologet* 2 (Münster 1928) 221 ff.; A. Beck, *Römisches Recht bei Tertullian und Cyprian* (Halle 1930;

repr. 1967) 13 ff.; and especially W. Kunkel, *Herkunft und soziale Stellung der römischen Juristen* (Weimar 1952) 236 ff. (note 237 n. 480 for strong doubts against Tertullian's purported senatorial status).

[227] See my article "The Secular Profession of Saint Cyprian of Carthage," *Latomus* 24 (1965) 633 ff., and arguing independently for the same conclusion, on different lines, A. Quacquarelli, *La retorica antica al Bivio* (Rome 1956) 99 ff.

[228] Jerome *De vir. illust.* 79, 80 (ML 23.723 ff.). Do we know that Arnobius was active as an advocate as well, as H. Leclercq claims (DACL 1.2 [1924] 3248)?

[229] Arnobius 2.5 (ML 5.816): *quod tam magnis ingeniis praediti oratores, grammatici, rhetores, consulti iuris ac medici, philosophiae etiam secreta rimantes, magisteria haec expetunt, spretis quibus paulo ante fidebant?* Arnobius places first the professions related to his own activities.

[230] For rhetoricians note also Malchion at Antioch, Euseb. *H.E.* 7.29.2 (c. 268); for schoolteachers (*grammatici*), Flavius, Jerome *Adv. Jov.* 2.6 (ML 23.306), *De vir. illust.* 80 (ML 23.726) at Diocletian's court; for doctors, Alexander the Phrygian, *H.E.* 5.1.49 (177), Theodotus bishop of Laodicea, *H.E.* 7.32.23; for philosophers, Anatolius at Alexandria, *H.E.* 7.32.6 (c. 264). Commodian (*if* he wrote at this time; see Schanz-Hosius-Krüger, *Geschichte der römischen Litteratur* 8.3 [Munich 1922] 398 f.) provides evidence for Christians acting as judges and advocates (*Carm. Apol.* 582 ff.; *Instr.* 1.31, 2.29).

[231] The evidence is collected by C. J. Cadoux, *op. cit.* in n. 180 above, 256 f., 364 ff., 538 f. Note that Tertullian would not allow a Christian magistrate to pass judgment on capital or moral offenses, to bind, imprison, or torture any prisoner; Tert. *De idol.* 17.3: *neque iudicet de capite alicuius vel pudore—feras enim de pecunia—neque damnet neque praedamnet, neminem vinciat, neminem recludat aut torqueat, si haec credibile est fieri potest.* He might, therefore, judge only civil suits.

[232] See n. 38 *ad Oct.* 5.4.

[233] See nn. 189–94 *ad loc.*

[234] Tertullian, with his characteristic blend of irony and disparagement, could describe the bulk of the faithful (*quae maior semper credentium pars est*) as *simplices . . . quique, ne dixerim imprudentes et idiotae* (*Adv. Prax.* 3.1). Eastern conditions may have been, and probably were, markedly different, though Orig.

C.Cels. 1.27 also admits that the great majority of Christians "are vulgar and illiterate persons"; but he implies the same might be said of pagans also.

[235] Cf. the banking activities of Callistus (see n. 190 above) and the heretical banker Theodotus (Euseb. *H.E.* 5.16.14), and note the already formed attitude to usury as found in Tert. *Adv. Marc.* 4.17, Cyp. *Test.* 3.48, etc.

[236] *Muratorium Canon* ll. 75 ff.: *Pastorem vero nuperrime temporibus nostris in urbe Roma Hermas conscripsit sedente cathedra urbis Romae ecclesiae Pio episcopo fratre eius* (*Some Early Lists of the Books of the New Testament*, ed. F. W. Grosheide [Leiden 1948] 11). See especially H. Chadwick, "The New Edition of Hermas," JTS n.s. 8 (1957) 274 ff. It is, however, highly dangerous to take the references to slavery and Rome (*Vis.* 1.1.1) and Cumae (*Vis.* 1.1.3, 2.1.1, 2.1.4) as securely autobiographical; see R. Joly, *Hermas le Pasteur* (Paris 1958) 17 ff. against, e.g., W. J. Wilson, "The Career of the Prophet Hermas," HTR 20 (1927) 21 ff. Can we safely say, therefore, that Pope Pius was a slave or an ex-slave (e.g., Frend, *op. cit.*, 297 n. 50)?

[237] E.g., *Vis.* 1.1.8, 3.6.5, 3.9.4; *Sim.* 1.2.4–5, 8.9.1, 9.30.4, 9.31.2 etc.

[238] *Mand.* 10.1.4.

[239] The context of the letter is unfortunately unknown; it seems to be an appeal to preserve ancestral traditions—or was it a begging letter? For similar aid sent by Pope Stephen to the Churches of Arabia and Syria, see Dionysius of Alexandria *ap.* Euseb. *H.E.* 7.5.2; cf. Dionysius of Rome sending funds to Cappadocia c. 259, Basil *Ep.* 70 (MG 32.436).

[240] Euseb. *H.E.* 6.43.11: the statistics are from Pope Cornelius himself. In the same context (6.43.12) he speaks of his Church as a "rich and multiplying number with an immense and countless laity"; contentious evidence, however: he is arguing for the primacy of the orthodox (versus Novatianist) Church in Rome; cf. salaried clerics in Africa at this period, Cyp. *Ep.* 34.4.2, and similar charitable funds, *Ep.* 52.1.2.

[241] The judgment is that of Hertling and Kirschbaum, *op. cit.* in n. 192 above, 58: cf. Duchesne, *Liber pontif.* 148: *et multas fabricas per cymeteria fieri praecepit* (of Pope Fabian, 236–50).

[242] The literature now reaches formidable proportions: see especially J. Toynbee and J. Ward Perkins, *The Shrine of St. Peter and the Vatican Excavations* (London 1956) 167 ff., and

H. Chadwick, *art. cit.* in n. 193 above. For a critical bibliography, see A. A. de Marco, *The Tombs of St. Peter* (Leiden 1964) esp. 70 ff.

243 The date is *Antonini fere principatu, sub episcopatu Eleutheri benedicti*, i.e., c. 180's; cf. the wealthy followers of the Gnostic Marcus in the Rhone valley, Iren. *Adv. haer.* 1.13.3 (MG 7.581).

244 E.g., Clem. *Quis. dives* 3, *Paedag.* 3.11.53.1 ff.; Euseb. *H.E.* 6.41.11 (Dionysius of Alexandria) etc.

245 See the interesting material collected by W. H. C. Frend, "A Note on the Influence of Greek Immigrants on the Spread of Christianity in the West," *Mullus* (Münster, 1964) 125 ff.

246 See J. P. Brisson, *Autonomisme et christianisme dans l'Afrique romaine* (Paris 1958) 370 ff. For Hermas the rich man was a barren elm, but capable of supporting the fruitful vine of the poor Christian, *Sim.* 1 f.; cf. *Oct.* 36.7: "we prefer to despise wealth than to amass it." For the East see esp. Clem. Alex. *Quis dives, passim,* and cf. Orig. *C.Cels.* 6.16: "Not even a stupid person would praise the poor indiscriminately; the majority of them have very bad characters."

247 Many of these sentiments are evident Stoic commonplaces: see V. Carlier, "Minucius Félix et Sénèque," *Musée belge* 1 (1897) 258 ff., at 285 ff.

248 A useful coverage of modern literature is also to be found in H. von Geisau, PW Suppl. Bd. 11 (1968) 952–1002, 1365–78. This book was effectively completed in Aug. 1968 and, consequently, it has not been possible, without major recasting, to do justice to material that has appeared after that date.

TEXT

1 The translator has to decide whether to make Octavius dead or alive. The language of chap. 1 is certainly not conclusive; but its whole tenor, as exemplified in the choice of tenses (e.g., *flagraverit* §3) and of turns of phrase (e.g., *iam transacta et decursa* §1, explanatory *ita* in §2 [?]), strongly suggests that the *Octavius* was written, like Cicero's *Brutus* and *Hortensius*, in part to enshrine the memory of a departed (i.e., deceased) friend. Indeed, the deliberate echo from *Brutus* 2.1 (*vir egregius . . . triste nobis desiderium reliquerat*) in §3 (*vir eximius . . . immensum sui*

desiderium nobis reliquit) helps somewhat to confirm this impression: in Cicero the *vir egregius* is explicitly *extinctus*. On such memorial dialogues see A. Cameron, "The Date and Identity of Macrobius," JRS 56 (1966) 25 ff., at 28f.; and *idem*, "Tacitus and the Date of Curiatus Maternus' Death," CR 17 (1967) 258 ff. The *Hortensius* regrettably survives only in fragments, and those fragments that can be assigned to the prologue are but few and scanty; for recent reconstructions, M. Ruch, *L'Hortensius de Cicéron: Histoire et réconstitution* (Paris 1958), with the strictures of C. O. Brink, JRS 51 (1961) 215 ff., and A. Grilli, *M. Tulli Ciceronis Hortensius*, (Varese-Milan 1962); and for parallels between the *Octavius* and the *Hortensius* as a genre, J. Wotke, "Der Octavius des Minucius Felix, ein christlicher λόγος προτρεπτικός," *Comment. Vinabonens.* 1 (1935) 110–28. See also M. Ruch, *Le préambule dans les oeuvres philosophiques de Cicéron* (Paris 1958) 257 ff. on the *laudatio funebris* and the dialogue.

Was Octavius a historical figure? M.F. is writing in clear and deliberate imitation of Cicero. Ciceronian practice ought, therefore, to be relevant. And while Cicero might unashamedly contrive fictitious speeches for his dialogues (for speeches so composed *honoris causa*, Cic. *Ad Att.* 13.19.3 ff.), the characters to whom he assigns them were undeniably historical. (For Ciceronian practice, A. S. Pease, ed. Cicero, *De natura deorum* 1 [Cambridge, Mass. 1955] 22 ff., and more fully, R. Hirzel, *Der Dialog* 1 [Leipzig, 1895; repr. Hildesheim 1963] 457–552.) Similarly, it was the clear custom of Aulus Gellius in his literary vignettes to have named historical characters, or *unnamed* lay figures (e.g., *Noctes Atticae* 18.1).

One can allow, therefore, that much of the prologue and detailed argument of this dialogue may well be literary fiction (for recent discussions on the essentially literary nature of the prologue and epilogue, W. Speyer, "Octavius, Der Dialog des Minucius Felix: Fiktion oder historische Wirklichkeit?" JAC 7 [1964] 45–51; P. Frassinetti, "Finzione e realtà nell'Octavius," *Athenaeum* 46 [1968] 327 ff.; and note the earlier studies by A. Delatte, "La réalité du dialogue de L'Octavius," *Serta Leodensia* [Liège 1930] 103 ff., and O. Immisch, *Berl. Phil. Woch.* 34 [1914] 1062 ff.); and certainly the commonly expressed but highly subjective argument that the prologue savors of such sincerity and sympathy that it must have a factual basis bears little or no weight.

But given the literary background of the composition, Octavius himself probably ought to be allowed at least to retain his personal identity. That identity is indeed obscure: he has a wife and young family and his domicile is away from Rome (2.1); he may be interested in sailing (3.4); he has had a legal past (if not present), *if* it is safe to take chap. 28 as autobiographical; he may possibly have come from Cirta in Africa, *if noster* is used in an inclusive sense in 9.6 (*Cirtensis nostri . . . oratio*—a possible but not compelling inference); and he may have been a patron of a *collegium* of bakers, if—and this is a highly remote possibility—*pistorum praecipuus* as applied to Octavius in 14.1 (where see n. 172) has some literal foundation.

² In this post-Freudian age, many Latin expressions for emotional attachment generally and for friendship in particular (especially between men) can no longer be translated literally into modern English without infelicity. I have therefore paraphrased such phrases as *tanta dulcedo et adfectio hominis inhaesit* (§1) and *tanto nostri semper amore flagraverit* (§3). A. Elter, in his *Prolegomena zu M.F.* (Bonn 1909) 21, laid great stress on *inhaesit* (§1); it indicated, he argued, that Octavius was recently dead and that M.F. was reporting an authentic incident. For justifiable doubts about this deduction, L. Valmaggi, "Sul prooemio dell' 'Ottavio' " *Riv. di filol.* 38 (1910) 65–66.

³ The rather contorted expression is used to achieve the equivalent of Eng. "imagination," for which concept the Latin language was somewhat deficient. For an excellent note on the very widespread notion of the eye of the soul, heart, mind, etc., see Pease on Cic. *De natura deorum* 1.19 *oculis* [*animi*]; cf. *ibid.* 2.43 *mentis aciem*, 2.45 *aciem mentis.*

⁴ integrity: the word used is *sanctus*. For a study of the pagan and Christian connotations of this word, H. Delehaye, "Sanctus," AnalBoll 28 (1909) 145–200 (repr. no. 17 *Subsidia hagiographica*, Brussels 1954). departed: the MSS read *discedens*, which by itself would suggest departure on a journey rather than departure from life; for the latter significance *decedens*, used absolutely, is the more standard expression. But parallels are to be found, e.g., Fronto, Naber 235 *caelum . . . consultabo discedens*, and the usage occurs not infrequently in funerary inscriptions, e.g., CIL 8.9747, 9751 (Mauret. Caesar.), and especially on Christian epitaphs, see TLL 5.1 *s.v.* 11B.1 (p.1283) and E. Diehl, *Inscriptiones*

latinae christianae veteres 3 (2nd ed. Berlin 1961) index *s.v.* (p. 515).

[5] The expressions used are *communes loci*. Consult Otto, *Sprichwörter* 176 ff. (gaiety and gravity = *et in ludicris et in seriis*); 19 (single will = *eadem velle nolle*, on which expression see also Pease's n. on Cic. *De natura deorum* 1.17 *velim nolim*); on the theme "one in two," E. Bréguet, "*In una parce duobus:* Thèmes et clichés," *Hommages à Léon Herrmann* (Collection Latomus 44; Brussels 1960) 205 ff., provides multiple parallels. There are, therefore, no real grounds for seeing here a reminiscence of Fronto, Naber 210 (*non minus ludicris quam seriis*) contra Beaujeu *ad loc.*, especially given the general weakness of the purported parallels between the *Octavius* and Fronto's extant correspondence (most recently catalogued by P. Frassinetti, "L'orazione di Frontone contro i cristiani," GIF 3 [1949] 238 ff., at 250 f. See also L. Alfonsi, "Appunti sull'*Octavius* di Minucio Felice," SC 1942, 70–73, and M. Schanz, "Die Abfassungszeit des Octavius des Minucius Felix," RhM 50 [1895] 114 ff., at 120 ff. —though that author's conclusion that "Der Dialog Octavius ist zu Lebzeiten Frontos geschreiben" [p. 131] does not persuade).

[6] *solus in amoribus conscius.* Much depravity has been needlessly deduced from this innocent phrase, even the sage Gronovius (1709) taking this as a subtle preparation for the later attack (31.4) on pagans: *quod Venerem promiscue spargerent. Id ita esse confirmat nunc suo exemplo.* . . . For some sensible remarks on the vagaries of interpretation and much unnecessary emendation, E. Löfstedt, "Annotationes criticae in M. Minucii Felicis Octavium," *Eranos* 16 (1905–6) 1 ff., at 3–5 (*ludicris* and *seriis* are paralleled in phrase and significance by *amoribus* and *erroribus*). Note also on the passage J.-P. Waltzing, "Notes sur Minucius Felix," *Musée belge* 1 (1897) 158 f.

[7] *socius in erroribus.* Error (Greek πλάνη) is regularly used of a mistaken or wrongheaded philosophy, and in particular by Christians of paganism and by pagans of Christianity; examples in A. Cameron, "Palladas and Christian Polemic," JRS 55 (1965) 17 ff., at 22 f. What follows clearly shows that M.F. is not talking about aberrations of moral behavior, as is sometimes interpreted. Significantly, at the close of this work, another *socius*, Caecilius, now converted, is made to declare himself to be *triumphator erroris*, triumphant over "error" (40.1).

[8] The metaphors of darkness for ignorance, light for truth are

so common in pagan classical literature (one thinks especially of
the Platonic analogies in *Republic* 6-7: see D. Tarrant, "Greek
Metaphors of Light," *CQ* n.s. 10 [1960] 181 ff., at 185 f.) that it
is vain to look for explicit biblical sources for the idea, though
many might be cited (e.g., Isa. 5.20, 9.2, 60.1). Three, apparently
independent, critics have seen here a covert reference to the
ceremony of baptism: F. J. Dölger, "Die Sünde in Blindheit und
Unwissenheit: Ein Beitrag zu Tertullian De baptismo 1," *AC* 2
(1930) 222 ff., at 224; F. di Capua, "La croce et le croci nell'
Ottavio di Minucio," *Rend. Acad. Arch. Lett. e Belle Arte* n.s.
26 (1951) 98 ff., at 112 n.2; Chr. Mohrmann, *Études sur le latin
des chrétiens* 1 (Rome 1961) 145, n. 13, and 3 (1965) 155: "chez
Minucius Félix la terminologie chrétienne est vraiment tabouée."
It is true that these metaphors of light and darkness are very
common in the language of initiation, whether Christian or pagan
(F. Cumont, *Lux perpetua* [Paris 1947] 422 ff.; A. D. Nock,
Early Gentile Christianity and Its Hellenistic Background [New
York 1964] 136), and for an example cf. Cyp. *Ad Donat.* 4: "as
soon as the stain of my former life was wiped away by the help
of the birth-giving wave [of baptism], and a calm pure light
from above flooded my purged breast . . . the dark grew light."
But here the tense of the verb (*emergerem*) is rather against such
a narrowly liturgical interpretation. The themes of light and
truth, darkness and error, are picked up again in 3.1. For parallel
note the rescript of the persecuting emperor Maximin (Euseb.
H.E. 9.7.3). He speaks of the Christian mind shaking off and
dispersing "all-blinding mists of error" (πλάνη), which were
enveloping it in "the baneful darkness of ignorance." And cf.
Cyp. *Ad Demet.* 25 (ML 4.562), *Epp.* 65.2.2, 74.10.2; Arnob. 2.72;
2 *Clem.* 1.6, etc. Note too Ennius, *Fab. inc.* 398 Vahlen², quoted
by Cic. *De off.* 1.51 to exemplify the nature of true friendship:
*Homo qui erranti comiter monstrat viam/quasi lumen de suo
lumine accendat, facit.*

⁹ Caecilius Natalis is thought by many to be characterized in
the *Octavius* as being possessed of youthful high spirits, zest, and
impetuous exuberance (see, e.g., H. J. Baylis, *Minucius Felix and
His Place among the Early Fathers of the Latin Church* [London
1928] 6 ff.). Certainly his *alacritas*, we are told, was habitual
(2.3), but the youthfulness depends on a slightly doubtful deduction drawn from 3.1 (where see n. 23), and the impetuous
exuberance (cf. 14.1, 17.5, 40.1 [*erupit*]) may well be more due

to the arrangement of the material of the dialogue than to deliberate characterization; Caecilius is making the attack (*actio*) on Christianity, Octavius, by contrast, the reply (*responsio*). The attack gives more literary scope for displaying zest and vigor. H. Dessau, "Über einiger Inschriften aus Cirta," *Hermes* 15 (1880) 471–74, and with further discussion in "Minucius Felix und Caecilius Natalis," *Hermes* 40 (1905) 373–86, attempted *inter alia* to identify this Caecilius with the (clearly pagan) local magistrate and benefactor of Cirta, Caecilius Natalis of CIL 8.6996 (dated 210), 7094–98 (dated 211–17 A.D.) (Cirta). Such direct identification is without warrant, but Caecilius' invocation of the testimony of Fronto by the oblique title *Cirtensis noster* in 9.6 (where see n. 123) is certainly strongly suggestive that he had family connections in that town.

[10] Throughout the dialogue there is an unmistakable leitmotiv of *superstitio* versus *religio* (*alterum vitii nomen, alterum laudis*, Cic. *De nat. deor.* 2.72). Caecilius sets out to establish that Christianity is a *superstitio*, as opposed to Roman *religio*, Octavius that Christianity is the true *religio*. (For a discussion and bibliography on the difference between *superstitio* and *religio*, see Pease on Cic. *De nat. deor.* 1.45, 1.117, 2.72 [noting the discussion of Cicero there on the distinction], *De divinat.* 2.148.) The words or their derivatives are used with precision and placed with care. Observe especially the matching perorations 13.5 (. . . *ne aut anilis inducatur superstitio aut omnis religio destruatur*) and 38.7 (*cohibeatur superstitio . . . vera religio reservetur*). On this leitmotiv see G. Lieberg, "Die römische Religion bei Minucius Felix," RhM 106 (1963) 62 ff.

[11] *disputatione gravissima ad veram religionem reformavit.* Many translate "converted by (sheer) weight of argument." The phrase *disputatio gravissima* is repeated, surely not idly, in 15.1, where such an interpretation, though possible, is barely suitable (for the turn of expression cf. Cic. *Tusc. Disp.* 2.61 *eum* [*Posidonium*] *graviter . . . disputavisse*). In 14.1 ff. and in 39, retrospective judgments are passed on the speeches supplied by (or for) the protagonists; so here too we may equally well have a prospective indication of the gravity of the fare about to be presented. The effect is to give a lifelike touch to the (purported) reminiscence.

[12] By contrast with the *superstitiosae vanitates* associated with the pagan Caecilius, Octavius is surrounded by prattling youthful

innocence. This is a well-established rhetorical *topos* to arrest sympathy; see H. Hertel, "Das unschuldige Kind," JAC 4 (1967) 146–62, esp. 160.

adhuc dimidiata verba temptantibus. The Plautine word *dimidiatus* was clearly highly prized by contemporary littérateurs (used again by M.F. in 34.6); a discussion of its merits is to be found in Aulus Gellius, *Noctes Atticae* 3.14; (characteristically Apuleius *Metam.* 5.18 even has *tertiata verba*). Fronto not only discusses *dimidiata verba* in Naber 225, suggesting additions to the Plautine catalogue (e.g., "vigil" = *vigiliae*, "mole" = *molestiae*), but he also surveys the words appropriate for the language of the *balbus* in Naber 149 and again in Naber 159. Clearly this was a topical subject.

[13] *loquellam ipso offensantis linguae fragmine dulciorem.* The derivation from Lucretius 5.229 f.: *nec cuiquam adhibendast/ almae nutricis blanda atque infracta loquela*, though often advocated, is hardly established. (Against the wide claims of Lucretian influence on Minucius Felix by J. Tomaselli Nicolosi, "Pagine lucreziane nell'Octavius di Minucio Felice," *Misc. stud. lett. crist. ant.* 1 [1947] 67 ff., see H. Hagendahl, *Latin Fathers and the Classics* [Göteberg 1958] 79. F. Dalpane, "Se Arnobio sia stato un epicureo: Lucrezio e gli apologeti cristiani Minucio Felice, Tertulliano, Cipriano, Lattanzio," *Riv. stor. ant.* 10 [1906] 403–35, 11 [1907] 222–36, discusses M.F. very cursorily on 417, 420.) Jerome in *Ep.* 108.26.5 *aviae et amitae nomina dimidiatis verbis frangere* and *Ep.* 79.6 *garrula atque balbutiens linguae offensione fit dulcior* may be imitating this passage (his employment of *Plautina prosapia* used in 14.1—where see n. 172—suggests that he was familiar with details of the text of the *Octavius* and that in his notices of M.F. [see Intro. p. 4 f.] he is, therefore, making not merely secondhand judgments).

[14] Cf. Cic. *Brut.* 10: *quos postquam salutavi;* Cic. *Hortens. fr.* 3 Grilli: *Lucullo noster adventus et gratus et iucundus fuisset;* Cic. *De rep.* 1.14: *quem cum comiter Scipio adpellavisset libenterque vidisset;* Sulp. Sev. *Dial.* 1.1.2: *conplexi hominem amantissimum,* etc.; i.e., a friendly *salutatio* is a very common ingredient of dialogue introductions: see M. Ruch, *Le préambule dans les oeuvres philosophiques de Cicéron* (Paris 1958) 372 ff. The gaiety of this arrival and greeting in the prologue is nicely balanced by the lighthearted separation and departure in the epilogue (40.4: *laeti hilaresque discessimus*).

[15] A common treatment. Sulphurous springs were especially
valued for this purpose (e.g., *Albula aqua*, Suet. *Aug.* 82.2, Mart.
1.12.3, Stat. *Silv.* 1.3.75, Pliny *N.H.* 31.6.10), as was sunbathing
(Vitruvius *De arch.* 5.9.123). Not only those suffering from
gout, rheumatism (cf. Pliny *N.H.* 31.38.72), or arthritis (Fronto—
ὁ ἀρθριτικός Artemid. *Onirocrit.* 4.22, 257 Pack—was advised
to take the waters, Naber 4), but even those who wanted to make
room for more drinking (Arnob. 1.9) might avail themselves of
such therapy. Note too the stories told of Heraclitus' dropsy:
he attempted to draw off the noxious humours by stretching himself in the sun plastered over with manure (*Diog. Laer.* 9.1.4),
and Aul. Gellius, *Noctes Atticae* 19.8.1 ff.—a discourse by Cornelius Fronto on *calentes harenae* (hot sands) used for curing the
same malady. *Hot* sea-baths were often used also (Pliny *N.H.*
31.33.62) for this cure, and J. van Wageningen, "De siccandis
umoribus," *Mnem.* n.s. 49 (1921) 102–5, takes this to be the intention here (*per aquam marinam calidam et sulfurosam*, 105);
so too J. del Ton, "Minucius Felix, Octavius Ianuarius, Caecilius
Natalis Ostiae litus petunt," *Latinitas* 1 (1953) 117 ff., at 118
(*aqua . . . apte calefacta*). But the language of 4.5 suggests that
open sea-bathing is intended, and Pliny *N.H.* 31.33.62 confirms
that cold sea-water (with its inherent warmth, Hippoc. *Regim.*
2.57, Littré 6.570) was also effective: *medendi modus idem et in
marinis erit quae calefiunt . . . corpora ad siccanda, qua de causa
et frigido mari utuntur.* There is little value, therefore, in investi-
gating the construction of *thermae* at Ostia for chronological
implications (as S. Rossi, " 'Feriae Vindemiales' e 'Feriae Iudiciariae' a Roma," GIF 15 [1962] 193 ff., at 197 ff.). The literary
effect of this information is perhaps to suggest a mature Roman
of solid standing (who, therefore, commands one's respect and
attention); cf. P. Frassinetti, "Finzione e realtà nell'Octavius,"
Athenaeum 46 (1968) 327 ff., at 331 ff.

[16] To place a debate on leisurely *feriae* was well-established
literary practice, e.g. Cic. *De orat.* 1.7.24, 3.1.2 (*ludi Romani*),
De re pub. 1.14, 1.33 (*feriae latinae*), *De nat. deor.* 1.15 (*feriae
latinae*), Macrob. *Saturn.* 1.1.1 ff. (*Saturnalia*), Lucian *Amores*
1.398, and note the many vignettes in Aul. Gellius, e.g; *Noctes
Atticae* 9.15 (*per feriarum tempus aestivarum*), 18.5.1 (*aestivae
feriae*), 11.3 (*ab arbitriis negotiisque otium*), 20.8.1 (at a *vindemia* house party). G. Boissier, *La fin du paganisme* 1 (Paris
1891) 335, suggests that this was originally a stratagem devised

by Cicero to disarm his Roman critics; philosophic debate, demanding leisurely hours (*otium;* for the appearance of *otium* in debate, see Pease on Cic. *De nat. deor.* 2.3 *otiosi,* and M. Ruch, *Le préambule* etc. [Paris, 1958] 83 ff.) could thus appear to be compatible with a life devoted to public service. M.F. may have intended something of the same sort of effect here, though an atmosphere of friendly and relaxed ease is the more obvious impression. It should also be remembered that the device had occurred already in the Greek dialogue, e.g., Plat. *Repub.* 1.327.

The legal recess during September (*feriae vindemiales*) was regularized by J. Caesar (Suet. *Caes.* 40) and by modifying legislation under Marcus Aurelius (*S.H.A.* M. Aur. 10.10; *Digest.* 2.12.1, 3, 4; and *Cod. Iust.* 3.12.6[7]). It continued to be held at least into the sixth century (A. della Casa, "Le due Date dell' 'Octavius,' " *Maia* 14 [1962] 26 ff., at 27 n.2). As it was also a period when attendance at the Senate was not compulsory (Suet. *Aug.* 35), the harvest time provided a popular season for festivities and house parties (e.g., Varro, *De re rustica* 1.2.1 f.; *S.H.A.* Ant. Pius 11.2 f.; *S.H.A.* Elagab. 11.2 ff.; cf. Fronto, Naber 83; Aulus Gellius, *Noctes Atticae* 20.8.1; and one recalls the famous celebration of a *simulacrum vindemiae* by Messalina and friends in Tac. *Ann.* 11.31.1ff.). Though Marcus Aurelius was especially fond of this season (Fronto, Naber 68, 69, 90), it is difficult to see how any secure chronological conclusions can be drawn from this casual reference (for a contrary view, S. Rossi, "L' 'Octavius' fu scritto prima del 161," GIF 12 [1959] 289 ff., at 295 ff., and " 'Feriae Vindemiales' e 'Feriae Iudiciariae' a Roma," GIF 15 [1962] 193–224). For further discussion see J. Beaujeu, "Remarques sur la datation de l'Octavius: Vacances de la moisson et vacances de la vendange," *Rev. de phil.* 41 (1967) 121 ff., at 124 ff.

Cyp. *Ad Donat.* 1 appears to imitate the idea for his prologue: *tempus est quo indulgente vindemia solutus animus in quietem sollemnes ac statas anni fatigantis indutias sortiatur;* for a discussion, see "The Secular Profession of St. Cyprian of Carthage," *Latomus* 24 (1965) 633 f., and note P. Courcelle, *Le Confessions de saint Augustin dans la tradition littéraire* (Paris 1963) 121 f., comparing Ennod. 334 (*M.G.H.* 7.245) for a similar conversational setting.

[17] One can trace here two traditional literary elements of the dialogue genre. For *ambulatio* note the frequently employed de-

vice of Cicero in *De or.* 1.7.28 (*cum . . . in ambulationem ventum esset*); *Brut.* 10 (*cum inambularem in xysto*); as also for *De div.* 1.8 (*ambulandi causa*); and cf. *De finibus* 5.24.70 (*Tiberina descensio*); Cebes *Tabula* 1 (περιπατοῦντες); Plut. *passim* (Hirzel, *op. cit.* 1 [1895] 528 n. 1, 537); Sulp. Sev. *Dial.* 1.1.2 (*cum . . . deambulassemus*), etc.; and see M. Ruch, *Le préambule* etc. (Paris, 1958) 374 ff. Note, too, the contrived arrangement of some of A. Gellius' settings, e.g., *Noctes Atticae* 11.3, a soliloquy on the uses of *pro* during a *vespertina ambulatio*, and while on "legal" vacation (*ab arbitriis negotiisque otium*).

For the *mise en scène* by the seashore, cf. Just. *Dial.* 3–7 (Ephesus?); Florus *Vergilius orator an poeta, init.* (canal side at Tarraco); [Clem.] *Recog.* 8.1.1; cf. [Clem.] *Hom.* 14.1.1; Cic. *Academ. post. fr.* 13 (*ut nos nunc sedemus ad Lucrinum*); Quint. 7.3.31 (a *ficta controversia* with a beach picnic for setting). Note especially Aul. Gellius, *Noctes Atticae* 18.1.2 f. (Ostia), though Beaujeu, xx ff., liii, manifestly overplays his case for the dependence of M.F. on this passage: "le choix du lieu de la scène provient certainement de la lecture d'Aulu-Gelle" (xxiii); "la dérivation est sûre" (liii); cf. Suet. *De rhet.* 1, reporting a *controversia* with its setting on the seashore of Ostia: the incident occurs *aestivo tempore* and the main protagonists have come from Rome (*adulescentes urbani cum Ostiam venissent litus ingressi*).

It can be seen, therefore, that the judgment of P. Monceaux, *Histoire littéraire de l'Afrique chrétien* 1 (Paris 1901) 489, does not carry conviction: "Minucius Felix n'apporte réellement rien de nouveau. On peut dire sans exagération qu'une seule chose appartient vraiment à l'auteur: la mise en oeuvre".

cum . . . inambulando litore pergeremus ut et aura adspirans leniter membra vegetaret. The precise construing of this passage has exercised much needless ingenuity and complications have been multiplied by unnecessary emendation. The theories of J. Le Gall (who wished to read *in amnis ambulando litore*), *Le Tibre, fleuve de Rome dans l'antiquité* (Paris 1953) App. 2, 334 ff., have been effectively demolished by Beaujeu *ad loc.* The latter, however, finds "une grave difficulté" in construing the *ut* clause here as final, a difficulty which it is hard to share; for, so construed, the sequence of action and the geography then make admirable sense. For a lucid exposition, R. Meiggs, *Roman Ostia* (Oxford 1960) App. 4, 490 ff. It is, therefore, quite unnecessary to conclude with W. Speyer (who regards the dialogue as a

"Phantasie"), *art. cit.* in n. 1, at 51, that "Minucius Felix kannte Ostia nicht. Es ist ziemlich unwahrscheinlich, dass er überhaupt je in Rom war." For further discussion see P. Frassinetti, "Finzione e realtà nell'Octavius," *Athenaeum* 46 (1968) 327 ff., at 333, 338 ff.

[18] *molli vestigio cedens harena.* For the combination of epithets, cf. Pliny *Ep.* 2.17.15: *vinea . . . nudis etiam pedibus mollis et cedens;* Cels. 7.6.2: *quaedam* [sc., *tubercula*] *mollia cedentiaque sunt.*

[19] For a work of art used to trigger off a discussion, cf. Gellius, *Noctes Atticae* 13.25.1 f.; Varro *De re rust.* 1.2.1 ff., Lucian *Amores* 12 ff. One is reminded of the role played by the altar to an unknown god in Acts 17.23. The worship of Serapis, an Egyptian cult much encouraged—some said initiated—by the Ptolemaic kings (Tac. *Hist.* 4.81; Plut. *Mor.* 361 f.; Orig. *C.Cels.* 5.38; Clem. *Protr.* 4.48.1 ff.), was extremely popular throughout the Mediterranean world and was especially favored by the Severan dynasty. Serapis gradually came to achieve the status of a universal solar deity, adopting attributes of Ascelpius, Zeus, Helios, Dionysus, etc.; he is, however, frequently found closely associated with the worship of Isis, Harpocrates, and Anubis, on which see nn. 287, 288 to 21.3. There is little chance of seeing in this casual reference any chronological indication (though some have attempted to do so). The cult enjoyed a lengthy popularity at Ostia: for evidence see L. R. Taylor, *The Cults of Ostia* (Bryn Mawr 1912) 66 ff.; R. Meiggs, *Roman Ostia* 366 ff.; M. F. Squarciapino, *I culti orientali ad Ostia* (Leiden 1962) 19 ff.; and see n. 294 on 22.1. The ancient literary references on Serapis are collected by T. Hopfner, *Fontes historiae religionis Aegyptiacae* (Bonn 1922–24) 905 ff.; for the development of the cult, H. C. Youtie, "The *KLINE* of Serapis," *HTR* 41 (1948) 9 ff., has a useful survey with ample bibliographical references; for a description of the cult, G. Lafaye, *Histoire du culte des divinités d'Alexandrie, Sérapis, Isis, Harpocrate et Anubis hors de l'Égypte* (Paris 1884) esp. 248 ff.

The contrast between worshiper of Christ and of Serapis appears to have become traditional. Hence the paradoxical behavior of some Egyptians in S.H.A. *Quad. Tyr.* 8.2 f. (*illic qui Serapem colunt Christiani sunt*); on this passage see W. Schmid, "Die Koexistenz von Serapiskult und Christentum im Hadriansbrief bei Vopiscus," *Bonner Historia-Augusta-Colloquium 1964/*

65 (Bonn 1966) 153 ff.; R. Syme, "Ipse ille Patriarcha," *Bonner Historia-Augusta-Colloquium 1966/67* (Bonn 1968) 119 ff.

[20] This ritual gesture of kissing the hand is common and well attested in literature: R. T. Meyer, "Note on Minucius Felix, Octavius, 2.4," *Class. Bull.* 31 (1963) 22, compares Pliny *N.H.* 28.2.25, Apul. *Met.* 4.28; to which add Apul. *Apol.* 56, Lucian *Sacrif.* 12, *Alex.* 30, etc.) and in art (used by both god and devotee, H. P. L'Orange, *Studies on the Iconography of Cosmic Kingship in the Ancient World* (Oslo 1953) 153 ff., with illustrations especially from Alexandrian coins—and associated with statues of Serapis, *ibid.* 154 ff.). The right hand was used—is this the gesture of "Alexamenos" in the celebrated Palatine graffito (DACL 1.2 [1924] *s.v.* Ane 2044 for illustration)?

The custom of this religious gesture continued (in modified form) in Christian liturgical practice, e.g., the kissing of the church threshold: F. J. Dölger, "Der Kuss der Kirchenschwelle," AC 2 (1930) 156–58, and, of course, "Der Altarkuss," *ibid.* 190 ff. (in "Zu den Zeremonien der Messliturgie"). See further DACL 2.1 (1925) *s.v.* Baiser (F. Cabrol); K. M. Hofmann, *Philema Hagion* (diss. Erlangen, Gütersloh 1938); F. J. Dölger, *Sol Salutis²* (Munich 1925) 11 ff.; PW Suppl. Bd. 5 (1931) *s.v.* Kuss (W. Kroll) 511 ff., at 517 ff.

It is unclear whether Caecilius merely raises his kissed hand in a gesture of salute (cf. Tac. *Hist.* 1.36: *nec deerat Otho protendens manus adorare vulgus, iacere oscula*) or whether he actually proceeds to place it on the image (if, as seems most likely, a street herm of Serapis is envisaged; for illustration see H. P. L'Orange, *Apotheosis in Ancient Portraiture* [Oslo 1947] fig. 59). The former alternative seems the more probable, but the latter may be implied by *impingere* in 3.1, where see n. 24). For a discussion W. Fauscher, *Die Einleitungskapitel zum "Octavius" des Minucius Felix: Ein Kommentar* (Zurich 1966) 44. For statues worn smooth by such veneration, cf. Lucr. 1.316 ff.; Cic. *Verr.* 2.4.43: the mouth and chin of a bronze image of Hercules was *attritius quod in precibus et gratulationibus non solum id venerari verum etiam osculari solent*); and see further H. Jucker, "Geküsste Götterbilder," *Antike Kunst* 3 (1960) 91 f.

[21] *Marce frater.* It is possible that this form of fraternal greeting (common, of course, in Christian circles from the earliest New Testament times; cf., among Jews, Deut. 15.2, 7, 9, 11, 12; 2 Mach. 1.1) is intentionally used as a preparation for the attack on (9.2)

and defense of (31.8) the Christian notion of brotherhood, and especially on the Christian practice in salutation; hence the repetition of *Marce frater* by the pagan Caecilius in 5.1 might possibly be understood as ironical (*frater* could have other derisive connotations, e.g., Cic. *Cael.* 13.32; Mart. 2.4.3, 10.65.14; Petron. *Sat.* 9.2). On the other hand, it is not unknown as a general form of coaxing address between friends (Apul. *Met.* 1.17, 8.9, 9.7; Hor. *Ep.* 1.6.54; Cic. *Verr.* 2.3.66.155) or even the unacquainted (Fronto, Naber 179, and esp. [Quint.] *Decl.* 321 [p. 259 Ritter]: *quoties blandiri volumus his qui esse amici videntur, nulla adulatio procedere ultra [hoc nomen] potest quam ut fratres vocemus*); and see further on general pagan usage H. Pétré, *Caritas: Étude sur le vocabulaire de la charité chrétienne* (Louvain 1948) 105 ff.; and it was also in use among initiates of other sects (e.g., Mithraic: examples in F. Cumont, *Textes et monuments figurés relatifs aux mystères de Mithra* 2 [Brussels 1896] inscr. nos. 34, 324, 336, 351, 355).

[22] *in hac imperitiae vulgaris caecitate. Imperitia* and *inscientia* and their derivatives are much used, and deliberately so, throughout the dialogue. Their exploitation helps to underline the assertion that the Christians, so far from being ill-educated boors (*indocti, imperiti*, etc.), are possessors in fact of the right knowledge, of the true philosophy (with the pagan *docti*, philosophers and poets, supporting their claims to this possession). Significantly it is this charge of *inscientia* that is used to start off the discussion (4.3). For an analysis of this theme, H. Wagenvoort, "Minuciana (*ad Oct.* 3.1; 29.2)," in *Mélanges offerts à Mme Christine Mohrmann* (Utrecht 1963) 66 ff. Behind the theme lay the often unquestioned, and Socratic, assumption that virtue was knowledge; cf. Orig. *C.Cels.* 6.13: "no one would expound the truths of divine wisdom to those who are very uneducated slaves or ignorant." But cf., too, Cic. *De nat. deor.* 2.45, 3.11, 3.39, 3.79: stupidity imputed to one's philosophical opponents was clearly standard polemic technique as well.

[23] There is a faint suggestion—though it is no more—that Caecilius was a *sector* of Minucius Felix, a young man who lived in the home of the more experienced advocate and accompanied him to the law courts to learn his skills (*domi forisque*); cf. Cic. *De amic.* 1.1, the youthful Cicero, as far as he could, never left the side of Q. Mucius Scaevola: *a senis latere numquam discederem;* Tac. *Dial.* 2.1: *domi quoque et in publico adsectabar,* and

34.2; Fronto, Naber 180). There is another possible but slight hint at disparity in station in 4.6. On the other hand, Fronto could enjoy the constant company and assistance of the more junior senator Gavius Clarus (PIR² G97) both *in foro* and *domi*, and there is no indication that he was a pupil (Fronto, Naber 133 ff.).

[24] *Impingere* is here used either absolutely or (less likely) with object unexpressed. We might possibly understand *oscula*, in which case the verb is hyperbole for the more usual *iacere*, *iactare* (cf. Petron. *Sat.* 31.1: *basia impegit*); or (much more probably) it is used here intransitively (see TLL 7.1 *s.v.* impingo 11A1, and Lact. *Div. inst.* 2.3.3: *quid ei facias qui cum errare se sentiat, ultro ipse in lapides impingat*). We seem to have then what forms part of a virtual literary *topos*, a catalogue of the characteristics of the *vir religiosus;* for an analysis of this *topos*, see O. Weinreich, "Zu Tibull. 1 1, 11–24," *Hermes* 56 (1921) 337 ff., at 339 f. Among the many passages he adduces, note especially for close parallel Theophras. *Charact.* 16.5: "when he passes one of the smooth (-oily) stones at the crossroads, he anoints it with oil from his flask, and will not go his ways till he have knelt down and worshipped it" (trans. J. M. Edmonds, Loeb Classical Lib.; London 1929, 81); Lucian *Alex.* 30: "if he but saw anywhere a stone smeared with holy oil or adorned with a wreath, he would fall on his face forthwith, kiss his hand and stand beside it for a long time making vows and craving blessings from it" (trans. A. M. Harmon, vol. 4, Loeb Classical Library; London 1925, 217); and Clem. *Strom.* 7.4.26.2: "worshipping every piece of wood and virtually every oily stone"; and see in general P. J. Koets, Δεισιδαιμονία: *A Contribution to the Knowledge of the Religious Terminology in Greek* (Utrecht 1929). There is also more than a suggestion that Marcus has, biblically, allowed Caecilius to be "scandalized," i.e., made to stumble; for elements of this notion in the classical tradition, see Otto, *Sprichwörter, s.v.* lapis (6).

[25] For such attention to cult objects (not only oil and garlands, but perfumes and wine, incense and spices, fillets and drapery, garments and jewellery, ritual washing and processions, etc.), see E. Bevan, *Holy Images* (London 1940) 23 ff.; and Frazer's nn. on Pausanias, vol. 4, 154 f.; cf. Plat. *Rep.* 3.398A; Paus. 10.24.6; Cic. *Verr.* 2.4.35.77; Lucian *Charon* 22; Sicul. Flac. *De condic. agr.*: . . . *et unguento velaminibusque et coronis eos* (sc., *lapides*)

coronabant (Lachmann, *Gromatici veteres* 141); Arnob. 1.39: *lubricatum lapidem et ex olivi unguine sordidatum.* Note, too, Jacob's holy pillar anointed with oil, Gen. 28.18 (on which see Just. *Dial.* 86 and Aug. *De civ. Dei* 16.38).

[26] *semper mare etiam positis flatibus inquietum:* a frequently observed phenomenon, e.g., Seneca *N.Q.* 5.1.1, 5.5.2 (*cum aqua motum suum habeat etiam ventis quiescentibus*), *Dial.* 9.2.1, 10.2.3; Suet. *fr.* 157 (p. 243 Reifferscheid); and cf. Aul. Gellius, *Noctes Atticae* 2.30.3.

[27] *Octavi disserentis de navigatione narratio.* This has been frequently taken as confirmation of the African provenance of Octavius: he had traveled from overseas to Rome (so, e.g., Beaujeu *ad loc.*). But as *navigatio* can be used not only in the particular sense of "a sea voyage" but also in the general sense of "traveling by sea, sailing" (cf. Cic. *Fam.* 16.4.1), it is unsafe to be so precise. As Lindner (ed., Langensalza 1773) cautiously remarked: "sermonibus familiaribus occasionem subministrant tempus, locus, personae, negotia et denique res quaevis oculis objectae." See also "Minucius Felix *Octavius* 4.6," CP 61 (1966) 252 f., at 253 n. 4.

[28] J. Le Gall, *Le Tibre, fleuve de Rome, dans l'antiquité* (Paris 1953) App. 2, 337, sees here a specific allusion to tunny-fishing boats; the season for that industry was summer and early autumn—hence they are drawn up to dry in September. But the allusion is too specific; there is nothing untoward in *naviculae* being drawn up in late autumn. Nor need one see (with Le Gall) any significance in M.F.'s failure to mention coverings against rain and sun (the boats being more or less ready if a strike did occur). It is simply that the setting is described quite adequately without such elaborate annotation of detail. For a discussion, Meiggs, *Roman Ostia,* App. 4, 490 ff.

[29] A famous description of what the Greeks called ἐποστρακισμός, but not the only description that survives from antiquity. Close parallels are found in (M.F.'s contemporary?) Julius Pollux 9.119 (p. 191 Dindorf) as well as in a Florentine MS (reproduced in A. Pastorino, "L' 'epostracismo' in Minucio Felice (*Oct.* 3.2–6)," ΑΝΤΙΔΩΡΟΝ *Hugoni Henrico Paoli oblatum* (Genoa 1956) 250 ff., at 256 n. 36; this bears very close resemblance to the description to be found *apud* Eustathius on Hom. *Il.* 18.543 (Eustathius drew heavily on Suetonius' *Ludicra historia,* now lost; see PW 4.A.1 [1931] 625 ff. *s.v.* Suetonius, [G. Funaioli]; for the literary references, C. L. Roth, ed. Suetonius [Leipzig 1858]

278 ff. The fragment is, therefore, likely to have come from
Suetonius' lost work). The relationship between these descriptions has been carefully examined by R. Reitzenstein, "Zu Minucius Felix," *Hermes* 51 (1916) 609 ff., at 616f.; A. Pastorino,
art. cit., and A. Labhardt, "Minucius Félix et les ricochets d'Ostie
(*Octavius* 3.5–4.1)," *Hommages à Jean Bayet* (Brussels 1964)
349 ff. The stance of the thrower and the victory granted partly
in terms of distance are not to be found in the other descriptions
as they survive. There is a fourth, though brief, description in
Arrian *Epictet.* 4.7 (p. 417 Schenkl, 1916), introduced to exemplify the single-mindedness of the children's competition but their
indifference to the object used in that competition. In the face
of this evidence it is difficult to avoid the conclusion that while
M.F. may have added a touch or two to this topic from his own
personal observations, the choice of the topic itself—as one might
suspect for much else of the prologue—was essentially a literary
affair.

[30] *inclinem ipsum et humilem quantum potest super undas inrotare.* Probably *quantum potest* ought to be construed with
inrotare rather than with *humilem* (contra Beaujeu), especially
as one of the objects in the game is to achieve distance (*longius*).

[31] *omnes* presumably embraces Octavius and M.F. together
with the *pueri:* so G. Sörbom, "Ad Minucium Felicem," *Eranos*
27 (1929) 146 f. (though *omnes* can on occasion be used for
ambo: cf. Valer. Flac. *Argon.* 8.426 [of Medea and Jason], [Cyp.]
Ep. 21.4.1: . . . *Statium et Severianum, omnes confessores* . . .).
The passage is also discussed by E. Löfstedt, *Beiträge zur Kennt-
nis der späteren Latinität* (Stockholm 1907) 107–9.

[32] <*non*> *ipsius sectae homo.* The sequence of thought and
argument urges the addition of *non* (for *ipse* = "same" cf. 11.7
ipso corpore). On the text see further K. Abel, "Minucius Felix:
Octavius: Das Textproblem," *RhM* 110 (1967) 248 ff., at 252 ff.
M.F. here neatly begs the question whether Christianity rightfully
constituted a philosophical school (*secta*, cf. usage in 5.4); he has
the pagan assume that it does outright. A claim to this effect had
been made since at least the 160's: Justin Martyr was converted
to "the safe and sound philosophy" (*Dial.* 8); Melito of Sardis
talked of Christianity as a "philosophy" of barbarous origin (*ap.*
Euseb. *H.E.* 4.26.7; cf. Tat. *Or.* 35); Miltiades' lost *Apology* may
have been entitled (Euseb. *H.E.* 5.17.5) "On the Philosophy of
the Christians"; and Athenagoras' *Legatio* (note esp. chap. 2) is,

in essence, a plea that Christianity should be judged on a par with other philosophical schools (like the Epicureans, notorious "atheists," who had been acknowledged as a *secta* in Athens by Hadrian; see H. Diels, "Zwei Funde," *Archiv. f. Gesch d. Philosophie* 3 [1890] 478 ff., at 486–91; cf. Tert. *Apol.* 3.6: from their name "Christians" are like *Platonici, Epicurei, Pythagorici*). See also R. Walzer, *Galen on Jews and Christians* (Oxford 1949) 14 ff., 43 ff.; W. Jaeger, *Early Christianity and Greek Paidaea* (Cambridge, Mass. 1961) *passim*. For a famous (roughly contemporary?) statue of a Christian qua philosopher, DACL 6.2 (1925) 2419 ff. *s.v.* Hippolyte (H. Leclercq); for other (later) examples, H.-I. Marrou, Μουσικὸς Ἀνήρ (Grenoble 1938) 269 ff.

The attempt by S. Rossi, "Ancora sull' 'Octavius' di Minucio Felice," GIF 16 (1963) 293 ff., to make all three participants actual or former initiates of the Isis-*secta* fails for lack of convincing supporting evidence; likewise the case of A. D. Simpson, "Epicureans, Christians, Atheists in the Second Century," TAPA 72 (1941) 372 ff., that Minucius Felix and Octavius were erstwhile Epicureans, is left unsupported by adequate evidence. (Besides, to impute Epicurean tendencies was standard abuse; see R. Jungkuntz, "Fathers, Heretics and Epicureans," JEH 17 [1966] 3 ff.) Similarly, the view of H. J. Baylis, *Minucius Felix and His Place among the Early Fathers of the Latin Church* (London 1928) 124, 134, that M.F. was once a member of the Stoic *secta*, is unnecessary.

[33] *residamus.* For this common literary turn in the dialogue genre, cf. Varro *De re rust.* 1.2.2 f.; Cic. *De leg.* 1.14, 2.1, 2.7; *De divin.* 2.8, 2.150; *De orat.* 1.7.29; *Brut.* 24 (*sed quo facilius sermo explicetur, sedentes, si vobis videtur, agamus*); *Acad. post. fr.* 13 (*et ut nos nunc sedemus ad Lucrinum pisciculosque exultantes videmus*); *De fato* 2.4 (*considamus hic . . .*); Cyp. *Ad Donat.* 1 (*petamus hanc sedem*); Sulp. Sev. *Dial.* 1.1.2 (*consedimus*); [Clem.] *Recog.* 8.3.1 (*et cum vidisset iuxta portum recessum quendam secretum residere nos fecit, et ita primus ipse incipit. . . .*). See also J. S. Reid on Cic. *Acad.* 1.14 (ed., London 1885, 164) and Hirzel, *Der Dialog* 1.537.

[34] *ut me ex tribus medium lateris ambitione protegerent.* Editors frequently compare Sall. *Iug.* 11.3: *Hiempsal . . . adsedit ne medius ex tribus quod apud Numidias honori ducitur, Iugurtha foret.* Beaujeu *ad loc.* thereby sees confirmation of an African origin of the participants of the dialogue. An erroneous deduction,

as a seat in the middle was a mark of honor among many other
nations apart from Numidians: Parthians, e.g. (Plut. *Sulla* 5.4–5),
as well as Romans (Dio 54.10.5, Appian *De bell. civ.* 4.2); see
further "Minucius Felix *Octavius* 4.6," CP 61 (1966) 252 f.

[35] A frequently employed proverb, Otto *Sprichwörter* 264.
R. Verdière, "Note de lecture," *Latomus* 29 (1970) 1072, draws
attention to O. Ribbeck, *Scaen. Rom. poes. frag.* 2 (repr. 1962)
291, Appendix Sentent. 21.

[36] On the "dialogue with arbiter," see the analysis in Hirzel
Dialog 2.122 f., 177 f. (to which W. A. Baehrens, "Literarische
Beiträge iii," *Hermes* 50 [1915] 456 ff. adds little). The pedigree
is traceable to Plato (*Protag.* 337E, *Sympos.* 175E) through
Cicero (*Tusc.* 5.120: *tamquam honorarius iudex . . . Carneades;
De fato* 39: *Chrysippus tamquam arbiter honorarius*) and Tacitus
(*Dial.* 4 f.), but only becomes common with Plutarch (*Mor.* 615E,
750A, 1096F, cf. 747B). Note too Favorinus' role as *iudex* in the
debate *de vita beata*, Aul. Gellius, *Noctes Atticae* 18.1 (the
reconstruction of a dialogue composed by Favorinus between
Epictetus and Onesimus from Galen 1 p. 40 f., 19 p. 44 [Kühn]—
see Beaujeu xxi f.—rests on flimsy foundations); compare also
Vulcan's role in Vespa's debate between a cook and a baker
(Baehrens, *Poetae Latini minores* 4 [Leipzig 1882] 326 ff.).

M.F. may have chosen this format because it was currently
fashionable but, as Prof. Momigliano has suggested to me, the
effect of having a committed partisan acting as the *honorarius
iudex* may perhaps be a trifle gauche. It seems (it might be argued)
to have called for, as a result, the lengthy preamble on impartiality
in chap. 5, the repeated insistence on open-mindedness in 15, and
perhaps the virtual abrogation of the arbiter's role itself in 40.
Is there perhaps a suggestion, therefore, that the *Octavius*, like
many works of apologetics (cf. V. Tcherikover, "Jewish Apologetic Literature Reconsidered," *Eos* 48 [1956] fasc. 3, 169–73),
was really intended largely for the pleasure of an already converted audience among whom such an incongruity would hardly
be noticeable? On the other hand, the arrangement of the characters could as readily be construed as an attempt to create the
impression of lifelike, autobiographical authenticity.

[37] Caecilius begins by announcing one of the central tenets of
the Middle Academy, viz., universal scepticism, or more accurately ἐποχή (see Pease on Cic. *De nat. deor.* 1.12), the suspension of judgment until the (impossible) time when one can be

certain of all relevant facts (impossible, because of the fallibility
of sense perception, *akatalepsia*, *nihil percipi posse*, Cic. *Acad.
pr.* 2.9.28). It appears that Caecilius intends to support this attitude by establishing two main theses; these theses established, he
will then be in a position to make the deduction (6.1) that, given
the obscurity or unpredictability of the universe, men ought to
fall back on *religiones traditae*, traditional religion, and this religion can be proved, empirically, from the facts of Roman history
to have been a continual and positive force, good for its own
devotees, damaging for the neglectful, in the world (6 f.)

The two theses adduced are (1) that man's talents are too
limited and circumscribed for any comprehension of the universe;
nature must remain obscure and it is therefore an improper study
of mankind—which should be man. And (2) there are, in any
case, hypotheses which can explain the origins and formation of
man and the universe; they require no demiurge and therefore
exclude superstitious dread, but they emphasize the paramount
factor of capricious and random chance in the workings of the
universe.

The chapter has been (rightly) subject to a number of criticisms. There can be no doubt that the transition in 6.1 (to a
support of traditional religion) is not very clearly enunciated,
and it is here, at the least, somewhat unrealistic. And in §§7 ff.
(the hypotheses posited to explain the universe) there are very
obfuscated lines of argument: the theories—if indeed they are
meant to be taken separately—receive very unequal emphasis, and
their logic is not consistently sustained. What has the status of
suggestion is soon quietly given the grammar of proposition—the
apparently factual statements in §§8–13 turn out to be, in the
end, to one's surprise, merely tentative explanations.

How far can this be securely taken—as it often is—as an in-
cisively accurate picture of contemporary Roman paganism
among the intellectuals: sceptic in theory, but in practice tradi-
tionalist and conservative? That sceptic-conformist role is neither
an impossible nor an unrealistic picture nor without supporting
evidence, but the literary provenance of the arguments ought to
make one somewhat hesitant of its strict historicity. Caecilius
here is given traits freely borrowed both from Velleius (the
atomist and Epicurean) and Cotta (the Academic and tradition-
alist) in Cicero's *De natura deorum*: he may reflect, therefore,
more literary and philosophical history than contemporary reality.

And there is the (often neglected) factor that this is apologetic writing: ulterior reasons might dictate that Caecilius' case ought not to be too convincing nor its internal consistency too strong, and indeed a confusion of philosophical theories against a providential dispensation would enable the Christian spokesman to deploy a wide and impressive variety of counterarguments. For further recent doubts about the historicity, W. Speyer, *art. cit.* in n. 1, and P. Frassinetti, *art. cit.* in n. 5; recent advocates for the contrary are G. Lieberg, *art. cit.* in n. 10, and A. Pastorino, "I compromessi di un intellectuale pagano alla fine del ll secolo D.C.," *Le parole e le idee* 5 (1963) 155–66.

[38] *studiorum rudes, litterarum profanos, expertes artium etiam sordidarum*. This is the language of polemic (see n. 22 on 3.1 above, and n. 105 on 8.4 below), but this charge of illiteracy and "vulgarity" was particularly iterated against Christians—and right from the New Testament era (Acts 4.13: *homines . . . sine litteris et idiotae*)—and it was one which the Christians were often at pains to refute; cf. Arnob. 1.28: *nos hebetes, stolidi, fatui, obtusi pronuntiamur et bruti*); 3.15 (Christians are *rudes*), 5.31 (the Christian is said to be *imperitum, indoctum et rusticum*); Orig. *C.Cels.* 1.27, 1.29, 3.18, 3.44: "their injunctions are like this. 'Let no one educated, no one wise, no one sensible draw near. For these abilities are taught by us to be evils. But as for anyone ignorant, anyone stupid, anyone uneducated, anyone who is a child, let him come boldly'" (trans. H. Chadwick), 6.1 ("the most stupid and uneducated yokels"), 6.14, etc.; Just. *Apol.* 1.60: (some of us) "who do not even know the forms of letters, who are uneducated and barbarous in speech"; Just. *Apol.* 2.10 (Christians include "skilled and completely unskilled workmen"); Theoph. *Ad Autol.* 2.35 (even the Hebrew prophets were "unlettered, shepherds, unskilled workmen"); Athenag. *Leg.* 11: "simple folk, artisans and old women"; Tat. *Or.* 32 characteristically makes a boast of the charge. There were, of course, a number of arguments devised to counter the charge (see, e.g., the retorts in 16.5 f., 32.6, 36.4 ff., 37.3 ff., and Intro. p. 18 f.), but it is worth noting that it was not really until the fourth century that Christians attempted to meet the charge directly and emphasized the number, rank, and occupation of socially prominent Christians (so Euseb. *H.E.* 7.32.2 ff., 8.1.2 ff., but, there, they are noticeably few and often not strong candidates, and thus provide corroborative but indirect evidence for the charge). See further

the still invaluable collection of material in A. von Harnack, *Die Mission und Ausbreitung des Christentums in der ersten 3 Jahrhunderten* 2⁴ (Leipzig 1923) 559 ff; C. J. Cadoux, *The Early Church and the World* (repr. Edinburgh 1955) esp. 287 ff.

There has been unnecessary bother with the last phrase of the triplet, *expertes artium etiam sordidarum.* E. Heikel, "Adversaria in Minucii Felicis Octavium," *Eranos* 21 (1923) 17 f., felt constrained to add *etiam <nisi> sordidarum* because of 14.1 (a Christian *pistor!*) and Tert. *Apol.* 46.9 (*opifex christianus*), but, of course, such pedantic nicety and exactitude is quite uncalled for in the language of polemic.

[39] Christians could exploit this fact too: the multiplicity of philosophical sects is used as a defense against the multiplicity of Christian sects by Orig. *C.Cels.* 3.12. In his reply Octavius does not take up the cue for ridicule on this point, unlike, e.g., [Just.] *Cohort. passim.*

[40] This passage is discussed by A. J. Festugière, *L'idéal religieux des grecs et l'évangile* (Paris 1932) 34 f.; and for a very full survey of this widely diffused idea of the temerity and inadequacy of man *caelum petere,* L. Delatte, "Caelum ipsum petimus stultitia . . . (Contribution à l'étude de l'ode 1.3 d'Horace)," *Ant. Class.* 4 (1935) 309–36: cf. esp. Xen. *Mem.* 4.7.6 (and note the parallel with Xen. *Mem.* 4.3.13 f. at 32.4 f; see also n. 257). Cf. also Isa. 14.13 f. On the text here see B. Kytzler, "Notae Minucianae," *Traditio* 22 (1966) 419 f.

[41] The frequently quoted *Delphica inscriptio* (Tert. *De an.* 17.12) γνῶθι σεαυτόν (know thyself), inscribed on the pronaos of the temple of Apollo at Delphi (along with μηδὲν ἄγαν and other apothegms, Paus. 10.24.1). The identity of the sage was a matter for dispute even in antiquity; candidates canvassed ranged over a wide field: they included Thales, Bias, Chilon, Phemonoe, Phanothea—or Apollo himself. See Diog. Laer. 1.39; Cic. *Tusc. disp.* 5.70; Mayor's excellent n. on Juv. *Sat.* 11.27; and note the commentary on the inscription in Xen. *Mem.* 4.2.24 ff. For a discussion of the implications of this adage on Greek religious attitudes, see M. P. Nilsson, *Greek Piety* (Oxford 1948) 47 ff.

[42] There are echoes here of Hor. *Od.* 1.3.38: *caelum ipsum petimus stultitia,* and Verg. 6.135: *insano iuvat indulgere labori.* Note the famous lines of Aristoph. *Nub.* 218 ff. and Lucian's *Icaromenippus* on this theme, and cf. Orig. *C.Cels.* 6.19.

[43] *formidulosis opinionibus.* Note the discussion of *-osus* epithets

in Aul. Gellius, *Noctes Atticae* 9.12, with a particular observation in §7 on the uncommon passive usage of *formidulosus*—as employed here = "caused by fear"—*in eam partem quae minus usitata est*. He illustrates from Sall. *Cat.* 7.5. The usage (see TLL, *s.v.*) would be a nice touch appreciated by the literary-minded.

[44] *natura in se coeunte*. According to most commentators, this first hypothesis seems designed to explain the existence of the world without a pre-existent demiurge; there thus seems to be—if the biological metaphor of self-fertilization can be pressed—a brief glance at some theory of spontaneous generation of matter. Such a theory was maintained in Orphic legend where Phanes (the god of light) or Protogonus was said to have been born of an egg fashioned by Chronos in the Aither (W. K. C. Guthrie, *Orpheus and Greek Religion*[2] [London 1952] 80, 95 ff.). He was considered to be the supreme power, and maker of heaven and earth, having the powers of creation within himself because he was a bisexual god (. . . *quasi aut ipse secum coierit, aut sine coitu non potuerit procreare*, Lact. *Div. inst.* 4.8.4). Such embryological analogies are common: see H. C. Baldry, "Embryological Analogies in Pre-Socratic Cosmogony," CQ 26 (1936), 27 ff.

The theory gets no further amplification, and M.F. goes on to deal exclusively with the materialistic explanations of atomism (and possibly to be taken separately, the four-element theory), for which systems the eternal existence of matter was an axiomatic truth. Note that in the reply at 17.1 this theory, if it is a separate one, has been tacitly overlooked.

But is it not possible that in fact no embryological metaphor of self-fertilization is intended and that the passage should simply mean: "let us suppose that in the beginning nature was gathered together and the seeds of everything were in a packed mass"? For this use of *coeo* cf. Lucr. 1.838: *sanguinis inter se multis coeuntibus guttis;* Lact. *Div. inst.* 1.11.54: *ut elementa . . . tanto intervallo separata in unum coirent*. In that case an atomistic picture of the cosmos is unfolded in three (rhetorically favored number) steps in a simple and straightforward manner.

[45] It is not altogether clear whether Caecilius here intends us to envisage the composition of the world by the *fortuitis concursionibus* of the *semina* of the first "theory."

The most famous exponents of atomism were the shadowy Leucippus (of Elea, Abdera, Miletus? *fl.* fifth century B.C.?), see

PW 12.2 (1925) 2266-77 (J. Stenzel) and Pease on Cic. *De nat. deor.* 1.66; Democritus of Abdera (*fl.* c.460-c.370 B.C.), renowned for his encyclopediac learning and his contributions to mathematics and physics, who probably added details to the outlines established by Leucippus (see Pease on *De nat. deor.* 1.29); Epicurus of Samos (342-270 B.C.), who seems to have adapted the theory to his ethical principles and to his vision of *ataraxia* or imperturbability; and of course the Roman poet Lucretius (c. 99-55 B.C.), who wrote his didactic poem *De rerum natura* in six books. For these see C. Bailey, *The Greek Atomists and Epicurus* (Oxford 1928) esp. 123 ff. (on their theories of the creation of the world).

fortuitis concursionibus: a reference to the famous and much criticized swerve which was added to the Democritean system of downward-raining atoms by Epicurus in order to avoid a blind and mechanistic necessity (and hence fatalism). It was an unashamedly arbitrary movement which caused the original atoms to collide at random and thus made possible their subsequent combinations and permutations which shaped the present world. See Pease on *De nat. deor.* 1.54, 1.66 (*nulla cogente natura sed concursu quodam fortuito*), 1.69, 2.93 (*concursione fortuita*).

[46] Again this may not necessarily be intended as an alternative theory—the four-element theory (associated especially with the older Greek cosmogonists)—for the atomistic philosophers not unnaturally tended to incorporate some explanation of the four great masses of earth, air, fire, and water into their own atomistic system. (They are, in fact, frequently mentioned together as a commonplace list of primary *phenomena;* cf. Cic. *De nat. deor.* 1.19, 1.22.) The four-element theory is traceable to Empedocles (see Lucr. 1.712 ff.) and is found throughout antiquity (there was a later fifth element of obscure significance and controversial authorship). The theory came to be associated with the four humors of the body (and the four seasons of the year) and thus enjoyed a long and flourishing medieval history. See Pease on Cic. *De nat. deor.* 1.29.

On the separation and location of the *elementa* according to the nature (specific gravity) of their substance, see Pease's exhaustive note on Cic. *De nat. deor.* 1.103 (*nam locus . . . suus est cuique proprius, ut terra infimum teneat, hanc inundet aqua, superior <aeri>, aetheriis ignibus altissima ora reddatur*), and cf. *De nat. deor.* 2.44, 2.116 f., 3.34.

⁴⁷ A theory of conservation of matter and balance in the elements was common to the mechanistic theories of the universe. See Pease's very full note on Cic. *De nat. deor.* 1.50 (ἰσονομίαν); for criticism of the theory, Cic. *De nat. deor.* 1.109, also Bailey on Lucr. 2.294 ff.

⁴⁸ *nullo artifice, nec iudice, nec auctore.* The correctness of *iudice* has been frequently queried (e.g., by B. Axelson, "Textkritisches zu Florus, Minucius Felix und Arnobius," *Bull. Soc. roy. des lettres de Lund* 1 [1944–45] 29) but unnecessarily. The three questions posed above asked for the source of (1) *auctor*, (2) *machinator*, (3) *formido* and *superstitio*. *Artifex* answers to (2), *auctor* to (1), and *iudex* to (3), i.e., there is no need for fear of judgment, fire, and punishments (35), because all things revert back into their *elementa*. See further E. Löfstedt, "Annotationes criticae in M. Minucii Felicis Octavium," *Eranos* 6 (1905–6) 1 ff., at 6 ff.

⁴⁹ Caecilius now turns to the standard philosophical activity of explaining meteorological phenomena by his cosmological theory. For this common analysis of the elemental flux, cf. Lucr. 5.656 ff.; Cic. *De nat. deor.* 2.101, 3.31, 2.84 (with Pease's n.).

⁵⁰ Caecilius has provided no data to explain the blowing of winds, though they formed a standard part of the discussion (see Pease on Cic. *De nat. deor.* 2.101); *flare ventos* may in fact have been added to complete the artistic *tricola*.

⁵¹ A commonplace observation: see Otto *Sprichwörter*, *s.v.* fulmen (1), 148, for examples.

⁵² Temples—and the undeserving—struck by lightning were favorite weapons in the antiprovidence arsenal; e.g., Lucr. 2.1101 ff., 6.416 ff.; Cic. *De divin.* 1.19, 2.44 f. (with Pease's nn. *ad loca*).

⁵³ There is an unannounced and somewhat unexpected turn of thought. It has been argued that capricious *meterologica* bring equal disaster for all. It is now claimed that there is in fact positive mismanagement and misjustice in the world which reinforces the lesson that there cannot exist a beneficent providence. Caecilius gives the impression that he has been carried away from the strict rigor of his argument by his facility in *sententiae*, but there are close parallels for the same train of thought in Epic. *fr.* 370 (*ap.* Lact. *Div. inst.* 3.17.8: *in bellis meliores potius et vinci et perire*) and Philo *De prov.* 1.37 (*probi viri paupertate pressi, impiis ditescentibus et vitam feliciter traducentibus*), 1.59

(Aucher) quoted by R. Reitzenstein, "Zu Minucius Felix," *Hermes* 51 (1916) 609 ff., at 612 f. There is quite a philosophical pedigree behind the notion that the virtuous die in battle: see G. S. Kirk, "Heraclitus and Death in Battle," AJP 70 (1949) 384 ff., and cf. Clem. *Strom.* 4.4.14.4 f.

⁵⁴ A standard topic for philosophical and rhetorical debate (cf. Cic. *De nat. deor.* 2.73 ff.) and often the subject of specialized treatises: see Intro. p. 28 f. and nn. on 11.5 and on the reply in 36.1. This particular point, that the wicked prosper, is countered in 37.7 ff.

⁵⁵ A list of standard *exempla* follow; they all occur in Cic. *De nat. deor.* 3.80 ff., save Camillus, cf. Orig. *C.Cels.* 4.67, 5.20 (Phalaris and Socrates), Sen. *De prov.* 3.4 (Rutilius and Socrates), etc. Phalaris, tyrant of Sicilian Agrigentum c. 570–54 B.C., was proverbial for his cruelty, especially for the brazen bull in which his victims were roasted alive. For references see Pease on Cic. *De nat. deor.* 3.82; PW 19.2 (1938) 1649–52 (Th. Lenschau).

⁵⁶ Dionysius I, tyrant of Syracuse 405–367 B.C., was associated with all the standard vices of classical tyranny: despotism, cruelty, sacrilege, avarice; see Pease on Cic. *De nat. deor.* 3.81; PW 5.1 (1903) 882–904 (A. Dieterich).

⁵⁷ P. Rutilius Rufus (*cos.* 105 B.C.), Stoic of uncompromisingly high ideals, was condemned to exile in 92 B.C. by his enemies on a false charge of peculation and went into exile (spent at Mytilene and Smyrna); see Pease on Cic. *De nat. deor.* 3.80; PW 1 A1 (1914) 1269–80 (F. Münzer). He figures as a frequent example of the innocent martyr.

⁵⁸ M. Furius Camillus, a second Romulus, was famed for the epic siege of Veii. He came from his exile at Ardea to be the great savior of Rome during the Gallic invasions (see 6.2). The trial and exile have been the subject of much modern debate (and clearly distortion in the Roman historical traditions). See Livy 5.32.8 f. and Ogilvie's nn. *ad loc.*

⁵⁹ See Plato *Phaedo;* and for further discussion on Socrates, see n. 165 on 13.1.

⁶⁰ The example is cited by the Stoic Balbus in Cic. *De nat. deor.* 2.167 as an objection against a belief in providence: cf. Philo *De prov.* 1.47, 1.56 (Aucher). Balbus replies (somewhat inconsistently with his argument): *magna di curant, parva neglegunt.* See Pease's n. *ad loc. (segetibus aut vinetis)* and Cic. *De nat. deor.* 3.86 (Cotta's retort to Balbus). M.F. does not meet this example

specifically, but see 18.3 for a general reply. (Arnob. 1.3 ff. reports that pagans claimed Christians were the cause of these crop disasters.) Columel. 3.20.2 remarks resignedly, in the age-old manner of farmers: *semper est aliquid quod vineas offendat.*

⁶¹ For *varietas* as the proper associate of Fortuna, cf. Cic. *De nat. deor.* 2.43: *fortunam quae amica varietati constantiam respuit; De divin.* 2.109: *ipsa varietas, quae est propria fortunae;* and *inconstantia,* Cic. *De nat. deor.* 3.61: *fortuna . . . quam nemo ab inconstantia et temeritate seiunget; De divin.* 2.18: *nihil enim est tam contrarium rationi et constantiae quam fortuna.*

⁶² *aut fortuna certa aut incerta natura.* For justification of the MS reading, E. Heikel, "Adversaria in Minucii Felicis Octavium," *Eranos* 21 (1923) 17 ff., at 21 ff.; see also L. Valmaggi, "Minucio Felice 6,1 e 7,1," *Didaskaleion* 1 (1912) 201 ff., and K. Abel, "Minucius Felix: Octavius: Das Textproblem," *RhM* 110 (1967) 248 ff., at 256 f.

⁶³ *antistites veritatis. Antistes* is much employed by Tertullian, with various supplements, of Christians, e.g., Tert. *De fuga* 2.1: *veri Dei antistites, sectatores veritatis* (see J. H. Waszink, "Minuciana," *VC* 8 [1954] 129 f.). From the pagan's lips the phrase might, therefore, perhaps be taken as ironical (see, also, n. 119 on 9.4 below). The switch from the plural (*antistites*) to the singular (*imbutus es*) within the same period has caused unease, but there are frequent changes from second person singular to plural (and vice versa) throughout the dialogue, often without apparent significance—both could be used for generalizations; cf. 34.10: *tu . . . credis; ut creditis.* There is a closely parallel *variatio* in Arnobius, e.g., 4.31: *existimetis . . . putes* (within the same sentence), 2.53: *quid ad vos, ineptissime, fatue?;* and cf. Cic. *De nat. deor.* 2.73: *nam vobis, Vellei, minus notum est. . . .*

⁶⁴ It was a frequent, and for the classical world a serious, charge that adherence to Christianity entailed a divorce from ancestral traditions (cf. Arnob. 2.66 ff.; Celsus *ap.* Orig. *C.Cels.* 5.32 f.: "I will ask them where they have come from or who is the author of their traditional laws. Nobody, they will say" [5.33]). The sense of the value of tradition was so strong that it was possible to put forward the claims for inherited religion merely because it was traditional. The classical statement along these lines is that of Cotta in *De nat. deor.* 3.5 f.: *debeo . . . maioribus . . . nostris etiam nulla ratione reddita credere,* with Pease's nn. *ad loc.;* and cf. *De nat. deor.* 3.10: *mihi enim unum* (sc., *argumentum*) *sat*

erat, ita nobis maiores nostros tradidisse; cf. the views attributed
to Varro (*ap.* Aug. *De civ. Dei* 3.4, 6.1 ff.) and Scaevola (*ibid.*
4.27) and the opening words of the "palinode" attributed to the
erstwhile persecutor Galerius in Lact. *De mort. pers.* 34.1; and
see for further evidence of the theme in Cicero, J. C. Plumpe,
Wesen und Wirkung der AUCTORITAS MAIORUM *bei Cicero* (Lang-
endreer 1935) esp. 34 ff. Quispel in ed. *ad loc.* appositely quotes
Sext. Empiric. *Adv. math.* 9.49 on the characteristics of the
sceptic who is quite prepared to claim the existence of the gods
and to worship them according to traditional custom though he
is unhurried in his philosophical research to prove their existence.
Such, apparently, is the attitude Caecilius is meant, rather awkwardly, to adopt. The reply to this abandonment of tradition is
countered especially at 21.1, and see further Intro. p. 13 ff.

[65] The phrase *nosse familiarius* is carefully repeated from 5.5.
Caecilius' point is thereby suitably underscored and is therefore
ready to be exploited by Octavius in 24.10 (idol worship due to
unthinking adherence to parental "error") and 35.4 f. (the wickedness of ignorance of God). The pagans are, in fact, the veritable
victims of the *formidulosis opinionibus* (5.6) that Caecilius de-
precates. For an ironical *sententia* on this theme, see Tac. *Germ.*
34.3: *sanctius ac reverentius visum est de actis deorum credere
quam scire.*

[66] *meruerunt deos vel faciles habere vel reges.* For the alleged
illogicality of this view, see Tert. *Apol.* 25.10 f. (who were the
kings' gods?). Note the stress laid on the continuity of paganism
from the remotest antiquity. Behind the stress lay the commonly
entertained notion that the first men "were better than we and
lived nearer the gods" (Plat. *Phil.* 16C); they were the pious
recipients of a primitively given truth, the original laws (Joseph.
Contr. Ap. 2.152; Celsus *ap.* Orig. *C.Cels.* 5.24; Lucian *Fugitivi*,
on the theme "the Greek sophists corrupt the primitive truth").
A corollary was that when the primordial truth became gradually
corrupted in later ages, remote barbarian peoples preserved the
original piety relatively unspoilt (Diod. 3.2.2 ff.). The reply to
the present claim is at 25.1 ff.

[67] The question of *dei peculiares* (Arnob. 4.4) and the relativity
of religious cults and practices was a much discussed topic at this
period; cf. Celsus *ap.* Orig. *C.Cels.* 5.25 f., 5.34, and see in general
C. Andresen, *Logos und Nomos* (Berlin 1955) esp. 308 ff. Indeed
a catalogue of local gods and their habitations was a frequently

employed *topos*, e.g., Ovid *Fast.* 3.81 ff., Tert. *Apol.* 24.7 (*Ad nat.* 2.8.4 f.), Sidon. Apol. *Carm.* 9.168 ff., and cf. below chap. 25.8. Presumably such gods are introduced here to establish two points: (1) all men adhere to their traditional religions, and so ought the Christians—an argument from normal practice; (2) of these religions that of Rome is paramount in the practice of piety and consequently in richness of benefaction—an argument from results.

M.F. does not exploit the counterargument that if others can worship such *peculiares deos*, Christians can worship theirs—a point made by Athenag. *Leg.* 1, 12 ff., Just. *Apol.* 1.24, Tert. *Apol.* 24.9 f., Orig. *C.Cels.* 5.27. Perhaps such an argument was avoided as it would savor of a "third race" theory of Christianity (e.g., *Barn.* 5.7, *Ad Diog.* 1, Arist. *Apol.* 16 f. [Syr.], Arnob. 2.69) with its clear implication that Christians were a race apart from Roman society; that notion is alien to the whole tenor of the *Octavius*. Paradoxically, the lack of national identity of the Christians was a stumbling block in an increasingly nonnationalistic era.

[68] Ceres (Demeter) was the object of celebrated mysteries at Eleusis in Attica. For a succinct account of the rites, A. D. Nock, *Early Gentile Christianity and Its Hellenistic Background* (New York 1964) 110 ff. See also E. Rohde, *Psyche*[8] (London 1925) 217 ff.; G. E. Mylonas, *Eleusis and the Eleusinian Mysteries* (Princeton 1962). For a useful collection of *testimonia*, N. Turchi, *Fontes historiae mysteriorum aevi hellenisti* (Rome 1930) 43–99. See also 22.2 below.

[69] For Cybele, the chief divinity of the Phrygians, H. Graillot, *Le culte de Cybèle, mère des dieux, à Rome et dans l'empire* (Paris 1912); PW 11 (1922) 2250–98 (F. Schwenn). For *testimonia* see Turchi, *op. cit.* 217–50, and see n. 87 on 7.3 for the introduction of the cult into Rome.

[70] At Epidaurus was the most famous shrine of the god of healing Aesculapius; for an ancient description of the site, Paus. 2.27 ff. (*Test.* 739 in E. J. and L. E. Edelstein, *Asclepius* 1 [Baltimore 1945] and see vol. 2 for interpretation). For rhapsodic praise of the god, see Aelius Aristides' *Sacred Discourses*, and for a satirical picture of his patients' sufferings, Arnob. 1.49.

[71] Baal, the great Semite deity, was often identified or confused with Zeus or Saturn in the Western Mediterranean. The word means "Lord," and being an epithet rather than a proper name

is properly the title of a masculine deity. For an euhemeristic account of the god, Theoph. *Ad Autol.* 3.29.

[72] Astarte, Astoreth of the OT, was a Semite Aphrodite (or Venus) and served quite possibly as the prototype of her Greek counterpart. For *testimonia* see Turchi, *op. cit.* 253–76, and Pease on Cic. *De nat. deor.* 3.59 ("Astarte").

[73] Diana (Greek Artemis) was identified with a similar virgin goddess worshiped among the people of the Tauric Chersonese; see 30.4 for her savage propensities.

[74] For a discussion of Mercury, the characteristic Gallic deity and identified with local Gallic divinity, or divinities, see P. M. Duval, *Les dieux de la Gaule* (Paris 1952) 19 ff., 67 ff.; PW 15.1 (1931) *s.v.* Mercurius (keltisch und germanisch), 982–1016 (Heichelheim), and for the cult in cisalpine Gaul, G. B. Pascal, *The Cults of Cisalpine Gaul* (Brussels 1964) 165 ff., and cf. chap. 30.4.

[75] Rome, the confluence of all religions, is a commonly expressed idea; for a full statement, see Claudian 24.160 ff. (p. 226 Birt); cf. Arnob. 6.7: *civitas maxima et numinum cunctorum cultrix;* Aristid. *Or.* 26.105 (1.122 Keil); and for the pessimistic side of the same phenomenon, Tac. *Ann.* 15.14.4 (in connection with Christianity): *urbem etiam quo cuncta undique atrocia aut pudenda confluunt celebranturque;* Jerome *Comm. in Gal.* 2.4.3 (ML 26.397): *Romanique omnium superstitionum sentina.* See also on this theme A. D. Nock, "The Praises of Antioch," *Journ. Egypt. Arch.* 40 (1954) 76 ff., at 77 ff., R. Klein, *Tertullian und römisches Reich* (Heidelberg 1968) 41 ff.

[76] A reference to Rome's most romantic territorial aspirations, "beyond the paths of the sun" (as shown by Verg. *Aen.* 6.796 *extra anni solisque vias* and Servius *ad loc.*), alluding probably to Aethiopia and to the south, beyond the tropics, "the very bounds of Ocean" to the north and to "Thule" much elaborated in imperial rhetoric (see "Ancient Knowledge of the Gulf Stream," CP 62 [1967] 25 ff.).

[77] For the notion that there was a direct relation between Rome's welfare and the vestals' chastity, note Pliny *Ep.* 4.11.7: Cornelia exclaims repeatedly, as she is about to be buried alive on a charge of unchastity, *me Caesar incestam putat qua sacra faciente vicit, triumphavit!*; cf. Livy 22.57.2 on the disaster of Cannae and the violation by two vestals of their virginity, and Symm. *Relat.* 3.11 ff.: *saluti publicae dicata virginitas.* For the

idea of religious fortifications, cf. Cic. *De nat. deor.* 3.99: *diligentius urbem religione quam ipsis moenibus cingitis*, and see the reply to this passage in 25.10. On the vestals note T. C. Worsfold, *The History of the Vestal Virgins of Rome* (London 1932).

[78] After a series of general remarks on Roman piety there is here a rather ungainly switch to a particular example (a very standard one, of course) followed by a shift back to further generalizations on the same theme. The example referred to is the ignominious capture, sacking, and burning of Rome by the Gauls in 390 B.C. The Capitol itself (it was said) was saved by Manlius roused by the warning cackling of the sacred goose (or geese)—an event still celebrated under the Empire with ceremonial procession: see Plut. *De fort. Rom.* 12. 325D; Aelian *De nat. anim.* 12.33. Despite the crisis Fabius Dorsuo insisted on carrying out the sacred ceremonies, over on the Quirinal hill, traditional for the *gens Fabia*. In this account the individual is generalized (see Livy 5.46.1 ff. and Ogilvie's nn.). Caecilius, following the usual story, says *citra solum Capitolium*, but there is in fact a suggestion in some sources that the Capitol itself was captured, an indignity patriotically suppressed or overlooked by later tradition: see O. Skutsch, "The Fall of the Capitol," JRS 43 (1953) 77 f. (with "Postilla" in *Studia Enniana* [London 1968] 141 f.); M. J. McGann, "The Authenticity of Lucan fr. 12 (Morel)," CQ 7 (1957) 126 ff.; and my note "The Capitol in 390 B.C.," CR 81 (1967) 138.

[79] Possibly a passing reference to the consequences of the Roman ceremony of *evocatio*, an invitation to the god or gods of a beleaguered city to quit and join the ranks of the besiegers before the sacking of the city. For this ritual the *loci classici* are Macrob. *Sat.* 3.9.2 ff. and Livy 5.21 f., and for further evidence consult Ogilvie on Livy *loc. cit.* and the monograph of V. Basanoff, *Evocatio: Étude d'un rituel militaire romain* (Paris 1947). (In the matching section of Octavius' reply, 25.7, there is perhaps a reference to the same ceremony). There is hardly here a specific allusion to one particular event, however (so Beaujeu, rightly, contra Pellegrino), and indeed the passage is perhaps better interpreted as simply a general observation on the ubiquity and *perpetuus tenor* of Roman piety.

[80] It is clear that there were such *arae* so dedicated specifically in Athens (Acts 17.22; see N. B. Stonehouse, *Paul before the Areopagus and Other New Testament Stories* [London 1957]

10 ff.; Tert. *Ad nat.* 2.9.4; Paus. 1.1.4) and elsewhere in Greece (Paus. 5.14.8). From the testimony of Tert. *Adv. Marc.* 1.9.2, *Invenio plane ignotis deis aras prostitutas, sed Attica idolatria est. Item incertis deis, sed superstitio romana est,* one might suspect that Caecilius is being vaguely general about Roman *dei incerti;* for examples see ILS 4015 (Rome), 4016 (Lanuvium), 4017 (Tibur), 4018 (Rome). But contra Quispel and Beaujeu *ad loc.,* Jerome *Comm. in ep. ad Tit.* 1.12 (ML 26.607) does not provide secure evidence for the existence of the cult of unknown gods in Rome itself, for the inscription on his altar dedicated *deis ignotis et peregrinis* could just as readily be a translation from the Greek as is the *ignoto Deo* in the same sentence. See E. Norden, *Agnostos Theos* (Leipzig 1913) 117 ff.; PW Supp. 1 (1903) 28–30 (Jessen); and (on unnamed gods) H. J. Rose, "Divine Names in Classical Greece," HTR 51 (1958) 3 ff., and A. D. Nock, "The Exegesis of Timaeus 28C," VC 16 (1962) 79 ff. at 84 f.

Observe that Apul. *De deo Socr.* 15.153 connects *di incerti* and *manes* (which here follow): *cum vero incertum est quae cuique eorum sortitio evenerit . . . nomine Manem deum nuncupant.*

[81] For the Roman cult of the Manes, see B. Santoro, "Il concetto dei 'Dii Manes' nell'antichità Romana," *Riv. di filol.* 17 (1889) 1–62; F. Cumont, *Lux Perpetua* (Paris 1949) 58 ff., 392 ff.; PW 14.1 (1928) 1051–60 (Marbach). For actual altars dedicated to the shades, note for parallel Verg. *Aen.* 3.63: *stant manibus arae,* cf. 3.303, 6.177; Tac. *Ann.* 3.3: *aras dis manibus statuentes;* Stat. *Silv.* 5.3.47: *dare manibus aras.* The essentially pagan monogramme D.M. (*Dis Manibus*) in fact became so stereotyped on funerary inscriptions that it is found not infrequently on Christian memorials; see E. Diehl, *Inscriptiones Latinae christianae veteres* 3 (Berlin 1961) 425 ff. for references.

[82] For this much-vaunted and iterated claim that it was Rome's piety that made her great, note Polyb. 6.56.6 ff. (with the commentary of F. Walbank [Oxford 1957] 741 f.), and esp. Cic. *De nat. deor.* 2.8, 3.5 (with abundant parallels supplied by Pease's nn.); and see A. Momigliano, "Livio, Plutarcho e Giustino su virtù e fortuna dei Romani," *Athenaeum* n.s. 12 (1934) 45 ff. = *Terzo Contributo alla Storia degli Studi Classici e del Mondo Antico* 1 (Rome 1966) 499 ff. There can be little doubt that similar thinking (in a more hysterical and irrational form) con-

tributed, at least in part, to the persecutions of the mid-third
century and later; cf. Euseb. *H.E.* 7.11.7; *Mon. Asiae min. ant.*
8.424.8 ff. (Aphrodisias). It was a claim that Christians had to
meet; they did so with various devices at various periods. Melito,
in a time of prosperity, could claim the coincidence of imperial
peace and Christianity: Euseb. *H.E.* 4.26.7; so, too, Eusebius
under Constantine. In a time of disaster Cyprian, notoriously,
resorted to the increasing senility of the world (*Ad. Demet.*).
M.F. (and Tertullian) answered by denying Rome's piety (see
on chap. 25). But it was to be a long time before the pagan argument could eventually be stood on its head and the decay of
Rome be put down to the survival of pagan practices (Salvian,
Gelasius). For counterevidence of Christians blamed for the
decline of the Empire, see P. Courcelle, "Propos antichrétiens
rapportés par saint Augustin," *Rech. Aug.* 1 (1958) 149 ff., at
178 ff. It is noticeable that Christians and pagans both tend to
argue from common ground—piety was something visited with
material rewards (the attitude of Cotta in Cic. *De nat. deor.* 1.116
being typical: "I fail to see why the gods should be worshiped
if we neither have received nor hope to receive benefit from
them"). For further evidence on these attitudes, K. Büchner,
"Drei Beobachtungen zu Minucius Felix," *Hermes* 82 (1952)
231 ff., at 234 ff.; H. Chadwick, "Pope Damasus and the Peculiar
Claim of Rome to St. Peter and St. Paul," in *Neotestamentica et
patristica* (Freundesgabe für O. Cullmann; Leiden 1962) 313 ff.;
E. A. Isichei, *Political Thinking and Social Experience* (Christ-
church 1964).

[83] The fulsomeness of the phraseology underlines the claims
made for and reverence paid to antiquity. For such claims and
reverence, cf. Cic. *Verr.* 2.4.108: *tanta enim erat auctoritas et
vetustas illius religionis;* Ovid *Fast.* 4.203: *pro magna teste vetustas
creditur;* even in the panic-stricken extirpation of the Bacchanalian "conspiracy" (186 B.C.), the Romans were careful to make
exceptions: *extra quam si qua ibi vetusta ara aut signum con-
secratum esset,* Livy 39.18.7; Tertullian's complaints in *Apol.* 6.9
laudatis semper antiquitatem like those in the *Acta Perpet. et
Felic.* 1.1: the record will be useful one day *si in praesenti suo
tempore deputantur auctoritati, propter praesumptam venera-
tionem antiquitatis.* Similarly Cyp. *Ep.* 74.9.2: *consuetudo sine
veritate vetustas erroris est.*

[84] *ausim enim interim et ipse concedere et sic melius errare.* This

rather compressed clause seems designed to keep up the sceptic pose which Caecilius represents himself as adopting, *melius errare* being an ironical joke referring back to 3.1 (and see n. 7). In the preceding chapter Caecilius, in fact, gives the appearance of having established to his satisfaction the value of ancestral Roman piety. Now once more the empirical argument is to be repeated, this time not from Rome's greatness, but from the evidence of augury, prophecy, etc. (This appeal to cumulative experience as a proof of the genuineness of divination is a commonplace; cf. Cic. *De nat. deor.* 2.162 f., *De divin.* 1.16.) For the sceptic's characteristic interim concession to keep the discussion alive, cf. Cic. *De nat. deor.* 1.64, 1.67, 1.75, 1.103, 3.23. Here Caecilius' sceptical pose appears to be rather transparent, for Caecilius is not conceding a point with which he disagrees or has confuted, as is usually the case with the Academic's concession; he is in fact producing other proofs for the support of *religiones traditae*.

[85] For references on these rites, consult A. Bouché-Leclercq, *Histoire de la divination dans l'antiquité* 4 (Paris 1882); PW 7.2 (1912), 2431–68 (C. Thulin); Pease's n. *ad* Cic. *De divin.* 1.16; also R. Schilling, "À propos des "exta": L'Extispicine étrusque et la 'litatio' romaine," *Hommages à Albert Grenier* (Coll. Lat. 58; 1962) 1371 ff. For the reply (a fairly standard Christian one to the effect that it is doubtful if the prognostications are genuine —and if they are genuine, then they are due to certain demons) see chaps. 26 f.

[86] M.F. does not take up directly this cue of *ira* attributed to the gods. Had he chosen to reply, he would have had strong support in the *argumenta et exempla* (39) of pagan philosophy, for both the Stoics and especially the Epicureans denied that the gods were ever angry (e.g., Cic. *De nat. deor.* 3.91: *quem omnino irasci posset negatis-deus;* Sen. *Dial.* 4.27.1; Cic. *De off.* 3.102: *At hoc quidem commune est omnium philosophorum . . . numquam nec irasci deum nec nocere;* cf. *Ad Diog.* 8.8; 1 *Clem.* 19.3; Arist. *Apol.* 1, and, of course, frequently in Arnobius and Lactantius: see E. F. Micka, *The Problem of Divine Anger in Arnobius and Lactantius* [Washington, D.C. 1943] 17 ff. for previous ecclesiastical writers; also C. Tibiletti, *Q.S.F. Tertulliani De testimonio animae* [Turin 1959] 165 ff.).

[87] Late in the Second Punic War (204 B.C.) the black meteoric stone which came from Phrygia near Mount Ida and *quam Matrem deum esse incolae dicebant* (Livy 29.11.7) was brought

with great pomp into Rome after the Sibylline Books and the Delphic oracle had been consulted the previous year. The orgiastic worship of Cybele was thus officially introduced into Roman religion (see n. 69) and Rome was thereby encouraged to overcome her enemies. One of the incidents which roused this enthusiasm and encouragement was that associated with the matron Claudia Quinta (some later accounts, e.g., Aurel. Vict. *De viris illust.* 3.46, Aug. *De civ. Dei* 10.16, make her a vestal virgin). Her chastity was under suspicion, and when the vessel carrying the stone stuck in the Tiber and could not be moved, she was able to draw the vessel along singlehanded (by her girdle, *zona*, in some accounts) as proof of her virtue. The *locus classicus* for the story is Ovid *Fast.* 4.247 ff., esp. 305 ff., where see Frazer's notes; cf. Livy 29.10.4 ff., 14.5 ff., Arnob. 7.49. See also, on the introduction of the cult, H. Graillot, *Le culte de Cybèle, mère des dieux, à Rome et dans l'empire* (Paris 1912) esp. 25 ff. For illustration of a Cybele procession (the meteoric stone drawn by elephants, etc.), see J. Quasten, *Musik und Gesang in den Kulten der heidnischen Antike u. christl. Frühzeit* (Münster 1930) *Taf.* 21.1.

[88] There were two especially famous instances in Roman history of this function of the heavenly twins Castor and Pollux—that of assisting at and later announcing Roman victories (Cic. *Tusc.* 1.28): (1) the Battle of Lake Regillus c. 499 B.C. (over Latin forces allied with Tarquin the Proud), see Livy 2.19.1 ff. and Ogilvie's notes *ad loc.*; and (2) the victory of L. Aemilius Paulus over Perseus, king of Macedon, at Pydna in 168 B.C. Both examples are given in Cic. *De nat. deor.* 2.6, where see Pease's excellent nn. for other references, parallels, and discussion.

There are some grounds for suspecting confusion in Caecilius' account here. He ought to be exemplifying the introduction of a rite to repay divine *indulgentia*, and that introduction, according to Livy, occurred not after the Battle of Pydna but after the Battle at Regillus (Livy 2.20.12 f.—though in fact the cult was clearly celebrated *intra pomerium* even before that date: see R. Schilling, "Les *Castores* romains à la lumière des traditions indo-européennes," *Hommages à G. Dumézil* [Brussels 1960] 177 ff., at 182). And there have been discovered fragments of statues, depicting the Dioscuri and their horses, in the *Lacus Juturnae* itself. This sounds like the group that Caecilius has in mind, but they seem to be of Greek workmanship of the early 5th century B.C.

(see A. Alföldi, *Early Rome and the Latins* [Ann Arbor 1965] 268 ff.). But Caecilius might possibly be accurate: was the statuary part of the notorious loot brought back from Greece by Aemilius Paulus himself? (For his penchant for Greek treasures, see Plut. *Aemil. Paul.* 28 ff., esp. 32: 250 carts were required to carry the captured statues and paintings alone.) See further my note "The Dioscuri of the *Lacus Juturnae*," *Latomus* 27 (1968) 147 f.

The Dioscuri appeared (the reading *sicut <se> ostenderant* for their epiphany is surely correct) washing and watering their white horses at the basin of the *Fons Juturnae* in the Forum immediately S.E. of the temple of Castor. (The hasty, and lengthy, journey from Pydna to Rome explains their being "steaming and foaming.") There is a quadrilateral base in the centre of the basin which apparently supported the statues; hence *in lacu* (against many editors) is to be taken quite literally. (The doubts of E. Nash, "Suggerementi intorno ad alcuni problemi topografici del Foro e del Palatino," *Arch. Class.* 11 [1959] 227 ff., are not decisive.) See Platner and Ashby, *A Topographical Dictionary of Ancient Rome* (Oxford 1929) *s.v.* Lacus Juturnae; E. Nash, *Pictorial Dictionary of Ancient Rome* 2 (London 1962) 9 ff.; and for commemoration on coinage, E. A. Sydenham, *The Coinage of the Roman Republic* (rev. ed. London 1952) no. 612; and on a new silver denarius (c. 211 B.C.), R. A. G. Carson, "Roman History and Roman Coinage," *Didaskalos* 1.3 (1965) 153 ff., at 156 f. and fig. 4.

The twin *Castores* were children of Leda (and Tyndareus, or in variant accounts of Zeus [Cic. *De nat. deor.* 3.11, 3.53]). Castor, the horse-tamer, was mortal, Pollux, the boxer, was immortal (though the immortality is reversed in some accounts); when Castor was slain, Pollux shared life with him on alternate days (referred to in 22.7). Their cult (of controversial origins) seems to have coincided in Rome with the emergence of the overwhelming military and political importance of the cavalry. For the cult, Roscher 1.1154–77 (A. Furtwängler). Such twin military protectors have many counterparts in Christian hagiography and legend; see J. R. Harris, *The Dioscuri in the Christian Legends* (Cambridge 1903), and H. Delehaye, "Castor et Pollux dans les légendes hagiographiques," *AnalBoll* 23 (1904) 427 ff. For a rich catalogue of victories similarly reported on the same day, Pease on Cic. *De nat. deor.* 2.6.

[89] This event is related, with many variants, in many sources

(see Pease on Cic. *De divin.* 1.55). Most agree that the *rusticus*, here and in Cicero *loc cit.* anonymous, was Titus Latinius and that the date was c. 491 B.C. (Livy 2.36; but Macrobius *Sat.* 1.11.2 ff. has, circumstantially, 279 B.C.). The games—again there are variants—were, according to the best sources, the *ludi romani* celebrated in the middle fortnight of September; the offense was the ill-omened punishment (variations on the details) of a slave in the circus on the morning of the *ludi*. Roman religion demanded *instauratio* for a religious ceremony interrupted or vitiated by some mistake or pollution. It had to be repeated from the beginning, possibly with added ritual for appeasement (cf. Verg. *Aen.* 5.94 ff.).

For general discussion on the events and details, see Ogilvie's commentary on Livy 2.36.

⁹⁰ The famous *devotiones* (PW 5.1 (1903) 277–80 [Wissowa]) of the Decian family. The formula and regulations for *devotio* are given in Livy 8.9.4 ff.; cf. Macrob. *Sat.* 3.9.9 f.: the general offers his life by plunging into the enemy's ranks in return for victory; if he fails to die, he is to be sacrificed. The first (P. Decius Mus) so died, according to the received account, at Veseris *bello latino* in 340 B.C. (Livy 8.9 ff.); the second, his son, in the Samnite wars, at Sentinum in 295 B.C. (Livy 10.28.12 ff.; cf. E. T. Salmon, *Samnium and the Samnites* [Cambridge 1967] 208 n. 1, 267). There is a third, son of the second, to whom, in some traditions, a *devotio* is attributed at Ausculum (279 B.C.), e.g., Cic. *Tusc.* 1.89, *De fin.* 2.61. But Cassius Dio 10.43 and Zonaras 8.5 report that it was intended but not carried out, an embarrassing episode which appears to have been later suppressed or emended (so O. Skutsch, "The Fall of the Capitol," JRS 43 [1953] 77 f., at 78; *idem*, "Enniana iii," CQ n.s. 10 [1960] 188 ff., at 193 ff.). F. Altheim, "Der Opfertod der Decier," FF 17 (1941) 112 ff., points out that only these three Decii are *mures*, the *mus* being a prophetic beast (cf. Apollo *Smintheus*) closely associated with death. But, contra Altheim, the name and tradition do not establish the authenticity of the third episode. For further references and discussion, see Pease on Cic. *De divin.* 1.51, *De nat. deor.* 2.10, 3.15; S. Stübler, *Die Religiosität des Livius* (Amsterdam 1964) 181 ff. Orig. *C.Cels.* 1.31 compares such *devotiones* with the self-sacrifice of Christ.

⁹¹ *Curtius qui equitis sui vel mole vel honore hiatum profundae voraginis coequavit.* This contains two rather difficult expressions:

eques seems to be best interpreted as = "horse and rider" (so R. Reitzenstein, "Philologische Kleinigkeiten," *Hermes* 51 [1916] 609 ff., at 618 ff., followed by J. H. Waszink, "Minuciana," VC 8 [1954] 129 ff., at 130), for Curtius sacrificed himself as well as his horse to bridge the gulf. The best supporting evidence for this (consciously archaic) usage seems to be the statement in Macrob. *Sat.* 6.9.9: *omnes enim antiqui scriptores ut hominem equo insidentem, ita et equum, cum portaret hominem, equitem vocaverunt* (cf. Aul. Gellius, *Noctes Atticae* 18.5.8, with the same observation), though an incontrovertible parallel is in fact rather hard to discover.

    vel mole vel honore. One ought naturally to take *equitis sui* with *honore* as well as *mole*. *Honor* would then simply be used in the sense of "sacrifice" (so G. Thörnell in *Strena philologica Upsaliensis* [Festscrift per Persson; Uppsala 1922] 383 f.), or even (but hardly possible) "trappings" (Curtius was *equo . . . quam poterat maxime exornato insidentem armatum*, Livy 7.6.5). But some commentators have attempted to see here an obscure and compressed allusion to a detail of the historical event. In 362 B.C. there opened up in the middle of the Forum a vast chasm which men were unable to fill; to satisfy the report of the *vates* on this portent, Marcus Curtius charged on horseback in full armor into the gap. Valerius Maximus 5.6.2 continues: *super quem* (sc., *profundum*) *universi cives honoris gratia certatim fruges iniecerunt, continuoque terra pristinum habitum recuperavit* (cf. Livy 7.6.5: *donaque ac fruges super eum a multitudine virorum ac mulierum congestas*). *Honor*, therefore, (the commentators argue) refers to these, to the *dona ac fruges*—a strained and unnecessary explanation. For further discussion on the passage, see K. Abel, "Minucius Felix: Octavius: Das Textproblem," RhM 110 (1967) 248 ff., at 258 ff. This was one of the reported origins of the *Lacus Curtius* in the centre of the Forum, which vied with the *Lacus Juturnae* in legendary fame. For a discussion of the archeological site and the variant legends, see Platner-Ashby *s.v.* Lacus Curtius (310 f.); Ogilvie's nn. on Livy 1.12 (75 ff.); D. R. Dudley, *Urbs Roma* (Aberdeen 1967) 95 ff.

    [92] *Allia nomen infaustum*. Cf. Verg. *Aen.* 7.717: *infaustum. . . Allia nomen* (on the characteristically altered word-order to avoid an hexameter ending, unsuitable for the forensic style, see H. Hagendahl, "Citation in Post-Classical Latin Prose," *Eranos* 45 [1947] 114 ff., at 124). The historical reference is to the overwhelmingly

disastrous battle of the Allia with the Gauls in 390 B.C. on July
18, though the casualty figures reported are mere conjecture
(70,000 in Diodorus, 40,000 in Plutarch). The day found an
unforgettable place in the Roman calendar as a *dies ater* (Aul.
Gellius, *Noctes Atticae* 5.17.2; Macrob. *Sat.* 1.16.23), on which
day neither law courts might be held nor assemblies convened
(for the effect on military life, A. D. Nock, "The Roman army
and the Religious Year," HTR 45 [1952] 187 ff., at 190 ff.). This
can be cited as an example of *contempta auspicia* not only because
the *tribuni militum* drew up for battle *nec auspicato nec litato*
(Livy 5.38.1) but also because the commander, Q. Sulpicius, is
said *rem divinam dimicandi gratia postridie Idus fecisse*, i.e., on
an ill-omened day (Aul. Gellius, *Noctes Atticae* 5.17.2; and cf.
Macrob. *loc. cit.*, Livy 6.1.12). For further discussion and evidence
on the event, see Ogilvie's nn. on Livy 5.37 f.

[93] This example and the following ones are given in Cic. *De
divin.* 1.29, 2.20 ff. (cf. *De nat. deor.* 2.7): they were part of a
stock catalogue of instances of lack of piety towards the gods.
Caecilius is here a little inaccurate in his compressed illustration.
Only L. Iunius Pullus lost his forces by shipwreck (Polyb. 1.54.1
ff.); his colleague P. Claudius Pulcher lost his in a naval engagement at Drepanum in 249 B.C. off the Sicilian coast (Polyb. 1.49.3
ff.). For the story of his having the sacred chickens, that refused
to eat, cast into the sea, see Cic. *De nat. deor.* 2.7 and Pease's nn.
ad loc.

[94] The disastrous battle at Trasimene took place in 217 B.C.
C. Flaminius, along with some 15,000 of his men, was slain. See
Livy's account of the battle in 22.3 ff. and Cic. *De divin.* 1.77,
with Pease's nn., for Flaminius' disregard of unfavorable omens
before the battle.

[95] Crassus was defeated by the Parthians at Carrhae in 53 B.C.,
with the notorious loss of three military standards. His expedition
had been visited both with unfavorable omens (*dirae*) and with
positive curses (*imprecationes* voiced by C. Ateius) even before
it left the *pomerium* of Rome (engineered by his political enemies). Caecilius seems here to combine the two methods of religious obstruction (*dirarum imprecationes*). For the evidence see
Pease at Cic. *De divin.* 1.29 with a good discussion, and A. D.
Simpson, "The Departure of Crassus for Parthia," TAPA 69
(1938) 532 ff.

Many have attempted to find here an allusion to events contemporary with M.F. (for a recent endeavor, see S. Rossi, "L' 'Octavius' fu scritto prima del 161," GIF 12 [1959] 289 ff., at 292 ff.) but without carrying any conviction (for a riposte to S. Rossi, see A. della Casa, "Le due date dell' 'Octavius,' " *Maia* 14 [1962] 26 ff., at 30 f.; and for a convincing defense of *repetamus*, F. di Capua, "Minucio Felice, Octavius 7.4," *Didaskaleion* 2 [1913] 175 ff.; B. Axelson, *Das Prioritätsproblem Tertullian-Minucius Felix* [Lund, 1941] 22). The effect of the present subjunctive is vivid and pictorial: "that we should be seekers of standards from Parthia"; cf. Verg. *Aen.* 2.663 with the note of R. G. Austin *ad loc.* (in ed., Oxford 1964).

The allusion is in fact to the long-drawn-out diplomatic negotiations with Parthia for the recovery of the lost standards, brought to a successful and much-vaunted conclusion in 20 B.C. (*Res. gestae* 29.2 with the notes of J. Gagé *ad loc.* [2nd ed. Paris 1950]).

[96] *praedicta etiam de oraculis fata transilio.* How far this is merely the (much-used) rhetorical trick of mentioning a topic by saying you do not intend to discuss it (a figure called *occultatio*) can be divined by Octavius' reply in 26.5 ff. There it is assumed *oracula* have been produced as an argument. To include "antique" as well as modern examples was standard rhetorical practice: cf. the model epistle 1 *Clem.* 4.6 ff; Cic. *De nat. deor.* 3.80: *sed haec vetera et alia permulta; propriora videamus;* 3.74: *superiora . . . posteriora;* 2.7, where see Pease's n. (*domesticis . . . exemplis*); Tac. *Dial.* 8.1, 12.4.

[97] *muneribus.* Perhaps the sense here should be "monumental (public) edifices" as in Cic. *De nat. deor.* 2.90: *tamquam architectum tanti operis tantique muneris;* cf. Cic. *Tusc.* 1.70; Vell. Pater. 2.48.2, 2.130.1.

[98] Note the effective liturgical formula to convey the *vates'* fervor. For parallel Christian prayer formulae, cf. Melito *Hom.* 82 f. (Bonner); *Apost. cons.* 8.12.6 ff.; Cyp. *Ep.* 31.1.2; Athenag. *Leg.* 13; 1 *Clem.* 59.4: "deliver those of us who are in stress, raise up the fallen, show thy face to those in need, heal the infirm, bring back the erring of thy people, feed the hungry, ransom our prisoners, set the infirm upon their feet, comfort the fainthearted." And see generally A. Hamman, *Early Christian Prayers* (London 1961).

[99] Proof from the occurrence of dreams comes, as here expressed, somewhat awkwardly affixed and, in appearance, by way

of an offhand appendage, but Cic. *De nat. deor.* 2.163 shows that
the inclusion of such an argument was standard in this sort of
discussion (*multa cernunt hauruspices, multa augures provident,
multa oraclis declarantur, multa vaticinationibus, multa somniis
. . .*). Cf. Cic. *De divin.* 1.39 ff., 1.60 ff. Dreams (in which
visions of gods appeared) were, of course, a famous proof for
the existence of the gods elaborated by Epicurus (see A. J.
Festugière, *Épicure et ses dieux* [Paris 1946] 86 ff.; C. Bailey,
The Greek Atomists and Epicurus [Oxford 1928] 438–81 and
his nn. on Lucr. 5.1161 ff.; see also Pease's nn. on Cic. *De nat.
deor.* 1.46). It is interesting that in antiquity generally, men
(Christian and pagan alike) tended to regard dreams not as
mere subjective phenomena but as states in which they experienced directly the influence of spiritual forces (thus, e.g., *in-
cubatio* rites). Hence Tertullian could remark (*De an.* 47.2) that
the majority of men *ex visionibus deum discunt;* cf. Orig. *C.Cels.*
1.48, 1.66, etc. Dreams were, therefore, the one form of pagan
divination that Christianity countenanced (F. Cumont, *Lux perpetua* [Paris 1949] 92) from New Testament times (e.g., Acts
16.9 f.). Even such a robustly practical man as Cyprian seems to
have acted constantly at the monition of dreams. So, too, in 27.4,
M.F. clearly believes dreams were *genuine* occurrences. For
further literature see Waszink's nn. on Tert. *De an.* 500 ff.; on
Constantine and the fourth century, A. Alföldi, *The Conversion
of Constantine and Pagan Rome* (Oxford 1948) 125 f.; on the
New Testament, A. Wikenhauser, "Die Traumgeschichte des
neuen Testaments in religiongeschichtlicher Sicht," *Pisciculi*
(Festschrift F. J. Dölger; Münster 1939) 320 ff.; and generally,
E. R. Dodds, *The Greeks and the Irrational* (Berkeley 1964) 102
ff. Note also that (M.F.'s contemporary?) Cassius Dio wrote on
the dreams and portents of Septimius Severus, and was upheld by
the support of dreams in the composition of his history (F.
Millar, *A Study of Cassius Dio* [Oxford 1964] 179 f.).

[100] A blatant argument from *consensus omnium* (used by
Octavius himself in 18.11, where see n. 228) which was especially
common in Stoic argumentation to prove the existence of the
gods (see M. Pohlenz, *Die Stoa* 1.56 ff., 1.94, and 2.88; and for
the allied Stoic notion of common ideas implanted in man's soul,
see n. 190 on 16.5). It is found frequently in Cicero, generally
(see Pease's nn. on Cic. *De nat. deor.* 2.12), and this particular
argument is formulated in *De nat. deor.* 1.44, 2.5 ff. The argument

could also be used by a *scepticus* (Sext. Emp. *Adv. math.* 9.33)
to establish the existence of the gods. It was, of course, an easily
vulnerable line of argument (for criticism, Pease's n. on *De nat.
deor.* 1.43). See also A. Michel, "Éclectisme philosophique et
lieux communs: A propos de la 'diatribe romaine,' " in *Hommages
à Jean Bayet* (Brussels 1964) 485 ff.

[101] Theodorus of Cyrene and Diagoras of Melos are among
the standard examples of "atheists" in antiquity. A third, Protagoras of Abdera, is cited below (the triad occurs in Cic. *De nat.
deor.* 1.2, where see Pease's n. for other candidates in the canon
of *atheoi*). Theodorus of Cyrene (*fl.* 310 B.C.), the teacher of
Euhemerus (another "atheist," see n. 274 on 21.1), was forced to
leave Athens for his notions on relative morality (Diog. Laert.
2.102 f.); his work *On the Gods* was said to have strongly influenced Epicurus (*ibid.* 2.97), himself another "atheist." See A.
B. Drachmann, *Atheism in Pagan Antiquity* (London 1922) 75 f.

Diagoras of Melos (*fl.* 420 B.C.) was even more notorious and
proverbial for his views, being frequently cited by Christians as
well as pagans. He is said to have lost his faith in the gods by
their failure to punish an act of perjury and even to have boiled
turnips using a wooden statue of Heracles. There is variation in
the evidence but he seems to have died in flight from Athens with
a price on his head (for references and a recent discussion, see L.
Woodbury, "The Date and Atheism of Diagoras of Melos,"
Phoenix 19 [1965] 178–211; also Drachmann, *op. cit.*, 31 ff.).

Christians were frequently the butt of a charge of "atheism":
e.g., Lucian *Alex.* 38; Just. *Apol.* 1.6, 1.13; Tert. *Apol.* 10.1 ff.;
Arnob. 1.29, 3.28, 5.30; Athenag. *Leg.* 4; *Mart. Polycarp.* 3.2, 9.2;
and see generally A. von Harnack, "Der Verwurf des Atheismus
in den drei ersten Jahrhunderten," TU 28 (N.F. 13.4; 1905);
RAC 1 (1950) *s.v.* Atheismus, 866–70 (W. Nestle). It is worth
noting that Caecilius does not lay any *formal* general charge
against the Christians partly because, characteristically of the
pragmatic Romans, there was no specific Roman statute against
believing the gods to be nonexistent; hence Tert. *Apol.* 46.4 ff.,
Orig. *C.Cels.* 8.38 can plead for treatment equal to that of other
philosophical "atheists." There were only legal regulations against
specific rites, acts of impiety, or sacrilege. Cicero might urge
(*De leg.* 2.19) *Separatim nemo habessit deos neve advenas nisi
publice adscitos; privatim colunto, quos rite a patribus cultos
acceperint;* but there was only public *social* pressure to enforce

this view. Caecilius, therefore, resorts to *Greek* examples of such impiety (legally penalized) and to the vaguely allied charges of illegal conspiracy, unnatural vice, sacrilegious rites, etc. In his reply Octavius does not face directly this charge of "atheism," partly because it had (deliberately?) not been posed openly, but partly, too, because if it meant "not worshiping the national gods" it was formally irrefutable.

[102] *timorem omnem quo humanitas regitur.* For the notion of fear of divine power acting as a restraint on man, Cic. *De nat. deor.* 1.77 (with Pease's ample note); and for the frequently allied view of the social and political value of religion destroyed by atheism, see *ibid.* 1.4, 1.118 (again with Pease's notes). Cf. Herm. *Mand.* 1.2; Athenag. *Leg.* 1.

[103] Protagoras of Abdera, agnostic rather than atheist, was a famous sophist of the fifth century B.C. (c. 485–c. 415) noted for his dictum that "man is the measure of all things." The opening words of his work *On the Gods* are often quoted) cf. Cic. *De nat. deor.* 1.63: *de divis neque ut sint neque ut non sint habeo dicere*) but were perhaps misinterpreted for "atheism" even in antiquity (see Pease on Cic. *De nat. deor.* 1.2). The story of this expulsion and the burning of his books, much repeated in non-contemporary sources, may well be an apocryphal invention (Pease on Cic. *De nat. deor.* 1.63, where the story is given, and C. A. Forbes, "Books for the Burning," TAPA 67 [1936] 114 ff., at 117 ff.) See further Drachmann, *op. cit.* 39 ff.; and for condemnation of even academic atheistic discussion *tout court*, cf. Cic. *De nat. deor.* 2.168: *mala enim et impia consuetudo est contra deos disputandi sive ex animo id fit sive simulate.*

[104] *homines . . . deploratae, inlicitae ac desperatae factionis.* Common epithets of abuse, the most important being *inlicitae* (the charge of disloyalty and illegality lay at the core of Celsus' attack, and Origen significantly made his first rejoinder to that charge, *C.Cels.* 1.1.). There has long been a much-debated controversy on the precise legal ground or grounds on which Christians were prosecuted. A frequent view, especially supported by the French Church historians, has been that the Christians were in fact proscribed as a sect (just when is a further matter for controversy) and, therefore, that they were formally illegal. It is true that the Apologists are at great pains to urge that their *factio* should be dissociated from other illegal groups (cf. Tert. *Apol.* 4.4 ff., 38 f., with the punch line 39.21 *non est factio*

dicenda sed curia), and there is plenty of evidence, esp. from *Acta martyrum*, to suggest that men were eventually tried simply qua Christians (cf. 28.4). But both these facts could still be attributed to a *de facto* prohibition of the sect based on the precedents established by Nero, Pliny, etc.; for examples might be invoked from time to time by the Church's enemies without any precise details of the *crimina cohaerentia nomini* which had caused them to be set in the first place under special or individual circumstances. A sort of "illegality" could thus be acquired by the accumulation of examples of condemned Christians, but there may well have been no formal outlawing of the sect as such until the Decian persecution. (The earlier general edicts attributed to Septimius Severus and Maximinus Thrax appear to be apocryphal; see K. H. Schwarte, "Das angebliche Christengesetz des Septimius Severus," *Hist.* 12 [1963] 185 ff., and my article "Some Victims of the Persecution of Maximinus Thrax," *Hist.* 15 [1966] 445 ff.) The best of much recent literature on the subject are A. N. Sherwin-White, "The Early Persecutions and Roman Law Again," JTS n.s. 3 (1952) 199 ff.; *idem*, "Why Were the Early Christians Persecuted?" *Past and Present* 27 (1964) 23 ff.; G. E. de Ste Croix, "Why Were the Early Christians Persecuted?" *Past and Present* 26 (1963) 6 ff., 27 (1964) 28 ff.; T. D. Barnes, "Legislation against the Christians," JRS 58 (1968) 32 ff.; for the Apologists, F. C. Grant, "Religio licita," *Studia patr.* 4 (1961) = TU 79, 84 ff.; and for an admirably succinct and judicious analysis, W. H. C. Frend, *Martyrdom and Persecution in the Early Church* (Oxford 1965) 165 f. See also n. 459 on 28.4 and Intro. p. 42 f. M. Sordi, "L'Apologia del martire romano Apollonio come fonte dell'Apologeticum di Tertulliano e i rapporti fra Tertulliano e Minucio," *Riv. di stor. chiesa in Italia* 18 (1964) 169 ff., at 184 f., sees in the omission of the illegality charge in the *Octavius* proof of the priority of M.F. (unconvincing).

[105] *qui de ultima faece collectis imperitioribus et mulieribus credulis sexus sui facilitate labentibus.* On this and the following chaps. consult DACL 1.1 (1924) *s.v. Accusations contre les chrétiens* 265–307 (H. Leclercq). On the *imperitiores* see n. 22 on 3.1. For the constant charge of the social and cultural inferiority of the Christian following, see Intro. p. 18 ff. and n. 38 above on 5.4. On the theme of feminine instability and weakness, cf. Livy 34.2.11, Arnob. 6.10, and, generally, Otto *Sprichwörter, s.v.* mulier (2) 231. It was an established charge to accuse proselytism among

the gullible (women) and stupid (children, old women, rustics); cf. Tat. *Or.* 33, Orig. *C.Cels.* 6.24, etc. And on the noticeable predominance of women in the Christian following at this period, see Intro. 38 f.; and see further J.-M. Demarolle, "Les femmes chrétiennes vues par Porphyre," JAC 13 (1970) 42 ff. This sort of abuse was, indeed, a traditional element in polemic against rival philosophical schools: note the attacks on Epicurus and his followers as uncouth, ill-educated, and uncultivated in Cic. *De nat. deor.* 1.58, 1.72, 1.85, 1.89, and esp. 2.74: *sine arte, sine litteris, insultantem in omnes, sine acumine ullo, sine auctoritate, sine lepore.*

[106] *plebem profanae coniurationis instituunt.* This is almost standard jargon to describe contemptuously any clandestine religious sect. The paradigmatic case in Roman history was that of the Bacchanalian *coniuratio* (186 B.C.), for which Livy 39.8–19 and CIL I²581 are our primary sources (and for an analysis see A. H. McDonald, "Rome and the Italian Confederation (200–186 B.C.)," JRS 34 [1944] 11 ff., at 26 ff.; H. M. Last, "The Study of the 'Persecutions,' " JRS 27 [1937] 80 ff., at 84 ff.). There the offenders are consistently described as constituting *coniurationes coetusque nocturi,* 39.14.4 (cf. 18.3 *nefanda coniuratio,* 15.10, 15.12, 16.3, 16.5, 16.10, 17.6, etc.). Similarly in CIL I² 581.14f.: *neve posthac sed coniora[se nev]e comvovise neve conspondise/ neve compromesise velet.* This episode strongly colored the Roman attitude towards such apparently subversive religious groups outside official religion (*profanae*). (This consideration weakens the case of R. M. Grant, "Pliny and the Christians," HTR 41 [1948] 273 ff., for a *direct* influence of Livy on Pliny in his letter on the Christians. Pliny's was a common Roman attitude.) Cf. Cyprian accused of being a member of a *nefaria coniuratio* (*Act. proc. Cyp.* 4).

It is a reasonable conjecture that Fronto would have used similar language (see n. 123 on 9.6 below), though there can be no doubt that being *Catonis simia,* he would have consulted, in strong preference to Livy's account, Cato's *De coniuratione* on the subject (if this, as seems probable, was concerned with the Bacchanalian *coniuratio:* see *fr.* 68 Malcovati). This point somewhat impairs the conjecture of P. Frassinetti, "L'Orazione di Frontone contro i cristiani," GIF 3 (1949) 238 ff., that in Livy's account we can trace Fronto's model; and furthermore the Livian account appears to be closer to the Hellenistic style of the senatorial historians than to the speeches of Cato (so McDonald, *art. cit.* 26 n. 118), so it is even more unlikely that we should find very strong remains of Cato's (and thus Fronto's) language via Livy.

[107] *nocturnis congregationibus et ieiuniis sollemnibus et inhumanis cibis.* *Nocturnae congregationes* were always suspect for Roman authorities (forbidden in the City by the Twelve Tables, *tab.* viii *leg.* 26: *ne quis in urbe coetus nocturnos agitaret*)—and particularly when connected with ritualism (see Livy on the Bacchanalian conspiracy *passim*, 39.8–19). There are a number of occasions which might be referred to here: the early-morning service (*ante lucem*) on the Lord's day, *stato die* (Pliny *Ep.* 10.96.7, and see the commentary of A. N. Sherwin-White, *The Letters of Pliny* [Oxford 1962, 702 ff.]), immediately followed by the agape in Just. *Apol.* 1.67?; the frequent (*Did.* 16.2; Ign. *Ephes.* 13.1) or daily meetings (*Barn.* 19.10) urged on Christians, which in Cyprian's day were early-morning Eucharistic services (*Ep.* 63.16; *De orat. domin.* 18) or the *nocturnae convocationes* (Tert. *Ad uxor.* 2.4.2) concerned with vigils, station days, and preparatory ceremonials for the Eucharist. The agape which lasted into evening might also be included (see n. 122 below).

ieiuniis sollemnibus. Added somewhat surprisingly as a charge, for not only did many pagans believe in and advocate such ascetic practices, but fasting was also associated with many pagan rites (e.g., those of Cybele). In fact, Galen could commend Christians because "in self-discipline and self-control in matters of food and drink . . . [they] have attained a pitch not inferior to that of genuine philosophers" (Walzer, *Galen on Jews and Christians* 15). Octavius does not reply to the charge. Christians were, of course, frequently enjoined and exhorted to persevere in fasting (e.g., Polyc. *Phil.* 7.2), whether to gain remission for their sins (Just. *Apol.* 1.61) or to make prayer more effective (Tert. *Apol.* 40.14 f.; Herm. *Vis.* 3.10.6) or as a preparation for ceremonies and feasts (e.g., before baptism, *Did.* 7.4, Just. *Apol.* 1.61, Tert. *De bapt.* 20; before Easter, Euseb. *H.E.* 5.24.12 [Irenaeus]); or to save food for almsgiving (Herm. *Simil.* 5.3.7, Arist. *Apol.* 15, *Const. apos.* 5.20.9), etc.

Sundays were exempted from fasting generally (H. Dumaine, *DACL* 4.1 (1920) *s.v.* Dimanche 858 ff., at 957 ff.) and, notoriously, Wednesdays and Fridays were especially urged, against the Jewish Mondays and Thursdays (*Did.* 8.1) as fixed days for this form of penance (see the commentary of J. P. Audet, *La Didachè, Instruction aux Apôtres* [Paris 1958] 170 ff., 367 ff.). For the whole question, R. Arbesmann, "Fasting and Prophecy in Pagan and Christian Antiquity," *Traditio* 7 (1949–51) 1–71; J. Schümmer, *Die altchristliche Fastenpraxis* (Münster 1933).

In fact, *nocturnis congregationibus et ieiuniis sollemnibus* sounds rather like a colorful translation of what Tertullian would have described, in military metaphors, as *vigiliae stationesque* (on *statio*, Chr. Mohrmann, "Statio," VC 7 [1953] 221–45; Schümmer, *op. cit.* 82 ff.; C. H. Dugmore, *The Influence of the Synagogue upon the Divine Office* [Oxford, 1944] 37 ff.).

inhumanis cibis: elaborated below in 9.5.

[108] *latebrosa et lucifugax natio, in publicum muta, in angulis garrula.* For the pejorative usage of *natio*, see Pease on Cic. *De nat. deor.* 2.74, and cf. the description of Christians in Orig. *C.Cels.* 4.23 (frogs round a marsh). The charge was the sort that could be leveled against any exclusive and generally retiring sect, especially with a strict catechumenate (on this see Orig. *C.Cels.* 3.51), and there need not be any more factual foundation for it than that the Christians were a quiet and unobtrusive society. However, there is some evidence for a so-called *disciplina arcani*, e.g., Lact. *Div. inst.* 7.26.8–10 (*deo iubente ut quieti ac silentes arcanum eius in abdito . . . teneamus*), though Tertullian *passim*, and Just. *Apol.* 1.65 ff. on the Eucharistic ritual, show how frank a Christian might be on Christian beliefs and practices; for further evidence see RAC *s.v.* Arkandisziplin (O. Perler) 667 ff., at 671 ff., and Baylis, *op. cit.* 162 ff.). Cf. Herm. *Mand.* 11.8 ff., who notes that the true Christian prophet gifted with tongues does not, unlike his pagan counterpart, answer any question from anyone but will speak forth only in the Christian "synagogue." These attitudes may have reinforced the slander; but nothing more need be implied than the charge as in Orig. *C.Cels.* 3.55: "In private houses also we see wool-workers, cobblers, laundry-workers, and the most illiterate and bucolic yokels who would not dare to say anything at all in front of their elders and more intelligent masters. But whenever they get hold of children in private and some stupid women with them, they let out some outstanding statements . . ." (trans. H. Chadwick). M.F. seems to have two replies to the charge of public silence: (1) In 19.14 f. Christians follow Plato in finding a declaration of God suitable

for the ears of the general public a difficult matter; (2) in 31.6 (plus 28.3) they do not speak out in public because pagans unfairly refuse to give them a proper hearing.

E. Griset, "Un cristiano di Sabrata," *Riv. di stud. class.* 5 (1957) 35 ff. at 38 compares Apuleius *Apol.* 16 *humilitate abdita et lucifuga,* but his conclusions both about the Christianity of Aemilianus and about the dating of the *Octavius* do not follow (cf. A. Birley, *Septimius Severus, The African Emperor* [London 1971] 58 deducing, on the same evidence, Fronto as the ultimate source). Apuleius need only be drawing—as indeed were the opponents of Christianity—on a rich and common tradition of rhetorical polemic and religious and philosophical abuse.

To remain *in angulis* was a proverbial taunt at those who took no part in public life; cf. Plat. *Gorg.* 485D f. on the academic philosopher (quoted by Aul. Gellius, *Noctes Atticae* 10.17.23); Plut. *Phil. princip.* 1.777B; Epict. *Diss.* 1.29.36,55, 2.13.26; Cic. *De orat.* 1.56: *in angulis . . . disserant;* Cic. *De re pub.* 1.2.2: *(res) quas isti (philosophi) in angulis personant.* Characteristically Tat. *Or.* 26 chides *pagans* for hiding their teaching "in corners." The description of the "Impious in Palestine" in Aelius Aristides *Or.* 46.402D ff. (Dindorf) is similar, but in view of the proverbial nature of the observations in diatribe it need not necessarily be about Christians (see A. Boulanger, *Aelius Aristides et la sophistique dans la province d'Asie au IIe siècle de notre ère* [Paris 1923] 256 ff.; and P. de Labriolle, *La réaction païenne* [Paris 1934] 79 ff.); and cf. Oros. *Hist.* 1.63: *quia de temporibus christianis rari et hoc in angulis murmurent.*

[109] *templa ut busta despiciunt. Ut busta* does not merely mean "as if they were sepulchres" (G. H. Rendall, trans. Loeb Classical Library [London 1960] 335), though there are plenty of parallels for this pejorative use of *bustum* etc. referring to something detestable; cf. Matt. 23.27; Anth. Pal. 5.20.6; Ign. *Philad.* 6.1; Tac. *Ann.* 4.38.2: *pro sepulcris spernuntur.*

But the significance here is more literal, for there is a wide variety of parallels for an insistent Christian claim that the pagan temples were merely charnel houses built over (*templa . . . superlata . . . bustis,* Arnob. 6.6) or filled with the corpses, bones, and ashes of those buried in them. Perhaps the fullest expression is to be found in Arnob. 6.6, where that apologist appends a long list of sanctuary graves. (Famous sanctuary graves, often with rival sites, were those of Aphrodite, Apollo, Asclepius, Ares,

Cronos, Dionysus, Hermes, Osiris, Poseidon, Uranus, and, of course, Jupiter [see 23.13]. For further discussion see Pease on Cic. *De nat. deor.* 1.38.) For the idea cf. Tert. *De spect.* 13: *nec minus templa quam monimenta despuimus;* Athenag. *Leg.* 28; Clem. *Strom.* 6.5.40.2, *Protrep.* 3.44.4 ff. In Arnob. 7.15 temples appear as *ustrinae, rogi, busticeta* not of men or heroes but of sacrificed animals.

Christian churches could, of course, be readily exposed to a similar charge of being places for worshiping the dead, e.g., Julian *Ep.* 114.438E (p. 178 Bidez and Cumont), *Adv. Galil.* 335C ff. (Christians grovel among tombs, "adding many recent corpses to the corpse of long ago"). And see A. Berthier, *Les vestiges du christianisme antique dans la Numidie centrale* (Algiers 1943) for Christian (and Donatist) churches built over or housing tombs.

[110] *deos despuunt.* I have translated this literally in view of the evidence amassed by F. J. Dölger on the custom of spitting to ward off evil spirits when passing by statues, temples, etc.: "Heidnische Begrüssung und christliche Verhöhnung der Heidentempel: *despuere* und *exsufflare* in der Dämonenbeschwörung," AC 3 (1932) 192–203; cf. Tert. *De idol.* 11.7: . . . *quo ore Christianus thurarius si per templa transibit, quo ore fumantes aras despuet et exsufflabit quibus ipse prospexit.* For further discussion see my article "Four Passages in Minucius Felix," *Kyriakon: Festschrift Johannes Quasten* (Münster 1970) 2.499–502. (For a refutation of the widely held view of sputation as part of the early baptismal liturgy, see B. Botte, "La sputation, antique rite baptismal?" *Mélanges Christine Mohrmann* [Utrecht 1963] 196–201.) A nonliteral meaning is also possible; cf. Arnob. 6.21 f.; Orig. *C.Cels.* 8.38, 8.41, etc.

[111] *honores et purpuras despiciunt, ipsi seminudi. Seminudi,* i.e., Christians do not wear the ceremonial toga, *de rigueur* apparel for the Roman in civilized and dignified public life (*vita togata*). Tert. *Apol.* 42.1, *Ad Diog.* 5.4, however, declare that Christians were not distinguishable from their fellow men in dress and appearance.

On the rarity of traceable Christian officeholders at this period, see Intro. p. 35 ff. Clearly, despite the assertions of Orig. *C.Cels.* 8.75, Tert. *Apol.* 38.3 (*nec ulla magis res aliena quam publica*), *De idol.* 17 f., *De pallio* 5.4 f., etc., there was no hard and fast rule against Christians holding public office. The question was partly one of involvement: how far ought Christians to be a race apart, especially when they would be judged ultimately not by any rank or office (cf. Ign. *Smyr.* 6.1; *Did.* 4.10; *Barn.* 19.7), and partly one of practical considerations. There seem to have been occasional Christian magistrates at this period, but the difficulties they encountered must have been considerable, especially if they had scruples about swearing oaths, or ordering the execution of criminals, or participating in ceremonial which had its origins in pagan ritual. There were, too, strong pressures to compromise (e.g., the Christian municipal officers holding the flaminate: *Counc. Elvira can.* 2 and 3, 55 and 56, ed. C. J. Hefele, *Histoire des conciles* 1.1 [Paris 1907] 222, 251 ff.).

The charge is part of a traditional one made against exclusive sects and had been particularly frequent against the Jews (*apanthropia* or, more positively, *misanthropia*), e.g., Dio 37.17.2; Philos. *Vit. Apol.* 5.33; Apollonius Molon *ap.* Josephus *Contr. Ap.* 2.148; Tac. *Hist.* 5.5 (*adversus omnes alios hostile odium*); it was a charge which the Christians inherited: Tac. *Ann.* 15.44 *odium humani generis* (see J. B. Bauer, "Tacitus und die Christen," *Gymnasium* 64 [1957] 497 ff., esp. 501 f.). Significantly, Celsus ended his attack on Christianity with an appeal to Christians to hold office, *ap.* Orig. *C.Cels.* 8.75.

For further discussion see C. J. Cadoux, *The Early Church and the World* (Edinburgh 1925) 358 ff., 393 ff., and Ch. Guignebert, *Tertullien: Étude sur ses sentiments à l'égard de l'empire et la société civile* (Paris 1901) 200 ff.

[112] For the Christians' notorious contempt of death, see from the pagan angle, Lucian *De mort. Pereg.* 13, Marc. Aur. *Med.* 11.3, Epict. *Diss.* 4.7.6, Celsus *ap.* Orig. *C.Cels.* 2.45; and from the Christian, *Ad Diog.* 1, 7.7 f., Tat. *Or.* 4, *Mart. Polyc.* 4, Tert. *Apol.* 50.10, and chap 37 below.

[113] *sacraria ista taeterrima.* The precise significance of *sacrarium* is obscure and it would, therefore, be incautious to press the passage, as has been done, for any indication as to dating. Some have interpreted the word as a translation of the Greek *thysiastérion* (= *altare*); so J. Stiglmayr, "Zur Priorität des 'Octavius' des Minucius Felix gegenüber dem 'Apologeticum' Tertullians," ZkTh 37 (1913) 221 ff. That word is indeed common in the epistles of Ignatius (*Magn.* 7.2, *Trall.* 7.2, *Philad.* 4.1; and cf. Hebr. 13.10; see J. Moffatt, "An Approach to Ignatius," HTR 29 [1936] 1 ff., at 9 f.; F. J. Dölger, "Die Heiligkeit des Altars und ihre Begründung in christlichen Altertum," AC 2 [1930]

183). But *sacrarium* clearly has been chosen here rather for its literary connotations: Livy uses it of the Bacchanalia in 39.15.14 (*his ex obsceno sacrario eductis*) and 39.16.2 (*ex illo uno sacrario*); cf. Cicero of the Catilinarians, *In Cat.* 1.9.24 (*sacrarium scelerum*), 2.6.13. The meaning of "rites" advocated by Beaujeu *ad loc.* is unlikely, for it is without any firm parallel. The *Digest* (1.8.9) provides the most likely answer to the significance: *sacrarium est locus in quo sacra reponuntur: quod etiam in aedificio privato esse potest.* That is to say, it means "cult centre" "a religious meetingplace," and this would be consonant with the claim made in 10.2 that Christians have *nullas aras . . . templa nulla, nulla nota simulacra;* that charge is not denied in the reply at 32.1 ff. See also Baylis, *op. cit.* 256 ff.

In the New Testament period there were naturally private houses used for religious gatherings (cf. Philem. 2; Rom. 16.23; 1 Cor. 16.19), following the example of the Cenacle. Thereafter Justin's *Acta* 2 provides the next real evidence of the continuation of this tradition of church houses (in Rome). The third-century evidence suggests that there were, in increasing numbers, separate church buildings (in Latin, *conventiculum* [Arnob. 4.36], *ecclesia* [Lact. *De mort. pers.* 12.3]; see F. J. Dölger, " 'Kirche' als Name für den christlichen Kultbau etc.," AC 6 [1940–50] 161 ff., esp. 190 ff.), but many may well still have been, as at Dura, converted private houses (M. Rostovtzeff, *Dura-Europos and Its Art* [Oxford 1938] 130 ff.). The evidence for separate church buildings is, as one might expect, predominantly from the East (Euseb. *H.E.* 6.34, ?7.13, 7.15.4, 7.30.10 and 19; Orig. *Comm. in Matt.* 39; Lact. *De mort. pers.* 12, 15; cf. Tert. ?*De pudic.* 4.5, ?*De idol.* 7.1, etc.).

The evidence of general imperial proclamations gives the appearance of being studiously ambiguous on the subject; e.g., Gallienus refers to "the places of worship" (Euseb. *H.E.* 7.13.1); under Valerian (*H.E.* 7.11.10) Christians are forbidden "to hold meetings or to gather at the so-called cemeteries"; the edict of Galerius (*H.E.* 8.17.9) allows Christians to build "the dwellings where they used to assemble," and the "Edict of Milan" (*H.E.* 10.5.9) speaks of the "places" at which it was the Christians' wont to assemble, etc.

Caecilius may thus be referring not to separate "churches" but merely to private houses (used for religious purposes), to *areae*, and so on. On the latter cf. Tert. *Ad Scap.* 3.1: *areae non sint!* and note that about this period Pope Fabian *et multas fabricas per cymeteria fieri praecepit* (*Lib. pontif.*, ed. Duchesne 148 f.), and there was said to be the ground held by the *popinarii* which was wanted by the Christians (*S.H.A.* Alex. Sev. 49.6—but not necessarily for "building a church," against J. G. Davies, *The Origin and Development of Early Christian Architecture* [London 1952] 15, but simply for worshiping God there).

The bibliography is extensive: J.-P. Waltzing, "Minucius Felix 9.1 et 34.5," *Musée belge* 14 (1910) 61 ff., at 62 ff.; DACL 4.2 (1921) *s.v.* Églises 2292 ff. (H. Leclercq); G. Dix, *The Shape of the Liturgy* (Westminster 1945) 19 ff.; J.-R. Laurin, "Le lieu du culte chrétien d'après les documents littéraires primitifs," *Anal. Greg.* 70 (1954) 39–57, esp. 47 f.; Davies, *The Origin and Development of Early Christian Architecture* 14 ff.

[114] An agricultural metaphor with, of course, biblical sanction (Matt. 15.13; cf. Ign. *Philad.* 3.1), but Livy 39.16.3 uses very parallel language of the Bacchanalia: *crescit et serpit cotidie malum.* Octavius flatly contradicts the proverb *fecundius nequiora proveniunt* in 31.6.

[115] *occultis se notis et insignibus noscunt.* Some have taken *notis* as referring to tattoo or painted marks on the body (as, e.g., in Mithraic practice; see F. Cumont. *Textes et monuments figurés relatifs aux mystères de Mithra* 1 [Brussels 1899] 319, and in other cults F. J. Dölger, *Sphragis* [Paderborn 1911] 89 ff.). But the evidence for this (esp. for crosses marked on the forehead) comes considerably later: see F. J. Dölger, "Die Kreuz-Tatöwierung in christlichen Altertum," AC 1 (1929) 202 ff.; H. Rondet, "Miscellanea Augustiniana: La croix sur le front," *Rech. de sc. relig.* 42 (1954) 388–94; and for a graffito, J. Carcopino, *De Pythagore aux apôtres* (Paris 1956) 93 f. In any case this interpretation would fit ill with the epithet *occultus.* It seems clear both from Octavius' reply (31.8 *notaculo corporis*) and from the parallel passage in Tert. *Apol.* 21.2 (*neque de ipso signaculo corporis neque de consortio nominis cum iudaeis agimus*) that the reference is to circumcision, a practice generally abhorred by the Romans and even, for a period, prohibited by their law (E. M. Smallwood, "The Legislation of Hadrian and Antoninus Pius against Circumcision," *Latomus* 18 [1959] 334 ff., with Addendum *ibid.* 20 [1960] 93 ff.). Justin (*Dial.* 16), too, could claim that Jews recognized each other "by the marks of circumcision." Most Christians, of course, at this stage merely practiced "circumcision of the heart" (*Ad Diog.* 4); they spoke

of their initiation ceremony, baptism, as _signaculum dominicum_ (Cyp. _Ep._ 73.9.2).

Are _insignia_ merely synonymous or meant to refer to something different? If the latter alternative is the case, Octavius fails to make any reply to the charge (31.8). The term could well embrace ritual gestures like the sign of the cross (the _locus classicus_ is Tert. _De cor. mil._ 3.4, cf. _Ad. uxor._ 2.5.2), on which see F. J. Dölger, _Sphragis_ (Paderborn 1911) 171 ff., and _idem_, "Beiträge zur Geschichte des Kreuzzeichens I," JAC 1 (1958) 5 ff., esp. 8. It could also embrace the use of well-known Christian symbols (e.g., on signet rings, Clem. _Paed._ 3.59.2): the anchor, dove, fish, boat, etc.

Note the charge against Gnostics that they could recognize each other by special handshakes (Epiphanius _Adv. haer._ 26.4 [MG 41.337]) and that against the Carpocratians (Iren. _Adv. haer._ 1.25.6 [MG 7.685]), who were said to have marked themselves on their ear. The present charge _need_ not, therefore, have any real objective evidence; it was a natural one to make against people regarded as forming a secret society. (Cf. also the Mark of the Beast, _Apoc._ 13.16, 14.9: _characterem in fronte sua aut in manu sua._)

[116] For "brother and sister" see n. 21. Such charges of "incest" were freely made: they were presumably a gross and deliberate distortion of the much-emphasized Christian "badge" of fraternal love (e.g., John 13.34 f.; cf. Tert. _Apol._ 39.7: _vide, inquiunt, ut invicem se diligant_) and the Christian gatherings called "agape" ("love feast") as an open manifestation of that brotherly love (see below n. 122 and cf. Lucian _De mort. Pereg._ 13). At these gatherings there could be abuse, as implied, e.g., in Ign. _Smyr._ 8.2: "it is not permitted without authorization from the bishop to hold an agape," and evidenced already in St. Paul's animadversions on misconduct in 1 Cor. 11.29 ff. The Christian custom of greeting with a kiss (Just. _Apol._ 1.65; cf. James, the brother of John, Euseb. _H.E._ 2.9.3; 1 Cor. 16.20) and the ceremonial kiss of peace (where abuse was possible, as implied in the regulation of one kiss only, Athenag. _Leg._ 32, and in the complaints of Clem. _Paed._ 3.11.81) would provide further evidence for these charges.

Both Tertullian (_Ad nat._ 1.14) and Origen (_C.Cels._ 6.27 f.) trace these calumnies to the Jews. Eusebius, on the other hand, refers the enormities in fact to the heretical sect of the Carpocratians (_H.E._ 4.7.10 ff; so too Clem. _Strom._ 3.2.10.1), whence they spread to the full body of Christians. But it is clear that, in any case, they formed part of the general language of religious abuse, Catholics freely making the same charges against the Montanists (Isid. Pelus. *Ep.* 1.242 [MG 78.329 ff.]), Montanists against Catholics (Tert. *De ieiun.* 17.3: *adulescentes tui cum sororibus dormiunt*), and see Epiph. *Adv. haer.* 26.4.1 ff. (MG 41.337) on the aberrations of Gnostic sects, and Iren. *Adv. haer.* 1.6.3 ff., 1.13.3 ff. (MG 7.508 ff., 583 ff.) on heretics debauching their converts (for discussion, see W. Speyer, "Zu den Vorwürfen der Heiden gegen die Christen," JAC 6 [1963] 129–35). One might suspect that the slanders, especially in the third century, were more reported by apologists for refutation than leveled in fact, but Origen *C.Cels.* 6.27 declares that some were still deceived by such stories (but they were generally rejected as false, 6.40). Euseb. *H.E.* 4.7.11 notes that no one continued these calumnies in his own day (but observe that Licinius forbade Christians to worship in mixed congregations, Euseb. *Vit. Const.* 1.53, and in 311 harlots were forced to confess to acts of lewdness in the Christian churches themselves, Euseb. *H.E.* 9.5.2, a match for the temple prostitution charged by Christians to paganism, as in 25.11). For all these pagan accusations, see the article by A. Henrichs, "Pagan Ritual and the Alleged Crimes of the Early Christians," *Kyriakon: Festschrift Johannes Quasten* (Münster 1970) 1.18–35.

vana . . . superstitio: cf. Verg. *Aen.* 8.187.

[117] It is possible that the reference to the reports of *fama* is merely commonplace material (so Pellegrino *ad loc.*); for such reports are abused by the Greek Apologists (Just. *Apol.* 1.1–3, 26–27; Athenag. *Leg.* 2, 31; cf. Herm. *Mand.* 3.3 and cf. the disparagement of *rumor* as a source of information in philosophical discussion in Cic. *De nat. deor.* 3.13, *De divin.* 2.27, 2.113). It is, however, hard not to see here an echo of Tertullian's diatribe against *fama* (*Apol.* 7.8 ff.; *Ad nat.* 1.7.1 ff.). If so, the material is, characteristically, broken up, the pagan here praising *fama* for being *sagax*, the Christian (in 28.7) inveighing against it as one of the works of the "demons."

[118] A famous and much-discussed calumny. The charge had clearly been made earlier against the Jews and passed thence (actively or passively) onto the Christians generally; the genesis of the charge is, however, rather less obvious. For the Jewish calumny, evidence is to be found in Tac. *Hist.* 5.3 f., reporting

the story that Moses, directed by a herd of wild asses, discovered
water in the wilderness whence *effigiem animalis . . . penetrali
sacravere* (see A. M. A. Hospers-Jansen, *Tacitus over de Joden,
Hist. 5.2–13* [Groningen 1949] 122 ff., with a summary in English
195 ff.). This compares with Diod. Sic. 34.1.3, who relates how
Antiochus Epiphanes found a statue of a bearded man (whom he
supposed to be Moses) seated on an ass in the Temple. Josephus,
Contra Apion 2.49, 2.80, 2.113 ff., attempts to deal with the
charge directly, and there are further elaborations in Democritus
ap. Suidas, ed. Ada Adler, vol. 2 (Leipzig 1931) 5 no. 49. For
the Christians, cf. Tert. *Apol.* 16.1 ff. (the Christian God is
auribus asininis), *Ad nat.* 1.11, 1.14.1 ff.: Gnostic angelology
would lend support—Sabaoth said by some to have "the shape of
an ass" (Epiph. *Adv. haer.* 26.10.3 ff. [MG 41.346]; cf. Thapha-
baoth or Onoel in Orig. *C.Cels.* 6.30). Does Arnob. 3.16 have this
slander in mind ("How great flames of passion would they
provoke . . . if the founder of the City, Romulus, were to
stand there with an ass's head?")?

Traditional fun at the expense of Egyptian animal gods (see
n. 466 and chap. 28.7 f.) may have contributed towards the survival of this form of slander (note the Egyptian terracottas using
an ass for various caricatures listed in J. Préaux, "Deus Christianorum Onocoetes," *Hommages à Léon Hermann* [Coll. Lat.
44, 1960] 639 ff., at 651). Note also Liban. *Or.* 4.37 (an onocephalic mask used for deriding a prisoner); see R. Pack, "An
Onocephalic Mask," HTR 48 (1955) 93 ff. But the ass as an
animal notoriously fabled for its erotic powers—and aberrations
—is a more likely influence (see Préaux, *art. cit.*, and for further
evidence P. Bruneau, "Illustrations antiques du coq et de l'âne de
Lucien," BCH 89 [1965] 349 ff.); hence the ass is here a *turpissima pecus* and the concluding remark *digna et nata religio talibus
moribus* is thereby explained. This phallic association would suit
the context of *honore praefanda* admirably. (There was a certain
amount of literary rivalry for the *turpissima pecus*: in Ennius
Sat. 69 [Vahlen] *ap.* Cic. *De nat. deor.* 1.97 it is an ape [*simia
quam similis turpissima bestia nobis*]. See Pease's n. *ad loc.* for
parallels.)

And there is the famous graffito in the Paedagogium on the
Palatine with an *orans* shown before a crucified figure with an
ass's head and with the legend "Alexamenos worships god" DACL
1.2 [1924] *s.v.* âne 2042 ff. [H. Leclercq]). To the left of the ass's

head is the letter Y, a magic Egyptian sign (also a Pythagorean symbol, see F. Cumont, *After Life in Roman Paganism* [New Haven 1922] 150 f.). Epiphanius *Adv. haer.* 39.1 ff. (MG 41.665 ff.) mentions the Gnostic sect of the Setheans who identified Christ and the Egyptian god Seth (or Typhon)—and the symbol of Seth was an ass. This may, therefore, be a document of that sect (so M. Sulzberger, "Le symbole de la croix et les mono- grammes de Jésus chez les premiers chrétiens," *Byz.* 2 [1925–26] 337 ff.). In any case, it illustrates neatly how the slander might be attached from an aberrant sect to the Christian following gener- ally. See further L. Vischer, "Le prétendu 'culte de l'âne' dans l'église primitive," *Rev. de l'hist. des relig.* 139 (1951) 19–35; J. Jacoby, "Der angebliche Eselskult der Juden und Christen," *Archiv. rel. Wissen.* 25 (1927) 265–82; D. Mallardo, "La calunnia onolatrica contro i cristiani," *Atti della Reale Accad. di Arch. Lett. e Belle Arti* 45 (1936) 115–38; C. Cecchelli, "Noterelle sul christianesimo africano," in *Studi dedicati alla memoria di Paolo Ubaldi* (Milan 1937) 189 ff., at 197 ff. with *addendum* at 481 ff.

[119] *antistitis ac sacerdotis colere genitalia et quasi parentis sui adorare naturam.* This bizarre story is not found elsewhere among the charges reported against the Christians. It sounds like the sort of *mendaciunculum* that Fronto qua orator (see below 31.2) would have felt quite free to use for effective rhetorical polemic (cf. Cic. *De orat.* 2.59.241, allowing invention in a speech on the grounds *quod . . . est mendaciunculis aspergendum*; cf. Titus Castricius *ap.* Aul. Gellius, *Noctes Atticae* 1.6.4). And besides, reporting it permitted the Christian to fling the charge back with considerably stronger virulence (28.10 f.). There is no real reason, therefore, to demand any objective evidence for the charge, but there may have been some foundation for the story in fact. R. Reitzenstein, *Poimandres* (Leipzig 1904) 33 ff., and *Zwei religions- geschichtliche Fragen* (Strasbourg 1901) 96 and n. 2, conjectures a syncretistic religious group who worshiped Christ under the symbol of a phallus, for Hippolytus *Philos.* 5.7.29 (GCS Hippoly- tus 3.85) reports on the Naassenes that they equated the Logos with Hermes, and Hermes was often depicted with phallus erect (see Pease on Cic. *De nat. deor.* 3.56: *excitata natura*). Note, too, the description of Epiphanius *Adv. haer.* 26.4,9 (MG 41.337 f., 343 f.) of the reputed phallic ceremonies among Gnostics. The charge sounds, therefore, to be merely an example of religious polemic.

There is perhaps another possible source: Christ was worshiped under the symbol of the fish, and that could also be used as a phallic symbol (so F. J. Dölger, ΙΧΘΥΣ 2 [Münster 1922] 444 n. 2, and for illustration see vol. 3 [1922] Taf. lxxvii.4. He refers to Athenaeus *Deip.* 3.65; cf. Ovid *Metam.* 5.331 (in Egyptian religion); *pisce Venus latuit;* Plut. *De Isid. et Osir.* 18.358B; Suet. *Tib.* 44: the victims of Tiberius' lust called *pisciculi,* also a Christian soubriquet, see Tert. *De bapt.* 1.3: *sed nos pisciculi secundum* ἰχθὺν *nostrum Jesum Christum;* and generally R. Eisler, "Der Fisch als Sexual-Symbol," *Imago* 3 [1914] 165–96). That is a highly fanciful, and unnecessary, explanation.

Another, but even less likely, source that has been suggested is a misinterpretation of the ceremonial of exomologesis as described by Tert. *De paenit.* 9: the penitent *inter alia* is enjoined *presbyteris advolvi,* [*et*] *aris dei adgeniculari* (9.4).

What is intended by *parentis* is not immediately clear. Tert. *Apol.* 8.7 and *Ad nat.* 1.7.23 reports the master of ceremonies of the initiation service as being described as *pater sacrorum, magister sacrorum vel pater.* That is also the language of Mithraic and other mystery cults. For Mithraic evidence: *pater et sacerdos,* inscriptions nos. 35, 36, 37, 136; *pater et antistes* 139; *pater sacrorum* 14, 21, 22, 23, 24, etc.; *pater patrum* 7 to 18; *sacerdos, pater patrum* 141, in F. Cumont, *Textes et monuments figurés relatifs aux mystères de Mithra* 2 (Brussels 1896). *Parens* is presumably a parody on such reported usage or of the use of *filius* by the clergy in addressing layfolk, e.g., Cyp. *Ep.* 69.1.1; it is, in any case, a more emotively suggestive word suitable for polemic.

Note that Caecilius does not use *episcopus vel presbyter*—that would have been out of character. Even in the fourth century Ammianus Marcellinus felt constrained to gloss the word *presbyter* apologetically in 31.12.8: *Christiani ritus presbyter* (*ut ipsi appellant*). *Antistes,* on the other hand, could serve as an acceptable Christian word as well. For discussion see Averil and Alan Cameron, "Christianity and Tradition in the Historiography of the Late Empire," CQ 14 (1964) 316 ff., at 323.

[120] *hominem summo supplicio pro facinore punitum et crucis ligna feralia.* One of the two allusions to Christ in the *Octavius,* the second, again by paraphrase, being in the rather embarrassed reply to the charge of worshiping a criminal in 29.2. For this charge cf. Lucian *De mort. Pereg.* 11; Just. *Apol.* 1.13; Orig. *C.Cels.* 2.29, 2.47 f., 6.10; Arnob. 1.36: *hominem natum et quod*

personis infame est vilibus crucis supplicio interemptum. For the allied charge of staurolatry, see Tert. *Ad nat.* 1.12.1 ff., *Apol.* 16.6 ff. The charge clearly persisted well into the fourth century; cf. Julian *ap.* Cyr. *Contra Jul.* 6.194 (MG 76.706 f.): "you adore the wood of the cross, you paint likenesses of it on your fore-heads and before your houses." The Christians often used the word "wood" to avoid the scandalous word "cross" (e.g., *Barn.* 5.13, 8.5; and for the "scandal," 1 Cor. 1.23, Ign. *Ephes.* 18.1), and they exploited, in heavy-handed fashion, the symbolism of the "wood" (e.g., Just. *Dial.* 86 f.; Commodian. *Instr.* 1.35); but this is not the explanation of the fulsome phrase *crucis ligna feralia;* the reference is to the ritual use of *arbor infelix* for execu-tions, for which see n. 357 on 24.6. In fact, actual crucifixes cer-tainly seem to be of later date, though crosses (e.g., equal-armed or tau-shaped, *Barn.* 9.7 f.) were not. See F. J. Dölger, "Beiträge zur Geschichte des Kreuzzeichens ii," JAC 2 (1959) 15 ff.; DACL 3.2 (1914) *s.v.* croix et crucifix 3045 ff. (H. Leclercq), and the notes on 29.6 f. below. But note the image-worshiping activities reported of the Carpocratians in Iren. *Adv. haer.* 1.25.6 (MG 7.685 f.) and, of course, those of "Alexamenos" (see n. 118 above).

Too much need not be made of the paucity of direct references to Christ (see Intro. p. 30 f.); there is a similar reticence in other Apologists (e.g., Theophilus, Arnobius).

[121] A famous description of a notorious slander made against the Christians. Pliny's remark about the Christians' food being harmless (*Ep.* 10.96.7) shows that he had heard the charge of cannibalistic meals in the early second century, and it is reported by most of the Apologists (e.g., Just. *Apol.* 1.26; Tat. *Or.* 25; Athenag. *Leg.* 31; Theoph. *Ad Autol.* 3.4; Euseb. *H.E.* 5.1.1-4, and esp. 25-26 (Lyons and Vienne); Orig. *C.Cels.* 6.27; Tert. *Apol.* 8.2 ff., *Ad nat.* 1.7.23 ff.). Ritual murder was in fact a not uncommon charge in religious polemic—already current against the Jews (Josephus *Contra Ap.* 2.91 ff.; Democritus *ap.* Suidas 2 (Adler) 5, no. 49)—and sacramental cannibalism could be charged in turn by Catholics against Marcionites (Just. *Apol.* 1.26), Carpocratians (Clem. *Strom.* 3.2.10.1), Montanists (Epiph. *Adv. haer.* 48.14.5 [MG.41.877]), or Gnostics generally (Epiph. *Adv. haer.* 26.5 [MG 41.339]). The ritual use of an embryo or a new-born child in black magic would help to make the charge a credible one: *Michigan Papyri* 6 (ed. H. C. Youtie and O. M. Pearl, *Papyri and Ostraka from Karanis;* Ann Arbor 1944) nos.

423-24, p. 124 f., with references and literature there cited, adding
M. Leglay, *Saturne Africain histoire* (Paris 1966) 323 ff. on ritual
murder in antiquity, and J. Hubaux, "L'enfant d'un an," *Hommages à Joseph Bidez et à Franz Cumont* (Brussels 1949) 143 ff.;
and stories reported of other initiation ceremonies would lend
further support (cf. Sallust *Cat.* 22: . . . *quom ad ius iurandum
popularis sceleris sui adigeret, humani corporis sanguinem vino
permixtum in pateris circumtulisse . . . quo inter se fidi magis
forent alius alii tanti facinoris conscii* [see 30.5 below] and cf.
Livy 39.13.13). But basically the charge is due to a misunderstanding of language about the Eucharist. See J.-P. Waltzing, "Le
crime rituel reproché aux chrétiens du IIe siècle," *Acad. roy. de
Belg., Bull. de la Classe des Lettres* 11 (1925) 205–39, and F. J.
Dölger, "Sacramentum infanticidii," AC 4 (1934) 188–228. To
use the passage to urge the priority of Minucius Felix over Tert.
Apol. 8.2 ff. is a treacherous proceeding, as many of the variant
details which M.F. provides *may* well have come from the oration
of Fronto (so G. Goetz, PhW 46 [1926] 753 f. against Waltzing
in *art. cit.*) For the real initiation ceremony, Just. *Apol.* 1.61 ff.,
esp. 65, elaborately described, though with tantalizing gaps.

[122] A parody description of the Christian agape (*dilectio*, Tert.
Apol. 39.16) or Christian communal meal. For details consult H.
Connolly, "Agape and Eucharist in the Didache," *Downside Review* 55 (1937) 477–89; G. Dix, *The Shape of the Liturgy* (Westminster 1945) 82 ff.; DACL 1.1 (1924) *s.v.* Agape 775–848 (H.
Leclercq); K. Völker, *Mysterium und Agape: Die gemeinsamen
Mahlzeiten in der alten Kirche* (Gotha 1927) esp. 99 ff. Tert.
Apol. 39.16 ff., in his defense of the agapes, describes the *coenulae*
as consisting of (1) prayer, (2) modest meal of food and drink,
(3) washing of hands, (4) the bringing of the lights, (5) the
recitation of Scripture or impromptu "singing to God," and (6)
concluding prayer. The agape is usually associated with the
charges of immoral behavior already discussed in n. 116, and cf.
the Bacchanalian *convivia*, Livy 39.8.5 ff., 39.13.10 ff. The retort
of *Ad Diog.* 5.7 is noteworthy: "they serve common board but
not bed."

[123] *id etiam Cirtensis nostri testatur oratio.* There can be no
doubt that this is a reference to Marcus Cornelius Fronto (PIR[2]
C1364), born at Cirta, Numidia (c. A.D. 100). In the reply to
this passage Octavius calls the man outright (31.2) *tuus Fronto.*
(For Fronto as patron, friend, and host of men from Cirta, see

Naber 169, 175, 200.) He was the foremost orator and rhetorician
of his day, being described in the *Panegy. Const. dictus, Panegy.
Lat.* (ed. Mynors) *or.* 8.14.2 as *Romanae eloquentiae non secundum sed alterum decus*). He rose to the rank of consul in 143
(earlier career, CIL 8.5350) and was tutor in Latin rhetoric to the
future emperors M. Aurelius and L. Verus. In Aulus Gellius he
appears as a *doyen* of a circle much given to discussing the
niceties of philology. He seems to have died in the late 170's
(Th. Mommsen, *Gesammelte Schriften* [Berlin 1906] 4.1: "Die
Chronologie der Briefe Frontos," 469 ff., at 486; G. W. Bower-
sock, *Greek Sophists in the Roman Empire* [Oxford 1969] 124
ff. The usually accepted doctrine of death c. 166 does not convince). Of all his works only a mutilated portion of his letters
survives (ed. Naber, Leipzig 1867). This speech in which he
attacked Christian practices is not attested elsewhere. The implications of this allusion to Fronto have aroused a great deal of
debate but only a measure of agreement.

Firstly, the form of the allusion *Cirtensis noster*, and the reply
tuus Fronto. These need not necessarily imply either contempo-
raneity or friendship with Fronto. *Tuus Fronto* could be paralleled
by *tuus Serapis* (21.3), i.e., signifying the one you support, invoke, etc. For *noster* one might compare Cicero's *noster Ennius*
(*De nat. deor.* 1.119), *Philo noster* (*ibid.* 1.59), *Euhmerus . . .
noster* (*ibid.* 1.119). Again, therefore, merely the support of
Fronto need be implied by *Cirtensis noster*. On the other hand,
the studiously allusive *Cirtensis* demands explanation. The natural
interpretation would be that the speaker Caecilius Natalis is a
fellow townsman (so J. H. van Haeringen, "Cirtensis noster,"
Mnem. 3 [1935] 29–32, neatly citing *Hipponensis noster*, Aug.
De civ. Dei 22.8.9): it would be the economic hypothesis to accept
the interpretation in view of the inscriptions from Cirta of
Caecilii Natales (though, contra Dessau, no direct identification
ought to be invoked; see n. 9 above). This interpretation does not,
of course, establish the provenance of the other protagonists,
though the proclivities of provincial for provincial might be
urged here (for these see esp. R. Syme, *Colonial Elites* [London
1958] *passim*, and *idem, Tacitus* 2 [Oxford 1958]). If the *Octavius*
is pure literary fiction, then the proud remark would rather reflect, instead, on the author's own *patria;* but that is another
hypothesis.

Secondly, the dating. A date of composition not too distant

from the time of the actual delivery of the speech has been advocated, but such advocacy is wholly unnecessary, for several reasons. (1) The speeches of Fronto were read and circulated in written form (Naber 25, 105, 111, 183), and note the quotation from the *Pro Ptolemaeensibus* by the grammarian Charisius c. 400 A.D.; as Origen might reply to the *Alēthēs Logos* some sixty-five years after Celsus wrote his polemic, or Josephus to Apion's attacks some fifty-five years or more after they were made, so Minucius Felix might reply to Fronto's gibes after just as lengthy an interval. They would be known from the circulated manuscripts of the speech. (2) The setting of the *Octavius* is in the past. If one can judge from Ciceronian practice, that can leave a wide interval between the narrated events and the time of writing (e.g., *De nat. deor.* set c. 30 years in the past, *De orat.* c. 35: for further details see Hirzel *Dialog* 1.457 ff. and A. S. Pease, ed. *De nat. deor.* 1.22 ff.).

All that is required is, therefore, that at the imagined or actual time of the debate an allusion to Fronto was possible or appropriate. A wide range of dates is thereby clearly allowable; cf. E. K. Rand, CAH 12 (1939) 595. And (3) the descendants of Fronto lived well on into the second half of the third century; for Fronto's grandson (cos. 199 A.D.) and great grandson, CIL 11.6334 (Pisaurum); for later progeny (256 A.D.), ILS 7218 (Cirta) (Petronius Victorinus and his son—who had *fratres* as well). An allusion to the illustrious forebear of any one of these descendants would be an appropriate compliment. This is merely a possibility, but it makes a date of composition contemporary or near-contemporary with Fronto's lifetime altogether uncertain or, at the least, unnecessary.

One might compare Martial, writing oddly in praise of Seneca about 25 years after the latter's death, *Epig.* 4.40. The simple explanation is that the wife of Lucan, Seneca's nephew, continued to be a patroness (Polla Argentaria), *Epig.* 7.21, 7.23, 10.64.

Thirdly, the indebtedness of Caecilius' speech to Fronto's oration. On this question much remains idle speculation. Some points can, however, be stated positively. Minucius Felix writes with careful metrical *clausulae*, Fronto does not. If Fronto's words do reappear, they must be in a somewhat transformed form (cf. H. Bornecque, "Les clausules métriques dans Minucius Felix," *Musée belge* 7 [1903] 247 ff., at 257). Fronto abhorred Seneca (Naber 155 ff.; for discussion see A. Beltrami, "Seneca e Frontone,"

Raccolta di scrit. per Felice Ramorino [Milan 1927] 508 ff.; M. Leroy, "Fronton et la philosophie," *Musée belge* 34 [1930] 291 ff.; F. Portalupi, *Marco Cornelio Frontone* [Turin 1961] 55 ff.); ideas and parallels from Seneca (collected by F.-X. Burger, *Minucius Felix und Seneca* [Munich 1904]) must therefore be added ingredients. On the other hand, so little of Fronto's oratorical writing is extant (note Naber 13 ff.) that it is unsafe to conjecture how or what he might have written in a speech. But it ought not to be overlooked that Fronto had a deep admiration for Cicero, making excerpts from his works (Naber 107), annotating and emending his text (Naber 190) analysing his oratorical methods (Naber 108), imitating his phrases (Naber 25, 98), and so on. (On Cicero and Fronto, see F. Portalupi, *op. cit.* 39 ff.) For all we know, Fronto might have written in a more Ciceronian manner—and thus more in the manner of Minucius Felix—on the right oratorical occasion (cf. Tacitus in his *Dialogus*). Alleged stylistic differences between the two authors are, therefore, hazardous tools of argument. The most sensitive discussion is that of P. Frassinetti, "L'Orazione di Frontone contro i cristiani," GIF 3 (1949) 238–54, who, however, overemphasizes (a) the apparent debt of Livy to the (nonextant) speech of Cato *De coniuratione* and (b) the apparent parallelisms between Livy 39.15 f. and phrases in chaps. 7–12. Similarity of context could easily explain much (see n. 106 above).

Finally, the context and nature of the speech. Fronto as *causidicus* pleaded either for or against individuals or communities (Naber 40, 111, 169, 184, etc.), and as senator he took part in senatorial debates (Naber 25). Christians, or Christianity, could well have figured in such speeches, for Fronto firmly believed *atrocia enim sunt crimina et atrocia dicenda,* and this was the period of the martyrdom of Polycarp, Justin, Tolemaeus, Lucius, etc. A senatorial debate leading to the "new decrees" mentioned by Melito of Sardis (*H.E.* 4.26.5) or the rescript on "superstition" (*Dig.* 48.19.30: Modestinus) would be an attractive setting.

See further A. della Casa, "Le due date dell' 'Octavius,' " *Maia* 14 (1962) 20 ff., at 36 f.; M. D. Brock, *Studies in Fronto and His Age* (Cambridge 1911) 92 ff.; and my article, "Four Passages of Minucius Felix," *Kyriakon: Festschrift Johannes Quasten* (Münster 1970) 2.502–504.

[124] It is curious that this colorful detail of the upsetting of the lamps plays an unusually prominent part in the tradition of this

particular slander (e.g., Just. *Apol.* 1.26 f., *Dial.* 10; Tert. *Apol.* 7.1, 8.3,7; Orig. *C.Cels.* 6.27; Clem. *Strom.* 3.2.10.1 [of Carpocratians]). It is legitimate to wonder why. Possibly the role that light played in Christian liturgy and rituals called attention to the *candelabrum* and made it an integral part of the calumny (e.g., prayers and ceremonies associated with the lighting of the lamp, as in Jewish custom and surviving in the paschal candle in the West, and, in the East, in the *lucenarium* or blessing of the evening lamp). See G. Dix, *The Shape of the Liturgy* (Westminster 1945) 85 ff.; F. J. Dölger, "Lumen Christi," AC 5 (1936) 1–43, esp. 26 ff. ("der christliche Licht-Segen im Abendland").

[125] *everso et exstincto conscio lumine.* For the notion cf. Sen. *Ep.* 101.15: *lucem videre tot consciam scelerum,* Phaedr. 107: *conscias . . . faces;* Apul. *Met.* 5.26: *conscio lumine,* 8.10: *nullo lumine conscio;* Verg. *Aen.* 4.167 f.: *fulsere ignes et conscius aether/conubiis;* and esp. Hor. *Carm.* 3.6.27 f.: *cui donet impermissa raptim/gaudia luminibus remotis.*

[126] A commonplace observation, cf. Sen. *Ep.* 97.12: *omnes peccata dissimulant . . . at bona conscientia prodire vult et conspici,* and *Ep.* 122.14: *gravis malae conscientiae lux est.*

[127] *nullas aras.* There can be a distinction between *ara* and *altare* difficult to reproduce in English. *Ara* was the more appropriate word for the high altars of important gods and sacrifices, *altare* the term for the shrines of cult heroes and minor rituals (hence in 12.5 *delibatos altaribus potus*). See the discussion of Servius *ad* Verg. *Ecl.* 5.66. The Christians used freely the latter term (*altare*) of their own rites in Latin (cf. Greek θυσιαστήριον versus βωμός); cf. Cyp. *Ep.* 65.12: *quasi post aras diaboli accedere ad altare Dei fas sit,* but note the exceptional Tert. *De orat.* 19.3: *ad aram Dei.* Such a distinction between *ara* and *altare* may be intended here; Christians do not take part in the bloody sacrifices of pagan public worship (for the charge see Orig. *C. Cels.* 8.17; Arnob. 6.1 [but there he has rhetorically *non altaria fabricamus, non aras*]; Tert. *Idol.* 7; Mart. *Polyc.* 12.2: "He teaches many not to sacrifice, not to worship." The Christian "altar" (cf. Iren. *Adv. haer.* 4.18.6 [MG 7.1029]; Ign. *Eph.* 5, *Magn.* 7, *Trall.* 7, *Philad.* 4; Cyp. *Ep.* 1.1.2, 43.5.2, etc.) at this stage usually consisted of a three-legged table (for illustration, bearing loaf and fish, see G. B. de Rossi, *La Roma sotteranea* 2, Tav. 16) which was made of wood (cf. Opt. *De schism. Donat.* 6.1 [CSEL 26.143]: Donatists break up a Catholic wooden altar;

Aug. *Ep.* 185.7 [CSEL 57.25 f.]: Bishop Maximianus almost beaten to death by boards from a destroyed altar), etc. But note the altar presented by Constantine in Rome; it was silver-gilt set with 400 precious stones (*Lib. pontif.*, ed. Duchesne 177).

For further evidence see RAC *s.v.* Altar iii (J. P. Kirsch) 334 ff.; DACL 1.2 (1924) *s.v.* Autel 3155 ff. (H. Leclercq); and F. J. Dölger, "Die Heiligkeit des Altars und ihre Begründung im christlichen Altertum," AC 2 (1930) 161 ff., esp. 173 ff.

[128] On "temples" see n. 113 above. As Arnobius and Lactantius can repeat this charge when there were definitely "churches" (in our sense) in use, the meaning must be "no places of (pagan) sacrifice" etc.

[129] *nulla nota simulacra.* The epithet (*nota*) is presumably intended to attack the cultural poverty of Christianity: they have no famous masterpieces like Pheidias' chryselephantine statues of Olympian Zeus or Athena Parthenos; it probably should not imply that there were *private* images—though there is some minor evidence for them.

Note, exceptionally, the statues Eusebius (*H.E.* 7.18) saw at Caesarea Philippi which he thought were of Christ and the woman suffering from an issue of blood, the statues of Daniel and the Good Shepherd erected by Constantine (Euseb. *Vit. Const.* 3.49), and cf. the contents of the *lararium* of Severus Alexander, S.H.A. *Sev. Alex.* 29.2. M.F. makes no mention of paintings, though Theophilus *Ad Autol.* 2.2 included them in his attack; cf. Euseb. *H.E.* 7.18 (pictures of Peter, Paul, Christ Himself), Euseb. *Ep. ad Constantiam* (MG 20.1545–49) condemning pictures of Christ (cf. the *imagines depictae* worshiped by the Carpocratians, Iren. *Adv. haer.* 1.25.6 [MG 7.685], and cf. Hippol. *Philos.* 7.32.8 [GCS Hippolytus 3.220]). The argument that Christ was in fact ugly (Clem. *Paed.* 3.1; Orig. *C.Cels.* 6.75) was part of the Christian, and "higher pagan," iconoclastic movement. For the Christian's reply, see 32.1 ff.

The bibliography is very plentiful: see H. Koch, *Die altchristliche Bilderfrage* (Göttingen 1917); DACL 7.1 (1926) 15 ff., 182 ff. *s.vv.* Iconographie, Images (H. Leclercq); the series of articles in the issues of JAC 1 (1958) ff. by Th. Klauser ("Studien zur Entstehungsgeschichte der christlichen Kunst"); W. Elliger, *Die Stellung der alten Christen zu den Bildern in den ersten vier Jahrhunderten* (2 vols. Leipzig 1930, 1934); and for a very readable account of idolatry and the early Church, N. H. Baynes, *Byzantine Studies and Other Essays* (London 1955) 116–43.

[130] For this charge see n. 108 above.

[131] The gibe at the solitude of a monotheistic god is not directly rebutted, but note 18.7: it was not without its tradition in the philosophical schools, esp. in the Stoic-Epicurean debate; cf. Cic. *Hortensius* fr. 47 (Grilli), *ap*. Lact. *Div. inst.* 1.7.4: *si deus unus est, quae esse beata solitudo queat;* cf. Cic. *De nat. deor.* 1.10.24 (Epicurean mockeries), and note the miller's wife in Apul. *Met.* 9.14: she has added to her long catalogue of vices the fact that she said that God was *unicus*.

[132] *non saltem romana superstitio*. The movement of thought is comparable to that in 6.1: Rome is the confluence of all religious practices. Hence *superstitio* may be used, as usual, rather pejoratively.

[133] Note, however, *simulacra* are not mentioned (cf. Tac. *Hist.* 5.5: *nulla simulacra in urbibus suis nedum in templis sistunt*). The Christians were, of course, scornful of Jewish *arae* and *victimae;* see *Ad. Diog.* 3; Just. *Dial.* 22; Tert. *Adv. Jud.* 5; such Jewish sacrifices may have continued until 135 A.D. at Jerusalem: see K. W. Clark, "Worship in the Jerusalem Temple after A.D. 70," JNTS 6 (1960) 121 n. 3.

[134] Reading *romanis hominibus* with the correcting hand of the Paris MS. The expression may be merely pleonastic; one might compare 8.3: *Athenienses viri* (some compare Cic. *De nat. deor.* 2.5: *romanisque hominibus gloriosum*, but there the phrase is probably dictated by considerations of clarity and balance with the following *graecis . . . litteris*), but the fulsome phrase is probably intended here for effective contrast, cf. Livy 5.51.3: *diique et homines romani* and Cic. *De fato* 2.4: *ut romanum hominem, ut timide ingredientem ad hoc genus disputandi.*

The theme of God's failure to vindicate His people is a very common one, e.g., Just. *Apol.* 2.5; Tert. *Apol.* 21.5, 41.2, *Adv. Jud.* 10.6 ff.; Orig. *C.Cels.* 5.41, 8.39 f., 8.69; Arnob. 2.76; Euseb. *H.E.* 5.1.60 ("Where is their god and what good to them was their worship?" [Lyons and Vienne]); Clem. *Strom.* 4.9.78 ff.; Cic. *Pro Flacco* 28 (on Pompey's conquest of 63 B.C.): *quam cara [illa gens Judaeorum] dis immortalibus esset docuit, quod est victa, quod elocata, quod serva facta;* Joseph. *Contr. Ap.* 2.215: "a clear proof according to him [Apion] that our laws are unjust, our religious ceremonies erroneous, is that we are not masters of our empire, but rather the slaves first of one nation, then of another, and that calamity has more than once befallen our city." The Christians in particular tended to gloat over the fate of Jerusalem, crushed first in 70 A.D., and then again in the disastrous uprising of 131–35 A.D.: on this theme see H. J. Schoeps, *Aus frühchristlicher Zeit: Religionsgechichtliche Untersuchungen* (Tübingen 1950) 144 ff., and cf. Tert. *Apol.* 21.4 f., *Adv. Jud.* 13.4; Orig. *C.Cels.* 2.8; Euseb. *H.E.* 3.5.6, and see chap. 33.3. See also 12.2 below and n. 153.

[135] Cf. Tatian *Or.* 4; Theoph. *Ad Aut.* 1.2 f.: "Show me your God"; Euseb. *H.E.* 5.1.60: "Where is their God?" (pagans at Lyons and Vienne).

[136] This theme of the interference of God in the administration of the world and of the tension between *providentia generalis* and *providentia specialis* has had a long and much-debated philosophical history, especially in the Epicurean (whose gods were *aut otiosos aut nullos*, 19.8 and n. 249) and Stoic debate. Note the typical argument in [Arist.] *De mundo* 398^{b}1 ff.: "If it was beneath the dignity of Xerxes to appear himself to administer all things and carry out his own wishes and superintend the government of his kingdom, such functions would be still less becoming for a god" (trans. E. S. Forster, 1914), and see E. Peterson, *Der Monotheismos als politisches Problem* (Leipzig 1935) 16 ff., and Pease's nn. on Cic. *De nat. deor.* 1.52–54, 3.93 for abundant parallels (esp. Cic. *Acad. prior.* 2.121, *De divin.* 2.105, 2.129; Apul. *De deo Socr.* 16; Pliny *N.H.* 2.20), adding Tert. *De test. anim.* 2.3. It seems not at all unlikely that this passage—and the replies, esp. 18.3, where see n. 214—come directly from the *De nat. deor.*

[137] The end of the world by fire—a notion occurring but briefly in the New Testament (2 Peter 3.7 ff.; cf. Apoc. 18.8 f.)—is heavily emphasized in early ecclesiastical tradition, e.g., Hermas *Vis.* 4.3.3, and see Spanneut, *Le stoicisme des pères de l'église* (Paris 1957) 358 ff. What is noticeable here is that the notion is urged as an objection against Christianity, whereas it is frequently brought forward by Christians either (in a rather gloating fashion) as part of a lurid depiction of the horrors awaiting the damned (2 *Clem.* 16.3; *Apoc. Peter* 21 ff. [James *Apoc. N.T.* 508–10]; Tert. *De spect.* 30 with luxuriance of detail), or to underscore the respectability of the Christian doctrine, the destruction of the world by fire being, *inter alia, Stoicis constans opinio* (see 34.2 and parallels

cited in n. 564). The immediate suspicion is that the objection is in fact here a literary contrivance to allow for the reply of 34.1 ff. with its emphatic line *philosophos eadem disputare quae dicimus* (34.5); however, Fronto's scorn of Stoics especially might be a possible source and we could have here, therefore, a genuinely reported objection against Christianity.

J. Bishop, *Nero, the Man and the Legend* (London 1964) 79 ff., has revived the idea that the arson charge leveled against Christians in 64 A.D. was not only a credible one (because of this much-iterated tenet), but one possibly possessing some basis in fact; there are some virtues in this thesis that Christians may have encouraged the eschatological flames, but note that the charge of arson was a traditional one, being leveled, e.g., against the Bacchanalian *coniuratio* (Livy 39.8.18) and the Jews at Antioch (Jos. *B.J.* 7.3.3–4, 67 A.D.)—and in these instances there was no question of eschatological beliefs dictating the charge. Given the inadequacy of fire precautions in the concentrated urban districts and the heavy use of timber as a building material, the threat would readily rouse genuine fears (cf. Juv. *Sat.* 3.197 ff.).

[138] *moles ista qua [mundus] continetur et cingitur subruatur.* For the language cf. the theory of *ardor* as Cleanthes held it (Cic. *De nat. deor.* 1.37: *omnia cingentem atque complexum ardorem*) or, as some would call it, *aether* (Cic. *De nat. deor.* 2.10: *omnia cingens et coercens caeli complexus qui idem aether vocatur;* cf. ibid. 2.58 and Pease's nn. there). Note, too, the biblical view of 2 Peter 3.5: *caeli erant prius, et terra de aqua et per aquam consistens Dei verbo.*

Caecilius here divorces himself from Epicurean views; they included a belief in the finality of the world, with conflagration, cf. 34.2 and Lucr. 5.95 f.: *una dies dabit exitio, multosque per annos/sustentata ruet moles et machina mundi.* For the language cf. Arnob. 1.2: *numquid machinae huius et molis qua universi tegimur et continemur inclusi, parte est in aliqua relaxata aut dissoluta constructio?*

[139] *aniles fabulas.* For this popular philosophical expression of abuse, see Otto *Sprichwörter* 28 s.v. anus (2); M. C. Sutphen, "A Collection of Latin Proverbs," AJP 22 (1901) 11 s.v. anus; Pease on *De nat. deor.* 1.55, 3.12, *De divin.* 2.19.

[140] Beaujeu *ad loc.* is right to stress that *post mortem et cineres et favillas* should be taken together. The rhetorical rule of three

will help to explain the unusual fulsomeness of expression, but there is also here some ironic reference to §1 and anticipation of §4 (objections to cremation): despite their hatred of cremation, Christians will turn to ashes according to their own teaching of the "conflagration."

[141] The resurrection of the body, one of the great "scandals" of Christian doctrine in a society habitually inclined, qua philosophers, to think of death as a merciful liberation "from the body, not with the body" (Plotinus *Ennead*. 2.9.15), a release from the soul's sleep (Plotinus *Ennead*. 3.6.6) or from the slough, mire, prison house, etc. of the body (Plat. *Phaed.* 62B, 69C). Hence, for all their ascetic practices, Christians might paradoxically be called scornfully "a flesh-loving crew," Celsus *ap*. Orig. *C.Cels*. 5.14 (for the standard objections raised here and the topic in general, see chap. 34.9 ff. and nn. *ad loc*.). As a result some Christians were reluctant to accept the doctrine of the bodily resurrection (e.g., 1 Cor. 15.12). For the objection that without the body there is no *mens*—not faced by Octavius in his reply—cf. Cic. *De nat. deor*. 1.87: *numquam vidi . . . animam rationis consiliique participem in ulla alia nisi humana figura* (an Epicurean viewpoint): see Pease *ad loc*.

[142] A proverbial idea; cf. Epicur. *Sent. Var*. 60: πᾶς ὥσπερ ἄρτι γεγονὼς ἐκ τοῦ ζῆν ἀπέρχεται (*Epicurus, The Extant Remains*, ed. C. Bailey [Oxford 1926] 114); cf. Lucr. 3.970 ff.

[143] There is no doubt that the Christian custom of inhumation was based ultimately on the Jewish practice (in which incineration was exceptional, e.g. 1 Reg. 31.12, Amos 6.10), and a practice, moreover, hallowed by the burial of Christ. Respect for the body, temple of Christ and destined for future resurrection, and a recoiling from funeral pyres associated both with pagan notions of apotheosis (see n. 318 on 22.7) and with pagan punishments for criminals (so Tert. *De an*. 33.5 ff., 51.4: *poenali exitu*), would have helped to confirm the tradition. There was in fact taking place at this time a notable shift in burial habits in the Roman Empire; by Macrobius' day (*Sat*. 7.7.5) cremation was quite in disuse. This alteration in burial custom—about equally divided between cremation and inhumation c. 200 A.D. (despite Tert. *De carn. resur*. 1.3, who characteristically exaggerates)—was perhaps due not so much to new religious beliefs or the prevalence of mystery religions as to merely changing fashion, especially as

ostentatious sarcophagi, and hence inhumation, became increasingly popular.

See DACL 5.1 (1920) *s.v.* Feu (supplice de) 1456 ff. (H. Leclercq); DACL 7.1 (1920) *s.v.* Incinération 502–8 (H. Leclercq); G. Schnitzner, "Minucio Felice e la cremazione," *Religio* 10 (1934) 32 ff.; A. D. Nock, "Cremation and Burial in the Roman Empire," HTR 25 (1932) 321–59, esp. 334 f.; A. G. Martimort, "La fidélité des premiers chrétiens aux usages romains en matière de sépulture," *Mél. Soc. Toulous. Ét. class.* 1 (1946) 167–89; F. Cumont, *Lux perpetua* (Paris 1949) 457 f. (App. by L. Canet); R. Turcan, "Origines et sens de l'inhumation à l'époque impériale," REA 60 (1958) 323–47; and nn. 577, 650 on 34.10, 38.3.

In the Christian tradition one of the background attitudes was a legacy from pagan beliefs: improper burial entailed not participating in a full life after death (cf. the legal penalty for traitors, murderers, incendiarists, etc). Hence many Christians feared they might risk not partaking of the resurrection if their bodies were burnt or scattered abroad (for desecration of already buried Christians, see Tert. *Apol.* 37.2 f.; Euseb. *Mart. Palest.* 9.10, etc). This fear was, notoriously, exploited deliberately at Lyons and Vienne (Euseb. *H.E.* 5.1.62 ff.)—the bodies of the victims were burned to ashes and swept into the Rhône, "that they might not even have any hope of resurrection. . . . Now let us see if they will rise again and if their God is able to help them and to take them out of our hands." The Christians' cemeteries were therefore objects of attack (e.g., edict of Valerian, Euseb. *H.E.* 7.11.10; Tert. *Ad Scap.* 3.1) and the Christians were consequently concerned with providing suitable burial for their dead, e.g., Cyprian *Ep.* 8.3.2, 12.1.2; Tert. *Apol.* 39.6—common funds used, besides other things, *egenis alendis humandisque*, cf. Julian *Ep.* 49.429^d (the Christians' care for the tombs of their dead). Note Tert. *De idol.* 14.5: *licet convivere cum ethnicis, commori non licet;* Cyp. *Ep.* 67.6.2 insisting on separate Christian burial grounds.

The Christians might defend their burial custom on the grounds of adherence to antique practice (34.10 and n. 577 there.)

Another consequence was that the early Christians were preoccupied with fire as a means of punishment by their persecutors (though natural repugnance and fear were also contributing factors for the prominence of the theme): e.g., Ign. *Rom.* 5.3,

Smyr. 4.2; *Ad Diog.* 10.8; *Mart. Poly.* 2.3, 5.2, 11.2; Euseb. *H.E.* 4.15; Just. *Dial.* 110, *Apol.* 1.71 (the third, and palpably forged, decree); Arnob. 1.26; Tert. *Apol.* 12.5, 20.7, 37.2, 49.4, 50.3, *Ad Scap.* 5.2, *De fuga* 5.3; *Mart. Tryph.* 2 (Ruinart, 1859, 208 ff.); *Mart. Fruct, ibid.* 264 ff. (note the Christians there severally gather the relics after the *vivicomburium* but are ordered by a vision to bury the remains together *uno . . . in loco*). Indeed, there was a certain tendency to make a virtue out of necessity and find grounds for special heroic glorification in death-by-fire: on this motif, especially in "martyr-enthusiastic literature," see F. J. Dölger, "Der Feuertod ohne die Liebe . . . Ein Beitrag zu 1 Korinth 13.3," AC 1 (1929) 254–70; J. Gagé, "Le livre sacré et l'épreuve de feu," *Mullus* (Festschrift Th. Klauser; Münster 1964) 130–42; and n. 625 on 37.3.

[144] A virtual literary *topos* on the theme *quid sepultura prodest:* here there appears to be a conscious echo of Seneca *Ep.* 92.34: *. . . ignis illud excidat, terra contegat, an ferae distrahant . . . utrum proiectum aves differant an consumatur "canibus data praeda marinis";* cf. [Sen.] *De rem. fort.* 5.1–2, 4–5; Sen. *Dial.* 9.14.3 ff. (a "cynic" doctrine); on these parallels see F.-X. Burger, *Minucius Felix und Seneca* (Munich 1904) 9 ff. Note too Fronto, Naber 16 (*de transmarinis testamentis*): *sive maria naufragos devorent, sive flumina praecipites trahant, sive harenae obruant, sive ferae lacerent, sive volucres discerpant, corpus humanum satis sepelitur ubicumque consumitur;* cf. *Ody.* 15. 133 ff.; Verg. *Aen.* 10.559 ff.; Tatian *Or.* 6.2; Athenag. *Resur.* 8; Prudent. *Cath.* 10.141 ff. For the theme of burial in rhetorical exercises, see [Quint.] *Declam.* 299, 329, 369; Sen. *Controv.* 4.4; and note especially Sen. *Controv.* 8.4.1: *omnibus natura sepulturam dedit: naufragos idem fluctus qui expulit, sepelit; suffixorum corpora a crucibus in sepulturam suam defluunt; eos qui vivi uruntur, poena funerat;* the theme is also treated at length in Cic. *Tusc. disp.* 1.43.102 ff. and Lucr. 3.870 ff.

[145] Cf. Sen. *Dial.* 11.5.1: *. . . . si nihil sentit, supervacuum est, si sentit, ingratum;* [Sen.] *De rem. fort.* 5.2: *istud non sentienti supervacuum, sentienti onus;* and compare 38.3, where see n. 650.

[146] *perpetem vitam mortui pollicentur.* It seems more natural, and therefore preferable, to take *mortui* as a bold potential (rather than, e.g., with E. Heikel, "Adversaria in Minucii Felicis Octavium," *Eranos* 21 [1923] 34 f., as = "these dead men," "these life-

in-death, biothanitoi characters," comparing 12.6 *nec interim vivitis* and 38.4 *iam vivimus*).

[147] On the heavily debated theme of fate and providence, a favorite topic among Christians and pagans alike, note among the many separate treatises those of Chrysippus (Aul. Gellius, *Noctes Atticae* 7.12); Panaetius (Cic. *Ad Att.* 13.8); Cicero, Philo, Favorinus, [Plut.], Alexander of Aphrodisias, Oenomaos of Gadara, and (among Christians) Tertullian (*De anim.* 20), Bardesanes, Origen, etc. For a full coverage, see D. Amand, *Fatalisme et liberté dans l'antiquité grecque* (Louvain/Paris 1945) 71 ff. (pagan), 191 ff. (Christian). See also Pease on Cic. *De nat. deor.* 1.55, 3.14. According to Arnob. 7.10, *fato fieri quaecumque fiunt* was a view held by the whole tribe of most learned scholars (*universus ille doctissimorum chorus*).

[148] *sic sectae vestrae non spontaneos cupere sed electos.* The point of the remark is that if it is only Christians who enjoy eternal bliss and if they are Christians merely by the random election of fate (God), then the whole system is one of injustice and wickedness. For the identification of providence and fate, cf. Apul. *De Plat.* 1.12: *si quid providentia geritur, id agitur et fato.* The reply is made in 36.1 f.

[149] *sine corpore? hoc, quod sciam, neque mens neque anima nec vita est.* For the meaning of *anima*, see J. H. Waszink's commentary on Tert. *De an.* 201, 254; for the general thought, a perennial philosophical problem, cf. Cic. *De nat. deor.* 1.30: *quod vero sine corpore ullo deum vult esse . . . id quale esse possit intellegi non potest; careat enim sensu necesse est, careat etiam prudentia, careat voluptate;* 1.33: *cum autem sine corpore idem* (sc., Aristoteles) *vult esse deum, omni illum sensu privat, etiam prudentia;* 1.48: *. . . nec virtus sine ratione constare nec ratio usquam inesse nisi in hominis figura;* 1.87: *numquam vidi . . . animam rationis consilique participem in ulla alia nisi humana figura.* Cf. 1.76 and Pease's nn. *ad loca* for this generally Epicurean viewpoint on corporeality; cf. Lucr. 5.132 f.: *sic animi natura nequit sine corpore oriri/sola neque a nervis et sanguine longiter esse.* Some of the objections were faced already by St. Paul, 1 Cor. 15.35: *sed dicet aliquis: Quomodo resurgunt mortui? qualive corpore venient?*

[150] The lack of trustworthy examples of bodily resurrection had been raised as objections already; see Just. *Apol.* 1.19; Theoph.

Ad Autol. 1.13; cf. Lact. *Div. inst.* 7.22.10; Commodian *Instr.*
1.24.15: *quis est, qui a morte redivit/ut credamus ei?;* Orig. *C.Cels.*
2.16, 5.57, 2.55 ff. has many other examples (apart from that of
Protesilaus) of those who are fabled to have returned from the
dead (Zamolxis, Pythagoras, Rhampsinitus, Orpheus, Heracles
and Theseus, etc.), the truth of which Celsus himself, however,
doubted.

Protesilaus (see PW 23.1 [1957] 932–39 [G. Radke] for the
myth in literature and in religious cult), a Homeric hero, fell in
landing at Troy (Hom. *Il.* 2.695 ff.)—some said because it was
fated that the first to land should be killed and P. thus heroically
volunteered his life (Hyginus *Fab.* 103); he prevailed upon the
god(s) below to see his newly-wedded wife Laodameia for a
short while (or others said that importunity came from his wife).
This was for "one day" in Lucian *Dial. mort.* 23.429, "three hours"
in Hyg. *Fab.* 103. Caecilius clearly follows the latter version; for
other accounts see Cat. *Carm.* 68.73 ff. and Ovid *Her.* 13.

[151] M.F., though prepared to criticize the fables elaborated in
poetry (23.1 f.)—for that he carefully cites the impeccable company of Plato—seems to have carefully arranged that the sympathetic disputant should rather be the one to enlist the testimony
of poetry generally in his support (19.1 f., 26.9, 35.1). The impression thus achieved is one of cultural sympathy for the Christian Octavius. For Caecilius' scorn cf. Tat. *Or.* 22; Theoph. *Ad
Autol.* 2.12; Sen. *De benef.* 1.4.5 f.; and see further n. 230 on 19.1.

[152] *pars vestrum et maior, melior, ut dicitis.* For the common
concatenation of *maior* and *melior* with *pars*, cf. Sen. *Dial.* 10.18.1:
maior pars aetatis, certe melior reipublicae data sit, N.Q. 7.30.3:
maior pars sui operis ac melior; Mart. *Praef.* 8.13 (Friedländer):
pars libri et maior et melior; Cyp. *De unit.* 22: *confessorum pars
maior et melior.*

On the question of poverty and wealth among the early
Christians, see A. Bigelmair, "Zur Frage des Sozialismus und
Kommunismus in Christentum der ersten drei Jahrhunderte"
(*Festgabe A. Ehrhard;* Bonn/Leipzig 1922) 73 ff., esp. 86, and
see the reply to this charge in 36.3. Poverty (an adversity) was
a serious charge in a mental context where adversities could be
considered evils and punishments, not only in paganism (e.g.,
Hor. *Odes* 3.24.42: *magnum pauperies opprobrium*) and Judaism
but also in Christianity (e.g., Herm. *Sim.* 6.3: the wicked
are punished with loss, deprivation, unsettlement, afflictions, etc.

in this world; conversely, *Sim.* 10.1.3: the good will prosper *in omni bono negotio*). In 36.3 Octavius claims that the Christians' poverty is really both illusory (poverty being a relative idea) and, in fact, a benefit.

[153] For this theme of God's impotence, see n. 134 above. Cf. also the discussion in Cic. *De nat. deor.* 3.79 ff., quoting Ennius' famous line from his *Telamo* 318: *nam si curent* (sc., *di*) *bene bonis sit, male malis; quod nunc abest,* and see Pease's n. *ad loc.* for discussions on this frequent topic.

For the turn of phrase *non vult aut non potest opitulari suis; ita aut invalidus aut iniquus est,* cf. Lact. *De ira Dei* 13.20, quoting Epicurus *fr.* 374 Usener: *si vult* (sc., *deus tollere mala*) *et non potest, imbecillus est . . . si potest et non vult, invidus . . . si neque vult neque potest, et invidus et imbecillus est.* For the thought cf. Cic. *De nat. deor.* 1.3: *sin autem dei neque possunt nos iuvare nec volunt,* and see Pease's nn. *ad loc.* and on *De divin.* 3 *fr.* 8.

[154] *cum periculo quateris. Periculo* has often been emended to some bodily ailment (e.g., *quercero*), but needlessly. For (1) *periculum* may be used in the sense of dangerous illness: cf. Pliny *N.H.* 23.1.24: *in acutis vero periculis nullis dandum est vinum;* Cyp. *Ep.* 30.3.3, 31.2; and (2) in any case, (external) mortal danger, serious illness, and severe pain are appropriately linked with *condicio, fragilitas, infirmitas.* For a defense of the reading on these lines, see E. Löfstedt, "Annotationes criticae in M. Minucii Felicis Octavium," *Eranos* 6 (1905–6), 1 ff., at 12. Note, too, in the Christian's reply, 36.9: *ingenium singulorum periculis pensitat.*

[155] For these crosses and the reported worshiping of them, see 9.4 above.

[156] *ignes etiam quos et praedicitis, et timetis.* Does this refer simply to the final conflagration (11.1) and to the Christians' horror of cremation (11.4) (so Pellegrino)? Should it not be taken more generally, embracing a reference to the fires of hell (and perhaps purgatory) as well? (See nn. 584 ff. on 35.1 ff.). For these fires, linked with fear, *Ad Diog.* 10.7 f.; Orig. *C.Cels.* 3.78; cf. Athenag. *Leg.* 31 and esp. Tert. *Apol.* 45.7: *pro magnitudine cruciatus non diuturni verum sempiterni, eum timentes quem timere debebit et ipse qui timentes iudicat, deum, non proconsulem timentes;* and for fear as an auxiliary of Christian faith, see *Barn.* 2.2.

[157] For this argument from superior power, see n. 72 above. One might also note Arnobius' reply to this point in 1.16: if, as is claimed, Alamanni, Persians, and Scythians have been defeated with Christians in their ranks, Rome has also expanded with Christians in hers.

[158] *spectacula, pompae, convivia publica, sacra certamina.* The Christians notoriously tended to refrain from these very popular aspects of public life and occasions of social intercourse and celebration. *Spectacula* will cover productions of stage, arena, and amphitheatre (denounced liberally by Christians: see Tat. *Or.* 22 ff.; Theoph. *Ad Autol.* 3.15; Athenag. *Leg.* 35; Tert. *De spect. passim, Apol.* 38.4; Cyp. *Ad Donat.* 7 f., [Cyp.] *De spect. passim;* Arnob. 7.33 etc.).

pompae: solemn processions where images of gods were carried (Tert. *Apol.* 35.2, and see further J. H. Waszink, "Pompa diaboli," VC 1 [1947] 13–41, esp. 31 ff.).

convivia publica: civic banquets celebrated on religious festivals, emperors' anniversaries, triumphs, etc.; see Tert. *Apol.* 35.2, 42.5; cf. Celsus *ap.* Orig. *C.Cels.* 8.21 ff.—the gods acted as hosts, A. D. Nock, "The Cult of Heroes," HTR 37 (1944) 141 ff., at 150 ff., 169 f.

sacra certamina: gladiatorial shows and *ludi* associated with certain gods or religious commemorations, e.g., *ludi romani, megalenses,* etc. (Theoph. *Ad Autol.* 3.15; Tat. *Or.* 23, etc.). The early Jews, too, shared the same reluctance to attend gymnastic contests, theatrical shows, and horse racing (Orig. *C.Cels.* 5.42); it all helped to reinforce the *odium humani generis* reproach (see n. 111 above), especially as *spectacula* in particular aroused such popular fervor and enthusiasm. Not all Christians conformed, however, and denunciations continued well into the "Christian" empire (though the use of the amphitheatre in persecutions no doubt also helped *de spectaculis* to be such an emotional and enduring theme in patristic literature). There were, of course, a number of grounds urged for rejecting these public occasions: idolatry or idolatrous associations, impurity, cruelty and bloodshed, worldly vanity, and so on (see nn. 507, 637 ff. on 30.6 and 37.11 f).

[159] *praecerptos cibos et delibatos altaribus potus.* Abstention from sacrificial food had been enjoined in Acts 15.29: *ut abstineatis vos ab immolatis simulacrorum;* and despite the later general relaxation of Judaic dietary regulations (see 30.6 and n. 508), this

particular regulation continued unabated (e.g., *Did.* 6.3; Orig. *C.Cels.* 8.24 f.; Tert. *De spect.* 13.4: *neque de sacrificato . . . edimus;* Novatian *De cibis Judaicis* 7 [ML 3.992]), for to eat meat known to have been offered to idols was to worship dead gods or to be in communion with devils, etc. (see 38.1). Hence Pionius was offered by a pagan priest *tepentia . . . exta, Mart. Pionii* 18 (Ruinart, 1859, 196). Beasts would be slaughtered in sacrifice at the temples and a token portion offered on the altars (Arnob. 6.9); the rest might be used at a ceremonial banquet but, generally speaking, it would go to the public meat market, being, in fact, the main source of the supply (cf. Tat. *Or.* 23). And libations might be poured by a religiously-minded host at even the most ordinary social dinner party. The social implications of these practices for Christians were considerable; note (on meat) the prudential advice of St. Paul, 1 Cor. 8 ff. Many scrupulous Christians must have resorted to the Kosher butcher shops (A. A. T. Ehrhardt, "Social Problems in the Early Church," in *The Framework of the New Testament Stories* [Manchester 1964] 275 ff.) or to vegetarianism, common at this period and practiced by Christian ascetics (Orig. *C.Cels.* 5.49; Clem. *Strom.* 7.6.32.8; Euseb. *H.E.* 5.3.1 f.; cf. Arnob. 7.4, 2.41, adding butcher shops to the bloody horrors of pagan life; Clement felt constrained to defend meat-eating in *Paed.* 2.1.9.2). See generally J. Haussleiter, *Der Vegetarismus in der Antike* (Berlin 1935).

The Christian abstention aroused, of course, social protest: cf. Philos. *Vit. Apol.* 5.33 on the Jews ("these people cannot share with the rest of mankind in the pleasure of the table, nor join in their libations or prayers or sacrifices") and the Bithynian suppliers of sacrificial animals, Pliny *Ep.* 10.96.10. On the general question, consult G. Resch, *Das Aposteldecret nach seiner ausserkanonischen Textgestalt* (*T.U.* n.f. 13.3; 1905).

[160] *unguenta.* According to Pliny the Elder (*N.H.* 13.1.3, 13.3.24), perfumes were introduced into Roman funerary customs when Rome came into contact with Syria in the Hellenistic period. Despite the fact that pagans frequently used these spices at burials (Ovid *Fast.* 3.561; Juv. *Sat.* 4.109, etc.), Christians felt free to use them also, and there can be no doubt that in this attitude they were strongly influenced by the details of Christ's burial (John 19.39 f.); cf., too, Christ's remark when Magdalene poured out the contents of the alabaster box: "She did it for my burial" (Matt. 26.12: *ad sepeliendum me fecit*).

On this theme cf. Tert. *Apol.* 42.7, *De carn. resur.* 27.4; Iren. *Adv. haer.* 1.21.3 ff. (MG 7.663 ff.); Lact. *Div. inst.* 2.4.9; and see DACL 13.2 (1921) *s.v.* Embaumement, 2718 ff. (H. Leclercq). Octavius makes no attempt to justify the Christian practice in his reply (38).

For the avoidance of *odores* on the living (as part of Christian penitence and asceticism), see Clem. *Paed.* 2.8 *passim;* DACL 13.2 (1938) *s.v.* Parfums 1692–94 (H. Leclercq). Their use is (strangely) not condemned in Tert. *De cultu fem.* and Cyp. *De habitu virginum.* Octavius confines his reply (38.2) to the use of flowers only. It is noteworthy that incense is not mentioned specifically—as it usually is in these contexts; see Arnob. 7.26 ff.; Tert. *Apol.* 30.6, *De idol.* 11.6 ff.; Just. *Apol.* 1.13; Athenag. *Leg.* 13; Clem. *Strom.* 7.6.32.5—with the same restrictions and qualifications applying as in the case of *unguenta:* see DACL 5.1 (1922) *s.v.* Encens 2 ff., at 8 ff. (F. Fehrenbach).

[161] The early Christians eschewed wreaths both for the living (worn at festivals, celebrations, as a mark of honor, used at sacrifices by both celebrant and victim [see 37.7] etc.) and for the dead. The basic reason for the Christian rejection of these common customs was that *coronae* had heavy religious connotations. Originally they may have been intended to ward off evil spirits, and certainly various flowers and leaves were closely associated with special pagan deities, e.g., violet (Atthis), rose (Adonis), myrtle (Venus), ivy (Dionysus), laurel (Apollo), etc. This connection is heavily stressed by Tert. *De coron. passim* esp. 7, 10, 12; cf. Clem. *Paed.* 2.8.72. In their funeral use such wreaths might have had as well the practical effect of counteracting evil smells at tombs: see P. Perdrizet, "Le mort qui sentait bon," *Mélanges Bidez* 2 (Brussels 1934) 719 ff.

On this theme of wreaths, cf. also Tert. *Apol.* 42.6; Just. *Apol.* 1.24; Arnob. 7.32; and the standard reply in 38.2 ff. below; F. Cumont, *Lux perpetua* (Paris 1949) 45 ff.; *idem, Recherches sur le symbolisme funéraire* (Paris 1942) 474. In fact, Christian practice appears to have become somewhat relaxed in the use of flowers etc. in funerary matters, e.g., Jerome *Ep.* 66.5: *ceteri mariti super tumulos coniugum spargunt violas, rosas, lilia floresque purpureos; Ep.* 60.1: *super tumulum . . . flores spargere;* Sulp. Sev. *Dial.* 3.18: *licet inani munere solum ipsum flore purpureo et suave redolentibus sparge graminibus.*

By contrast, in the Jewish tradition, flowered crowns had been freely used both in rituals and funerary memorials: see E. R. Goodenough, *Jewish Symbols in the Greco-Roman Period* 12 (New York 1965) 139 ff.; C. H. Kraeling, *The Excavations at Dura-Europos: Final Report* 8.1 (The Synagogue) (New Haven 1956) 114ff.

There were, of course, other pagan funerary customs that tended to survive despite strictures from authorities, e.g., lamps and candles lit at tombs (continued in modern Greece), cf. Jerome *Adv. Vigil.* 7 (ML 23.361); Counc. Elvira *can.* 34 (F. Cumont, "Cièrges et lampes sur les tombeaux," *Misc. Giov. Mercati* 5 [Vatican City 1946] 41–47); *parentalia* ceremonies (food and wine taken to tombs, offered to the dead, and eaten at the graveside as a meal), see Aug. *De civ. Dei* 8.27.1, *Conf.* 6.2 (Cumont, *Lux perpetua* 435 f.; H. Delehaye, "Refrigerare, Refrigerium," *Journ. des savants* n.s. 24 [1926] 385–90). This latter continues as a practice in the Balkans; see M. P. Nilsson, *Greek Piety* (Oxford 1948) 164.

[162] *desinite caeli plagas . . . rimari; satis est pro pedibus aspicere.* This, according to Donatus *ad* Terence *Andr.* 386, is a *pervulgatum ancillae dictum.* The story goes back in philosophical legend to Thales who fell down a well while walking along stargazing (Plato *Theaet.* 174A); cf. Diog. Laer. 1.34 (with variations); Hippoly. *Philos.* 1.1.4; Tert. *Ad nat.* 2.4, *De an.* 6.8, etc. For discussions of the proverbial anecdote, see Pease's n. on Cic. *De divin.* 1.30 (where Cicero quotes Enn. *Iphig. fr.* 244: *quod est ante pedes nemo spectat, caeli scrutantur plagas*); I. Vahlen, *Ennianae poesis reliquiae*[2] (Leipzig 1928) 160 f.; Otto *Sprichwörter* 274; P. Courcelle, "Le retentissement profane et chrétien d'un vers d'Ennius," REL 48 (1971) 107 ff. The associations of Claudius' grand aspirations (*deus fieri vult*) and halting gait is neatly exploited by Seneca *Apoc.* 8.3 by this proverbial idea: the same effect is intended here for the Christian "clodhoppers." For *caeli plagas . . . rimari* compare Varr. *Men.* 233B: *oculis caeli rimari plagas.*

[163] *maxime indoctis inpolitis, rudibus agrestibus:* see n. 38 above.

[164] *quibus non est datum intellegere civilia.* For the essentially practical and civic-minded Romans, a very damning accusation indeed; cf. Cicero's advice to his son: *philosophiae quidem praecepta noscenda, vivendum autem esse civiliter* (Cic. *ap.* Lact. *Div. inst.* 3.14.17 = 4.3.302 *fr.* 4 Müller). For Christians and public office, see n. 111 above. Octavius replies in 17.2 with the

reverse proposition: you have to understand the world as a whole before you can *pulchre gerere rem civilem.*

[165] The turn of phrase *quisque vestrum tantus est, si potuerit, imitetur* might be merely pleonastic: "whoever is equal to the task, let him imitate, if he can. . . ." For the expression used of Socrates, *princeps philosophiae,* see Cic. *De nat. deor.* 2.167 and Pease *ad loc.* for parallels (to which add Fronto, Naber 52), and cf. Cic. *De nat. deor.* 1.93: *parentem philosophiae.* It is a virtual quotation, as is the *scurra Atticus* ("buffoon of Attica") applied to Socrates in 38.5, the studiously matching reply of Octavius.

The passages provide rather typical evidence of the ambivalence with which the figure of Socrates might be regarded not only in philosophical circles generally, but especially in the early Christian tradition. For in that tradition Socrates frequently appears not as a "humbug" but as a pattern of philosophical integrity, vindicating Christian martyrs in their resistance to the tyranny of the state (the latter often spurred on by the instigation of demons), e.g., Just. *Apol.* 1.5, *Apol.* 2.7; Tert. *Apol.* 14.7 f.; Clem. *Strom.* 4.9.80.4; *Acta Apollon.* 41 (AnalBoll 14 [1895] 292 f.); or as a Christian before his due time, e.g., Just. *Apol.* 1.46, cf. *Apol.* 2.8; or as a Christlike model *sapiens,* e.g., Just. *Apol.* 2.10; Orig. *C.Cels.* 3.66. Note that Peregrinus was called by his fellow Christians "the new Socrates," Lucian *De mort. Pereg.* 12.

On the other hand, for Socrates as a typical pagan philosopher—declared to be the wisest of them all, but superstitious, in league with demons, a hypocrite and corrupter of youth, cf. Tat. *Or.* 25; Tert. *De an.* 1.5, *Apol.* 46.5 f.; Orig. *C.Cels.* 7.6; and 38.5 below.

For further analysis on Socrates, see A. von Harnack, *Sokrates und die alte Kirche* (Berlin 1900) esp. 16 ff.; E. Benz, "Christus und Sokrates in der alten Kirche," ZNTW 43 (1950/51) 195–224; E. Fascher, "Socrates und Christus: Eine Studie zur aktuellen Aufgabe der Religionsphänomenologie," ZNTW 45 (1954) 1–41. The question is a reflection of the ambivalent attitude of early Christians towards philosophy generally: see M. Pellegrino, *Gli apologeti greci del II secolo* (Rome 1947) 53 ff., 158 ff.

[166] *quod supra nos, nihil ad nos.* As so formulated, this adage is quoted only by Christian writers, by Lact. *Div. inst.* 3.20.10 (*celebre hoc proverbium*), cf. *Epit.* 32.3; Jerome *Adv. Ruf.* 3.28 (ML 23.500); Tert. *Ad nat.* 2.4.15. Unlike the former two, who ascribe the saying, with Caecilius, to Socrates, Tertullian ascribes

it to Epicurus. There has, consequently, been much discussion as to the correct attribution (e.g., Axelson 101 ff. and Beaujeu and Pellegrino *ad loc.*). But Ariston *ap.* Stobaeus *Flor.* 80.7 (3.104 ed. Meineke) shows that the saying was proverbial; cf. Apostol. 15.95C τὰ ὑπὲρ ἡμᾶς οὐδὲν πρὸς ἡμᾶς (2.654, *Corp. paroem. Graec.* ed. Leutsch); and suitably interpreted, both Epicurus and (more readily) Socrates might have been reasonably accredited with the *nostrum* in the philosophical tradition. For Epicurus see H. Usener, *Epicurea* (repr. Rome 1963) 229 no. 342 (*de meteoris*), cf. 71 (Κυρ. Δοξ. 2). For Socrates, Cic. *Acad. post.* 1.4.15: *caelestia autem vel procul esse a nostra cognitione . . . vel . . . nihil tamen ad bene vivendum;* Aul. Gellius *Noctes Atticae* 14.3.5: *Xenophon negat Socraten de caeli atque naturae causis rationibusque umquam disputavisse.*

[167] The famous reply of the Pythian oracle at Delphi to the inquiries of Socrates' disciple Chaerephon whether Socrates was the wisest of men. The fullest version appears to have been

σοφός Σοφοκλῆς, σοφώτερος δ'Εὐριπίδης
ἀνδρῶν δὲ πάντων Σωκράτης σοφώτατος

("Wise is Sophocles, wiser Euripides, but wisest of all Socrates"). See H. W. Parke and D. E. W. Wormell, *The Delphic Oracle* 2 (Oxford 1956) no. 420, and the references there cited. But there are many variants: Plato's form (the earliest) is in paraphrase and is carefully negative: "no one is wiser than Socrates," Plat. *Apol.* 20E and Parke and Wormell, *op. cit.* no. 134. For a good discussion, see Parke and Wormell, *op. cit.* 1.401–5. The oracle is quoted by Christian writers and exploited by them with the same mixture of approval (e.g., Tert. *Apol.* 46.5 f.; [Just.] *Cohort.* 36) and disapproval (e.g., Tert. *De an.* 1.5; Orig. *C.Cels.* 7.6) that they gave to Socrates' life and character generally. To Parke and Wormell's references one might add these patristic passages and Arnob. 2.21 etc.

[168] The reference is to philosophers of the Academy, a residential school founded by Plato c. 385 B.C. and situated on the outskirts of Athens. It had an apparently continuous existence right through to its final dissolution by Justinian in 529 A.D. Of its many illustrious members Caecilius singles out two of the most influential for the "sceptical" phase of the Academic *secta* The works of Sextus Empiricus (*fl.* c. 280 A.D.) give a full account of the whole system; and cf. V. Brochard, *Les sceptiques grecs* (2nd ed. Paris 1923).

Arcesilaus (c. 315–240 B.C.) was a pupil of Theophrastus and founder of the sceptical Middle Academy. He denied the validity of sense perception and hence the possibility of any certain knowledge; suspended judgment (*dubitatio*, see Pease on Cic. *De nat. deor.* 1.1: *adsensionem cohibuisse*) was, therefore, the proper philosophical attitude. He was arguing largely against the prevailing dogmatism of the contemporary Stoa. See PW 2.1 (1895) 1164–68 (H. von Arnim); Diog. Laer. 4.28 ff.; Pease on Cic. *De nat. deor.* 1.11.

Carneades (c. 214–128 B.C.) was the founder of the so-called Third or New Academy; while adhering to the scepticism of Arcesilaus, he admitted degrees of probability in human perception and thus gave the Academy a more positive direction by this modification. He did much to systematize ancient scepticism. See PW 10.2 (1919) 1964–85 ((H. von Arnim); Diog. Laer. 4.62 ff.; Pease on Cic. *De nat. deor.* 2.1 f.

See Cic. *De nat. deor.* 1.11 and Pease *ad loc.* for this emphasis on the direct philosophical descent of Arcesilaus and Carneades from Socrates with his critical inquisitiveness and suspension of judgment (*ratio contra omnia disserendi nullamque rem aperte iudicandi*).

[169] By a slip, Beaujeu reads here *Simonidis Melici* (MSS *melchi*) and translates "Simonide de Mélos." The epithet of Melos is, however, *Melius*. For *Simonides melicus*, i.e. the melic or lyric poet (to match *Hiero tyrannus*), cf. Pliny *N.H.* 7.24.89, 7.56.192; *Marius Victorinus gramm.* 6.194.15 (Keil); *Audax gram.* 7.325.5 (Keil). See also on this point L. Hermann, "Notes de Lecture 188," *Latomus* 25 (1966) 949 f. Simonides, from Iulis in Ceos (c. 556–468 B.C.: see C. M. Bowra, *Greek Lyric Poetry from Alcman to Simonides* [Oxford 1936] 317–401) was one of the many poets —Pindar and Aeschylus included—attracted to the brilliant court of Hiero, tyrant of Syracuse 478–67 B.C. (PW 8.2 [1913] 1496–1503 [Th. Lenschau]). For the evidence connecting Simonides and Hiero, see Pease on Cic. *De nat. deor.* 1.60, where this same anecdote is related; this Ciceronian passage is undoubtedly the source here. Tert. *Ad nat.* 2.2.11 and *Apol.* 46.8 has a variant version making the protagonists Thales and Croesus. Contra Baylis, *op. cit.* 314 ff., little can be exploited from this discrepancy for the question of priority, as variations are common in the already common theme of wise counselor advising a king, e.g., Hdt. 1.27 (Bias of Priene, *or* Pittacus of Mytilene, and Croesus);

Thrasyboulus and Periander in Hdt. 5.92.6 become Sextus
Tarquinius and Tarquin the Proud in Livy 1.54.6 ff. For the
theme see C. Bonner, "A Note on Mark 6.20," HTR 37 (1944)
41 ff., at 43 f., and also Axelson 39 f., 58.

[170] For this notion cf. *Orac. deor. gr.* 84 (K. Buresch, *Klaros*
[Leipzig 1889] 124, recounting this same story); Orig. *C.Cels.*
7.42.

[171] On *superstitio* and *religio* see n. 10; and for the idea of
steering a proper course between neglect of religion and acceptance of superstition, cf. Cic. *De divin.* 1.7: *est enim periculum
ne aut neglectis iis* (sc., *auspiciis rebusque divinis religioneque*)
impia fraude aut susceptis anili superstitione obligemur; ibid.
2.148: *nec vero . . . superstitione tollenda religio tollitur.*

[172] *homo Plautinae prosapiae, ut pistorum praecipuus, ita post-
remus philosophorum.* The general significance of these notoriously debated phrases is clear, but there is some obscurity about
the choice of specific details. The over-all meaning is that Octavius, being a member of a Christian following and therefore ill-
educated, must be no philosopher (cf. 8.3, 12.7); this charge is
rebutted in 20.1; it appears to be intended as a retort to the snub
of Octavius in 3.1 ("such blindness and crass ignorance").

homo Plautinae prosapiae. Jerome uses a variant *Plautinae
familiae* twice (*Ep.* 48.18 [ML 22.508]; 50.1 [ML 22.512]) and
leaves us in no doubt as to how he interpreted the phrase: he
uses it of ill-educated and ill-informed abusive braggarts, like
many a Plautine comic figure, *prosapia* being here a suitably
archaic (Cic. *Tim.* 11.39)—and Plautine (*Curc.* 3.23; *Merc.* 3.4.49)
—word for added mock-heroic effect. This being so, to look for
other explanations seems to be misspent labour (e.g., A. Beltrami,
"M. Minucio Felice *Octavius* 14.1," RFIC 47 [1919] 271 ff.
interprets the phrase as *homo caninae prosapiae = unus de grege
advocatorum vel causarum patronorum.*) Note the hit-back in
34.7: *non philosophi . . . sed mimi convicio digna ista sententia.*

In the correlative expression *ut . . . ita . . .* , the internal
meaning should be beyond dispute: a supreme *pistor* implies the
meanest *philosophus*. *Pistor* was a byword for unreflecting stupidity, his work the nadir of banausic drudgery; hence Cic. *Rosc.
Amer.* 46.134: *mitto hasce artes vulgares, coquos, pistores, lecti-
carios;* Cassius *ap.* Suet. *Aug.* 4: *crudissimum pistrinum;* Tert.
De cor. 13.8 lists in order brothels, lavatories, bakeries, and
prisons (*et lupanaria et latrinae et pistrina et carcer*); Plaut. *Pers.*

3.3.15 uses *pistrinorum civitas* as a term of abuse (of slaves, by a procurer: see S. Lilja, *Terms of Abuse in Roman Comedy* [Helsinki 1965] 39 and 55); hence *pistrinum* was a place of punishment (of the future pope Callistus, Hipp. *Philos.* 9.12.4 [GCS Hippolytus 3.247]) and Celsus derisively describes Joseph as the "chief baker" of Pharaoh, Orig. *C.Cels.* 4.47; Christians could make similar fun of the pagan cult of Jupiter Pistor (Lact. *Div. inst.* 1.20.33, and see Frazer on Ovid *Fast.* 6.350). Cicero can thus jocularly use *pistrinum* in *De orat.* 1.46 and 2.144 of the company of hard-working orators (versus easeful philosophers). On *pistrinum* see also Otto *Sprichwörter* 281. This contrast between philosophy and *pistrinum* is also found in Varro (*Sat. Menipp.* p. 194 Riese) *ap.* Aul. Gellius, *Noctes Atticae* 15.19, to the effect that the more one is a *pistor* the less one is a *philosophus;* and Sen. *Ep.* 90.22 (in the company of cobbler, shipwright, etc.). The contrast between *pistor* and *philosophus* seems, therefore, to have been traditional.

The next question is, what is the connexion of *pistorum praecipuus* with (a) *Plautina prosapia* and (b) Octavius? The former is readily answered: Plautus (Aul. Gellius, *Noctes Atticae* 3.3.14) was at one time reduced to working in a *pistrinum* (on Plautus' life see G. E. Duckworth, *The Nature of Roman Comedy* [Princeton 1952] 49 ff.). The latter is the problematical question. The simplest explanation is that Octavius can be so called by the company he keeps: it is irretrievably working-class, and *pistores* are the quintessence of that class (thus Tert. *Apol.* 46.9 on the *opifex christianus;* cf. Athenag. *Leg.* 12, Tat. *Or.* 32, Orig. *C.Cels.* 3.44 ff. So, too, Octavius does not deny the fact that the majority of Christians are *pauperes* in 36.3). But the specific nature of the trade, despite its well-documented literary use, has proved to be still a little disconcerting to many scholars, and has consequently provoked a variety of hypotheses (e.g., a pun on πιστοί = *fideles*, Th. Birt, "Marginalia zu lateinischen Prosaikern," *Phil.* 83 [1927] 164 ff., at 177; a reference to an easily traced slander on Matthew as a miller, preserved in a fragment of Porphyry, *Adv. christ.* [Harnack 13], P. Frassinetti, "Explanationes ad Porcium Licinum, Petronium et Minucium Felicem," *Athenaeum* 32 [1954] 384 ff., at 390 ff.; or—an attractive but unfortunately quite unprovable suggestion—Octavius was in fact a *patronus collegii pistorum* or the like, so E. Cocchia, *Studi critici e scritti varii* 2 [Naples 1927] 115 ff., at 123 ff.; see further CIL 6.1690, 1693;

J.-P. Waltzing, *Les collèges professionels* 2 [Brussels 1896] 78
ff., and 4 [1900] 37 ff., 114 f.; also A. Stöckle, "Spätrömische und
byzantinische Zünfte," *Klio* Bft. 9 [1911] 1 ff., at 47 ff.). Other
theories are summarized in E. Magaldi, "Della controversia su
'Homo Plautinae prosapiae etc.' (Min. Fel. *Octav.* xiv.1),"
Didaskaleion 7 (1929) 41 ff., and G. Révay, " 'Pistorum praecipuus': Un passo difficile nell'Octavius de M. Minucio Felice,"
ibid. 1.2 (1923) 3 ff. Any emendation—and there are many—
which destroys the alliteration, common in M.F., ought to be
eschewed; see E. san Giovanni, "L'Allitterazione in Minucio
Felice," *Boll. di filol. class.* 17 (1910) 87–91 (who, however,
omits this passage).

Fronto was notoriously fond of Plautus and Plautine vocabulary, e.g., Naber 61, 26, 178, 224; see R. Marache, *Mots nouveaux
et mots archaïques chez Fronton et Aulu-Gelle* (Paris 1957) 97
f. One suspects, therefore—but this is merely suspicion—that the
original conceit may have been devised by him in the speech in
which he attacked Christianity. Octavius' speech which follows,
with its heavy use of such Plautine features of style as pleonasm
(often with asyndeton), alliteration, assonance, etc., is fittingly
Plautine in pedigree. Cf. my article, "Four Passages of Minucius
Felix," *Kyriakon: Festschrift Johannes Quasten* (Münster 1970)
2.504–506.

[173] The *locus classicus* of this interlude on the snares of eristic
eloquence is Plato *Phaedo* 88B ff. There can be little room for
doubt that Plato, or a literal translation of Plato, is used directly
here (though it is not necessary to believe that Plato was so used
elsewhere, in 19.14, 23.2, 26.2, 34.3–6, *pace* J.-P. Waltzing, "Platon,
source directe de Minucius Felix," *Musée belge* 8 [1904] 424–28:
a handbook of philosophical δοξαί would be a sufficient source;
it is clear that they all formed part of the *sententiarum suppellex*
of the educated mind). The theme of the duplicity and the
deceptiveness of rhetoric is a common one, particularly among
Christian writers sensitive to the unrelieved literary aridity and
naïveté, if not barbarity, of the biblical style: Iren. *Adv. haer.*
praef. 1.3 (MG 7.443 f.); Tert. *Apol.* 48.1; Arnob. 1.58 f., 2.11;
Theoph. *Ad Autol.* 1.1; [Just.] *Cohort.* 8, 35 f.; Just. *Apol.* 2.10;
Tat. *Or.* 29,32; Athenag. *Leg.* 11; Cyp. *Ad Donat.* 2; Clem.
Strom. 1.10.48; Orig. *C.Cels.* 1.62, 3.39, 4.50, 6.2, 7.41, 7.59 f.,
etc.; for further discussion see Intro. p. 16 ff. and n. 194 below.

[174] *sic adsidue temeritate decepti.* It is a little uncertain whether

the *temeritas* should belong to the audience (= impetuosity; they assent *sine dilectu*) or to the speakers (= sheer effrontery; they assert falsehoods with authoritative eloquence). The former interpretation suits the context better.

[175] On this point Theoph. *Ad Autol.* 3.7 quotes the Greek comic poet Philemon (Koch, *Comic. Attic. Frag.* 2.252, no. 143: "What is intolerable is an unintelligent audience; because of their stupidity they do not find fault with themselves"); cf. Plat. *Phaed.* 90D.

[176] *ut damnatis omnibus malint universa suspendere:* the sceptical ἐποχή or *dubitatio* (13.3) which, says Arnob. 2.10, results from the constant disputes of philosophers; cf. Plat. *Phaed.* 88C.

[177] Cf. Plat. *Phaed.* 89C ff. for a detailed description of this passage from misology to misanthropy.

[178] *utrimque omni negotio disseratur et ex altera parte plerumque obscura sit veritas. . . .* Translators have varied in taking these clauses generally or specifically, i.e., "in every question there are arguments to be said on both sides and on the one hand the truth is generally obscure . . ." as opposed to the more specific translation given in the text. In the context both appear to be possible interpretations.

[179] *religiosus.* On the meaning of the word, see Aul. Gellius, *Noctes Atticae* 4.9. Aul. Gellius *ibid.* 14.2 has a disquisition from Favorinus on the topic *officium iudicis;* note especially §§17 ff. on the controversial subject of the propriety, or impropriety, of *interlocutiones* on the part of the judge.

[180] *intergressu gravissimae disputationis.* The phrase *gravissima disputatio* is repeated from 1.5, on which see n. 11.

[181] Not, as at first sight it appears to be, a rather odd (unanswered) appeal for intervention addressed to Minucius Felix, after he has just protested his good faith as a *iudex religiosus*, but a neat way of saying that the meretricious tinsel of rhetorical polemic will be found on the pagan side only.

[182] *conviciorum amarissimam labem verborum veracium flumine.* For this idea cf. Plat. *Phaedr.* 243D: "I desire to wash out the bitterness from my ears with the sweet water of discourse." Plato need not be a direct source, however; cf. Cic. *De nat. deor.* 2.20: *sic orationis flumine reprensoris convicia diluuntur,* and Athenaeus 121e: "to wash away bitter words with sweet streams" (so P. Shorey, "Plato and Minucius Felix," CR 18 [1904] 302 f.). The

metaphor of the stream of speech is commonplace: see Pease's n. on Cic. *De nat. deor.* 1.2 for abundant parallels.

[183] Elaborate metaphors of roads and paths are very common in the language of philosophy and religion: Cic. *De nat. deor.* 2.1: *de dis immortalibus habere non errantem et vagam . . . sed . . . stabilem certamque sententiam* (echoed here); cf. *idem, Acad. prior.* 2.66, *De off.* 2.7. It is particularly common in Christian writings, no doubt receiving stimulus from such biblical passages as Matt. 7.13–14 and especially from the doctrine of the "Two Ways" (*Did.* 1.1 f.; Hermas *Mand.* 6.1.3, cf. Hermas *Vis.* 3.7.1; Tert. *Apol.* 47.9; Orig. *C.Cels.* 8.16, etc. And see n. 186 and chap. 35.6 below).

[184] To underline the inconsistencies and internal contradictions of the pagan case was standard procedure in Christian apologetics. For abundant parallels see Pellegrino *ad loc.* For the same trick in Jewish apology, compare Joseph. *Cont. Ap.* 2.6: "His argument is difficult to summarize and his meaning to grasp. But so far as the extreme disorder and confusion of his lying statements admit of analysis, one may say that . . ." (trans. H. St. J. Thackeray, Loeb Classical Library 1926).

[185] Some irony is presumably intended, in view of what Caecilius has just said about the Christians' social and cultural attainments (7.3 ff., 12.7).

[186] There seems to be a reminiscence of Verg. *Aen.* 6.540: *Hic locus est, partes ubi se via findit in ambas;* there are elaborations of this situation of *aporia* or indecisiveness at the crossroads in Ovid *Fast.* 5.3–6; Oppian *Halieut.* 3.501–6; Plato *Legg.* 7.799C; cf. Cic. *De divin.* 1.123. Indeed the idea was proverbial: see Hes. *Theog.* 911 f. and Zenob. 3.78 ἐν τριόδῳ εἰμί (1.76 *Corp. paroem. Graec.* ed. Leutsch and Schneidewin). The famous myth of Hercules choosing between the path of *voluptas* or *virtus* is comparable (attributed to Prodicus of Ceos); see Xen. *Mem.* 2.1.21 ff.; Cic. *De off.* 1.32.118; cf. Lact. *Div. inst.* 6.3.6 (the fork in the road of life).

[187] *una veritate confirmata probataque.* This could also be translated "by confirming and proving. . . ."

[188] On this see n. 21 above.

[189] *inliteratos, pauperes, inperitos* (the charges against Christians in 8.3 ff., 12.7; see also on *inperitos* n. 22 above). These three epithets are countered in turn: (a) lack of education is no bar, because all men have innate wisdom; (b) neither is lack of money:

wisdom is not given for riches, and the wealthy are in fact tied to their earthly possessions; and (c) lack of literary skill is actually a blessing: the truth is thereby clearer. But in the characteristic style of the *Octavius*, the lines of the divisions in the reply are somewhat blurred together.

[190] *natura insitos esse sapientiam*. Octavius appeals to *emphytoi* or *koinoi ennoiai* implanted in every man by nature. It was a notion particularly favoured by the Stoic school, e.g., Sen. *Ep.* 90.1 f., 44.3: *bona mens omnibus patet, omnes ad hoc sumus nobiles. . .* , 117.6: *omnibus insita de dis opinio est;* Dio Chrys. *Or.* 12.27,39; Aët. *Plac.* 4.11.3; but the Epicurean prolepsis was closely allied (Cic. *De nat. deor.* 1.44: *insitas . . . vel potius innatas cognitiones habemus;* Lucr. 5.1161 ff.; Epic. *fr.* 227ª, Usener = Lact. *Div. inst.* 3.25.4), and indeed the idea is formulated in a wide variety of sources, being closely connected with the equally general use of *consensus omnium* (on which see nn. 100, 228); cf. Cic. *De fin.* 4.2.4, *De legg.* 1.7.18; and see Pease on Cic. *De nat. deor.* 1.43 f. for a heterogeneous collection of references. It is, of course, a very frequent idea in Christian writers starting from Rom. 2.15 *opus legis scriptum in cordibus;* cf. Clem. *Protrep.* 2.25.3, *Strom.* 1.29.181.4 ff., 4.8.58.3, 5.14.133.7 ff. (for other Clementine passages, see A. Beltrami, "Clemente Alessandrino nell'Ottavio di M. Minucio Felice," RFIC 47 [1919] 366 ff., at 373, and E. Molland, "Clement of Alexandria on the Origin of Greek Philosophy," *Symb. Oslo.* 15/16 [1936] 57 ff., at 66 ff.); Orig. *C.Cels.* 1.4; Arnob. 1.33; (see P. Krafft, *Beiträge zur Wirkungsgeschichte des älteren Arnobius* [Weisbaden 1966] 43 ff.); Just. *Apol.* 2.8,13; and possibly the *testimonium animae* argument associated with Tertullian (on this see n. 228 on 18.11). See further Pohlenz 1.56 ff., 78, 123 f., 195 ff., 2.221.

[191] *plebeios, indoctos, seminudos:* a rejoinder to 8.4, where see n. 111.

[192] For this classic theme of more profound knowledge of God to be found among the poor and simple than among the wealthy and the philosophic, see Just. *Apol.* 2.10, *Apol.* 1.60; Tat. *Or.* 32; Athenag. *Leg.* 11.

[193] A commonly expressed point: cf. Cic. *De nat. deor.* 1.10; Plato *Charm.* 161C; Varro *Sentent.* 22 (*Menipp.* ed. Riese 266); Cyp. *Ad Donat.* 2; *Imitation of Christ* 1.5: *non quaeras quis hoc dixerit sed quid dicatur attende* etc.

[194] Chr. Mohrmann takes this to be "la défense de l'usage populaire des cercles chrétiens," *Études sur le latin des chrétiens* 1 (Rome 1961) 403 ff. It is certainly a common theme in the Christian tradition: for references see n. 173 above, to which one might add Cyp. *Ad Donat.* 2 (ML 4.197 f.); Jerome *In Eccles.* 9.17 (CCSL 72.332) disapproving of preachers who indulged in rhetoric and provoked applause (so, too, *In Ezech.* 10.33.22–33 [CCSL 75.479]); Aug. *Enarr. in Ps.* 138.20 (CCSL 40.2004): *melius est reprehendant nos grammatici, quam non intellegant populi;* (see further Hagendahl, *Latin Fathers and the Classics* 314 n.1; R. MacMullen, "A Note on *sermo humilis*," JTS 17 [1966] 108 ff.); but the theme had a well-established classical tradition as well. Note, e.g., the *verbum illud vetus et pervulgatum* quoted by Aul. Gellius, *Noctes Atticae* 12.5.6: ἀμαθέστερόν πως εἰπὲ καὶ σαφέστερον λέγε (i.e., Aristoph. *Frogs* 1445: "speak with less learning—and more clarity"). It was a common theme among Stoics: see C. N. Smiley, "Seneca and the Stoic Theory of Literary Style," *Classical Studies in Honor of Charles Forster Smith*, Univ. of Wisconsin Stud. in Lang. and Lit. 3 (1919) 50 ff.

[195] *regula recti.* A term with philosophical overtones: note esp. Diog. Laert. 10.27: Epicurus' work called περὶ κριτηρίου ἢ κανών, and *ibid.* 10.31 κριτήρια τῆς ἀληθείας; the Stoics also used the expression περὶ κανόνων καὶ κριτηρίων (Diog. Laert. 7.41.); Isid. *Etym.* 6.16.1 equates|κανών and *regula*, and see H. Oppel, ΚΑΝΩΝ, *Philol. Suppl.* 30.4 (1937) esp. 80–94 on the philosophical use of *regula* in Latin.

[196] This refers back to 5.5, where see n. 41. It is always an effective technique in an *ad hominem* argument to concede the opponent's premise, but then to reinterpret its implications. Clem. *Paed.* 3.1.1 draws the same implications more precisely: "It seems, then, that the greatest of all knowledge is to know yourself; if you know yourself, you will also know God." And for the prominence of this "know thyself" theme in teleological philosophizing, see R. Beutler 12 ff.

[197] The materialistic theory, or theories, put forward in 5.7 ff., where see nn. 44, 45, 46.

[198] For this line of thought, frequent in Stoic discussions being based on their notion of the organic unity of the world (for which see Pease on Cic. *De nat. deor.* 2.29), cf. M. Aurel. *Med.* 8.52; Persius *Sat.* 3.66 ff. and Schol. *ad loc.*, etc. See also Beutler 12–17, who *inter alia* aptly quotes *Vit. Pythag.* 18 (O. Immisch,

Agatharchidea, Sitz. Heidelb. Akad. Phil.-Hist. Kl. 10.1 [1919]
32): "To know oneself is nothing other than to know the nature
of the entire universe"; and cf. Asclepius 10 (ed. Nock-Festigière,
308): "he who knows himself, also knows the world" (*is novit
se, novit et mundum*).

[199] The contrary of the attitude to be found in 12.7. The appeal
is to the commonly expressed notion of the cosmopolis or world-
city to which the whole race of mankind belongs—"Every land
is one's homeland" being a proverbial notion first attributed to
Diogenes the Cynic, *Epict.* 3.24.66. Expressions of this idea become particularly frequent in the Hellenistic world after the
breakdown of the narrow political barriers of the city-states that
resulted from the conquests of Alexander (W. W. Tarn, *Alexander the Great* 2 [Cambridge 1948] Ap. 2, 399–449). The Stoic
school, with their "natural law" theory, adopted the idea with
repetitious enthusiasm (Sen. *Ep.* 28.4, 48.3, 95.52; *Dial.* 8.4.1; M.
Aurel. *Med.* 2.10, 3.11, 6.44, 9.9, 10.15, etc.; and Pohlenz 1.135 ff.,
315 f., 351); and the theme had a vigorous life both in Hellenistic-
Judaic writings (Philo *De somn.* 1.243) and of course in those
of Christianity (Tert. *Apol.* 38.3; Tat. *Or.* 28; Orig. *C.Cels.* 8.72;
Ad Diog. 5.5), culminating in the Augustinian concept of the
civitas Dei. See Spanneut 254 ff. for further passages. To introduce
the idea here was doubly useful; it not only demonstrated that
the proper study of mankind included God; it reinforced the idea
that all men, including Christians, can properly examine the
Universal Commonwealth of Nature, of which they are all equal
citizens. For further discussion on the idea, see Pease's nn. on Cic.
De nat. deor. 1.121, 2.154, and A. G. McCready, "Cosmopolitanism
and the Roman Empire," in *For Service to Classical Studies:
Essays in Honour of Francis Letters* (Melbourne 1966) 131 ff.

[200] This argument distinguishing man from beasts by their
posture—beasts being essentially intent on food, but men, with
upward gaze, meant to understand heaven—is a cliché of ancient
philosophy. For a multifarious collection of references, see S. O.
Dickermann, *De argumentis quibusdam e structura hominis et
animalium petitis* (diss. Halle 1909) 92 ff., and additions supplied
by Pease on Cic. *De nat. deor.* 2.140 (see also Cic. *ibid.* 2.37: *ipse
autem homo ortus est ad mundum contemplandum,* and Pease's
n. *ad loc.*). For discussion see Beutler 18 ff.; M. Pellegrino, "Il
'Topos' della 'status rectus' nel conteso filosofico e biblico,"
Mullus (Münster 1964) 273 ff.; H. Chadwick, "Origen, Celsus

and the Stoa," JTS 48 (1947) 34 ff., at 36 ff. (part of the Stoa-versus-Academy debate). Note the variant in Just. *Apol.* 1.55: man differs from animals in having his head erect, his hands extended, his nose protruding from his forehead—whereby he resembles the form of the Cross!

[201] *sermo et ratio.* This almost seems to be a calque, being closely parallel to *Ad Diog.* 10.2: οἷς λόγον ἔδωκεν οἷς νοῦν; but the resemblance is perhaps only accidental, for this combination of words is particularly common in Tertullian and seems basically designed to express the Stoic distinction between λόγος προφορικός (the external logos) and λόγος ἐνδιάθετος (the internal logos); see esp. Tert. *Apol.* 21.10: *apud vestros quoque sapienter* ΛΟΓΟΝ *id est sermonem atque rationem, constat artificem videri universitatis;* cf. *Apol.* 21.11, 17.1, and for discussion R. Braun, *"Deus christianorum": Recherches sur le vocabulaire doctrinal de Tertullien* (Paris 1962) 260–65; Spanneut 310 ff.; Pohlenz 1.439 ff. (he says on this phrase of M.F.: "wo er neben Cicero wohl auch ein stoiches Kompendium benutzt" [2.215]). See also Beutler 17–19, esp. for the common connexion made between knowledge and imitation; he compares Sen. *Dial.* 4.16.2: *ex omnibus animalibus ut solus imitetur solus intellegit* [*homo deum*].

[202] A further rebuttal of 5.7 (*in terram proiecti*) and 12.7 (*pro pedibus aspicere*); for the general line of thought, Manilius *Astronom.* 4.920 ff.: *ipse vocat nostros animos ad sidera mundus/ nec patitur, quia non condit, sua iura latere./quis putet esse nefas nosci, quod cernere fas est?* For the specific notion of the wickedness of ignorance, see Tert. *Apol.* 17.3, *Adv. Marc.* 5.16; Orig. *C.Cels.* 3.77, 4.65; and cf. chap. 35.4 f. and n. 597. Note, too, the complaint of the Anonymous *ap.* Euseb. *H.E.* 5.28.14 (on the Theodotians): "They abandon the holy scripture of God and study geometry [lit. = measurement of the earth], for they are of the earth and they speak of the earth, and Him who comes from above they do not know."

[203] Here begins a relatively brief statement of the so-called "argument from design," which had a flourishing history in ancient philosophizing. There were, of course, references to such a notion in biblical literature, e.g. Sap. 13.1–5, esp. for the notion here adumbrated *et de his quae videntur bona, non potuerunt intelligere eum qui est neque operibus attendentes agnoverunt quis esset artifex;* Ps. 18.2: *Caeli enarrant gloriam Dei et opera manuum eius annuntiat firmamentum;* Rom. 1.20 f.; Acts 17.24 ff.; and in

Christian apologetics (e.g., Theoph. *Ad Autol.* 1.4, 1.6, 2.10; Arist. *Apol.* 1; Tert. *Apol.* 17). But Octavius' main source in this and the following chapter is without any doubt Cicero's *De natura deorum*, Book 2, where the "natural" theology of the Stoic partisan Balbus is expounded at length (for other possible sources, see the discussion in Beutler 21 ff.). Socrates, according to the philosophical autobiography in Plato *Phaedo* 97A ff., declared that he had discovered the argument for himself; a full statement of it seems to have been made in the no longer extant, but very influential, youthful treatise of Aristotle *De philosophia*. And the later Stoic school was especially associated with the argument. For general discussion see K. Reinhardt, *Kosmos und Sympathie* (Munich 1926) (esp. for the Posidonian contributions to the topic); G. Lazzati, *L'Aristotele perduto e gli scrittori cristiani* (Milan 1938) esp. 62 ff.; Spanneut 371 ff., esp. 383 f. As so much of chaps. 17–19 is paralleled in Cicero *De natura deorum*, the annotation here largely consists of references to Pease's commentary, for little has been overlooked in the meticulous references and bibliography of that work.

For the ideas here, see Pease's nn. on Cic. *De nat. deor.* 2.4 (for *hunc mundi totius ornatum* = κόσμος; cf. Tert. *Apol.* 17.1), *De nat. deor* 2.82 (for *frustis quibusdam temere cohaerentibus*), 2.147 (for *mentem, sensum etc. non habere*).

[204] This passage is a virtual quotation from Cic. *De nat. deor.* 2.4: *quid enim potest esse tam apertum tamque perspicuum, cum caelum suspeximus caelestiaque contemplati sumus, quam esse aliquod numen praestantissimae mentis quo haec regantur*, combined with a modified verbal tetracolon from Cic. *De nat. deor.* 1.100. For comment see Pease's n. on *De nat. deor.* 2.4.

[205] The thought is to be found in a splendid passage in Cic. *De nat. deor.* 2.95, quoting from the lost Aristotelian work *De philosophia* (fr. 12 Rose): *cum . . . caelum totum cernerent astris distinctum et ornatum lunaeque luminum varietatem, tum crescentis tum senescentis. . . .* In the argument from design, the proof from the beauty-in-variety of the firmament is, of course, standard—as again is the proof from its utility (§6 below); for parallels see Pease on Cic. *De nat. deor.* 2.15, 2.55 (on celestial harmony), 2.95. Especially noteworthy is the brilliant eulogy of the harmony of the cosmos in 1 *Clem.* 20; cf. Athenag. *Leg.* 16; Theoph. *Ad Autol.* 1.6; etc.

[206] For the common theme of *diei noctisque vicissitudo*, see

Pease on Cic. *De nat. deor.* 2.95, 101, 132; Beutler 26. Xen. *Mem.*
4.3.3 is an early statement; cf. Aug. *De civ. Dei* 22.24 (in a closely
parallel discussion): *quam grata vicissitudo diei alternantis et noctis.* For the stars generally, see Pease on Cic. *De nat. deor.* 2.15,
2.43, 2.104 ff. (esp. 2.105 f. on the *cursum navigandi*); for the
sun, Cic. *De nat. deor.* 2.49; the moon, *ibid.* 2.50; for the plough
and harvest time, cf. Hesiod *Works and Days* 383 f. (cf. the more
general observation in Cic. *De nat. deor.* 2.155). Characteristically
Tat. *Or.* 27 denigrates this sort of inquiry.

[207] Again a direct copy of Cicero, *De nat. deor.* 2.115 (on the
arrangement of the stars and the beauty of the heavens): *Aut
vero alia quae natura mentis et rationis expers haec efficere potuit?
Quae non modo ut fierent ratione eguerunt sed intellegi qualia
sint sine summa ratione non possunt?* Compare, too, *ibid.* 2.97:
*quae (tam certos caeli motus, tam ratos astrorum ordines etc.)
quanto consilio gerantur nullo consilio adsequi possumus.* For
parallels see Pease's commentary on Cic. *De nat. deor.* 2.115. To
translate, as is frequently done, "requires a supreme effort of
intelligence" is to miss the punch of the deliberate paradox in a
context which consciously endeavors to analyze by rational discussion the workings of the universe.

[208] There are four main themes in this section common in the
argument from natural phenomena to demonstrate that there is
a providential dispensation. They are (a) the maintenance of
ordered regularity in the world, as shown by the unvarying four
(on the number, which in fact could vary, see Pease on Cic. *De
nat. deor.* 2.49) seasons. For the argument from constant order,
which made even Lucretius admit (5.1183 ff.) that it caused
some men to believe in the existence of a superhuman being, see
Pease's nn. on Cic. *De nat. deor.* 2.43, 2.56, *De divin.* 2.146; and
specifically illustrated by the seasons, see *De nat. deor.* 2.101, and
compare esp. Cic. *Tusc. disp.* 1.68 ff.

b) The rich variegation in the crops characteristic of those
seasons: see Cic. *De nat. deor.* 2.98, cf. 2.156, 1.4; 1 *Clem.* 20;
Theoph. *Ad Autol.* 1.6; Philo *Leg. alleg.* 3.39.97. Winter—usually
set down as a time of agricultural rest, see Cic. *De rep.* 4.1.1 (cf.
chap. 34.11 below)—has its early December crop of olives (Colum.
De re rust. 12.52.1) to complete the balance and symmetry; cf.
Gratiarum actio Mamertini (*Panegy. Lat.* ed. Mynors *Or.* 3) 22,
where, in a more elaborate conceit, the same agricultural phenomenon is exploited (*una certe unius hiemis est olivitas*); so too

[Tert.] *De iudicio domini* 2–5 (ML 2.1089) has each season with a characteristic produce concluding with *quisve hiemi placidas semper laudabit olivas;* Verg. *Georg.* 2.519, imitated by Proba in her Vergilian cento (CSEL 16.573 l.78). The *olivitas* is *necessaria* as it formed a staple of agricultural produce, being used for food, cooking, lighting, medicine, etc.; see Verg. *Georg.* 2 *passim*, and cf. Orig. *C.Cels.* 8.67.

c) The benevolence of providence in providing the mean seasons of spring and autumn: cf. esp. Sen. *De benef.* 4.28.1: *diem, solem, hiemis aestatisque cursus et media veris autumnique temperamenta . . . (di) invenerunt;* Verg. *Georg.* 2.343 ff.: *nec res hunc tenerae possent perferre laborem/si non tanta quies iret frigusque caloremque/inter, et exciperet caeli indulgentia terras.* By contrast Tat. *Or.* 20 does not think the changing seasons the perfect climatic arrangement; Arnob. 2.59 f. dismisses the question.

d) The corollary of the previous theme, the safety in the slow and peaceful transitions between the seasonal extremes, shows the workings of providence; this is emphasized by Xen. *Mem.* 4.3.9; Dio Chrys. *Or.* 3.79 f; cf. Cleomedes ed. Ziegler 52.14 ff.; 1 *Clem.* 20.9, etc.

The fact that the stars indicate the time for harvest and plough (§6), and that the mean seasons and slow seasonal changes are highly beneficial, though well-established themes, are not specifically elaborated by Cicero; hence speculation about further (Posidonian?) source material. For discussion see Beutler 27 f. (but on the safety theme, note Cic. *De nat. deor.* 2.98: *impetum caeli . . . constantissime conficientem vicissitudines anniversarias cum summa salute et conservatione rerum omnium*).

209 An enumeration of such phenomena can have many variations in this argument: e.g., 1 *Clem.* 20.10 has ocean, sea, earth's fruits, sun, moon, etc., seasons, winds, perennial springs; cf. Arnob. 1.30; Theoph. *Ad Autol.* 2.36.

For the sea (of course, the Mediterranean primarily) and the bounds imposed upon it by the land, see Cic. *De nat. deor.* 2.100: *ipsum autem mare sic terram appetens litoribus eludit,* and Pease's n. *ad loc.* (*orarum ac litorum*); cf. *De nat. deor.* 2.116; Job 38.10: *Circumdedi illud* (sc., *mare*) *terminis meis;* Clem. *Protrep.* 1.5.1; Firmicus Matern. *Math.* 7.1.2: *qui maris fluctus intra certos terrae terminos coarctavit;* Sedulius *Carm. pasch.* 1.22f. Note the parallel in Philo *De provid.* 1.33: *maris situs secundum legem;* 1.70: *mare regulam mandati non excedit* (Aucher)—due to Posidonian sources, as there was little rabbinical interest in the argument from design? See Beutler 28 f.

For the trees and their sustenance, see Cic. *De nat. deor.* 2.83, 2.120: *e terra sucum trahunt quo alantur ea quae radicibus continentur;* cf. Aug. *De civ. Dei* 11.27: *arbusta omnesque frutices . . . aliud terrae radicis adfigunt, quo alimentum trahant* and other pages cited by Pease *ad loca.* It is a characteristically Stoic point.

For the Ocean (i.e., Atlantic) and its tides (generally speaking, hardly a Mediterranean feature; cf. Cic. *De nat. deor.* 3.33: *aestus maritimi vel Hispanienses vel Britannici*), see Cic. *ibid.* 2.132: *aestus maritimi accedentes et recedentes* and Pease's nn. on Cic. *De nat. deor.* 2.19 and *De divin.* 2.34; and generally, my article "Ancient Knowledge of the Gulf Stream," CP 62 (1967) 25 ff., adding to the references Lucan. *Phars.* 1.409 ff and Amm. Marc. 27.8.4. They were popular topics of interest both in science and in rhetoric.

For springs and rivers, see Cic. *De nat. deor.* 2.98: *fontium gelidas perennitates, liquores perlucidos amnium;* cf. Apul. *De mund.* 4: *haec* (sc., *terra) fontium perennitate recreatur, haec fluminum frigidos lapsus nunc erroribus terrenis vehit . . .* ; *idem, Flor.* 10: *ubique distinxit amnium fluores;* Theoph. *Ad Autol.* 1.6.

[210] For hills and plains, cf. Cic. *De nat. deor.* 2.98: *impendentium montium altitudines, inmensitatesque camporum;* cf., too, Apul. *De mund.* 4: *(terra) altitudine montium, camporum aequore . . . variatur; idem, Flor.* 10: *alibi montium arduos vertices extulit, alibi camporum supinam planitiem coaequavit.* For animals and their means of defense there is a doublet in Cic. *De nat. deor.* 2.121 and 2.127. It was a hardy commonplace of ancient literature; for the *spicatas aculeis* (sea urchins, hedgehogs, porcupines, etc.) see Pease on Cic. *De nat. deor.* 2.121 and for the general theme, with abundant documentation, on *ibid.* 2.127.

[211] For man's beauty cf. Cic. *ibid.* 1.47, and for the military deployment of his senses Cic. *ibid.* 2.140 *tamquam in arce* (a very common figure, from Plat. *Tim.* 70A onwards, in the teleological argument); see Pease's commentary *ad loca;* Beutler 31 ff.

[212] The argument from *formae pulchritudo* of man appears to be elaborated in §§1–2, and the corollary, the *providentia specialis* in the physical world of man, in §§3–4; the nature and char-

acteristics of that *providentia* in §§5–10. The emphasis laid on this regard of Providence for detail is, in part, a reply to chap. 10.5: God cannot attend to both the whole and the parts.

For the commonplace argument from beauty and utility in man's *membra*, cf. Cic. *De nat. deor.* 1.47: . . . *quae compositio membrorum, quae conformatio liniamentorum, quae figura, quae species humana potest esse pulchrior? Vos quidem . . . soletis . . . quam sint omnia in hominis figura non modo ad usum verum etiam ad venustatem apta describere; ibid.* 1.92: [*descriptio*] *omnium corporis partium in qua nihil inane, nihil sine causa, nihil supervacuum est, itaque nulla ars imitari sollertiam naturae potest; ibid.* 2.133–9 on the same proof from *tota hominis fabricatio . . . omnisque humanae naturae figura atque perfectio* (largely on the face, digestive system, and bones). For the dissimilarity in uniformity, cf. Sen. *Ep.* 113.16: *etiam quae similia videntur cum contuleris diversa sunt;* and particularly Apul. *Asclep.* 35: . . . *ut hominum genus quamvis sit uniforme . . . singuli tamen in eadem forma sui dissimiles sunt.*

[213] For procreation as illustration of divine providence, see Cic. *De nat. deor.* 2.128; Xen. *Mem.* 1.4.7; Joseph. *Contra Ap.* 2.192; Athenag. *Res.* 12; Theoph. *Ad Autol.* 1.6; and cf. Dio 56.2.3 f. (Augustus on his marital legislation); for the phenomenon of lactation, see Cic. *loc. cit.* and Pease's note *ad loc.;* Lucr. 1.258 ff., 5.813 ff.; Clem. *Paed.* 1.6.44.2; cf. Aul. Gellius, *Noctes Atticae* 12.1 (Favorinus on the virtues of mothers' breast-feeding their own children). Both are frequent illustrations. Note that Octavius' language is general, and the reference need not necessarily be about man specifically, although the rhythm of the context suggests that it is. (The word translated by "offspring" [*fetus*] is used more frequently of human beings than Lewis and Short suggest. See TLL *s.v.*) For the language *ubertate lactei roris,* cf. Cic. *De divin.* 1.20 (a quotation from his own poem *De consulatu*): *uberibus gravidis vitali rore rigabat* (Pease incorrectly observing *ad loc.* that *ros* is used only there of milk).

[214] The examples of Nile, Euphrates, and Indus—though a rhetorically frequent triplet for illustrations from exotic geography—are clearly derived ultimately from Cic. *De nat. deor.* 2.130, where see Pease's excellent nn. Britain has been added to the catalogue—a standard example for northern geography—to complete the coverage of the *universitas,* but the precise point of the illustration lacks a parallel. Its genesis seems to lie in a combi-

nation of fact and theory: (a) the fact that Britain's sun-deficient island climate (Strabo 4.200; Herodian 3.14.8, etc.) was milder than that of the Continent opposite (Caes. *B.G.* 5.12.7; Tac. *Agr.* 12.3; cf. *Panegy. Lat. or.* 6.9 ed. Mynors), and (b) the theory that inherent warmth in the sea was released by movement or agitation (as warmth is released in one taking exercise), and with its tides, estuaries, and storms, the waters around Britain were fit subjects of this agitation; for the theory cf. Cic. *De nat. deor.* 2.26 (on *maria agitata ventis*).

Any reference to the Gulf Stream is, therefore, rather due to the accidents of theory and of rhetoric than to any empirical knowledge of the temperature of the British waters. For further discussion and details, see my article "Ancient Knowledge of the Gulf Stream," CP 62 (1967) 25 ff.

The emphasis on the balanced equilibrium in nature, lacking in the Ciceronian passage (*De nat. deor.* 2.130) suggests the influence of some Stoic source (Beutler 35).

For the care of *singula* as well as the *universitas* by providence, cf. Cic. *De nat. deor.* 2.164, *De divin.* 1.117; Plat. *Legg.* 10.900C ff.; M. Aurel. *Med.* 6.44; Just. *Dial.* 1; Clem. *Strom.* 7.2.9.1.

²¹⁵ This particular formulation of the argument from design has been often used, and especially with the favored metaphor of the universe as a dwelling place (see Pease's nn. on Cic. *De nat. deor.* 2.15 and Spanneut 254, 283 ff. for parallels). Cicero *De nat. deor.* 2.15 ff. appears to be the immediate source of the present passage, but there is more precisely emphasized here the idea that "the Creator is superior to His creation" (though that type of argument appears frequently elsewhere in the *De nat. deor.*: note esp. 2.29 ff., where see Pease's nn.); cf. Acts 17.24; Rom. 9.21; Athenag. *Leg.* 15; Arist. *Apol.* 3; Just. *Apol.* 1.20, quoting Menander. It is not a surprising conclusion, for it was the common Stoic view that the whole of anything was not to be identified with the sum of its parts (see Pease's nn. on Cic. *De nat. deor.* 2.30 ff., and H. Chadwick, "Origen, Celsus, and the Stoa," JTS 48 [1947] 34 ff., at 44 f., for a collection of references) and it was standard rhetorical procedure to argue "from the greater" (ἐκ τοῦ μείξονος) to demonstrate that what is greater automatically embraces what is less (e.g. Aelius Theon, *On Theses* 12, p. 122 Spengel). God must, therefore, be surpassing beautiful.

²¹⁶ This political analogy for the *principatus* of providence has a long classical pedigree; cf. Hom. *Il.* 2.204 *ap.* Arist. *Meta-*

phys. 12.10.1076a.: "The world should not be governed badly: 'The rule of many is not good; let there be one ruler,'" also quoted by [Just.] *Cohort.* 17, Acts of Codratius, F. C. Conybeare, *The Armenian Apology and Acts of Apollonius* etc. 196, and see the many other passages collected by E. Peterson, *Der Monotheismos als politisches Problem* (Leipzig 1935) 13 ff. It is an argument much favored by Roman writers, for whom *providentia* was a word closely associated with the ruler cult and therefore with political flavor (see M. P. Charlesworth, "Providentia and aeternitas," HTR 29 [1936] 107 ff.), and among whom the connected Stoic theory of *optimus princeps* had considerable currency. See also Cic. *De nat. deor.* 2.29 with Pease's nn.

For the widespread notion of earthly rulers obtaining their authority from the divine (Rom. 13.1 ff.), see K. M. Setton, *Christian Attitude towards the Emperor in the Fourth Century* (New York 1941) 25 f.; cf. Celsus *ap.* Orig. *C.Cels.* 8.63; *Acta Apollon.* 9 (AnalBoll 14 [1895] 288); the earliest *official* formulation of the divine right of emperors to rule seems to come under Aurelian, see A. D. Nock, "*A dis electis* etc.," HTR 23 (1930) 251 ff., at 263–68.

Porphyry attacked the general analogy, *ap.* Makar. 4.20 = *fr.* 75 Harn. (a monarch is not alone: he rules over others like himself; god has to rule over other gods to be truly a monarch).

[217] *quando umquam regni societas . . . sine cruore discessit?* This passage has been badly mishandled in the desperate endeavor to trace some datable remark in the *Octavius:* the remark must have been made, it is variously concluded, before the peaceful condominium of Marcus Aurelius and Verus (161–69 A.D.), or a generation or so afterwards when that peaceful condominium was forgotten, or with the murder of Geta (d. 212) and Elagabalus (d. 222) fresh in mind, both killed during partnerships in imperial power. Advocates for such conclusions are Baylis 234 ff; H. V. M. Dennis, "The Date of the Octavius," AJP 50 (1929) 185 ff.; G. de Sanctis, "Minucio Felice e Lucio Vero," RFIC 55 (1927) 233 ff.; S. Rossi, "L' 'Octavius' fu scritto prima del 161," GIF 12 (1959) 289 ff., at 297 ff., and "Ancora sull' 'Octavius' di Minucio Felice," GIF 16 (1963) 293 ff., at 298 ff. But the premise is mistaken. The remark and the illustrations belong to a standard *thema* "That Monarchy Is Best"; for a collection of purple passages and quotable quotations for use in composition, see Stobaeus *Flor.* 4.6, ed. Hense 4 (Berlin 1909) 239 ff. The precise

formulation seems to be partly indebted to Ennius (*Scen.* 404, Vahlen²), *ap.* Cic. *De off.* 1.8.26 (cf. *De repub.* 1.32.49): *nulla sancta societas nec fides regni est;* and for the proverbial notion generally, Otto *Sprichwörter* 296, adding Dio 48.1.2, 69.20 ff. etc. Such gnomic *topoi* could readily be invoked without any consciousness of contemporary realities; they, and the standard illustrations that went with them, were part of the literary tradition. Compare Fronto, Naber 125, who (in a very fragmentary text) can talk to the coemperor Lucius Verus himself of treachery and conspiracies together with illustrations from Romulus and Remus, and the Persians and the neighing of a horse. No chronological conclusions may, therefore, be drawn, nor any direct borrowing from Fronto deduced. For further discussion see Axelson 25 ff.; A. Gudeman, "Nochmals Minucius Felix und Tertullian," PhW 46 (1926) 1067 ff., at 1069 f.; A. della Casa, "Le due date dell' 'Octavius,' " *Maia* 14 (1962) 26 ff., at 30; and Beaujeu in ed. xlix ff. and "Remarques sur la datation de l'*Octavius* etc.," *Rev. de phil.* 41 (1967) 121 ff., at 122 ff.

²¹⁸ The rhetorical dismissal of the reference (cf. n. 96 above) does not make clear the precise point of the story here: it is simply that any form of partnership in power the Persians found to be undesirable, Darius having won his point that monarchy was to be preferred to oligarchy or democracy. The (clearly apocryphal) story is first found in Hdt. 3.82 ff., where there is described in detail the stratagem whereby, of the contestants for the throne, Darius got his horse to neigh first after daybreak and thereby was selected as the Great King of the Persian Empire. The same incident occurs in the list of illustrations of Stobaeus referred to in n. 217 (p. 246 f.); cf. Val. Max. 7.3.2; Just. Trog. 1.10.1 ff.

²¹⁹ *Thebanorum par*, i.e., Eteocles and Polynices, sons of Oedipus, who agreed to reign over Thebes in alternate years, but at the end of his year Eteocles refused to relinquish the throne. Polynices returned with the Seven, and the two brothers killed each other. See Aeschylus, *Septem contra Thebas*, and H. J. Rose, *A Handbook of Greek Mythology*² (London 1964) 189 ff. For the expression cf. Petron. *Sat.* 80.3: *Thebanum par* (*par* being particularly appropriate as the word used also to signify a gladiatorial "match").

²²⁰ Romulus and Remus: see Livy 1.7.2 for the fighting; for the *casa Romuli* (there were, in fact, two such primitive huts pre-

served in historical times, one on the Capitol, one on the south-west corner of the Palatine) see Verg. *Aen.* 8.654; Prop. 4.1.10; Ovid *Fasti* 1.199 and Frazer's n.; and Platner-Ashby *s.v.* Casa Romuli.

[221] The reference is to Caesar and Pompey (who married Caesar's daughter Julia) and the Civil War that began in 49 B.C. The expression *duos fortuna non cepit* may come from Lucan *Phars.* 1.111 *non cepit fortuna duos* with altered word order to avoid the poetic rhythm (cf. H. Hagendahl, "Methods of Citation in Post-Classical Latin Prose," *Eranos* 45 [1947] 114 ff., at 124), the examples of Romulus and Remus, on the theme *nulla fides regni sociis*, occurring just before in Lucan 1.92 ff., but cf. Florus 2.14: *tamquam duos tanti imperii fortuna non caperet.*

[222] For such (Stoic) illustrations drawn from nature, cf. Sen. *De clem.* 1.19.2: *natura enim commenta est regem, quod et ex aliis animalibus licet cognoscere et ex apibus;* Dio Chrys. *Or.* 4.62 (bees); Cyp. *Ep.* 66.6 is closely parallel: *apes habent regem et ducem pecudes et fidem servant;* and the analogies criticized by Celsus, Orig. *C.Cels.* 4.81. As usual in classical antiquity, the sex of the leader of the beehive is mistakenly thought to be masculine; e.g., Arist. *Hist anim.* 9.40; Verg. *Georg.* 4.68,75.

[223] The passage is very close to Tert. *Apol.* 17.1 f., with additions, particularly on the eternity and self-sufficiency of God. For a discussion of the (Posidonian?) source of these additions, see Beutler 43 ff. They were in any case widespread ideas; for early Christian formulations on the eternity, see Theoph. *Ad Autol.* 2.10; Athenag. *Leg.* 4, 6. etc.; Tat. *Or.* 4; Just. *Apol.* 1.14, *Apol.* 2.5, etc.; and the self-sufficiency of God, Athenag. *Leg.* 16; Theoph. *Ad Autol.* 2.10; Tert. *Adv. Prax.* 5.2: *ante omnia enim Deus erat solus, ipse sibi et mundus et locus et omnia.* See also Spanneut 312 f.

[224] Such passages listing God's attributes (in largely negative form) are not only standard ingredients of early apology (see Spanneut 271 ff. for a catalogue; also M. H. Shepherd, "The Early Apologists and Christian Worship," *Journ. of Rel.* 18 [1938] 60 ff., at 64 f.); they can also be paralleled from other sources (Beutler 47 ff.). Here, however, the immediate source appears to be Tert. *Apol.* 17.2 f., which is followed closely.

[225] The lack of a proper name for the unique God is a very common theme in Stoic literature (see Dio Chrys. *Or.* 12.78; Sen. *N.Q.* 2.45), as well as in Hermetic sources (*Corp. Herm.* 5.1a,

5.10a, ed. W. Scott: "He who is too great to be named God"),
Judaic (on Philo see H. A. Wolfson, *Philo* 2 [Cambridge, Mass.
1947] 110 ff., and H. Chadwick, CR 63 [1949] 24 f., reviewing
Wolfson), and Christian (Arist. *Apol.* 1 [Syr.]; Clem. *Strom.*
5.12.82.1; Euseb. *H.E.* 5.1.52 [Attalus]; [Just.] *Cohort.* 21, Just.
Apol. 2.6; Orig. *C.Cels.* 6.65). See also Pease's n. on Cic. *De nat.
deor.* 1.30; Spanneut 272; Beutler 50 ff. (overplaying, as often,
Posidonian influence but providing useful illustrative parallels).
There is an interesting discussion on the topic by E. Bikerman,
"Anonymous Gods," *Journ. Warb. Inst.* 1 (1937) 187 ff.

[226] *carnalis:* a word first found in Christian writings, (a "Christianism," to use the jargon of the school of Schrijnen), no doubt
formed as a calque for the Greek σαρκινός (versus πνευματικός,
Ign. *Eph.* 7.2) and used again in 32.6. Such terms are normally
avoided by Minucius Felix and we might have expected *corporalis*
or *corporeus* instead (Chr. Mohrmann, *Études sur le latin des
chrétiens* 1 [Rome 1961] 25, 89, 119; 2 [1961] 14, 16, 105, 238;
3 [1965] 46, 52, 60, 113).

[227] *dominum.* Octavius reflects nothing of what appears as a
terminological controversy in Tert. *Apol.* 34, where *dominus* is
declared to be the cognomen of God and of God alone (cf. *Mart.
Poly.* 8.2: Polycarp is to say "Caesar is Lord"). Minucius Felix,
however, uses the word without demur here and, despite his
present assertions, again in 26.11, 35.4 (along with *parens omnium*). A. Gudeman, PhW 44 (1924) 90 ff., at 91 f., and *idem*,
"Minucius Felix und Tertullian," *Phil.* 82 (1937) 353 ff., at 356 f.,
uses the passages to clinch his argument for the priority of Minucius Felix, but unconvincingly. Tertullian freely uses the word
elsewhere (see generally for Tertullian's usage, R. Braun, *"Deus
christianorum"* 91–97) without apology; and it would be out of
character for Minucius Felix to insist on Tertullian's rather
idiosyncratic and cantankerous terminological definition.

[228] There now begins the supporting argument for the uniqueness of God. It is based logically on the *consensus omnium* (see
n. 100 above), here of the *vulgus* and in the next chapter of
poets and, at length, of philosophers. To support an argument in
this way was standard rhetorical procedure; it is among the
"proofs" on the thesis *de providentia* drawn up by Aelius Theon,
Progym. 12, *Rh.Gr.* 2.126; and, in fact, both Velleius and Balbus
begin with such an argument (Cic. *De nat. deor.* 1.43 f., 2.4;
Cotta opens with a criticism of it, 1.62, 3.11). In Tertullian, how-

ever, *Apol.* 17.5 ff. and elsewhere (especially in the treatise *De test. anim.*, *De an.* 41), there is a closely similar argument from the popular use of the singular *deus* (for the parallel Greek phenomenon of singular words for deity, see G. Français, *Le polythéisme et l'emploi au singulier des mots* ΘΕΟΣ, ΔΑΙΜΩΝ *dans la littérature grecque d'Homère à Platon* [Paris 1957] esp. 305 ff.); but in Tertullian the argument has a slightly different logical basis—not universal agreement but the instinctive, the natural expression of the soul (though *Adv. Marc.* 1.10 assimilates to the present passage—an appeal to what *maior popularitas generis humani* instinctively says). Hence a vigorous controversy from the passages for the priority question, and the provenance of the doctrine generally.

It is clear that Tertullian believed that he had discovered himself a *novum testimonium* (*De test. anim.* 1.5) for which some of his formulations (e.g., *De test. anim.* 5.2: *meminit sui auctoris*) suggest the Platonic *anamnēsis* or doctrine of spontaneous recall provided the ultimate basis (so C. Tibiletti, "Una presunta dipendenza di Tertullian da Minucio Felice," *Att. Accad. Scienz. Tor.* 91 [1956–57] 60–72, and in his edition of Tertullian's *De test. anim.* [Turin 1959] 174–80). A case can also be put forward for the influence of the Stoic-versus-Epicurean debate (so G. Lazzati, "Il 'De natura deorum' fonte del 'De testimonio animae' di Tertulliano?" *Atene e Roma* 7 [1939] 153–66, and see Pease's n. on Cic. *De nat. deor.* 1.44 for the difficulty of disentangling the philosophical provenance of an expression such as *innatas cognitiones*); but the biblical origin advocated by J. del Ton, "Monotheismos sensus apud antiquos ethnicos," *Latinitas* 3 (1955) 275 ff., at 278, is less persuasive. A mixed origin is, however, by no means impossible for such a theory.

On the whole, it is an inherently more probable construction that in this very brief passage Minucius Felix has assimilated the doctrine, as devised and elaborated by Tertullian, to a standard rhetorical format (so Axelson 103 ff.); but that point need not be pressed, and, in any case, a comparison of the passages involved certainly does not seem to provide any adequate warrant for claiming priority for the formulation of Minucius Felix (against G. Quispel, *"Anima naturaliter christiana,"* *Latomus* 10 [1951] 163 ff.).

The threefold appeal to the *vulgus*, the poets, and the philosophers, here elaborated, is traditional (and characteristically Stoic,

like the *consensus* argument itself); compare Aug. *De civ. Dei*
4.27: *relatum est in litteras doctissimum pontificem Scaevolam
disputasse tria genera tradita deorum: unum a poetis, alterum a
philosophis, tertium a principibus civitatis; ibid.* 6.5 (quoting
Varro on the three types of theology): *Mythicon appellant quo
maxime utuntur poetae; physicon, quo philosophi; civile quo
populi* (cf. Tert. *Ad nat.* 2.1); Cic. *De nat. deor.* 1.46: *non
philosophos solum sed etiam indoctos;* Celsus, *ap.* Orig. *C.Cels.*
7.41 (Christians are urged to turn to the divinely inspired poets,
the wise men, and the philosophers for guidance). See P. Boyancé,
"Sur la théologie de Varron," *Rev. ét anc.* 57 (1955) 57 ff., and
J. Pépin, "La 'théologie tripartite' de Varron (Essai de reconsti-
tution et recherche des sources)," *Rev. étud. aug.* 2 (1956) 265 ff.

²²⁹ This notion of variation in name but agreement in fact about
the Godhead was common in an increasingly monotheistic-minded
society, e.g., Diog. Laer. 7.135 (God is one and the same as
Reason, Fate, and Zeus; he is also called by many other names);
Max. Tyr. 39.5; Dio Chrys. *Or.* 31.11; Celsus *ap.* Orig. *C.Cels.*
1.24, 5.45 urged the same point—Origen's reply is weak (correctness of certain names proved by their superior efficacy in spells
and exorcisms); Maximus of Madaura, Augustine's pagan friend,
in Aug. *Ep.* 16.1 (ML 33.82): *deus omnibus religionibus commune
nomen est;* Porphyry *ap.* Aug. *Ep.* 102.10 (ML 33.374). See
generally, E. Peterson, Εἷς Θεός (Göttingen 1926) esp. 254 for
pantheus as an epithet applied to gods and for *idem* identifying
two or more gods), and J. Lortz, "Das Christentum als Mono-
theismus in den Apologien des zweiten Jahrhunderts," *Festgabe
A. Ehrhard* (Leipzig/Bonn 1922) 301–27. (Cic. *De nat. deor.* 2.4
plus Tert. *Apol.* 24.3 could well have provided the genesis of the
present passage.)

²³⁰ In the first two sections of this chapter there is an appeal to
the testimony of poets. Such an appeal is frequent even in serious
philosophizing, and the basic reason was perhaps that there survived vestigially some of the primitive superstition that poetic
utterance was (literally) divinely "inspired." But the attitude towards such appeals tended to be ambiguous; they certainly
brought sympathetic attention to a cause (they are, therefore,
reserved for Octavius) and to be able to reproduce suitable
quotations was a hallmark of rhetorical training. But the full corpus of poetry might, as frequently happened, offer contradictory
evidence (a fact exploited, e.g., by Theoph. *Ad Autol.* 2.5 ff. and

[Just.] *Cohort. passim*), so a tirade against irresponsible poetic fantasies became standard polemic (see Cic. *De nat. deor.* 1.42 f., 2.70, and Pease's splendid nn., and cf. chap. 11.9 and n. 151 above). Hence Octavius can appeal here and in 26.9, 35.1 to the evidence of poetry, but equally—and inconsistently—in 23.1 ff. he can attack the viciousness and incongruities of poetic fables (similarly with philosophy, 19.3 ff., 26.9—and 38.5 f.). Theophilus could explain away the inconsistency (*Ad Autol.* 2.8) by claiming that poets could sometimes get rid of the demons who inspired them and thus speak the truth, following the prophets. Cf. the famous appeal of St. Paul, Acts 17.28: "As certain of your poets have said. . . ," and Jerome *Ep.* 70.3 (ML 22.666): Cyprian criticized by Lactantius because he did not appeal in his *Ad Demet.* to the testimony of philosophers and poets *quorum auctoritati, ut ethnicus, contraire non poterat.* On such appeals see C. Tibiletti, in ed. Tertullian *De test. anim.* (Turin 1959) 151 ff., and cf. Pease's n. on Cic. *De nat. deor.* 1.41 (Homer and *veterrimi poetae* claimed by a wide variety of philosophical schools.)

The first two quotations come ultimately from the Greek "national" poet Homer; those that follow from his Roman counterpart, Vergil.

231 *patrem divum atque hominum*: the formulaic Homeric verse πατὴρ ἀνδρῶν τε θεῶν τε (*Il.* 1.544 etc.) translated, with variations, by Ennius (*Ann.* 175, 580 f. Vahlen: *patrem divumque hominumque*), copied by Verg. *Aen.* 1.65 etc., and quoted by Cic. *De nat. deor.* 2.4, where see Pease's n. for other (frequent) references, adding Just. *Apol.* 1.22, [Just.] *Cohort.* 2.

232 The often-quoted lines of Hom. *Od.* 18.136 f.

τοῖς γὰρ νόος ἐστὶν ἐπιχθονίων ἀνθρώπων
οἷον ἐπ'ἦμαρ ἄγῃσι πατὴρ ἀνδρῶν τε θεῶν τε

and translated—freely—by Cic. *De fato fr.* 3 *ap.* Aug. *De civ. Dei* 5.8; the quotation was rhetorical material considered suitable in the appeal to the testimony of wise men, lawyers, poets, etc., e.g., Aelius Theon, *Progym.* 213. *Rhet. Gr.* 2.103 *Spengel*.

233 I.e., Vergil.

234 Broken quotations from Verg. *Aen.* 6.724 ff., and a combination of *Georg.* 4.221 f. and *Aen.* 1.743. These are the only *direct* quotations from poetry in the *Octavius*, the rest being paraphrased to conform to the rules of the oratorical style of Minucius Felix. See H. Hagendahl, "Methods of Citation in Post-Classical Latin Prose," *Eranos* 45 (1947) 114 ff., at 117; W. Krause, *Die Stellung*

der frühchristlichen Autoren zur heidnischen Literatur (Vienna 1958) 142 ff. On Vergil's "divine immanence" (a notably Stoic tenet), see P. Courcelle, "Vergile et l'immanence divine chez Minucius Felix," *Mullus: Festschrift Th. Klauser* (Münster 1964) 34–42; and generally P. Boyancé, "Le sens cosmique de Virgile," REL 32 (1954) 220–49. See also on this passage P. Courcelle, "Les pères de l'église devant les enfers virgiliens," *Arch. d'hist. doctr. et litt. du moyen âge* 22 (1955) 5 ff., at 37 ff., 68; *idem*, "Interprétations néo-platonisantes du livre vi de l'Énéide," *Fondation Hardt: Entretiens sur l'antiquité classique* 3 (1955) 95 ff., at 107; D. S. Wiesen, "Virgil, Minucius Felix and the Bible," *Hermes* 99 (1971) 70 ff., esp. 79 ff., 85 ff.

[235] *mens et ratio et spiritus.* The quotations have provided *mens* and *spiritus* but not *ratio*. Rhetorical—and threefold—plenitude is the simple explanation—hardly an allusion to the Trinity (contra Beutler 45, 80).

[236] Here begins the appeal to philosophy. There can be little doubt that Octavius is borrowing, selectively, from the doxographical survey of the Epicurean spokesman Velleius in Cic. *De nat. deor.* 1.25 ff., but with a clearly different purpose: to establish a consistent philosophical belief in monotheism. Velleius' object, on the other hand, was to demonstrate the inconsistencies and mistakes of pre-Epicurean philosophers *de natura deorum.* Hence the selectivity of the catalogue here. There are closely parallel lists to be found elsewhere, e.g., [Just.] *Cohort.* 3 ff.; Philo *De somn.* 1.4.21 ff.; Joseph. *Contr. Ap.* 2.167 ff.; and especially Clem. *Protr.* 5.64 ff. (on which see A. Beltrami, "Minucio (Octavius)—Cicerone (D.n.d.)—Clemente Alessandro (Opere)," *Att. R. Accad. dell Scienz. Torin.* 55 [1919/20] 179 ff., who, however, concludes that Minucius Felix probably borrowed from Clement, an uncompelling conclusion). It is possible that a compilation such as the *Placita* of Aëtius is the explanation. See Beutler 73–82; H. Diels, *Doxographi Graeci*[2] (Berlin/Leipzig 1929) 531 ff.; C. Becker, *Der "Octavius" des Minucius Felix* (Munich 1967) 10 ff.; and Pease's n. on Cic. *De nat. deor.* 1.25. For (the variable) Christian attitude towards pagan philosophy, see n. 165 above and chap. 38.5 below.

[237] The so-called "Seven Sages," for whom the *locus classicus* is Diog. Laer. 1.40 ff. listing the many variations to be found in the catalogue of Sages (some seventeen candidates according to Hermippus). Socrates came to be added later (see Intro. n. 70).

Note, too, Plato, *Protag.* 343A; Plut. *Septem sapientium convivium, Mor.* 146B ff. (Thales 147B ff.); Ausonius, *Ludus septem sapientium* (Thales ll. 163 ff.; characteristic *dicta* ll. 52 ff.). Thales is regularly included (save apparently in Ephorus? [Diog. Laer. 1.40]), though the language of Minucius Felix might suggest his exclusion here, for Thales, unlike the other Sages who were noted as men of practical wisdom, was also a serious philosopher (cf. Diels, *Doxog. Gr.*² 555 = Hippol. *Philos.* 1.1).

²³⁸ Thales (c. 624–550 B.C.) is regularly listed as the pioneer of philosophers; his view that the world originates from, consists of, and returns to water marked the beginnings of Greek physical science. See PW 5 A1 (1934) 1210–12 (W. Nestle); D. R. Dicks, Thales, CQ 9 (1959) 294 ff.; W. K. C. Guthrie, *A History of Greek Philosophy* 1 (Cambridge, 1962) 45–72. The present passage follows closely Cic. *De nat. deor.* 1.25, where see Pease's nn.

²³⁹ A difficult passage, variously emended, and which I have obelized, following Gronovius. The present text certainly reads like a pious Christian gloss, for it seems to allude both to the story of the creation (Gen. 1.2: *Spiritus Dei ferebatur super aquas*) and to the waters of baptism (cf. Theoph. *Ad Autol.* 2.16), allusions which, certainly if this dialogue was intended for pagan ears, would have been completely lost, and therefore pointless, without further elaboration. Contrast the tirade in Arist. *Apol.* 5 against those who considered water to be God; cf. Herm. *Irris.* 4, [Just.] *Cohort.* 2. (Note that Porphyry *De antro nymph.* 10, Nauck 63, refers to the Platonizing Pythagorean Numenius as citing "the prophet" who said "the spirit of God was borne above the waters".) Indeed, to insist on the derivation of the theory from divine revelation seems to weaken the whole line of the present argument. In defense, J. H. Waszink, "Minuciana," VC 8 (1954) 129 ff., at 130 ff.; J. G. P. Borleffs, "De Lactantio in epitome Minucii imitore," *Mnem.* 57 (1929) 415 ff., at 421, seeks to derive Lact. *Epit.* 3.1 from this passage: *sublimior enim ac maior (deus) est, quam ut possit . . . cogitatione hominis . . . comprehendi,* but the derivation is not probant. For further discussion on the passage, K. Abel, "Minucius Felix: Octavius: Das Textproblem," RhM 110 (1967) 248 ff., at 265 f.

²⁴⁰ Anaximenes of Miletus (*fl.* c. 546) was a pupil of Anaximander (who is omitted from Velleius' list, Cic. *De nat. deor.* 1.25, because of his polytheistic views). He introduced the notions of condensation and rarefaction to explain changes in the cosmos.

See PW 1.2 (1894) 2086 (E. Wellmann); Guthrie, *op. cit.* 115–40; Pease's n. on Cic. *De nat. deor.* 1.26, which is close to the present passage.

²⁴¹ Diogenes of Apollonia (*fl.* c. 440) has been added from Cic. *De nat. deor.* 1.29, because he revived the teaching of Anaximenes that the primary substance was Air; he insisted, however, on its divinity (unlike Anaximenes, who could be condemned as an atheist by Clem. *Protrep.* 5.64.3). See PW 5 (1903) 764–65 (E. Wellmann); Guthrie *op. cit.* 2 (1965) 362–81; Pease's n. on Cic. *De nat. deor.* 1.29.

²⁴² A compressed and rather distorted version of Cic. *De nat. deor.* 1.26: *Anaxagoras . . . primus omnium rerum discriptionem et modum mentis infinitae vi ac ratione dissignari et confici voluit,* and with (an incorrect) variant reading *motum* for *modum* (on which see Beaujeu *ad loc.* and Pease's n. *loc. cit.* [*modum*]). The reference is to the celebrated doctrine of Nous, the intelligent initiator of cosmic motion and animating principle of plants and animals. Anaxagoras of Clazomene (c. 500–c. 428) was a teacher and friend of Pericles and was forced to flee from Athens indicted for impiety by Pericles' political enemies. See PW 1.2 (1894) 2076–77 (E. Wellmann); Guthrie, *op. cit.* 2 (1965) 266–338; and Pease's nn. on Cic. *De nat. deor.* 1.26.

²⁴³ Pythagoras of Samos (c. 582–10), famous especially for his mathematical investigations, founded in Southern Italy a religious-like community of philosophers, and thus a sect which was to have a long and influential history (see also chap. 34.6). See PW 24 (1963) 171–209 (K. von Fritz); Guthrie 1.146–319; Pease's n. on Cic. *De nat. deor.* 1.27, which is closely parallel to the present text except that *ex quo nostri animi carperentur* has become *animalium omnium vita* (a view paralleled elsewhere: see Pease's n. *ad loc.* and esp. Sext. Emp. *Adv. phys.* 1.127 [the same *pneuma* throughout the entire cosmos, and not only for men but even for irrational animals]); cf. Clem. *Protr.* 6.72.4. Beutler 73 ff. concludes from such alterations that Minucius Felix also consulted the source Cicero had doctored himself for his own purposes. Pythagoras is condemned (along with Euhemerus and Epicurus) for denying providence in Theoph. *Ad Autol.* 3.6 f., but in [Just.] *Cohort.* 19 he is credited with believing in the unity of God (via his Egyptian sojourn, cf. Joseph. *Contr. Ap.* 1.162 ff.). (Alcmaeon of Croton is here omitted from Velleius' list: he believed in astral divinities, and hence blatant polytheism.)

²⁴⁴ Xenophanes of Colophon (c. 570–c. 470), who migrated to Magna Graecia in S. Italy and Sicily, is associated with Elea (the source of the series of Eleatic philosophers, though there is no positive evidence that he actually founded the school himself). He was trenchantly critical of traditional mythological fables and anthropomorphism. See Guthrie, *op. cit.* 1.360–402; Pease on Cic. *De nat. deor.* 1.28.

For *omne* = τὸ πᾶν, see J. B. Hoffmann, "Die lateinischen Totalitätsausdrücke," *Mélanges . . . offerts à J. Marouzeau* (Paris 1948) 285 ff., at 287. Octavius proceeds to pass by Parmenides (Cic. *De nat. deor.* 1.28), Empedocles (1.29), and Protagoras (1.29), the latter already cited as an "atheist" by Caecilius, chap. 8.3, and the former two having some reputation for "atheism" (Clem. *Protr.* 5.64.2 f.; Theoph. *Ad Autol.* 3.2).

²⁴⁵ Antisthenes of Athens (c. 455–c. 360): a devoted follower of Socrates and founder of the Cynic school. See PW 1.2 (1894), 2538–45 (P. Natorp); R. Dudley, *A History of Cynicism* (London 1937) 1–16; and Pease's n. on Cic. *De nat. deor.* 1.32 (closely followed). For the idea of exoteric doctrines (for popular consumption) and esoteric doctrines (for the educated elite), frequently repeated throughout antiquity, see Pease's collection of references on Cic. *De nat. deor.* 1.61 and cf. §14 below.

²⁴⁶ Speusippus of Athens, son of Plato's sister, Potone, and successor to Plato as head of the Academy, c. 347–39. See PW 3 A2 (1929) 1636–69 (Stenzel) and Pease's n. on Cic. *De nat. deor.* 1.32 (closely followed).

²⁴⁷ Democritus of Abdera (c. 460–c. 370), the famous formulator—though not strictly the inventor (who was the shadowy Leucippus)—of the "atomic theory" (see n. 45 above). For his theory of *eidōla* (images), see Pease's n. on Cic. *De nat. deor.* 1.29 (of which we have an abridged version with less emphasis on the inconsistencies), and for criticism of it Cic. *ibid.* 1.107, and of his views of gods *ibid.* 1.120; and see, generally, PW 5.1 (1903) 135–40 (E. Wellmann); Guthrie, *op. cit.* 2.386–502.

²⁴⁸ Straton of Lampsacus, disciple of Theophrastus, and successor to him as head of the Peripatetic school for eighteen years (d. c. 269); he was noted as a physical theorist. See PW 4 A1 (1931) 278–315 (W. Capelle) and Pease's n. on Cic. *De nat. deor.* 1.35, here again followed closely.

²⁴⁹ Epicurus lived from 342/1 to 271/70, founding his famous school in Athens and preaching the gospel of the untroubled

mind, freed from the morbid fear of death and the gods. The latter he considered lived happily and harmlessly in the *intermundia*, or the spaces between the different Epicurean worlds (see Pease's n. on Cic. *De nat. deor.* 1.18), though some claimed this view was only meant to appease the Athenian public (Cic. *ibid.* 1.85, 3.3) and that he was in fact an atheist (Cic. *ibid.* 1.123: *nullos esse deos Epicuro videri* [from Posidonius]); see Pease's n. *ad loca*, and for a vigorous refutation, A. J. Festugière, *Épicure et ses dieux* (Paris 1946) 88 ff.: also C. Bailey, *The Greek Atomists and Epicurus* (Oxford 1928) 438 ff. For *natura* (the impersonal force which caused the swerve in the atoms and hence the creations) see Bailey 320 ff.; Pease on Cic. *De nat. deor.* 1.53 (*natura effectum esse mundum*); and Lucretius 1.56: *unde omnis Natura creet res*, 2.1116 f.: *donec ad extremum crescendi perfica finem/ omnia perduxit rerum Natura creatrix*, etc. This notice is, of course, not to be found in the compendium of Velleius the Epicurean: it may well have been compiled from the passages of the *De nat. deor.* cited above, but Tert. *Apol.* 47.6 is also close: (*deum*) *Epicurei otiosum et inexercitum, et ut ita dixerim, neminem humanis rebus.*

[250] These views of Aristotle (384–22) come from the third book of his youthful, and lost, work *De philosophia* (*fr.* 26 Rose). They are to be found in Cic. *De nat. deor.* 1.33, where see Pease's nn. "The Ruler of the Universe" appears to be the *Mens* (= *Nous*, *Noēsis*) qua Prime Mover. See also E. Bignone, *L'Aristotele perduto* 2 (Florence 1936) 335 ff.; W. Jaeger, *Aristoteles* (Berlin 1923) 125–70; L. Alfonsi, "Traces du jeune Aristote dans la 'Cohortatio ad Gentiles' faussement attribuée à Justin," VC 2 (1948) 65 ff., at 67 f.

[251] The text followed is the reconstruction of Beaujeu, based on Cic. *De nat. deor.* 1.34 f. (although his alteration of *divinae* to *divinum* [following Cicero] is unnecessary, for it is a variation consonant with other paraphrases and adaptations of this section of Cicero); there seems to have been some mechanical confusion both in the names and in the assignation of theories at this point. (The text of J. C. M. Winden, "Minucius Felix, Octavius 19,9," VC 8 [1954] 72–77, retaining the confusion of theories, is less plausible.) Theophrastus of Lesbos (c.370–c.287), faithful pupil of Aristotle and voluminous author, succeeded Aristotle as president of the Lycaeum. See PW Suppl. 7 (1940) 1354–1562 (O. Regenbogen) and Pease's n. on Cic. *De nat. deor.* 1.35. Octavius

alters *caelo* to *mundo* and omits the embarrassing assignation of divinity to the stars.

²⁵² A very emasculated and somewhat garbled extract from Cic. *De nat. deor.* 1.34 (in particular, the divinity of stars, earth, and sky is expunged). Heraclides Ponticus (c. 390–10) was a pupil of Speusippus and later of Plato. See PW 8.1 (1912) 472–84 (R. Däbritz) and Pease's n. on Cic. *De nat. deor.* 1.34.

²⁵³ There are here grouped together the three most famous names of the early Stoa. The founder Zeno of Citium (335–263) (*Oxford Classical Dictionary* [Oxford 1949] 965 [K. von Fritz]); his pupil for seventeen years and successor, Cleanthes of Assos (331–232) (PW 11.1 [1921] 558–74 [H. von Arnim]); and Chrysippus of Soli (c. 280–207), the third head of the Stoic School and a prodigiously prolific writer (PW 3.2 (1899) 2502–9 [H. von Arnim]), about whom it was currently said "Had there been no Chrysippus, there would have been no Stoa," Diog. Laer. 7.7. The views assigned to Cleanthes are a very abridged and freely paraphrased version of Cic. *De nat. deor.* 1.37, with the notable omission, once again, of the astral theology. See Pease's nn. *ad loc.* for exegesis.

²⁵⁴ Zeno's views on the *principium* alluded to are from Cic. *De nat. deor.* 1.36 (with characteristic omissions of the astral theology), where see Pease's excellent nn. The allegorical interpretation of myths had a long and rich history in the Greco-Roman world. It seems to have started as an attempt to reconcile the revered Homeric text with Ionic natural philosophy; it was enthusiastically adopted by the Stoic following with a similar aim—to bridge the gap between philosophical Stoicism and popular religion. It is frequently closely associated with (often very popular) etymological explanations for the origins of myths. A tradition was thus established that continued well into the Neoplatonic world (e.g., in Porphyry's Homeric questions: *Quaest. Hom. ad Iliadem* ed. H. Schrader [Leipzig 1880–82], *ad Odysseum* [1890]). See Pease's n. on Cic. *De nat. deor.* 2.63 ff., where there is an exposé of these particular Stoic theories (and criticism of them in 3.62 f.); Jupiter = sky (occurring in 2.63–65); Juno = air (2.66), Neptune = sea (2.66). Octavius adds Vulcan = fire (for which common identification compare Varro *L.L.* 5.70; Arnob. 3.33, Aug. *De civ. Dei* 7.16, Isid. *Etym.* 8.11.39 ff.; he was a difficult god to etymologize (see Pease on Cic. *De nat. deor.* 3.62 "Volcano"). On this Stoic exegesis of the popular theogony,

P. Decharme, *La critique des traditions religeuses chez les grecs des origines au temps de Plutarque* (Paris 1904) 305 ff., is still useful.

[255] A précis drawn from sections of Cic. *De nat. deor.* 1.39–41, where see Pease's nn.

[256] Diogenes of Babylonia (Seleucia, in fact), c. 240–152, succeeded Chrysippus as head of the Stoic school, and through his visit to Rome in 155 B.C. and his pupil Panaetius did much to stimulate Roman interest in Stoicism: PW 5.1 (1903) 773–76 and Pease's n. on Cic. *De nat. deor.* 1.41. The reference is, of course, to the birth of Athena (Latin: Minerva) from the head of Zeus (Jupiter), for the many allegorical interpretations of which see A. B. Cook, *Zeus* 3 (Cambridge 1940) 726 ff. (The usual is that Athena = Logos, or Reason; cf. Orig. *C.Cels.* 8.67, Arnob. 4.16, and for a Christian adaptation, Just. *Apol.* 1.64. Diogenes' particular version identified Zeus with the universe and Athena with its highest part, the Ether; see Diels, *Doxograph. Graec.*² 548 f. [Philodemus *De pietat. fr.* 15].)

[257] Octavius now collects together for the finale to his doxography—and as a partial reply to the Simonides story recounted by Caecilius in 13.4—philosophers who drew the correct conclusion from the difficulties encountered in the investigation of divine matters.

The reference in Xenophon (c. 430–354) is to his *Memorabilia* (or "Memoirs of Socrates") 4.3.13 f.; cf. Cic. *De nat. deor.* 1.31. It is possible, owing to an addition to the section from Cicero ("cannot be seen"), that M.F. referred to the original text or to an extract based on it (see again 32.5 and n. 40 above; K. Münscher, "Xenophon in der griechisch-römischen Literatur," *Philologus* Supp. Bd. 13, Hft. 2 [1920] 58 and 97; Beutler 78).

[258] Ariston of Chios (*fl.* c. 250), a friend and pupil of Zeno, and founder of a more Cynically-minded branch of the Stoic *secta*. See PW 2.1 (1895) 957–59 (H. von Arnim) and Pease's n. on Cic. *De nat. deor.* 1.37.

[259] Plato, the *doyen* of philosophers, is reserved for the end. For praise of his clarity of style, cf. Orig. *C.Cels.* 6.2, Joseph. *Contr. Ap.* 2.224, etc., the point being the contrast with the wavering opinions (*varie, variat, interim, multiformes*, etc.) of the preceding philosophers (see V. Carlier, "Authenticité de deux passages de Minucius Felix," *Musée belge* 1 (1897) 176 ff., at 181 f., defending the genuineness of these lines which have, on occasion,

been doubted). For the (common) laudation given to Plato in terms of quasi divinity, see Pease on Cic. *De nat. deor.* 2.32: *Platonem quasi deum philosophorum.* The *civilis persuasio* is a little obscure: (1) Plato's own political aspirations may possibly be envisaged, the *Timaeus,* e.g., providing the metaphysical structure that lay behind the *Republic* (see F. M. Cornford, *Plato's Cosmology* [London 1937] 5 f.). On Plato's political aspirations, for an extreme view, see K. R. Popper, *The Open Society and Its Enemies* 1 (London 1945); for a more moderate estimate, R. B. Levinson, *In Defense of Plato* (Cambridge, Mass. 1953) esp. 499 ff. Less sophisticated but more likely, (2) is the charge that Plato added "popular prejudices" to his own personally held monotheistic views (e.g., *Timaeus* 40D–41A); for the charge is to be found in [Just.] *Cohort.* 22 ff., 32, that Plato, for fear of the hemlock cup or the Areopagus, dissimulated the source (Moses) and nature (monotheism) of his own theological beliefs; cf. n. 245 above, and Pease's n. on *De nat. deor.* 1.30, referring to many ancient criticisms of Plato for his inconsistent theological views.

[260] The passage referred to in particular is *Tim.* 28C ff. The observation on the difficulty (or, as a later variant, danger) of describing God provided one of the most hackneyed quotations of all classical literature and it enjoyed particular popularity with the Christian apologists. For formidable lists of references, see E. Norden, *Agnostos Theos* (Leipzig 1913) 84 f.; J. Geffcken, *Zwei griechische Apologeten* (Leipzig/Berlin 1907) 174 f.; on the interpretation and variants of the passage, A. D. Nock, "The Exegesis of Timaeus 28C," VC 16 (1962) 79–86; and for the use of the *Timaeus* text, and Plato generally, by the early Christian apologists, J. Daniélou, *Message évangélique et culture hellénistique* (Paris 1961) 103–22. This notice on Plato does not come from Cic. *De nat. deor.* 1.30; for discussion, Beutler 78 f.

[261] Referring, no doubt, to the charge of public silence (8.4), on which see n. 108; see also 31.6; it is an adroit use of the Platonic quotation.

[262] On the construing of this period, see E. Löfstedt, "Annotationes criticae in M. Minucii Felicis Octavium," *Eranos* 6 (1905/6) 1 ff., at 18 ff. Note the neat but often overlooked echo of Plat. *Republic* 473C f.: "Either the philosophers of the past were kings or present-day kings are philosophers." The opening words of this section are unmistakably reminiscent of those of Velleius (Cic. *De nat. deor.* 1.42) at the end of his doxography. For this

central theme of the *Octavius,* claiming the support of the philosophical tradition for Christianity, see Intro. p. 26 ff., nn. 230 and
236 above and 655 below, and cf. the parallel conclusion of
Athenag. *Leg.* 7 after a similar doxography. For the notion of
"Christians before Christ," either by plagiarism of Moses and the
prophets (a classic expression in Theoph. *Ad Autol.* 1.14, and
cf. chap. 34.5 below) or by the influence of the spermatic word
(Just. *Apol.* 2.13), etc., see Intro. p. 15. That general theme
continued into the fourth century (e.g., Greg. Naz. *Or.* 15.1
[MG 35.912]: Christian martyrs before Christ's passion), and
note the concern of early Christianity on the salvation of the
righteous dead before Christ (1 Peter 3.18 ff.; 1 Cor. 15.29;
Clem. *Strom.* 2.2.9; Hermas *Sim.* 9.16.5, etc.).

²⁶³ To attack the fables of antiquity was an accepted procedure
(see n. 230 above). But to attack the value of tradition generally
was less in favor, and accordingly (unlike many other Apologists
in their attacks on traditional errors) Minucius Felix carefully
invokes the testimony of pagan philosophical tradition itself for
this refutation of the "ignorant generations of the past" (*antiquitas
imperitorum*—on the latter word see n. 22 above). This is a reply
to the uncritical claims for the virtue of *antiquitas* and *vetustas*
in 6.3; the retention of respect for the past is typical of the general
attitude of the *Octavius* (Axelson 91 f. criticizes the logic of this
position here).

²⁶⁴ After Octavius established not only that providence does
exist but also that it is a monotheistic providence, he adduced the
opinions of the common people, the poets, and the philosophers
to defend his monotheistic conclusion. He now proceeds to more
offensive manoeuvres, firstly—and briefly—attacking the paramount claim based on the authority of the *maiores* (cf. 6.1 ff.)
for pagan polytheism, and then—at greater length—the actual
origins of these pagan gods.

²⁶⁵ Beaujeu, following many editors, alters the MSS *mira
miracula* to *mera miracula* ("sheer marvels"—a readily paralleled
phrase [Aul. Gellius, *Noctes Atticae* 14.6.3] and confusion of
vowel [cf. 32.5 MS *mereris* for *mireris*]); but probably needlessly. See B. Axelson, *Gnomon* 24 (1952) 420 f., and note the
penchant of Minucius Felix for such etymological figures (e.g.,
8.4 *miserentur miseri,* 13.2 *merito . . . meruit,* 20.5 *creduli . . .
crediderunt,* 26.8 *perditi . . . perdere,* 27.8 *inserti . . . serunt,*
38.7 *impietas expietur,* etc.) and the praise of Fronto for such

paronomasia (quoting Sallust's *simulator ac dissimulator* with approval), Naber 108.

[266] There follow standard examples of composite (save the Hydra) mythical creatures, the *numen biforme* being traditional grist for the satirist's mill; cf. Cic. *De nat. deor.* 2.5; Lucr. 5.878 ff.; Tert. *Apol.* 16.13; and chap. 28.7 below.

Scylla, a sea monster with six heads and a girdle of dogs' heads, and twelve feet, irresistibly seized and devoured six men at a time from ships passing near the straits of Messina: Hom. *Od.* 12.73 ff. etc.

[267] The Chimera, a triple-bodied monster, lion in front, she-goat in the middle, serpent behind, was slain by Bellerophon; Hom. *Il.* 6.181 etc.

[268] The Hydra provided one of the labors of Hercules; it was a many-headed poisonous water snake that lived in the marshes of Lerna near Argos. As soon as one of its heads was cut off, others grew in its place.

[269] The Centaurs were hybrids of man and horse who once dwelt in Thessaly; see Pease's n. on Cic. *De divin.* 2.49 and *De nat. deor.* 1.105, and, of course, the sculptures of the temple of Zeus at Olympia for an illustration of their fight with the Lapithae.

[270] The stories of Procne (swallow), Philomela (nightingale), Leucothoe (tree), Hyacinthus (flower), etc. as recounted in Ovid *Metamorphoses.* Arist. *Apol.* 9 has Zeus transformed into bull, swan, eagle, etc. for his amorous escapades.

[271] For the (sophistic and vulnerable) line of argument, cf. Cic. *De divin.* 2.97: *si enim esset factitatum, non esset desitum.* Octavius clearly does not intend to base any arguments on the miracles of Christ.

[272] The gage of the epithets applied to the Christians in 12.7 is once again (see also 16.5 ff.) cast back to the pagan. The alert reader might be expected to detect some irony in the use of *simplicitas*—applied, somewhat ambiguously, to Caecilius in 16.2 and now revealed in its full significance.

[273] Here begins a brief outline of the euhemeristic explanation (from Euhemerus, on whom see n. 276 below) of the existence of the gods: that they were in origin flattered rulers or heroes (*fortis aut claros aut potentes viros* in Cic. *De nat. deor.* 1.119; cf. *ibid.* 3.50, stressing the *futuris . . . exemplum* aspect of

apotheosis). This doctrine is elaborated in the following chapter; cf. Sap. 14.14–21, where it is explained that idolatry began when (1) a father erected a statue of his dead child and ordered his household to worship it, and (2) the people set up likenesses of their absent king and by degrees came to worship them. There is no need to believe that Minucius Felix echoes this passage, however (contra J. D. Cooke, "Euhemerism: A medieval Interpretation of Classical Paganism," *Speculum* 2 [1927] 396 ff.); see Cic. *De nat. deor.* 1.118 f., 2.60 ff., 3.39, 3.50, and Pease's nn. *ad loca*, esp. on 1.119, for this common line of argument; cf. too Clem. *Protr.* 4.55.3 f., and other passages cited in A. Beltrami, "Clemente Alessandrino nell'Ottavio di M. Minucio Felice," RFIC 48 (1920) 239.

[274] A partial reply to the "national" deities of 6.1; see also 25.8 below.

[275] Beaujeu's text reads: *Lege historicorum scripta vel scripta sapientium.* In the rest of this chapter, it appears, one is to take, in order, Euhemerus as historian ([h]isto[r]icorum), Prodicus and Persaeus as philosophers (*sapientium*), and Alexander the Great as historian. It is odd categorization for Alexander. The reading of the main manuscript (*stoicorum*), which would refer to Persaeus alone, might be preferable—love of balance and *concinnitas* overriding strict accuracy and sense.

[276] Euhemerus of Messene, of the late fourth century B.C., wrote a work called the *Sacra historia*, a novel of fabulous travel in which he describes how he read on Panchaia in the Indian Sea, accounts of the mortal deeds of Uranus, Cronos, and Zeus, who were but beneficient kings and conquerors deified by their grateful people. This work was translated into Latin by Ennius, provided stock material (much used by Stoicism) for discussing ancient mythology, and was exploited (with evident relish) by Jewish and Christian apologists; to them, in fact, we owe most of the surviving fragments (cf. Tert. *Apol.* 10.3 ff.; Theoph. *Ad Autol.* 1.9 f., though in 3.7 Euhemerus is condemned as an atheist; Athenag. *Leg.* 28 ff.; Clem. *Protr.* 2.24.2; Arnob. 1.37 f.; esp. Lact.—see E. Laughton and Ed. Fraenkel, "The Prose of Ennius," *Eranos* 44 [1951] 35–56, etc. J. W. Schwippers, *De Ontwikkeling der Euhemeristische Godencritiek in de Christelijke Latijnse Literatur* [diss. Utrecht 1952], has collected the allusions in Latin patristic writings.) See further P. Decharme, *La critique*

des traditions religieuses chez les grecs des origines au temps de Plutarque (Paris 1904) 371 ff.; PW 6.1 (1907) 952–72 (F. Jacoby), and Pease's n. on Cic. *De nat. deor.* 1.119.

[277] For the Dictaean cult of Zeus, see especially A. B. Cook, *Zeus* (Cambridge 1925) 927 ff. Dicte was a mountain in Crete where, according to some accounts, Zeus was said to have been born and reared, or, according to others, buried. For further evidence of Euhemerus on Cretan Zeus, see Columel. *De re rust.* 9.2.3 and nn. 296, 347 below on chaps. 22.3 (birth) and 23.13 (the cave and tomb), and Pease's n. on Cic. *De nat. deor.* 3.53. Cook supposes that Euhemerus modeled his explanation of the Cretan Zeus on the stories of King Minos.

[278] Delphi, scene of the renowned oracle of Pythian Apollo and a major cult centre for the Greek world. Apollo is said to have wrestled with a serpent there and thus to have got possession of the oracle. See Plut. *De defect. orac.* 15f., 417F ff. for this and other variant legends of Apollo's mortal origins. (See also Pease's n. on Cic. *De nat. deor.* 3.42 [*de tripode*] for other evidence; Lucian *De sacrif.* 3 ff.).

[279] Before Alexandria stood the famous lighthouse, the Pharos, one of the wonders of the ancient world (on an island of the same name). Isis was especially worshiped there (Ovid *Amores* 2.13.8: *quae colis . . . palmiferamque Pharon; Ars amat.* 9.77.3 f.: *Pharonque/quae colis*); and there swallows (see n. 287 below for their association with Isis) each year were said to gather stones to prevent the rising Nile from inundating the land ([Plut.] *De fluv.* 16.2 [Bernard 7.309]). On Isis and her rites see below 21.3 and 22.1.

[280] Ceres was said to have fled from her native Sicily to Attica in pursuit of Pluto, the ravisher of her daughter; in recompense for hospitality given her at Eleusis, she gave the gift of corn, hitherto unknown; see Firm. Matern. *De error. prof.* 7; Pease on Cic. *De nat. deor.* 2.60 (*nomine ipsius dei*); Ovid *Fasti* 4.503 ff. and Frazer's ample nn. *ad loc.* See also chaps. 6.1 and 22.2.

[281] Prodicus of Ceos, famous sophist and contemporary of Plato, teacher of Isocrates and noted for his naturalistic interpretation of religion (notably the deification of things beneficial to man). See PW 23.1 (1957) 85–89 (K. von Fritz)and Pease's n. on Cic. *De nat. deor.* 1.118. Sext. Emp. *Adv. math.* 9.18 exemplifies the theory: Ceres = bread, Liber = wine, Neptune = water, Vulcan = fire, etc. Like Persaeus, he was noted as an etymologist (Plat.

Charm. 163D, *Crat.* 384B), the two philosophers being, in fact, closely associated (esp. Philodem. *De pietat.* 9–11, pp. 75–77 Gomperz). Indeed, Octavius (or his unknown source) may possibly have coalesced their theories, for the gods as the *discoverers* of beneficial foods, while an opinion, clearly attested for Persaeus, is not so certainly for Prodicus (see Pease's discussion on Cic. *De nat. deor.* 1.38, where, however, he interprets the passage of Philodemus cited above as attributing the discovery theory to Prodicus as well). For a valuable discussion of the *testimonia* related to this passage, see W. K. C. Guthrie, *A History of Greek Philosophy* 3 (Cambridge 1969) 238 ff.

[282] Persaeus of Citium (c. 306–c. 243), pupil of Zeno and defender of Stoic orthodoxy. See Pease's n. on Cic. *De nat. deor.* 1.38 and PW 19 (1937) 926–31 (K. Deichgräber). For passages illustrating gods said to be named after useful discoveries, see Pease's n. on Cic. *De nat. deor.* 1.38 (*a quibus . . . utilitas*).

[283] Ter. *Eun.* 432, quoted by Cic. *De nat. deor.* 2.60; see Pease's n. for the common use of this line to illustrate the figure of metonymy, and for parallels on this theory. It is fortuitous, therefore, that the line should mention together bread (Ceres) and wine (Liber = Dionysus), the elements of the Eucharist; they were proverbially the staples of life, one dry, one liquid. (Arnob. 1.38 adds Minerva = olive, another staple, cf. chap. 17.7 above; Tert. *Apol.* 11.8 characteristically remarks, what bad luck for Lucullus; he introduced the cherry into Italy from Pontus, but missed out on divine honors.)

For Bacchus (Liber) as the discoverer of wine, see Eur. *Bacch.* 278 ff.; Tert. *Apol.* 11.8 etc.; and see Pease on Cic. *De nat. deor.* 2.62 (Liber). For Ceres and corn, see above n. 280, and for an etymological explanation, Cic. *De nat. deor.* 2.67: *Mater autem est a gerendis frugibus Ceres tamquam gerere*, with Pease *ad loc.*

[284] Alexander consulted the famous oracle of Ammon (Zeus/Jupiter) at Siwah, a Libyan oasis (see G. Radet, "La consultation de l'oracle d'Ammon par Alexandre," *Mélanges Bidez* 2 [Brussels 1934] 779 ff., esp. 790; and generally, A. B. Cook, *Zeus* 1.376 ff.); he is reported to have written afterwards a letter to his mother containing "some ineffable oracles" (Plut. *Alex.* 27). This incident gave rise to some forged correspondence which appears to have had the purpose of ridiculing Alexander's own claim to divinity (see L. Pearson, "The Diary and Letters of Alexander the Great," *Historia* 3 [1955] 429 ff., at 447; W. W. Tarn, *Alexander the*

Great 2 [Cambridge 1948] 348 n. 2 is less sceptical). The forger was Leon of Pella (*fl.* late fourth century B.C.?); see PW 12.2 (1925) 2012–14 (Geffcken): he is cited, as one might expect after the example of Euhemerus, especially by Christian writers (Clem. *Strom.* 1.21.106.3; Tert. *De cor.* 7.6; Tat. *Or.* 27; Arnob. 4.29; cf. Athenag. *Leg.* 28; Augustine, *De civ. Dei* 8.5, 8.27 apparently conflates, citing "Leon an Egyptian priest" interviewed by Alexander; in Aug. *ibid.* 12.11 it is "a certain Egyptian priest"). It is clear from these examples and from Hyg. *Astron.* 20 that a euhemeristic explanation for Egyptian gods and for their attributes was presented. (*Schol.* Apoll. *Argon.* 4.262 cites "Leon in the First Book to the Mother," where apparently "of Alexander" has fallen out: Müller, FHG 2.331.) For further discussion see E. Amann, "Notes et communications," *Bull. d'anc. litt. et d'archéol. chrét.* 1 (1911) 123–26; D. Kuijper, "Minuciana," VC 6 (1952) 201 ff. W. Kroll, "Randbemerkungen," RhM 60 (1905) 307 ff., at 310, suggests, citing Joseph. *Antiq.* 11.317 ff. (Alexander and the Jewish highpriest), that the story came in Jewish apologetic also; E. Norden, "Varroniana," *Kleine Schriften zum klassischen Altertum* (Berlin 1966) 88 ff., esp. 90f. (suggesting Varro as the source employed). See also J. R. Hamilton, *Plutarch Alexander. A Commentary* (Oxford 1969) 71 ff.

[285] Vulcan = Greek Hephaistos = Egyptian Ptha (cf. Cic. *De nat. deor.* 3.55 and Pease's n.); for the theory of his being the head of the divine race, cf. Diod. 1.13.3.

[286] Jupiter = Greek Zeus = Egyptian Ammon (see chap. 22.6, where he wears "horns"; Leon of Pella, *ap.* Hyginus *Astronom.* 20, explained why: he introduced cattle from Africa; see Cook, *Zeus* 1.348 ff., for a full coverage, and Pease's nn. on Cic. *De nat. deor.* 1.82, and *De divin.* 1.3).

[287] In direct line of descent from Jupiter was Isis (Jupiter's daughter by Hera/Juno); Osiris was his son and Isis' husband (Diod. 1.13.4 ff.; there are variants, cf. Diod. 1.27.4). The "ears of corn" are explained by the myth that just as Ammon brought cattle to Egypt, Isis revealed the secrets of *spicae;* it was so reported by Leon of Pella (see Tert. *De coron.* 7.6; Aug. *De civ. Dei* 8.27, where Leon is, mistakenly, identified with the Egyptian priest, Alexander's informant; cf. Diod. 1.14.1 ff., 27.4). For a coherent discussion, see D. Kiujper, "Minuciana," VC 6 (1952) 201 ff.

Osiris (also a benefactor of mankind, see Plut. *De Isid. et Osir.*

13.356A-B) was murdered by Typhon, his monstrous brother, who dismembered and hid his corpse; cf. Athenag. *Leg.* 22. Isis, in her mourning for him, took the form of a swallow (see Plut. *ibid.* 16.357C; Roscher *s.v.* Isis 2.470; and for this soul-bird identification, generally, R. Turcan, "L'Ame-oiseau et l'eschatologie orphique," *Rev. de l'hist. des relig.* 155 [1959] 33 ff.; G. Weicker, *Der Seelenvogel in der alten Literatur und Kunst* [Leipzig 1902]). She searched for his limbs, timbrel in hand— whose shrill sounds (like those of her swallow) were a sign of grief. For further details see Plut. *De Isid. et Osir.*

The search was ritually celebrated annually (see chap. 22.1; Juv. *Sat.* 8.29 f. with Mayor's n.; Theoph. *Ad Autol.* 1.9; R. Merkelbach, *Isisfeste in griesch-römischer Zeit: Daten und Riten* [Meisenheim am Glan 1963]); it was often interpreted as a fertility analogy for the death of winter and the rejoicing of renascent spring (Tert. *Adv. Marc.* 1.13.5). There were other allegorical interpretations; on these see R. Merkelbach, *Roman und Mysterium in der Antike* (Munich/Berlin 1963) 53 ff.; and for possible influences on Christian ideas and practice, R. E. Witt, "The Importance of Isis for the Fathers," *Stud. patr.* 8 (1966) = TU 93, 135 ff.

[288] In popular parlance Serapis might be identified with Osiris (the latter being in fact rather in the background in this Hellenistic cult, and Serapis being by far the more prominent deity: Macrob. *Sat.* 1.20.16: *quem Aegyptii deum maximum prodiderunt*); cf. Lact. *Div. inst.* 1.21.22: . . . *Osiris quem Serapin vel Serapidem vulgus appellat;* and see generally F. Cumont, *Les religions orientales dans le paganisme romain*[4] (Paris 1929) 69 ff. Minucius Felix here exploits the confusion. Serapis, as a pantheistic, universal deity, might also be loosely identified with Zeus, Pluto, Helius, Asclepius, etc.

The allusion is to the story that Osiris had been enclosed in a chest; Typhon chanced upon his body and divided it into fourteen parts: hence the "scattered limbs and empty tomb." See Plut. *De Isid. et Osir.* 18.358A for the myth.

[289] Octavius appears to proceed to exemplify his point about these "human gods" further: the stories explaining their *sacra* and *mysteria*—those of Isis, Ceres, Jupiter, already mentioned, and in addition of Cybele of Dindymus—prove also that they are human beings. But this point merges into another: even in their humanity the gods are ridiculous and absurd (as shown by their

grief and greed). There is thus a gradual and concealed transition to another and distinct theme, which is then elaborated. By a process of "ring composition" Octavius returns to this basic theme of the human origins and the ridiculous rites of the gods in 23.9 ff. and 24.11 ff. This somewhat repetitious and meandering order has dissatisfied many editors, especially the uneasy transition here in 22.1, and they have accordingly advocated various rearrangements; the basic argument for an *interversion* in the MS archetype is that of J.-P. Waltzing, "Une interversion de deux feuillets dans l'Octavius de Minucius Felix," *Musée belge* 10 (1906) 83–100, examined at length in E. Heikel, "Adversaria in M.F. Octavium 3," *Eranos* 21 (1923) 130–50; and recently rediscussed by F. Scheidweiler, "Zu Minucius Felix," *Hermes* 82 (1954) 489 ff. But their results are no more satisfactory than the original text, and the length of the archetypal *feuillet* (to judge from the mistakenly-repeated phrase in 40.1 of *eadem tranquillitate qua vivimus* from 38.4) does not seem to admit of the transposition of an exactly even number of pages (see A. D. Simpson in ed. *ad loc.*). For further objections see A. J. Kronenberg, "Ad Minucium Felicem," *Phil.* 69 (1910) 126 ff., at 133 ff.; A. Kurfess, "Zu Minucius Felix," *Theol. und Glaube* 30 (1938) 546–52, and Beaujeu *ad loc.* The discussion continues; see K. Abel, "Minucius Felix: Octavius: Das Textproblem," RhM 110 (1967) 248 ff., at 269 ff., and C. Becker, *Der "Octavius" des Minucius Felix* (Munich 1967) 29 ff. It is perhaps worth remarking that (a) even in the most organized of Apologists this standard section on the pagan theogony tends to be ill-ordered and even downright scrappy (e.g., Clem. *Protr.* 2 f.; Athenag. *Leg.* 17 ff.), and (b) given the possibilities of confusion in the MS tradition, it is wise not to argue from rather *non sequitur* passages in the unaltered text of Minucius Felix for the priority of Tertullian (so Kurfess, *art. cit.*) or from a rather arbitrarily altered text for the priority of Minucius Felix. The unaltered text is followed here.

[290] There seems to have been some mistake here: Isis ritually searched for the remains of her brother-husband Osiris, not for those of Horus-Harpocrates, their posthumous son—though he, too, was eventually torn to pieces according to some accounts (Plut. *De Isid. et Osir.* 18.358E; *idem, De libidine et aegritudine* 6 [7.7 Bernadak.]); hence presumably the confusion which reoccurs only in Lact. *Div. inst.* 1.17.6, 21.20 (and *Epit.* 18.5) (derivative from Minucius Felix?).

A fragment (35 Haase) of Seneca *De superstit. ap.* Aug. *De civ. Dei* 6.10 is closely parallel.

For the ritual search, see n. 287 above.

[291] Cynocephalus (dog-headed god) = Anubis (strictly = jackal-headed), often equated with Hermes (Mercury) and hence a suitable guide for finding the remnants of Osiris (PW 1.2 [1894] 2645–49 [R. Pietschmann]). The search lasted three days (on this point see A. D. Nock, *Early Gentile Christianity and its Hellenistic Background* [New York 1964] 105 ff.).

[292] The Romans were particularly scornful of baldness and were themselves sensitive to loss of hair as a source of derision. Thus Julius Caesar was pleased with his perpetual olive wreath: it concealed his embarrassingly balding head; Suet. *J. Caes.* 45, cf. *ibid.* 51: he was heralded in song by his soldiers as the "bald adulterer." Domitian, troubled by a similar complaint, wrote a treatise *De cura capillorum* (Suet. *Dom.* 18) and he could be derided as the *calvus Nero,* Juv. *Sat.* 4.38; in Tacitus *Ann.* 4.57.3 the fact that Tiberius was *nudus capillo vertex* is suggested as one of the causes for his withdrawal from Rome; and note CIL 1.685 (*L. Antoni Calve . . .*), a taunt on a leaden bullet thrown at the siege of Perusia, and cf. CIL 1.684 and n. The priests of Isis had shaven heads (cf. Juv. *Sat.* 6.533 *grege calvo;* Mart. *Epig.* 12.29.19). Reasons (of mourning, ritual purity, etc.) are proffered in Plut. *De Isid. et Osir.* 4.352B ff.) for this practice. Note the observations on the subject of voluntary baldness by Artemid. *Oneirocrit.* 1.22 (p. 29 Pack).

[293] The lugubrious rites of Isis (see J. Burel, *Isis et Isiaques sous l'empire romain* [Paris 1911]; G. Lafaye, *Histoire du culte des divinités d'Alexandrie, Sérapis, Isis, Harpocrate et Anubis, hors de l'Égypte* [Paris 1884]; for illustration, J. Quasten *Musik und Gesang in den Kulten der heidnischen Antike und christlichen Frühzeit* [Münster 1930] *Taf.* 23,24,27) provided a standard example (e.g., Athenag. *Leg.* 14, 28; Clem. *Protrep.* 2.24.3) for the standard theme on the absurdity of honoring as gods those who have died and of worshiping them with a cultus of lamentation (Cic. *De nat. deor.* 1.38 and Pease's n. for abundant parallels; Sen. *De sup. fr.* 35 *ap.* Aug. *De civ. Dei* 6.10 is here very close). For lamentation, grief, condemned as evil, cf. Herm. *Mand.* 10— as opposed to the Christian virtue of ἡ ἱλαρότης (cheerfulness).

[294] Some have attempted to extract from this passage a chronological indication—the attempt, indeed, goes back to the disserta-

tion of Baudouin (see Intro. p. 3)–mostly notably E. Buonaiuti, "Il culto d'Iside a Roma e la data dell'Ottavio," *Athen.* 4 (1916) 91 ff. He appeals to S.H.A. *Commod.* 9.4 ff., *Carac.* 9.10 f., *Alex. Sev.* 26.8 (on the Severan devotion to the *sacra Isidis*), and urges that we therefore have evidence that the *Octavius* was written "al terzo decennio del terzo secolo" (add, e.g., Dio 77.23.2; S.H.A. *Nig.* 6.8; *Sept. Sev.* 17.4; H. Mattingly and E. A. Sydenham, *Roman Imperial Coinage* 4.1 [London, 1936] Caracalla nos. 193–94, 208, 244, 263, 280, 289, etc.). But such arguments must be totally inconclusive. The cult not only continued to have great, but declining, popularity *after* this period (Roscher 2.1.406 ff.; L. Vidman, "Die Isis–und Serapisverehung in 3 Jahrhundert u.Z.," *Neue Beiträge zur Geschichte der alten Welt* 2 [Berlin 1965] 389 ff.); but earlier, despite periodic suppressions as a public cult under the Republic (Tert. *Apol.* 6.8; Dio 40.47.3 f., 42.26.2) and under the early Empire (Augustus, Dio 53.2.4, cf. Suet. *Aug.* 93; Tiberius, Jos. *Ant. Jud.* 18.65 ff.; Suet. *Tib.* 36; Tac. *Ann.* 2.85.5), the cult continued privately (Tibull. 1.3.23 ff.; Ovid. *Amores* 1.8.73 f., 2.13.7 ff.) and public worship was restored when the temple of Isis Campestris or Campensis was established on the Campus Martius under the Julio-Claudians (by Caligula?–rebuilt by Domitian after fire, Dio 66.24.2, Juv. *Sat.* 6.528 f., Apul. *Met.* 11.26) and when emperors themselves figured as devotees of Isis (e.g., Otho, Suet. *Otho* 12). The remark could, therefore, have been made at least at any date from about the principate of Caligula (so A. D. Simpson, *Prolegomena* in ed. 10 ff.; Axelson 23; A. della Casa, "Le due date dell' 'Octavius,'" *Maia* 14 [1962] 26 ff., at 28; S. Rossi, "L' 'Octavius' fu scritto prima del 161," GIF 12 [1959] 289 ff.).

295 For Ceres and the Eleusinian rites, see n. 68 above. Ceres searched for her daughter Libera or Proserpine (see Pease on Cic. *De nat. deor.* 2.62, 2.65) abducted by Pluto as she gathered flowers on the Nysian plain: her pine torches were lit from Mount Aetna (Ovid *Fasti* 4.491 f. with Frazer's nn. *ad loc*; Arnob. 5.24, 5.35) and she is usually represented as being drawn by serpent(s) in a chariot (Ovid *Fasti* 4.497 f. and Frazer's nn. *ad. loc.*; Florus *Verg. orator an poeta* 2.4, etc.). Gronovius makes the imaginative but unlikely suggestion that Ceres had torches entwined with a serpent. See for the legend esp. Ovid *Fasti* 4.393 ff.; also Arnob. 5.24 ff.; Tat. *Or.* 8; Hyginus *Fab.* 146, etc.

296 Cronos (identified with Latin Saturn) sought to devour his

sons Hades, Poseidon, and Zeus because he was fated to be over-come by one of them. He succeeded with the first two, but Zeus was absconded by Rhea (often identified with Cybele) his mother, onto Mount Ida (there are several variants of location) in Crete. There he was cared for by a she-goat called Amalthea, or by a nurse (Amalthea) with a she-goat (for details, Roscher 1.262 ff, 2.1538 ff.). The sound of Zeus' infant cries was drowned by the noise made by the Curetes, attendants of Rhea, often iden-tified (as here) with the Corybantes, attendants of Cybele (see H. J. Rose, *Handbook of Greek Mythology* [London 1928] 170 f.). See also Frazer's nn. on Ovid *Fast.* 4.207 ff.; Cook, *Zeus* 3.1 (1940) 927 ff.; and Pease on Cic. *De nat. deor.* 2.64 *natos comesse*. This bizarre legend is, of course, frequently exploited by the Apologists: Arnob. 1.34, 3.30, 3.41; Athenag. *Leg.* 20; Orig. *C.Cels.* 3.43; Tat. *Or.* 25; Theoph. *Ad Autol.* 1.9, 3.3; Tert. *Apol.* 9.4, 25.7, etc.; and cf. chap. 30.3 below.

[297] On Cybele see n. 69 above: her sanctuary on Mount Dindy-mus in Phrygia was one of her most sacred; it overhangs Pessinus, the sacred city of Cybele.

[298] The castration of the youthful consort of Cybele, Attis (often a herdsman) has many variants, especially as to whether the act was self-inflicted or not, or whether Attis had been un-faithful or not. Generally speaking, the Apologists chose the variants placing the responsibility on Cybele as being the more discreditable; it is a frequent motif (Arnob. 5.5 ff.; Theoph. *Ad Autol.* 1.9, 1.10; Tat. *Or.* 8; Tert. *Apol.* 15.2, 15.5; Aug. *De civ. Dei* 6.7, following this account here). See also Catul. *Carm.* 63; Ovid *Fasti* 4.223 ff. with Frazer's nn.; and below chap. 24.12.

[299] For the eunuch priests of Cybele, the Galli, who imitated Attis in his emasculation, see especially H. Graillot, *Le culte de Cybèle, mère des dieux, à Rome et dans l'empire* (Paris 1912) 285 ff.; Roscher 1.2.1582–83. They were called Galli, it was said, after the river Gallus in Phrygia near Pessinus, whose waters drove them into their castrating frenzy (Ovid *Fast.* 4.361 ff. and Frazer's nn.). They are a constant motif of Roman satire (Juv. *Sat.* 2.110 ff., 6.513ff., 8.176; Pers. *Sat.* 5.186, etc.), and though the Christians follow them in this derision (see below 24.12 and cf. Athenag. *Leg.* 26; Tat. *Or.* 8; Tert. *Apol.* 25.4 f.), there are scattered references to early Christians prepared to castrate them-selves (Just. *Apol.* 1.29; Euseb. *H.E.* 6.8.1 [Origen], [Cyp.] *De sing. cleric.* 33; ?Athenag. *Leg.* 33–34; Tert. *De res. mort.* 61.6

(metaphorical?), *De virg. vel.* 10.1 (metaphorical? *spadones voluntarii*); "*Acts of John*" 53 f. Cf., too, the eunuch presbyter (?) Hyacinthus, Hippol. *Philos.* 9.12.11, and the strong tradition of eunuch martyrs (see B. de Gaiffier, "Palatins et eunuques dans quelques documents hagiographiques," AnalBoll 75 [1957] 17–46).

[300] In this section euhemerism is now clearly abandoned for the time being and the theme of the *ludibria* of the gods' features is further elaborated. It is a theme with a rich past in pagan (esp. Stoic) and Jewish writings as part of antianthropomorphism (cf. Cic. *De nat. deor.* 2.70, and see J. Geffcken *Zwei griechische Apologeten* [Leipzig/Berlin 1907] xvi–xxxi for references) before it was exploited by Christian writers (e.g., Athenag. *Leg.* 20 f., Arnob. 3.14 ff. for a vast catalogue, etc.).

[301] Vulcan (Hephaistus), god of fire, was lame as the result of his being hurled from heaven to earth by his father Zeus, Hom. *Il.* 1.590 ff. (or he was cast out of heaven by his mother, Hera, because he was misshapen, Hom. *Il.* 18.395 ff.). His physical deformity caused endless amusement (for references see Pease's n. on Cic. *De nat. deor.* 1.83).

[302] For Apollo traditionally beardless, see Pease's n. on Cic. *De nat. deor.* 1.83: *Apollinem semper inberbem.* There were, however, occasional bearded images, e.g., Lucian *De Syr. dea* 35.

[303] For Aesculapius bearded, Apollo not, cf. Cic. *De nat. deor.* 3.83 (the famous bon mot made by Dionysius as he removed the golden beard of Aesculapius at Epidaurus); Arnob. 6.21; Val. Max. 1.1. Ext. 3, etc. For a beardless Aesculapius, however, Paus. 2.13.5. For the general theme, Jos. *Contr. Ap.* 2.242. For his kinship with Apollo see Cic. *De nat. deor.* 3.57 and Pease's nn.

[304] *glaucis oculis*: appropriately colored for the sea-god (see TLL *s.v.* "*glaucus*" and J. André, *Étude sur les termes de couleur dans la langue latine* [Paris 1949] 175–78).

[305] For Minerva (Athena) *caesiis* (*oculis*), see Pease's n. on Cic. *De nat. deor.* 1.83; André, *op. cit.* 178–80; TLL *s.v.* "caesius." The phrase translates the Homeric epithet γλαυκῶπις, itself of controversial significance.

[306] The Homeric epithet βοῶπις applied to Hera (Juno).

[307] Mercury (Hermes), the god of commerce, was also a messenger of Zeus and the other gods; hence his winged feet (or sandals).

[308] Saturn (Cronos) enchained by Zeus, his son; cf. Arnob. 4.24; Macrob. *Sat.* 1.8.5, etc.

[309] Janus was a god of doors, thresholds, entrances, and thus of beginnings (e.g., the month *Januarius*) generally, and was often represented with a double-faced head (see Ovid *Fast.* 1.89 ff. and Frazer's nn. *ad loc.*, and Pease on Cic. *De nat. deor.* 2.67: *principem . . . Ianum*).

[310] A subtheme of the *ludibria deorum*, the multiple aspects of gods, is now exemplified by Diana and by Jupiter. For the theme in general, cf. Cic. *De nat. deor.* 3.53 ff. (where pluralities of Jupiter, the Dioscuri, the Muses, Vulcan, Mercury, Aesculapius, Apollo, Diana, etc. are elaborated). We have here Diana (Artemis) as the virgin huntress (e.g., the stories of Actaeon and his hounds and of the slaying of Orion), Diana as a many-breasted fertility goddess (often associated popularly as a moon-goddess with gestation and parturition—see Pease's nn. on Cic. *De nat. deor.* 2.69; she was especially cultivated at Ephesus—see Cook, *Zeus* 2.1 [1925] 405–17), and Diana (closely associated with Hecate) as a chthonian goddess haunting crossroads (hence multiple attributes) and appeased by monthly meals offered to her there (cf. Verg. *Aen.* 4.511 and 609, and Pease's nn. *ad loc.* [ed. *Aeneid* 4, Cambridge, Mass. 1935], Ovid *Fast.* 1.141 f. and Frazer's nn.); see also Rose, *A Handbook of Greek Mythology* 112 ff.; Pease's nn. on Cic. *De nat. deor.* 3.58 on the *tres Dianae* and their pedigrees, and Roscher 1.1002 ff.

[311] The general theme of the plurality of Jupiters is a common one, and Cicero tells us that it occurs *in priscis Graecorum litteris* (Cic. *De nat. deor.* 3.42 with Pease's n.). *Tres Ioves* are discussed in Cic. *ibid.* 3.53; so, too, in Clem. *Protr.* 2.28.1 and Arnob. 4.14 (along with 5 Mercuries, 5 Minervas, etc.); in Theoph. *Ad Autol.* 1.10 there are eight, in Tert. *Apol.* 14.8 (*Ad nat.* 1.10), on the authority of Varro, there are 300! See further Pease on Cic. *De nat. deor.* 3.53 for other catalogues. Provincial variants of Jupiter can, in fact, be startling and varied; for examples see C. B. Pascal, *The Cults of Cisalpine Gaul* (Brussels 1964) 77 ff.

For variations on Jupiter's facial *ornatus*, cf. Arnob. 6.10. Normally he was mature and bearded: *Iovem semper barbatum* (Cic. *De nat. deor.* 1.83), *barbati quidem Iovis* (1.101), though youthful and beardless Jupiters were to be found: Juv. *Sat.* 6.15 f.; Ovid. *Fast.* 3.437 with Frazer's n.; Servius *ad* Verg. *Aen.* 7.799 (Jupiter Anxurus).

[312] On Jupiter Hammon see n. 286 above.

[313] I.e., Jupiter Optimus Maximus, whose shrine was on the Capitol at Rome; see PW 10.1 (1917) 1135–39 (C. O. Thulin). P. H. Damsté, "Ad Minucii Felicis Oct. 22.6," *Mnem*, n.s. 39 (1911) 241 suggests *trina* (for *tunc*) *gerit fulmina*, comparing Ovid *Amor.* 2.5.52 *tela trisulca*. An unnecessary emendation.

[314] Jupiter Latiaris, in whose honor the *feriae Latinae* were celebrated annually on the Alban Mount with sacrifices (for the sacrifices see Dionys. Halic. *Antiq. Rom.* 4.49.763 [rams, bull]; Arnob. 2.68 [bulls]; Varro *De ling. lat.* 6.25 *ex sacris carnem;* Pliny *N.H.* 3.69 *carnem; visceratio,* Servius *ad* Verg. *Aen.* 1.211, Pease on Cic. *De divin.* 1.18). Blood is perhaps emphasized also because according to a tradition much exploited by Christian writers (Just. *Apol.* 2.12; Theoph. *Ad Autol.* 3.8; Tat. *Or.* 29; Tert. *Apol.* 9.5, *Scorp.* 7.6) he was also honored with human blood (see chap. 30.4 and n. 502). See further PW 10.1 (1917) 1134 f. (C. O. Thulin), Roscher 2.1.686 ff.

[315] The reading is quite uncertain and much emended, e.g., *quercina induitur* (W. H. Shewring, RB 41 [1929] 367, comparing CIL 8.6981) or *corona quercea cingitur* (A. Kurfess, *Th. Gl.* 30 [1938] 349) or *manu iacitur* (cf. Fest. 92.1; Simpson in *ed., ad loc.*) or *in lapide videtur* (B. Kytzler, "Notae Minucianae," *Traditio* 22 [1966] 419 ff., at 424 f.) or *sanguine verrino aditur* (L. Hermann, "Notes de Lecture 189," *Latomus* 25 [1966] 950). Jupiter Feretrius was concerned with the striking of treaties, and the *spolia opima* were dedicated in his shrine on the Capitol; see Roscher 2.1.670–79.

[316] There now follow four examples, intended to arouse derision, of the apotheosis of mortals and the bizarre methods used for that metamorphosis into pagan godhead.

Erigone, daughter of Icarius, found her father murdered and hanged herself. Athenian virgins began to do the same until her ghost was appeased by her elevation: Hygin. *Fab.* 130; Rose, *op. cit.* 154 f.; cf. Tert. *Scorp.* 10.4, Tat. *Or.* 9 (on the Dog of Erigone; an ironic inquiry whether the heavens were unadorned before the various deeds were performed that won animals a celestial place). It is perhaps worth noting that some of the Fathers actually debated whether the stars were rational beings or not (cf. Plat. *Tim.* 40B and see Pease on Cic. *De nat. deor.* 2.40 [*sideribus eadem divinitas*] for the many philosophers who accepted astral divinity). Orig. *C.Cels.* 5.10, *Comm. in Joann.*

1.24 (MG 14.67 ff.), etc., found that they were, because Job 25.5 ("the stars are not clean in His sight") implied that they were capable of sin. For a refutation of the idea, see Lact. *Div. inst.* 2.5.7 ff.

317 On the *Castores* see n. 88 above.

318 On Aesculapius see n. 70 above. He was slain by a thunderbolt of Zeus for combining the exercise of his healing craft with avarice—or, as in variant accounts, for raising men to life. The Apologists tended to choose the former version for derision (e.g., Tert. *Apol.* 14.5, *Ad nat.* 2.14; Arnob. 4.24; Clem. *Protr.* 2.30.1; Just. *Apol.* 1.21), the latter for parallels with Christ (e.g., Orig. *C.Cels.* 3.24, and see F. J. Dölger, "Der Heiland," AC 6 [1940–50] 241 ff., esp. 248 ff.). For *testimonia* on Aesculapius' death and deification, see E. J. and L. Edelstein, *Asclepius* 1 (Baltimore 1945) 232 ff., esp. 265, and for discussion 2.46 ff. On the significance of lightning as a means of "heroization," see E. Rohde, *Psyche*[8] (London 1925) App. 1, 581 f., and cf. chap. 35.3. See also Pease's n. on Cic. *De nat. deor.* 3.57 *fulmine percussus.*

319 Hercules, the great national hero of Greece, was sent as a gift from his wife, Deianira, a shirt daubed with the blood of the centaur Nessus whom he had slain; it was thus still impregnated with the poison of Hercules' own arrowhead; unable to remove the shirt, in agony he mounted a funeral pyre on Mount Oeta and died. On Hercules see Roscher 1.2135 ff. On the frequent theme of a fiery death as a means of apotheosis, see Pease on Cic. *De divin.* 1.47; on the event generally, Pease on Cic. *De nat. deor.* 3.41, 3.70; F. Stoessl, *Der Tod des Herakles* (Zurich 1945); and for the Christian exploitation of the legend, M. Simon, *Hercule et le christianisme* (Paris 1955), and *idem*, "Remarques sur la catacombe de la Via Latina," *Mullus* (Münster 1964) 327 ff.

The Castores, Aesculapius, and Hercules (along with Dionysus) are frequently mentioned together (as examples of apotheosis etc.; cf. Tat. *Or.* 21; Just. *Dial.* 69, *Apol.* 1.21 [with Ariadne among the stars]; Arnob. 1.41; Celsus *ap.* Orig. *C.Cels.* 7.53, cf. 3.22, 3.42; Cic. *De nat. deor.* 3.39, 3.45, 2.62, with many examples in Pease's n. *ad loc.*). On this passage see also Axelson 110.

320 A riposte to chap. 6.1, where Christians are urged to follow the teachings of their parents. For *imperitus* see n. 22.

321 On the *errores poetarum* see n. 230 above and esp. Pease on Cic. *De nat. deor.* 1.42 (a general passage on the theme of this chapter); there is also a reply intended to the gibe in chap. 11.9.

Homer, Vergil, etc. were, of course, standard school textbooks
(there being no children's books as such in classical antiquity)
which would be studied for learning by heart and repetition, cf.
Arnob. 4.33; Euseb. *H.E.* 9.5.1: the persecuting emperor Maximin,
in the war of counterpropaganda, orders primary-school teachers
to use the Memoirs of Pilate and the Saviour as such a school text.
This educational procedure caused embarrassment to those Christians who came to identify pagan literature with idolatry—and
Christian teachers clearly criticized such textbooks, cf. Julian *Ep.*
423d. Octavius manages to reject *en passant* the vital charge (for
conservative Romans) of abandoning ancestral tradition, by
elaborating on the generally admitted absurdities (so Caecilius
himself, 11.9) of the literary mythological tradition.

[322] Plato's celebrated expulsion of poets from his ideal state
(*Repub.* 3.398A) was a congenial theme for Christian and Jewish
apologists (Tert. *Ad nat.* 2.7.11; Orig. *C.Cels.* 4.36; [Just.] *Cohort.*
24, Just. *Apol.* 2.10; Joseph. *Contra Ap.* 2.256; cf. Philo *De gigant.*
59, *De ebriet.* 109) but it is of course mentioned frequently elsewhere as a commonplace of literature; see Pease on Cic. *De nat.
deor.* 1.42 (*poetarum*) for a vast list of references. J.-P. Waltzing,
"Platon, source directe de Minucius Felix," *Musée belge* 8 (1904)
424 ff., at 428, wishes to find in the epithet *laudatum* proof that
Minucius Felix consulted the Platonic text itself; it is omitted in
many parallel Latin passages (but note Joseph. *loc. cit.*)—but that
is an unnecessary deduction. A. Kurfess, "Zu Minucius Felix,"
Th. Gl. 30 (1938) 546 ff., at 550 n. 5, excises the word. Also
unnecessary.

[323] The present passage bears close resemblance to Tert. *Apol.*
14.2 ff., *Ad nat.* 1.10.37 ff., and has subsequently been much
discussed for the "priority question"; but each author has details
not to be found in the other's work, and while the lines of argument are slightly clearer in Tertullian, the impression to be gained
from a study of these particular passages cannot be conclusive for
either school of thought. The most balanced discussion is to be
found in Axelson 55 ff.

Etsi ludos facit. This may mean (1) Homer makes sport (fun)
of the gods—as in the scenes of courtly frivolities in, e.g., *Il.*
1.493 ff. or Hera's nagging of Zeus in the *Iliad passim.;* or less
possibly (2) Homer writes of the gods for sport, is not serious
about them—*ludo* and its derivatives being commonly used for
poetic frivolities (cf. 11.9: *in dulcedine carminis lusa*). On the

use of Homer in early Christian polemic, see G. Glockmann, *Homer in der frühchristlichen Literatur bis Justinus* (TU 105; Berlin 1968) esp. 76 ff., 85, 191 f.

[324] *Eorum paria composuit*. For *par* cf. 18.6 *Thebanorum par;* Tert. *Ad nat.* 1.10.38 is rather clearer: *gladiatoria quodammodo paria composuit;* cf. Tert. *Apol.* 14.2, Axelson 58 n. 24. For an example of the gods fighting, see Hom. *Il.* 20.31 ff. The indignity and incongruity of the gods fighting each other, and being wounded as a consequence, was a common theme; cf. Cic. *De nat. deor.* 1.42, and Pease's n. *ad loc.* (*eorum bella, proelia, pugnas*), *De nat. deor.* 2.70 f.

[325] For Venus wounded (by Diomedes) see Hom. *Il.* 5.330 ff., an absurdity much exploited, e.g. Tert. *Apol.* 14.2, *Ad nat.* 1.10.39; Arnob. 3.21; Theoph. *Ad Autol.* 1.9; [Just.] *Cohort.* 2, etc.; see Pease's n. on Cic. *De nat. deor.* 1.42 (*vulnera*) for other examples.

[326] For Mars enchained (by Otus and Ephialtes) see Hom. *Il.* 5.385 ff.; cf. Pease on Cic. *De nat. deor.* 1.42 *vincula;* wounded, see Hom. *Il.* 5.855 ff. (by Diomedes with the aid of Pallas Athena); cf. Athenag. *Leg.* 21; Arnob. 4.25; [Just.] *Cohort.* 2; Tert. *Apol.* 14.3, *Ad nat.* 1.13.39, etc.

[327] Hom. *Il.* 1.396 ff., cf. Tert. *Apol.* 14.3, Joseph. *Contr. Ap.* 2.241, [Just.] *Cohort.* 2 (all, with the two following examples as well, in the same context), Lucian *Deor. dial.* 21.2 etc.

[328] Hom. *Il.* 16.431 ff. (at the hands of Patroclus). A notorious example of theological inconsistency, or at least confusion, in Homer, much exploited by later writers, e.g., Athenag. *Leg.* 21 (with the following example); Clem. *Protr.* 4.55.3; Cic. *De divin.* 2.25 with Pease's n. *ad loc.* for references to other ancient literature on the incident.

[329] For the story see Hom. *Il.* 14.214 ff., and cf. Seneca *fr.* 84 Haase. For Jupiter's adulteries cf. Theoph. *Ad Autol.* 1.9, and, at great prolixity, Arnob. 4.22, 4.26; for further parallels see Pease's n. on Cic. *De nat. deor.* 1.42 (*libidine furentis, adulteria*); cf. esp. Sen. *fr.* 119 *ap.* Lact. *Div. inst.* 1.16.10: Jupiter's amorous adventures are dismissed as so much salacious rubbish.

[330] "Elsewhere" (*alibi*) is rather curious: the cleansing of the Augean stables (one of the Herculean labours) does not occur in Homer; the two accompanying illustrations do, however. On the passage see C. Becker, *Der "Octavius" des Minucius Felix* (Munich 1967) 87 ff., n. 54 (suggesting adaptation from Tertullian). For the story see Hygin. *Fab.* 30 (the stables had 3,000

cattle, uncleansed for 30 years; Hercules removed the dung in one day). The event is referred to by [Just.] *Or. ad Graec.* 2. Again it is the unseemly character of the role assigned to the god that is the point (stablehand and, in the following examples, herdsman and builder).

[331] For a reference to the story, see Hom *Il.* 2.763 ff., and see the prologue to Eurip. *Alcestis.* Listed among the foolish tales of the gods by Clem. *Protr.* 2.35.1; Arnob. 4.25; Tert. *Apol.* 14.4; Joseph. *Contra. Ap.* 2.247 (all with the following example); Tat. *Or.* 21; Athenag. *Leg.* 21.

[332] Hom. *Il.* 21.441 ff. and the passages cited above.

[333] Verg. *Aen.* 8.424 ff., cf. Cic. *De divin.* 2.43, and generally Roscher, 2.1.1676 ff. For the line of argument—natural phenomena are prior to birth of the gods—cf. Arnob. 1.30; Tert. *Apol.* 11.6 (including the same example).

[334] Hom. *Od.* 8.266 ff. for Mars and Venus; cf. Athenag. *Leg.* 21; Tert. *Apol.* 14.3; Joseph. *Contra Ap.* 2.245, etc.; Arnob. 5.41 for the allegorization of this story (the wedding of strength with beauty). Hom. *Il.* 20.232 ff. for Ganymede, carried off to be Jupiter's youthful cupbearer (Arnob. 4.26; Just. *Apol.* 1.21, 25; Tert. *Ad nat.* 2.10.10, etc.), and the subject of many famous statues (cf. Tat. *Or.* 34; Pausan. 5.24.5, and the colored clay group from Olympia; for illustration see John Boardman, *Greek Art* [London 1964] fig. iii). Both are famous illustrations of scandalous immoralities among the gods.

[335] This and the following observation (the stories of mythology providing a precedent for vice and corrupting men's minds, especially those of impressionable youth) are commonplace remarks of antianthropomorphic polemic and are to be found in a wide range of literature; cf. Arnob. 5.29; Tat. *Or.* 22; Just. *Apol.* 1.21; Plat. *Rep.* 2.378B, 3.391E; Ter. *Eun.* 583 ff.; Sen. *Dial.* 7.26.6: *quibus nihil aliud actum est quam ut pudor hominibus peccandi demeretur si tales deos credidissent* (cf. *Dial.* 10.16.5); Ovid *Amor.* 2.8.14: *quod decuit reges, cur mihi turpe putem;* and for many other references see Pease's nn. on Cic. *De nat. deor.* 1.42 (*poetarum* and *nocuerunt*); cf. also Cic. *ibid.* 1.102.

[336] A very Stoic, and ultimately Platonic, outlook; on the phenomenon of *synkatathesis* or understanding, see Pohlenz 1.88 ff., 2.32, 88, and contrast Octavius' concluding remark in 38.6: *gloriamur nos consecutos quod illi summa intentione quaesiverunt nec invenire potuerunt.* One is reminded of the controversial

findings of the First Vatican Council (Constitution *Dei Filius* c. 11): *Divinae revelationi tribuendum est, ut ea, quae in rebus divinis humanae rationi per se impervia non sunt, in praesenti quoque generis humani conditione ab omnibus expedite, firma cum certitudine et nullo admixto errore cognosci possint.*

[337] A rather abrupt transition back to an euhemeristic discussion of Saturn and Jupiter, and consequently frequently transposed. If the present passage is in place, a rather unrelated phrase like *principem huius generis et examinis* (closely parallel to Tert. *Apol.* 10.11, where it is appropriate), would point to the priority of Tertullian. Indeed, the passage as a whole bears strong resemblance to Tert. *Apol.* 10.7 ff. and has, consequently, been frequently discussed for the question of priority; see especially Axelson 35 ff. The narrative of Tertullian is somewhat clearer on some points (e.g., on the coining of money, Tert. has *imagine signatus nummus et inde aerario praesidet* for Octavius' less explicit *nummos signare*); but there are a number of details in the two accounts that are divergent, those of Octavius being especially related to Verg. *Aen.* 8.320 ff. The same story is told in *Origo gent. Rom.* 1.2 f., 2.4, 3.1 ff., (see A. Momigliano, "Some Observations on the 'Origo gentis Romanae,'" JRS 48 [1958] 56 ff., at 64), but it is unnecessary to suppose that it is derived from M.F., as Beaujeu suggests (see Baylis 346 f.). Note the appeal to antiquity for support.

[338] Cornelius Nepos (c. 99–c. 24 B.C.), a minor Roman historian and biographer (*De viris illustribus*); his universal history in three books (*Catul.* 1.3 ff.) does not survive. See PW 4.1 (1900) 1408–17 (Wissowa).

[339] Cassius Hemina seems intended, one of the first Latin annalists; he wrote a history of Rome from the earliest Italian times and, to judge from the surviving fragments, he seems to have been especially interested in the religious and social antiquities of Italy; see H. Bardon, *La littérature latine inconnue* 1 (Paris 1952) 73–77; PW 3.2 (1899) 1723–25 (Cichorius); and fragments, H. Peter, *Hist. Rom. frag.* (Leipzig 1883) 68 ff. See also PW 6.1 (1907) 1378 (Schwartz), where it is suggested Cassius Longinus is intended (unconvincing).

[340] Thallus, according to Africanus *ap.* Euseb. *P.E.* 10.10 and Euseb. *Chron.* 1.41 (ML 19.267), dealt with Syrian history from Troy to Olymp. 167 (112–109 B.C.); Theoph. *Ad Autol.* 3.29 clearly indicates his euhemeristic tendencies. See PW 5A1 (1934) 1225–26 (R. Laqueur).

[341] Diodorus Siculus, of the last century B.C., writer of the 40 books of world history. The reference to Saturn is at 5.70 ff.; PW 5.1 (1903) 662–704 (E. Schwartz). Much discussion has centered on this sentence; for Minucius Felix has *Nepos et Cassius, Thallus ac Diodorus* (cf. Lact. *Div. inst.* 1.13.8, who adds Varro), whereas Tert. *Apol.* 10.7 has *Diodorus Graecus aut Thallus, Cassius Severus aut Cornelius Nepos*, and *Ad nat.* 2.12.26: *apud Cassium Severum, apud Cornelios Nepotem et Tacitum, apud Graecos quoque Diodorum* (copied by Arnob. 2.12). Cassius *Severus* appears to be an error; he was an *orator* of the late Republic and early Empire (H. Bornecque, *Les déclamations et les déclamateurs d'après Sénèque le père* (Lille 1902) 157–59; PW 3.2 (1899) 1744–49 (Brzoska).

Has Minucius Felix, elegantly reducing the authorities to single *nomina* or *cognomina*, inadvertently or designedly corrected the error? Or has Tertullian added Severus for his own *concinnitas* or for clarity (so H. V. M. Dennis, "The Date of the *Octavius*," AJP 50 [1929] 185 ff., at 187 ff.–to avoid confusion with Cassius Dio: improbable)? The latter procedure is inherently the less likely; for discussion, Th. Rheinach, "Minucius Felix et Tertullien," *Rev. de l'hist. des rel.* 83 (1921) 59 ff., at 65 ff.; Baylis 305 ff., esp. 307 ff.; Axelson 35 ff.; and A. Klotz, "Zu Minucius Felix und Tertullian," *Würzb. Jahrb. für die Altertumswiss.* 4 (1949–50) 379 ff., on Minucius Felix' general habit of inverting the order of his borrowings; by no means a compelling point, but it helps to weigh the balance further towards the priority of Tertullian. On the ultimate source (Varro?), see E. Norden, *Kleine Schriften* etc. (Berlin 1966) 88 ff., esp. 90 ff.

[342] The epithets, already applied to the Christians in 12.7, are now returned to the Roman *maiores*–and to be found in their own mythology! Cf. Verg. *Aen.* 8.321: *genus indocile;* Macrob. *Sat.* 1.7.21.

[343] *Ut Graeculus et politus.* If the milieu of Minucius Felix was Roman and Severan, it was perhaps rather indiscreet of him to use the scornful diminutive (cf. Juv. *Sat.* 3.78, 6.186) in a community heavily represented in the governing circles with Greek-speaking Easterners (see M. Hammond, "Composition of the Senate, A.D. 68–235," JRS 47 [1957] 74 ff., at 78 f., and the literature there cited). Perhaps, therefore, a hint that his environment was Latin-speaking African, but this hint must be very slight, for denigration of the Greek "national character" was a

literary pose (so G. La Piana, "Foreign Groups in Rome during the First Centuries of the Empire," HTR 20 [1927] 183 ff., at 229 f., for evidence; and A. N. Sherwin-White, *Racial Prejudice in Imperial Rome* [Cambridge 1967] 71 ff.). Note for comparison Cic. *Pro Flacco* 4.9: *hoc dico de toto genere Graecorum: tribuo illis litteras, do multarum artium disciplinam, non adimo sermonis leporem, ingeniorum acumen, dicendi copias . . . testimoniorum religionem et fidem numquam ista natio coluit.*

[344] *Litteras inprimere, nummos signare, instrumenta conficere.* Tert. *Apol.* 10.8 has *ab ipso primum tabulae et imagine signatus nummus, et inde aerario praesidet.* There *tabulae* would appear to mean legal records; cf. Verg. *Aen.* 8.322: *legesque dedit;* Plut. *Quaest. Rom.* 22.269A, 41.274F. It is possible, therefore, that M.F. may have misinterpreted Tertullian's *tabulae.* On the other hand, *litterae* can be used (unusually) of ordinances (cf. Cic. *Verr.* 2.5.22.56: *praetoris litterae*) and this, just conceivably, might be the significance here; or M.F. may be simply alluding to Saturn's traditional civilizing role in more general terms.

Nummos signare. The treasury of the Senate was called *aerarium Saturni;* for the introduction of coined money, see Ovid. *Fast.* 1.239 f. and Frazer's nn.; Macrob. *Sat.* 1.7.22; Plut. *Quaest. Rom.* 41.274f; Athenaeus 692E; Isid. *Etym.* 16.18.3 f.

Instrumenta; i.e., farm tools. Saturn had many aspects as an agricultural deity; see Macrob. *Sat.* 1.7.24; Verg. *Georg.* 2.406 (the gift of the sickle, *Saturni dens*); Ovid. *Fast.* 1.234 (*falcifer deus*); Arnob. 3.29, 6.12.

[345] The popular (aetiological) etymology is common; cf. Verg. *Aen.* 8.322 f.: *Latiumque vocari/maluit, his quoniam latuisset tutus in oris;* 8.357 f.: *Hanc Ianus pater hanc Saturnus condidit arcem,/Ianiculum huic, illi fuerat Saturnia nomen.* See also Arnob. 1.36, 3.29; Ovid. *Fast.* 1.237 f., 1.245 f., 6.31 and Frazer's nn.; Varro *De ling. lat.* 5.42; Athenaeus 692D f.

[346] Tert. *Apol.* 10.9 is a little clearer: *cuius parentes ignoti erant, facile fuit eorum filium dici, quorum et omnes possumus videri.* The expressions are proverbial; see Otto *Sprichwörter* 62, 344 f. There are many variations of terminology, e.g., *fraterculus gigantis* (Juv. *Sat.* 4.98), *progenies terrae* (Pers. *Sat.* 6.57); compare with *terrae filios* (glossed by Fronto, Naber 37, with *cellae filios,* "offspring of the garret") the Stoic theory of autochthonous races born from the earth without sexual intercourse; cf. Celsus *ap.* Orig. *C.Cels.* 4.36.

For Caelus (Uranus) as a diety, the father of Cronos (Saturn), see Cic. *De nat. deor.* 2.63 and Pease's nn. for the relevant literature.

³⁴⁷ The birth and death of gods was a constant source of derision (see n. 276 on 21.1 above, and cf. Cic. *De nat. deor.* 1.42 and Pease's nn.) especially after the style of Euhemerus (Cic. *ibid.* 1.119: *ab Euhemero autem et mortes et sepulturae demonstrantur deorum*). The story of Jupiter's birth in a cave on Crete (Mt. Ida or Dicte) has already been alluded to in 22.3 (see Pease's n. on Cic. *De nat. deor.* 3.53 for a long catalogue of allusions to this event). The tomb of Zeus was even more renowned: references in the early Apologists alone include Orig. *C.Cels.* 3.43; Tat. *Or.* 27; Tert. *Apol.* 25.7; Theoph. *Ad Autol.* 1.10, 2.3; Clem. *Protr.* 2.37.4; Athenag. *Leg.* 30; Arnob. 4.14, 4.25; for further references and for a description of the tomb on Mount Juktas, see Cook 1.157 ff.; candidates for the site in antiquity included Knossos, Ida, and Dicte (see also Pease on Cic. *De nat. deor.* 3.53: *sepulcrum ostenditur*).

³⁴⁸ Arnobius, with typical lack of reticence, proceeds to trace the descent of the major gods from their parentage (2.70 ff.). For an *argumentum ad absurdum* based on the reverse process (if Saturn and his brothers are gods, then Caelus, then . . . are gods too), see Cic. *De nat. deor.* 3.44 ff.

This whole passage (§§1–4) bears close resemblance to Tert. *Apol.* 10.6 ff. and other snatches of Tertullian (esp. *Apol.* 21.3 ff.). Though the order of thought is not indefensible here, there can be no doubt that the elements to be found in common with Tertullian are much happier and more logically in place in that apology than they are here. The *non sequitur* at the beginning of §3 is particularly noticeable, as is the inappositeness of the concluding remark of §4. Well discussed in detail by J. van Wageningen, "Minucius Felix et Tertullianus," *Mnem.* 51 (1923) 223 ff., at 224 ff.; Axelson 105 ff.; Beaujeu, Intro. lviii ff.

³⁴⁹ Proculus Julius, by tradition a farmer from Alba Longa, declared that he had witnessed Romulus' epiphany after his death—genuinely (Livy 1.16) or, as in some other accounts, his announcement of Romulus' apotheosis came *impulsu patrum:* Cic. *De repub.* 2.20, *De legg.* 1.3 (hence "perjury"); for Romulus, with fratricide and rape to his credit (chap. 25.2 f.), was a controversial figure of Roman historiography, and the justification for his apotheosis was a subject for debate. See Ogilvie on Livy

1.16, Frazer's nn. on Ovid *Fasti* 2.492 ff., and Pease's n. on Cic.
De nat. deor. 2.62 (*Romulum* and *quidam*); cf. Cic. *De nat. deor.*
3.39. Similar eyewitnesses were to be equal to the occasion for
later apotheoses (Suet. *Aug.* 100; Dio 56.46.2 [Augustus]; Dio
59.11.4 [Drusilla]; cf. Herodian 4.2.11) and were equally a source
for derision.

[350] The deification of Juba II, ruler of the Mauretanians from
25 B.C. for nearly fifty years, has excited much discussion. Tertullian (from Africa) *Apol.* 24.8 has a generalized statement on the
reguli of Mauretania being regarded as gods; Minucius Felix has
a particular instance (to parallel Romulus). Which author came
first?

1) That other Numidian leaders were so reverenced, as well
as Juba, is known from inscriptions but from inscriptions only
(Masinissa, Gulassa, Hiemsal; see J. Toutain, *Les cultes païens
dans l'empire romain* 3.1 [Paris 1920] 39, to which add Masgava,
ILS 4488). Either author could, therefore, have made such statements independently—Minucius Felix instancing the best-known
Numidian chief—*if* they both had African backgrounds. In this
(commonly drawn) supposition we have another possible hint of
M.F.'s background (cf. n. 123 above).

But (2) Isid. *Etym.* 8.11.1 has the same example of Juba—the
only other literary source to mention the precise fact and
apparently independently of Minucius Felix; Lact. *Div. inst.* 1.20.6
and [Cyprian] *Quod idola* 2 have, like Tertullian, a general remark; the reading of Arnob. 1.36 on the religious cults of the
Mauri is corrupt. Therefore, M.F. may have culled the fact from
a common literary source and the passage cannot, accordingly,
be used to *prove* an African origin for M.F. or to settle the
priority question (so, rightly, J. van Wageningen, "Minucius
Felix et Tertulliananus," *Mnem.* 51 (1923) 223 ff.—hardly answered by G. Hinnisdaels, "Minucius Felix est-il antérieur à
Tertullien," *Musée belge* 28 [1924] 25 ff.). See also Th. Rheinach,
"Minucius Felix et Tertullien," *Rev. de l'hist. des rel.* 83 (1921)
59 ff.; J.-P. Waltzing, "Encore Minucius Felix et Tertullien,"
Musée belge 25 (1921) 189 ff.; Baylis 302 ff.; Axelson 46 ff.

[351] Note the careful reticence on the imperial cult (cf. the
equally guarded remarks in 29.5): to be too specific would rouse
unnecessary hostility and rancour. Typically, Tert. *Apol.* 28.2–
35, *Ad nat.* 1.17.8 is less general and restrained; cf., too, Theoph.
Ad Autol. 1.11. For the idea cf. Vespasian's famous dying bon

mot (Suet. *Vesp.* 23.4: *vae . . . puto deus fio*) or the remark of
Caracalla concerning his brother Geta (S.H.A. *Geta* 2.8): *sit divus
dum non sit vivus.* For discussion on the relationship with Tertullian, see Axelson 106 f.

[352] A collection of philosophical commonplaces; cf. 34.2 and
see Cic. *De nat. deor.* 1.20 with Pease's nn. (*ortum . . . aeternum*); Cic. *ibid.* 1.90 with Pease's nn. (*di enim semper fuerunt*);
Cic. *ibid.* 3.29 with Pease's nn. (*si nullum* etc.). For the line of
argument (often repeated), cf. Cic. *ibid.* 1.68: *Sint sane (dei) ex
atomis, non igitur aeterni. Quod enim ex atomis, id natum aliquando est; si natum, nulli dei ante quam nati; et si ortus est
deorum, interitus sit necesse est, . . . ubi igitur illud vestrum
beatum, et aeternum, quibus duobus verbis significatis deum?* Cf.
Arist. *Apol.* 1 (Syr.); Orig. *C.Cels.* 3.43; Cyp. *Ad Demet.* 3:
haec Dei lex est ut omnia orta accidant et aucta senescant; Sen.
Dial. 11.1.1; Sall. *Iug.* 2.3; Lucr. 5.235 ff., etc.

[353] The point (senility, impotence and, overpopulation among
the gods) was clearly a *topos* of antipolytheism; cf. Seneca *ap.*
Lact. *Div. inst.* 1.16.10 (= *fr.* 119 Haase): *Quid ergo est, . . .
quare apud poetas salacissimus Iuppiter desierit liberos tollere?
Utrum sexagenarius factus est;* cf. Juv. *Sat.* 6.59: *adeo senuerunt
Iuppiter et Mars?;* Cic. *De nat. deor.* 3.41; Pliny *N.H.* 2.7.16;
Tat. *Or.* 21; and combined with the idea of overcrowding, Arnob.
3.8 f.; Theoph. *Ad Autol.* 2.3 (citing *Orac. Sibyl. fr.* 2); Lact.
Div. inst. 1.16.5 ff.; Constant. *Orat. ad ss. coet.* 4 (GCS Eusebius
1.157). The question of sexual differentiation and activity among
the gods generally was an allied theme; see Cic. *De nat. deor.*
1.92, 1.95 and Pease's parallels *ad loca.*

[354] There now begins an anti-idolatry section, a favorite topic
of Christian and Judaic propaganda, and a reply to the gibe in
10.2: *nulla nota simulacra.* For the theme cf. Arnob. 6.8 ff.; Just.
Apol. 1.9; Tat. *Or.* 33 f.; *Ad Diog.* 2; 2 *Clem.* 1.6; Theoph. *Ad
Autol.* 2.1 f.; Athenag. *Leg.* 17 f.; Tert. *Apol.* 12; Jos. *Contra Ap.*
2.252; and for the relevant passages in Clement of Alexandria, see
A. Beltrami, "Clemente Alessandrino e Minucio Felice," RFIC
48 (1920) 239 ff., at 245 (esp. *Protr.* 4.60 ff.). One wonders
whether the Christians are often fair to the pagan position—but
to appreciate the niceties of their opponents' tenets was not their
particular purpose; it was more to score a palpable debating-point
even at the expense of accuracy. For downright idolatry, involving the complete identification of cult-image and god, was the

vulnerable attitude generally attributed by the Apologists to paganism. It was, however, an attitude much scorned by pagan intellectuals themselves: e.g., Heraclitus B5, Diels, quoted *inter alios* by Celsus *ap.* Orig. *C.Cels.* 1.5; cf. *ibid.* 3.40, 3.76, and esp. 7.62: "who but an infant imagines that these things are gods and not votive offerings and images of gods?" See also Sen. *fr.* 121 (Haase) *ap.* Lact. *Div. inst.* 2.2.14 on the absurdity of the veneration of images; Cic. *De nat. deor.* 1.77 (and Pease's nn.); the pagan in Arnob. 6.24; Porphyry *ap.* Euseb. *P.E.* 3.7, 9, 11, etc. There are, however, passages which do imply that the *vulgus* tended to identify god and image, notably Plut. *Is. et Osir.* 71.379C, *De superstit.* 6.167D; Lucian *De sacrif.* 11, etc. M.F. is, therefore, careful to confine his attack to the gullibility of the uncritical *vulgus:* it would surely have left many of his (intellectual) readers personally unmoved. For further discussion see H. Chadwick, "The Evidences of Christianity in the Apologetic of Origen," *Stud. patr.* 2 (1957) 331 ff.; M. P. Nilsson, *Greek Piety* (Oxford 1948) 168 ff.; E. R. Bevan, *Holy Images* (London 1940) *passim,* esp. 21 ff.; C. Clerc, "Plutarque et le culte des images," *Rev. de l'hist. des relig.* 70 (1914) 252 ff.

[355] For the idea of the exploitation of the splendors of gold and silver to attract the devotion of the masses, cf. Cic. *De legg.* 2.11.26, *De nat. deor.* 1.77 (with Pease's nn.); Polyb. 6.53.5 ff.; Arnob. 6.12, 6.24 etc. Note, too, the remark of Lucian that gods are held in greater honor when they are in gold (*Iupp. trag.* 7).

[356] Cf. Tert. *Apol.* 12.3 ff., a comparison of the Christian's sufferings under persecution with what the gods suffer as they are being made.

[357] *Infelicis stipitis:* a technical expression; see Macrob. *Sat.* 3.20.2–3 for a list of *arbores felices* and *arbores infelices.* The *infelices* are those which are barren (Orig. *C.Cels.* 8.31 makes demons directly responsible for barren vines and fruit trees), thorny, uncultivated (e.g., tamarisk, wild pear), or which bear dark fruit, the color of the infernal gods (e.g., black fig), or which have been struck by lightning. The wood of such trees was, notoriously, used for executions (hence the translation); cf. Livy 1.26.11; Sen. *Ep.* 101.14, *Dial.* 5.15.4; Cic. *Pro C. Rabir.* 4.13; Lucan *Phars.* 1.590 f., etc. The wood was also used for burning evil *portenta prodigiaque;* hence *ligna infelicia* were an appropriate wish for the funeral pyres of one's enemies or their works (Catul. 36.8; Cic. *Pro Mil.* 13.33). See R. Bloch, *Les prodiges dans*

l'antiquité classique (Paris 1963) 67 ff.; J. André, "Arbor Felix, Arbor Infelix," *Hommages à Jean Bayet* (Brussels 1964) 35 ff. Do we have here a partial retort to the *ligna feralia* attributed by Caecilius to Christ's cross in 9.4?

[358] The allusion is to Amasis' golden foot pan turned into a statue of a god, Hdt. 2.172.3 ff., and an anecdote much welcomed by the Apologists (e.g., Just. *Apol.* 1.9; Athenag. *Leg.* 26; *Acta Apoll.* 17 (AnalBoll 14 [1895] 289); Theoph. *Ad Autol.* 1.10 even has Egyptians adoring foot pans!); and for the general theme, cf. also *Ad Diog.* 2; Tert. *Ad nat.* 1.12, *Apol.* 12.2; Arnob. 6.12 (trinkets of harlots, pots and pans, and still more repulsive vessels etc.); Lucian *De sacrif.* 11; and Waszink's catalogue on Tert. *De an.* 57.2 (p. 578).

[359] This idea is commonplace: note especially Zeno *S.V.F.* 1, no. 264): nothing could be regarded as of much value or holy which was the work of builders and common laborers: cf. Just. *Apol.* 1.9; Tert. *Apol.* 12.2; Orig. *C.Cels.* 1.20; it is a point generally made in the passages cited above, as is the following one on the insensitivity of the pagan statues.

[360] Gods were equipped with appropriate *ornatus* to make them distinguishable from each other, e.g., thunderbolt, trident, aegis, caduceus, winged sandals, bow, etc.; cf. Cic. *De nat. deor.* 1.101. Paint, jewellery, drapery, etc. might also be applied to them.

[361] Consecration ceremonies were performed to attract the god to inhabit the image—by spells and ceremonies, by magic stones, by herbs, scents, and enticing sacrifices. (The god had to be made of the appropriate materials in the first place, however, with which he would have affinity). See Bevan, *Holy Images* 31 ff.; Cumont, *Lux Perpetua* 436 ff.; W. Scott, *Hermetica* 1 (Oxford 1924) 358.

[362] A similar point made by Arnob. 6.15; Theoph. *Ad Autol.* 2.2; Athenag. *Leg.* 17; Tert. *Apol.* 5.1: *nisi homini deus placuerit, deus non erit;* cf., too, Mart. *Epig.* 8.24.5 f.: *qui fingit sacros auro vel marmore vultus/non facit ille deos; qui rogat, ille facit.* For discussion of this quotation in relation to M.F. and Tertullian, see Axelson 34, 109. Typically, Tertullian exploits the ease of the reverse operation (*Apol.* 13.4: *in caccabulum de Saturno . . . in trullam de Minerva*).

There is heavy emphasis in Tertullian (*Apol.* 12.3, 16.7, and *Ad nat.* 1.12.1 ff.) on the fact that when terra-cotta images were made, a wooden framework (shaped like a cross) was used as a support for the friable material (see H. Zehnacher, *Les statues du sanctuaire de Kamart (Tunisie)* [Brussels 1965] 59 ff.). S. Rossi, "Tertulliano e l'origine degli dei," GIFC 19 (1966) 65 ff., concludes that as M.F. is unaware of this transformation of the cross into a pagan god, he is prior to Tertullian. An unconvincing deduction. Terra-cotta is simply omitted as a material altogether: *saxum, lignum, argentum* provided a suitable rhetorical triplet with which triple sets of verbs could be effectively associated. It is noteworthy that painting is also omitted (not so, e.g., Theoph *Ad Autol.* 2.2); see above n. 129.

[363] A traditional satirical observation to be made on divine images; cf. Hor. *Sat.* 1.8.37 f.; Aristoph. *Ran.* 366; Theoph. *Ad Autol.* 2.36 (quoting *Orac. Sibyl. fr.* 3 Geffcken); Tert. *Apol.* 12.7; a very expanded form in Arnob. 6.16 (with newts, shrews, mice, cockroaches, spiders, swallows, etc.); and cf. Theodor. *H.E.* 5.22: when Theophilus, bishop of Alexandria (391 A.D.), had the axe laid to the gigantic statue of Serapis, mice came out in droves, "for the god of the Egyptians was the house of mice."

[364] The pagans are hoist with their own attacks on the impotence (10.4, 12.2) of the Christian God, and the fear which He is said to inspire (12.4 f.). For other parallels to this commonplace notion (shared by Christian and pagan alike) on the material power that a deity ought to show in this world, see Pellegrino in ed. *ad loc.* For the oddity of providing police protection for valuable statues, cf. Arist. *Apol.* 3; Tert. *Apol.* 29.2; *Ad Diog.* 2.7; Arnob. 6.20; Cyp. *Ad Demetr.* 14; Juv. *Sat.* 14.260 ff. and Mayor's n. *ad loc.*

[365] A confutation of Caecilius' claim made in 6.1. Note the emphasis laid on reprehensible ignorance (see n. 22 above) and cf. 17.2: *ignorare nec fas nec licet,* and 36.4; cf. Arnob. 3.42. And on *sibi credere* cf. 15.5 and Sen. *Ep.* 31.3: *unum bonum est quod beatae vitae causa et firmamentum est, sibi fidere;* it was a prominent Stoic idea.

[366] This appears to be intended as an artistic conclusion to the discussion of idolatry, picking up the opening remarks on the attraction of gold and silver in artistic shapes, and providing at the same time an alternative account of the origins of Roman *superstitio* (versus Roman *religio* in 6.2 ff.). But the remark is tied awkwardly into the context and nothing has been said on the elegance of form given to the gods (as idealized men, see Pease on Cic. *De nat. deor.* 1.77 for this aspect). For the general

notion, see Lact. *Div. inst.* 2.6.2f.: *sub obtentu deorum avaritia et cupiditas colitur,* and cf. n. 355 above.

[367] The inclusion of a survey of apparently absurd ceremonials of paganism is standard apologetic practice; cf. Tert. *Apol.* 14.1 for a brief notice on the theme (and for discussion, Axelson 39). The Luperci, at their festival of the Lupercalia, celebrated on February 15, as they ran round the old line of the *pomerium* or city boundary, wore only a goat's skin (the festival being in honor of Faunus, though others, e.g., Varro *ap.* Arnob. 4.3, connected it with Luperca, the she-wolf who suckled Romulus and Remus). See Ovid *Fasti* 2.359 ff. and Frazer's nn. for a description.

[368] In March and in October the Salii, priests of Mars, paraded in solemn regalia, wearing their conical caps (*apices*) and their 12 *ancilia,* the shields sacred to Mars, the original of which was believed to have been worn by him and to have fallen from heaven. See Ovid *Fasti* 3.377 ff. with Frazer's notes, and Livy 1.20.3 f. with Ogilvie's notes.

[369] This appears to be a description of another group of pagan devotees (though V. Basanoff, *Evocatio* [Paris 1947] 116 ff. refers the beating of *pelles* to the *Mamuralia* also). The passage would appropriately refer to the mendicant priests of Cybele, beating their leather-covered tympana (Ovid *Fasti* 4.209 ff. and Frazer's nn.) and dragging their goddess' shrine behind drawn by oxen. For a description of their annual procession and *lavatio,* see Frazer on Ovid *Fasti* 4.337. For their notorious mendicancy, see Ovid *Fasti* 4.350 ff. with Frazer's nn. The Christians proudly pointed out that no charge was made at their liturgical ceremonies; donations were voluntary (Tert. *Apol.* 39.5, cf. 42.8 and 13.6: *circuit caupones religio mendicans*).

[370] Thus the shrine of Cybele at Boeotian Thebes was opened only once a year (Paus. 9.25.3 with Frazer's nn.); that of Ceres and Proserpine in Arcadia could be visited by men but once a year (Paus. 8.31.8); that of Athena Polias at Tegea could be entered by a priest only and then but once a year (Paus. 8.47.5 with Frazer's n. for other examples).

[371] So the temple of Poseidon at Matinea (Paus. 8.5.5, 8.10.2), the grove of Ceres and Proserpine in Arcadia (Paus. 8.31.5); cf. Paus. 8.30.2, 8.38.6 for other examples.

[372] The Bona Dea mysteries would be the most obvious candidate; see Cic. *De harusp. respon.* 8.37; Macrob. *Sat.* 1.12.21 ff.;

and generally J. Gagé, *Matronalia* (Brussels 1963) 137 ff. Certain shrines and rites of Ceres were similarly taboo for men (Lact. *Div. inst.* 3.20.4; Cic. *Verr.* 2.4.45.99; cf. Paus. 8.36.3, etc.).

[373] E.g., the rites in honor of Hercules; see Frazer on Ovid *Fasti* 1.581 for references and the various legends adduced for the prohibition; or those of Silvanus (Cato *De agric.* 83).

[374] Thus in the rites of Mater Matuta (the *Matralia*); see Frazer's n. on Ovid *Fasti* 6.481 for references and discussion, and Ogilvie's n. on Livy 5.23.7; and for a collection of instances of other ceremonies where slaves were explicitly excluded (*Megalesia*, Secular Games, etc.), Frazer on Ovid *Fasti* 6.551.

[375] A common requisite; cf. Tert. *De monog.* 17.4: *Fortunae Muliebri coronam non imponit nisi univira sicut nec Matri Matutae.* See also Frazer on Ovid *Fasti* 6.475; Servius *ad* Verg. *Aen.* 4.29, 4.166. The ideal of marriage to one husband is an ancient Roman one; for discussion and many references, see G. Williams, "Some Aspects of Roman Marriage Ceremonies and Ideals," JRS 48 (1958) 16 ff., at 23 ff. See also 31.5 below and n. 518.

[376] This sounds like a gratuitous addition merely for rhetorical flourish, and in such a polemical context it would be dangerous to press the passage for any implicit condemnation of second or subsequent marriages as "adulteries" (on this point see 31.5). Rites where prostitutes participated (e.g., *Floralia;* see 25.8) may be envisaged.

[377] For the orgiastic blood-spilling rites of the Cappadocian goddess Bellona, during which her devotees slashed their arms and legs with sharp knives, see Tibul. 1.6.43 ff.; Hor. *Sat.* 2.3.223; Juv. *Sat.* 4.123; Lucan 1.565 f.; S.H.A. *Commod.* 9.5; Tert. *Apol.* 9.10; and chap. 30.5 below.

[378] For the contrasting rites of Cybele, see above 22.4. March 24 was the *dies sanguinis.* Flint stone and bronze knife were also appropriate instruments; see H. Graillot, *Le culte de Cybèle* 296 f.; the mystical metaphor of harvesting is standard, apposite for Attis the handsome shepherd and corn god, see Graillot, *op. cit.* 294 f. For the rites see also F. Cumont, *Les religions orientales dans le paganisme romain*[4] (Paris 1929) 47 ff. (and notes, 224 ff.).

[379] Cf. Sen. *fr.* 34 Haase (*ap.* Aug. *De civ. Dei* 6.10): *ubi iratos deos timent qui sic propitios merentur;* the whole fragment is closely related to this section.

[380] Cf. Euseb. *H.E.* 7.32.3 on the Christian eunuch Dorotheus;

he was, prodigiously, by nature a eunuch, having been so from his very birth; see also n. 299 above.

[381] Cf. Sen. *loc. cit.* in n. 379: . . . *ut nemo fuerit dubitaturus furere eos, si cum paucioribus furerent; nunc sanitatis patrocinium insanientium turba est;* Juv. *Sat.* 2.45 f.: *sed illos/defendit numerus, iunctaeque umbone phalanges;* contrast Cyp. *Ep.* 31.6.3: *Nec hoc animentur quia multi sunt, sed hoc ipso magis reprimantur quia non pauci sunt. Nihil ad extenuationem delicti numerus impudens valere consuevit.*

[382] Octavius here replies to the defense of Roman religion advanced by Caecilius in chap. 6 ("it must be good because it has made Rome great"). The greatness of Rome it was unthinkable to deny. So the first proposition had to be attacked. This is done by (a) suggesting that the *maiorum disciplina* which the Christians had been urged to accept in 6.1 was positively wicked and, in fact, irreligious; by (b) demonstrating that Rome's material advance was due to acts of sacrilege, not of religious devotion; by (c) observing that the local gods of Rome (6.1) are risible—and harmful—and that others' native gods would not in any case have aided Rome; by (d) claiming that the vestal virgins and priests of Rome are lewd and corrupt (and therefore no protection); and by (e) denying that there is any direct correspondence between pagan religion and Empire—it all depends on the dispensation of God.

Note here the ironic echo from 6.1 (the gods, or kings, at the cradle of the world). The legend of the notorious first king of Rome is now to be exploited, as by many other Christian apologists (cf. Tert. *Ad nat.* 2.9.19, *De spect.* 5.5 f.; Arnob. 1.64; Lact. *Div. inst.* 1.15.29; cf. Aug. *De civ. Dei* 3.6,12 ff., 15.5, etc.). Monceaux, accordingly, declared of this passage (*Hist. de l'Afrique chrét.* 1.465): "il y parle de la Ville éternelle comme n'en aurait jamais parlé un vrai Romain" (cf. 1.466: ". . . L'*Octavius* évoque, presque à chaque page, quelque souvenir d'Afrique"); cf. with a parallel argument Baylis 13: "But a highly bred Roman gentleman under the Empire could hardly bring himself so to outrage even conventional patriotism as to assert, as Minucius Felix does (xxv), that. . . ." That is to overlook seriously the fact that criticism of Rome's *iustitia* and origins was a rhetorical *topos*; cf. Just. (Trog) 28.2.8 ff.; Caes. *B.G.* 7.77; Tac. *Agr.* 30 ff.; Sall. *Hist. fr.* 69.17 ff.; Cic. *De repub.* 3.12. Note the discussion of the *Romulus in caelo* graffiti from Pompeii (e.g., CIL 4.3135, 7353, 8568, 8995), with the literary parallels, by O. Skutsch, "Enniana vi," CQ 14 (1964) 85 ff., at 90 f., and the article of K. Scott, "Humor at the Expense of the Ruler Cult," CP 27 (1932) 317 ff. See also on the Romulus legend H. J. Krämer, "Die Sage von Romulus und Remus in der lateinischen Literatur," *Synusia: Festgabe für Wolfgang Schadewaldt* (Pfullingen 1965) 355 ff.; O. Seel, *Römertum und Latinität* (Stuttgart 1964) 219 ff.; and more generally, G. Lieberg, "Die römische Religion bei Minucius Felix," RhM 106 (1963) 62 ff., at 72 ff. (and for a discussion on the relationship with Tertullian [*Apol.* 25.14, *Ad nat.* 2.17.14 ff.] R. Heinze, *Tertullians Apologeticum* [Leipzig 1910] 426 ff.).

The verb *auspicata est* was perhaps chosen with irony (as below in §2, *haec prima sunt auspicia*). It was the notorious observation of the auspices that led to the fratricidal strife and the beginnings of Rome's career in crime. The *locus classicus* is Ennius *Ann.* 1.77–96 (Vahlen) *ap.* Cic. *De divin.* 1.107 f., where see Pease's nn., adding the discussion of O. Skutsch, "*Enniana iv*," CQ 11 (1961) 252 ff.; cf., too, such expressions as *Romulum auspiciis . . . fundamenta iecisse nostrae civitatis* (Cic. *De nat. deor.* 3.5 with parallels cited by Pease *ad loc.*).

383 For the story of the gathering at Asylum (PW 2.2 [1896] 1881–86 [Stengel]) at the deep dip in the ground between the two peaks of the Capitoline Hill where Romulus promised refugees protection and sanctuary, see Livy 1.8.5 ff. and Ogilvie's nn. *ad loc.;* Ovid *Fasti* 3.429 ff. and Frazer's nn. *ad loc.;* and Pease on Cic. *De divin.* 2.40.

384 For the rape of the Sabines, see Livy 1.9–13 and Ogilvie *ad loc.;* Ovid *Fasti* 3.189 ff. and Frazer *ad loc.* There is a Vergilian echo from *Aen.* 8.635: *raptas sine more Sabinas.* The Roman respect for virginity (6.2) is now shown in its historical reality; the intrepidity of Roman piety (*audacia*, 6.2) is now transformed into audacity (*audacius*) in outrage; the defenses of Rome are no longer religious rites and priesthoods (6.2), they are self-assured crimes; Rome stands at the confluence not of religions (6.1) but of criminals, etc.

385 This is the reinterpretation of the *maiorum . . . disciplina* and the injunction *prioribus credere* of 6.1.

386 There is close resemblance with Tert. *Apol.* 25.14, though the inappropriateness here of Tertullian's phrase *caedes . . . sacerdotum* has been much overstressed (e.g., by Beaujeu *ad loc.*:

"motif superflu, ajouté mal à propos"). The *impietas* of Roman activities is a connecting theme that runs through the individual arguments (blood of kindred §3, altars and temples §4, desecrations §6, seizure of arms against the gods §7, etc.). More superfluous, in fact, would be *id est de ruinis urbium*, excised (but unnecessarily) by S. Colombo, "Osservazioni sulla composizione litteraria e sulle fonti dell'Octavius di M. Minucio Felice," *Didaskaleion* 3 (1914) 79 ff., at 119 n. 2.

[387] A reply to the *numina victa* of 6.2.

[388] Directly related to Tert. *Apol.* 25.15: *Tot igitur sacrilegia Romanorum quot tropaea, tot de deis quot de gentibus triumphi, tot manubiae quot manent adhuc simulacra deorum;* cf. *Ad nat.* 2.17.16. The relationship is discussed by Axelson 44 f. Trophies of victory (*tropaea*) consisted primitively of tree trunks decorated with spoils taken from the defeated enemy.

[389] The text *quos postulaverant* is difficult as it stands: a significance such as "decide" ("began to worship those whom they chose to so honor") is possible but very strained. I have taken the meaning, with no great conviction, to be "challenge" and the allusion to be to the ceremony of *evocatio* or the like, thus providing a suitable match for 6.2 (where see n. 79; so, too, Quispel and Simpson in edd. *ad loc.*). K. Abel, RhM 110 (1967) 292, suggests reading *post v<io>laverant;* alii alia. It is noteworthy that Minucius Felix does not challenge the assumption of Rome's greatness; it is reasonable, therefore, to deduce that he is writing before the Roman world appeared to be in collapse—or in decadence (e.g., Cyp. *Ad Demet.*). Nor, prudently, does he raise the question why Rome's wickedness has gone unpunished (unlike that of the Jews, 33.4 f.).

[390] The train of thought is not immediately stated. It is that, if others' gods did not help Rome in her advance, then it must have been Rome's native gods: these are, accordingly, put under scrutiny and there is thus an incidental reply to the value of worshiping *deos municipes* as advocated in 6.1. On these *indigetes, indigitamenta* see n. 67 above and Roscher 2.129–233; PW 9.2 (1916) 1334–67 (F. Richter). Seneca *De superstit. fr.* 33 (Haase), *ap.* Aug. *De civ. Dei* 6.10, appears to be the direct source here; see F.-X. Burger, *Minucius Felix und Seneca* (Munich 1904) 20 ff. Cf. Arnob. 4.6 ff., with a recondite collection of (often obscure) *indigitamenta;* Lact. *Div. inst.* 1.20; Aug. *De civ. Dei* 4.23, etc.

[391] On Romulus see n. 349 above. The parallel passage from Seneca *De superstit. fr.* 33 suggests Romulus should properly figure as the inventor of the accompanying gods, not as one of them himself.

[392] Picus figures in Rome's aetiological myth as an old Italian king, son of Saturn, father of Faunus and grandfather of Latinus; he was changed by Circe, whose love he had slighted, into a woodpecker (*picus*). In fact, he appears to have been a primitive totemic deity, the woodpecker being sacred to Mars and highly valued for its augural powers. See Frazer on Ovid *Fasti* 3.54 for a full discussion, PW 20.1 (1941) 1214–18 (G. Rohde); the deity figures prominently in Iguvine augury, *Tab. Igu.* vi a. 1 ff. (and see the commentary of J. W. Poultney *ad loc.*).

[393] Tiberinus, in legend, was an Alban king who was drowned in the river Albula and thus gave his name to that river (Tiber), Ovid *Fasti* 2.389, 4.47; he was also the god of the river, Ovid *Fasti* 2.597, 6.237 with Frazer's nn. *ad loca*, PW 6A (1936) 784–88 (G. Rohde), 792–94 (H. Phillipp); and for a valuable discussion, A. Momigliano, "Thybris Pater," in *Terzo contributo alla storia degli studi classici e del mondo antico* 2 (Rome 1966) 609–39, and R. Meiggs, *Roman Ostia* (Oxford 1960) 339 f., 483 ff.

[394] Consus, an agrarian deity, god of crops and their safe-keeping in bin and granary (*condere*) and honored with the festival of the Consualia (Aug. 21, Dec. 15) (Livy 1.9 and Ogilvie *ad loc.*; Tert. *De spect.* 5.5); by false etymology (*deus consilii*) he also came to be regarded as the god of good counsel (Arnob. 3.23; Varro *ap.* Aug. *De civ. Dei* 4.11). See also Ovid *Fasti* 3.189 ff. and Frazer *ad loc.*; PW 4.1 (1900) 1147 f. (A. Aust.).

[395] Pilumnus, usually closely associated with his brother Picumnus, and said to be a personification of the pestle (*pilum*): hence reverenced by *pistores;* see Serv. *ad* Verg. *Aen.* 9.4. He was also honored as the protector (against Silvanus) of very young children; cf. Varro *ap.* Serv. *ad* Verg. *Aen.* 10.76; Varro *ap.* Aug. *De civ. Dei* 6.9. In mythology he was an ancestor of Turnus: Verg. *Aen.* 9.3 f., 10.76; and see PW 20.2 (1950) 1369–72 (V. Blumenthal).

[396] Volumnus, protecting deity of the newly-born, who "wished them well": Aug. *De civ. Dei* 4.21 and see PW 9A.1 (1961) 884–86 (W. Eisenhut).

[397] Sewer = (Venus) *Cloacina*, goddess of the Cloaca Maxima,

where, according to Lact. *Div. inst.* 1.20.11, Tatius found her statue and so dedicated it after the place of its discovery. The bizarre name of the cult was much exploited by Christians (Tert. *Adv. Marc.* 1.18.4, *De pall.* 4.7; Aug. *De civ. Dei* 4.8); but see Pliny *N.H.* 15.29.119 and Serv. *ad* Verg. *Aen.* 1.720 for the derivation as *Cluacina*, a goddess of purification. See Ogilvie on Livy 3.48.5 and J. Gagé, *Matronalia* 91 ff. for the cult.

398 Tullus Hostilius, third king of Rome, dedicated shrines to *Pallor* and *Pauor* during a critical period of the fighting with Veii: Livy 1.27.7, where see Ogilvie's n., adding Tert. *Adv. Marc.* 1.18.4, Arnob. 1.28 (worshipers of *Pavores*). On such apotropaic cults (averting injurious powers) see Pease's n. on Cic. *De nat. deor.* 3.63 (*perniciosis rebus*).

399 Febris had as her principal shrine an *ara vetusta* (Cic. *de legg.* 2.11.28) and a *fanum* (Cic. *De nat. deor.* 3.63) on the Palatine, no doubt designed to avert the attacks of malaria in particular; see also Val. Max. 2.5.6: *Febrem autem ad minus nocendum templis colebant*, and cf. dedications to *Tertiana* and *Quartana* (i.e., periodic malarial attacks?). See PW 6.2 (1909) 2095–96 (G. Wissowa).

400 Acca Larentia has a richly varied and disputed mythology: she was Romulus' nurse (according to Masurius Sabinus, see Aul. Gellius, *Noctes Atticae* 7.7.5; Livy 1.4.7; Macrob. *Sat.* 1.10.17 [quoting Licinius Macer]), or a notorious whore who left her money to Romulus (according to Antias) or to the Roman people (see Macrob. *Sat.* 1.10.11 ff.; Aul. Gellius, *Noctes Atticae* 7.7.5 ff.). The latter version, with the profession of prostitution, is the one usually followed by the Fathers: Tert. *Apol.* 13.9, cf. 25.3 ff., *Ad nat.* 2.10.1 ff.; Lact. *Div. inst.* 1.20.1 ff. for an ample collection of stories and etymologies. See Ogilvie on Livy 1.4.7; Ovid *Fasti* 3.55 ff. and Frazer's nn.; and A. Momigliano, "Tre figure mitiche," in *Miscellanea della Facoltà di Lett. e Filos. della R. Università di Torino* 2 (Turin 1938) 16 ff. Flora, goddess of flowers; her spring festival (the Floralia, April 28–May 3) was celebrated with notorious license (Lact. *Div. inst.* 1.20.6; Arnob. 3.23, 7.33); see also Ovid *Fasti* 4.945 ff. with Frazer's nn.; Mayor on Juv. *Sat.* 14.262. Beaujeu states that M.F. is the first to make of Flora a courtesan (in ed. *ad loc.*); she may, however, be the *scortum* in Cato's speech *De re floria fr.* 212, 3 Malcovati; and for a beautiful courtesan named Flora, whose portrait was dedicated in a temple, see Plut. *Pomp.* 2.4.

[101] *Mars Thracius*. For Ares dwelling in Thrace, see Hom. *Il.* 13.301; *Od.* 8.361; for Jupiter and Crete, see chap. 22.3, 23.13, and cf. Tert. *Apol.* 25.7.

[402] Juno *Argiva*, for Hera (Juno) was said to have been born in Argos and the Heraeum was in Argos, perhaps the most noted centre of her worship (Pomp. Mel. 2.41: *templum Iunonis vetustate et religione percelebre*). See Pease's n. on Cic. *De nat. deor.* 1.82 (*non est talis Argia*) for further discussion.

Juno *Samia*, Samos providing another noted cult centre of Hera; cf. Orig. *C.Cels.* 4.48; Varro *ap.* Lact. *Div. inst.* 1.17.8: *ibi Iuno adolevit ibique etiam Iovi nupserit*. She figures not infrequently on Samian coins; see J. Barron, *The Silver Coins of Samos* (London 1966) 92, 114 f., 124, 134 f., 141 f., etc.

Juno *Poena*, i.e., Juno identified with the Phoenician deity (Tanit) as *dea caelestis*, providing a very popular African cult. Note Verg. *Aen.* 1.15 f.: *(Carthago) quam Juno fertur terris magis omnibus unam/posthabita coluisse Samo*, and cf. Arnob. 3.30 for an outlandish list of Juno's titles.

[403] For *Diana* and *Mater Idaea* see 6.1, and on the *Aegyptia portenta* 28.8 below.

[404] A reply to the protection claimed by virtue of the vestals' virginity in 6.2. The traditional punishment for violated vows was to be buried alive (e.g., Livy 8.15.7 f., 22.57.2; Serv. *ad* Verg. *Aen.* 11.206; Suet. *Dom.* 8.3 f.; Pliny *Ep.* 4.11; Herodian 4.6.4). See the discussion of G. Wissowa, "Vestalinnenfrevel," *Archiv. rel. Wiss.* 22 (1923–24) 201 ff., on the treatment of fallen vestals, and Frazer's nn. on Ovid *Fasti* 6.458. The incidence of unchastity is, of course, much exaggerated.

Vesta sane nesciente: a retort to the connivance attributed to the God of the Christians at His followers' lack of material well-being (in 12.2).

[405] The passage is closely related to Tert. *Apol.* 15.7, on which see the discussion of Axelson 108 n. 14. Temple prostitution was a frequent literary *topos* (if not frequent in actuality under the Empire; but see Joseph. *Antiq.* 18.65 ff., priests of Isis in 19 A.D.); cf. Ovid *Amor.* 2.2.25, *Ars amat.* 1.77; Juv. *Sat.* 6.314 ff., 6.489, 9.24: *quo non prostat femina templo*.

[406] This important point, inserted here rather as an aside between the discussion of priesthoods and auguries, is argued more emphatically, and effectively, in Tert. *Apol.* 26.1 ff. For the argument cf. Joseph. *Contra Ap.* 2.125 ff.; Orosius *Adv. pag.*

7.1.7 ff.; and for the relationship with Tertullian, see Axelson 53 ff. For the (traditional) list of Empires, cf. *Orac. Sibyl.* (Geffcken) 3.158 ff., 3.167 ff., 4.49 ff., 8.6 ff.; Lact. *Div. inst.* 7.15.13 (Egyptians, Persians, Greeks, Assyrians).

[407] The Arval Brethren (a brotherhood of twelve) were established by Romulus as priests of Dea Dia and Bacchus: Pliny *N.H.* 18.6; Aul. Gellius, *Noctes Atticae* 7.78; the college was revived by Augustus. The extant records of their meetings, celebrating, with ritual, official imperial events, provide valuable primary documentation for the early Empire (collected by G. Henzen, *Acta fratrum Arvalium* [Berlin 1874]; later additions to be found in A. Pasoli, *Acta fratrum Arvalium* [Bologna 1950]).

[408] On the Salii see n. 368.

[409] See n. 93 above and n. 411 below.

[410] This chapter is designed as a reply to chap. 7 of Caecilius' discourse; the examples collected are in 7.3 f. To criticize and reject divination was respectable philosophically; it was a special activity of the Peripatetic and Epicurean schools (for divination implied direct providential interference in the world). See Cic. *De divin.* 1.5 for a historical survey, with Pease's nn., and cf. Orig. *C.Cels.* 8.45.

[411] For the historical references, see nn. 93, 94 on 7.4. The phrase used for the chickens' feeding is an augural technical term, *solistimum tripudium,* applied when animals ate so greedily that bits of food fell from their mouths to the ground; it is explained in Cic. *De divin.* 1.27 f. (where see Pease's nn.) and 2.72.

[412] M. Atilius Regulus (cos. 267, 256 B.C.), a great Roman hero and byword for courageous honesty (cf. Horace's "Regulus" Ode, *Carm.* 3.5; for Ciceronian references to Regulus as an *exemplum virtutis,* see Pease on Cic. *De nat. deor.* 3.80.; cf. Tert. *Apol.* 50.6, *De test. anim.* 4.9, *Ad nat.* 1.18; and chap. 37.5). After defeat and capture in the First Punic War (255 B.C.), he was sent to Rome to arrange an exchange of captives; faithful to his word, he returned to Carthage to be tortured to death (tortures recounted in detail by Aul. Gellius, *Noctes Atticae* 7.4, from Tubero; cf. Livy *Epit.* 18); PW 2.2 (1896) 2086–92 (E. Klebs). Many of the stories associated with his name may well be apocryphal (H. H. Scullard, OCD [1949] 757); and see H. Kornhardt, "Regulus und die Cannaegefangenen," *Hermes* 82 (1954) 85 ff., esp. 101 ff., for a thorough examination of the tradition.

[413] Caius Hostilius Mancinus (cos. 137 B.C.) concluded a shame-

ful treaty in the campaigns against Numantia. The Senate refused
to ratify the treaty and Mancinus was thus delivered back into
the hands of his enemies. It is doubtful whether his army was
ever actually sent beneath the yoke. See Val. Max. 1.6.7; Flor.
2.18.5 ff.; PW 8.2 (1913) 2508–11 (Münzer).

⁴¹⁴ At the crushing defeat at Cannae in the Second Punic War
(216 B.C.) Rome is said to have lost at the hands of Hannibal
more than 40,000 men (Livy 22.43 ff.). One of the generals was
L. Aemilius Paulus. The example is given in Cic. *De divin.* 2.71
(along with Clodius, Flaminius, and Junius); for his auguries cf.
Livy 22.42.8 ff. See PW 1 (1893) 581 (E. Klebs); 3.2 (1899)
1483–84 (C. Hülsen).

⁴¹⁵ Julius Caesar in his campaign against the Pompeians, in late
47 B.C., sailed from Sicily to Africa; his object in sailing in wintry
weather, as often in his campaigns, was to take the enemy by surprise. The days before the winter solstice (Dec. 25 in the Julian
Calendar) were ominous, but the day of the solstice itself was
highly auspicious (see Pease on Cic. *De divin.* 2.33: *puleium . . .
florescere*). This example occurs in Cic. *ibid.* 2.52, where see
Pease's nn. For Caesar's scorn of contrary omens, see Suet. *Jul.
Caes.* 59 (this campaign), 77.

⁴¹⁶ A reply to the fleeting observation in 7.5: criticism of
oracular responses formed part of the philosophical rejection of
divination generally (see n. 410 above). Note also the 2nd century
A.D. treatise against oracles by the Cynic Oenomaos of Gadara,
and cf. Orig. *C.Cels.* 3.25, 7.3.

⁴¹⁷ Amphiaraus (who also took part in the Argonautic expedition and the Calydonian boar hunt) lay concealed during the
campaign of the Seven against Thebes, having foreseen his death
if he took part. His whereabouts were revealed by his wife,
bribed by a necklace. He was swallowed up by the earth, according to many accounts, and was subsequently worshiped as a god
(Athenag. *Leg.* 29) especially at Oropus, the seat of his oracle,
which appears to have long been active. See Hyginus *Fab.* 70,
73, and Pease's nn. on Cic. *De divin.* 1.88 and *De nat. deor.* 2.7
(in both passages mentioned with Tiresias and others) for further
discussion. For similar stories, cf. Joseph. *Contra Ap.* 1.201 ff.
(from Hecataeus): a bird being observed by a seer for information
about the future is shot by a skilful archer; it could not foresee
its own death. Cf. Orig. *C.Cels.* 4.90 f., etc. They are as old as
Hom. *Il.* 2.858 f.

[418] The Theban Tiresias was celebrated as the type of seer in antiquity, and occurs frequently as such in Athenian tragedy; despite his blindness he practiced divination from the stars, from sacrifices, and especially from augury. See Pease's nn. on Cic. *De divin.* 1.88 (*de altero . . . Homero*), and *De nat. deor.* 2.7 for references, and Hyginus *Fab.* 75.

[419] This famous anecdote comes from Cic. *De divin.* 2.116, and the amphibole as given in Ennius (*Ann.* 179 Vahlen) reads *aio te, Aeacide, Romanos vincere posse.* See Parke and Wormell, *The Delphic Oracle* 2.441, for *testimonia* on this spurious Latin oracle, and discussion *ibid.* 1.247 f.; note the Greek variant reported by Dio 9 *fr.* 40.6. The cessation of Delphic verses is also Ciceronian; but it is, in fact, not true that the Pythia had ceased to deliver oracles in verse in Pyrrhus' day. The question of prose and verse oracles was the cause of much debate: it was a subject of Plut. *De Pyth. orac.* (but poetry, contra Cicero and Octavius, had not altogether disappeared, §20, 403F); cf. Strabo (of Augustan date) 4.419 (metrical and unmetrical responses at Delphi) and Philos. *Vit. Apol.* 6.11.15 (Apollo's commands are versified "by way of adornment," κόσμου ἕνεκα). Hexameters, in fact, were even composed for the occasion of Hadrian's visit to Delphi (Parke and Wormell, *op. cit.* 1.285 and 2 no. 465). One might also compare the serious discussion in [Just.] *Cohort.* 37 on the reason why the Sibyl's prophecies were often unmetrical (they were taken down by illiterate men who failed to record the metres accurately). See also P. Amandry, *La mantique apollinienne à Delphes* (Paris 1950) 165 ff.

[420] For the thought, cf. Cic. *De divin.* 2.117: *Quando ista vis autem evanuit? An postquam homines minus creduli esse coeperunt?* and chap. 24.3. The oracles had long suffered from declining prestige (largely displaced by popular mediums and astrologers); cf. Cic. *De divin.* 1.38; Strabo 7.327, 17.814; Juv. *Sat.* 6.553 ff.; and see Plutarch's examination of the problem in the treatise *De defect. orac.* Clem. *Protr.* 2.1.11.1 ff. claims the silence of the Delphic oracle, though Orig. *C.Cels.* 3.25, 7.3 and Arnob. 3.23 still write of Pythia's activities in the present tense, and Porphyry, *Phil. ex orac.* p. 172 Wolff, claimed that the only surviving oracular shrines were those of Apollo at Didyma, Delphi, and Claros. See generally on the imperial decline, Parke and Wormell, *op. cit.* 1.283 ff., and for some brief resurgence in oracular activity in the second century, F. Cumont, *Les reli-*

gions orientales dans le paganisme romain[4] (Paris 1929) 285 n. 2.
For Christian interpretation of the decline, cf. Prud. *Apoth.* 435
ff. (coincident with the Incarnation).

[421] This is also derived from Cic. *De divin.* 2.118 and ultimately
from Aeschin. *Contr. Ctes.* 130; cf. Plut. *Dem.* 20. Bribery (cf.
Orig. *C.Cels.* 8.46) and political favoritism were by no means
unknown in the history of the Oracle. See Pease's nn. *ad* Cic.
loc. cit., and H. W. Parke, *A History of the Delphic Oracle*
(Oxford 1939) 248 ff. on "Philippizing." (The readings of E.
Orth, PhW [1931] 1135 f. *Philippi zelo*, and A. Kurfess, *Jahrb.
für die Altw.* 2 [1947] 193 f. *philippizare*, an ugly neologism, do
not commend themselves.)

[422] A solemn and fulsome prelude to the subject of demonology,
a topic very much in favor at this period among pagan and
Christian alike. Octavius has already given rationalistic explanations for the pagan gods and disparaged the proof from divination.
He now proceeds, rather inconsistently, to claim that the pagan
gods are in fact demons, and whatever truthful divination there
is can be assigned to the influence of these "demons." The literature on this topic is voluminous; particularly useful are F. Cumont,
"Les anges du paganisme," *Rev. de l'hist. des relig.* 36 (1915) 159
ff.; J. Daniélou, *Les anges et leur mission d'après les pères de
l'église* (Éditions de Chevotogne 1953); PW Suppl. 3 (1918) 101–
14 (F. Andres); RAC 5 *s.v.* Engel 53 ff. (J. Michl); F. Andres,
*Der Engellehre der griechischen Apologeten des zweiten Jahr-
hunderts und ihr Verhältnis zur griechisch-römischen Dämonologie* (Paderborn 1914). I have been unable to see R. Berge,
*Exegetische Bemerkungen zur Dämonenauffassung bei Minucius
Felix* (diss. Freiburg-Kevelaer, 1929).
The language is (significantly) very reminiscent of 1.4: *obscurantism = caligo*, and cf. Cyp. *Ep.* 74.10.2. There is also an
echo of Cic. *De divin.* 2.49: *potest . . . veritatem casus imitari.*

[423] Octavius refers, without any specific explanations, to the
fall of the angels; most of the Apologists are not so reticent, and
recount, in greater or less detail, how they became earth-laden
as *amatores feminarum* (Tert. *De idol.* 9) and begot a yet more
corrupt brood of "demons" (Tert. *Apol.* 22.3). For fuller accounts see Athenag. *Leg.* 24 f.; Just. *Apol.* 2.5; Tat. *Or.* 12 ff.;
Arnob. 1.23; Orig. *C.Cels.* 4.92, 5.54 f. (taking Gen. 6.2 "daughters
of men" in a figurative sense, "a desire for life in a human body").
Clem. *Protr.* 4.55.5 is close to the present passage (see W. Den

Boer, "Clémente d'Alexandrie et Minucius Félix," *Mnem.* 11
(1943) 161 ff., at 172 f.); so, too, Cyp. *De lapsis* 12 (ML 4.475)
and *De habit. virg.* 14 (ML 4.453), but hardly, contra Beaujeu,
Intro. lxix, to be listed as "emprunts sûrs"). "Wander abroad":
vagi, repeated again in §11. This appears to have been virtually
a technical term, translated by Arnob. 1.23 as *errones* (MS
errores), which word Ulp. defines (*Dig.* 21.1.17.14) *qui non
quidem fugit, sed frequenter sine causa vagatur et temporibus in
res nugatorias consumptis serius domum redit* (cf. Ambrose,
Aeterne rerum conditor 1.11: *hoc omnis erronum chorus*). On
the topic see G. J. M. Bartelink, "Les démons comme brigands,"
VC 21 (1967) 12 ff.; S. Eitrem, "Varia," SymbOslo 32 (1956)
110 ff.

424 For the idea of *solatium*, cf. Tert. *Apol.* 22.6. Their machinations are more fully explained in the following chapter. The
intricate wordplay, especially on *perdere, perdiditi, depravati,
pravitatis, pravis*, is notable; these are words that were applied
earlier in chaps. 9.1, 9.4 and chaps. 5.11, 10.1 to the Christians
(and by Livy to the Bacchanalians: see n. 106).

425 "Demons" (*daemones*, δαίμονες) did not necessarily have
among the pagan writers any connotation of evil. For the appeal
to the testimony of poets and philosophers, see n. 230 and cf.
Tert. *Apol.* 22.1 f. (adding his favorite *vulgus indoctum—testimonium animae* argument); and for discussion of the relationship
with Tert. here, Axelson 92 ff.

Poets: cf. Just. *Apol.* 1.18, who for support cites Hom. *Od.*
11.25, Ulysses' pit to collect souls of the dead; Clem. *Protr.* 4.55.2
f. cites Hom. *Il.* 1.221 f.; Lact. *Div. inst.* 2.15.7 cites *grammatici*,
and in particular Hes. *Works and Days* 122 f.; Athenag. *Leg.* 24
f. cites the stories of the giants, offspring of maidens and fornicat-
ing angels, and Eurip. *fr.* 901 (Nauck).

On philosophers cf. Just. *Apol.* 1.18, who cites Empedocles,
Pythagoras, Plato, Socrates. The Stoics would be especially in
mind, for they had a rich demonology. As in the case of the
Hesiodic lines cited above, they were much given to the theory
of a protecting "demon" for each individual: M. Aurel. *Med.* 5.27;
Epict. 1.14.12 ff., 3.22.53; cf. Orig. *C.Cels.* 8.34; and for discussion,
E. Rohde, *Psyche*[8] (London 1925) 514 f.

426 The celebrated *daemonium* of Socrates, on which the *locus
classicus* is Plat. *Apol.* 19 (31D); it was a sort of voice which
dissuaded him from certain courses of action, especially politics.

It became a favorite topic for debate: note especially the works of Apul. *De deo Socr.*, Plut. *de genio Socr.*, Max. Tyr. 8 and 9 (see Pease on Cic. *De divin.* 2.122 for the modern literature) and Christian writers (Tert. *Apol.* 22.1, 46.5 f., *De an.* 1.2 ff., 39.3; Orig. *C.Cels.* 6.8, cf. Joseph. *Contra Ap.* 2.263 (and see the literature cited in n. 165 above). The negative character of the daemon of Socrates is almost universally stressed; but here, contra Beaujeu *ad loc.*, this aspect appears to be overlooked, perhaps largely for the sake of verbal *concinnitas* and a favored pair of words *vel declinabat . . . vel petebat;* cf. Cic. *De nat. deor.* 3.33: *adpetitio . . . et declinatio; adpetuntur . . . declinantur;* Aul. Gellius, *Noctes Atticae* 14.1.23: *adpetitionesque et declinationes.* For similar passages where this dissuasive role is forgotten, Xen. *Mem.* 1.1.4, 4.3.12; Plut. *De genio Socr.* 11.581B. For further discussion, W. K. C. Guthrie, *A History of Greek Philosophy* 3 (Cambridge 1969) 402 ff.

[427] The priestly Persian caste of the Magi, frequently mentioned in classical literature, features prominently in Herodotus for the interpretation of dreams; they were also interested in astrology and divination generally. Their principal figure was Zoroaster. See J. Bidez and F. Cumont, *Les mages hellénisés* 1 (Paris 1938) 30 ff., and Pease on Cic. *De divin.* 1.46 and *De nat. deor.* 1.43. The attribution of their feats to the agency of "demons" was not exclusively Christian (cf. Apul. *De deo Socr.* 133), but it is certainly frequently mentioned by them: Tat. *Or.* 17; Clem. *Protr.* 4.58.3; Orig. *C.Cels.* 1.60; Tert. *Apol.* 23.1. Arnobius gives examples of their tricks in 1.43 (again in 1.46, 1.52, 2.6, etc.); they open locked doors without keys, they decrease or increase the speed of horses at races, cf. Hippol. *Philos.* 4.41 (GCS Hippolytus 3.64)—they make a skull speak. Often there is a "double-think" in the Christian literature: they are mere tricksters, or they are demon-instructed; on this see W. L. Knox, *St Paul and the Church of the Gentiles* (Cambridge 1938) note 1, 204 ff. M.F. prudently eschews the question of Christ's miracles: he has said that others worked wonders via demons; the same could be, and was, said of the works of Christ: He was merely another, and inferior, *magus.* For that charge cf. Orig. *C.Cels.* 1.6, 1.68, 2.48 ff.; Arnob. 1.52 f.; Lact. *Div. inst.* 5.3; Tert. *Apol.* 21.17, etc.

[428] On Hostanes, of the fifth century B.C., see Bidez and Cumont, *op. cit.* 167 ff.; and for this fragment, 178 ff., 186 ff.

Much apocryphal material has gathered round his famous name and it is doubtful how far M.F. provides accurate information on Hostanes' doctrines. It does seem, however, that he did adhere to the view of a dualistic supernatural system, inhabited by good and evil beings, as ascribed to him here. It is also possible that M.F. alludes to angel worship—Hostanes (unlike others) gave due recognition to their Lord; on this worship see F. Cumont, "Les anges du paganisme," *Rev. de l'hist. des relig.* 36 (1915) 159 f.; and for the same charge laid against the Jews, see Aristides *Apol.* 14 (Syr.) and Celsus *ap.* Orig. *C.Cels.* 1.26, 5.6. See also, on this passage, PW Suppl. 3 (1918) 108–9 (Andres).

[429] *angelos, id est ministros et nuntios.* The word *angelus*, originally a Hebraism via Greek (see Chr. Mohrmann, *Études* 1.47, and Ch. Guignebert, *Le monde juif vers le temps de Jésus* [Paris 1935] 129 ff.), seems to have made its appearance in Latin literature somewhat reluctantly: it is used, with explanation, by Cornelius Labeo (contemporary with M.F.?) *ap.* Aug. *De civ. Dei* 9.19: *nonnulli istorum, ut ita dixerim, daemonicolarum, in quibus et Labeo est, eosdem perhibent ab aliis angelos dici, quos ipsi daemones nuncupant.* The word, however, occurs frequently on inscriptions, e.g., CIL 14.24: *I(ovi) O(ptimo) M(aximo) Angelo Heliop(olitano) pro salute imperator. Antonini et Commodi Augg.* (see PW, *loc. cit.* in n. 428, 105, Cumont, *art. cit.* in n. 428, 159 f., for further inscriptional dedications to *Diis Angelis*). But in classical letters the word remained somewhat a foreignism, and it was therefore avoided even in Christian Latin poetry, being replaced by *minister* or *nuntius* (Chr. Mohrmann, *Études* 1.156 f., 3.143). This is probably the reason for the explanatory gloss here (cf. Arnob. 2.35: *dii angeli daemones aut nomine quocumque sunt alio*). The word appears primitively to have covered both the good and the fallen angels (cf. 2 Cor. 12.7; *Ep. Barn.* 9.4, 18.1; Hermas *Mand.* 6.2.1; Tert. *De idol.* 6.2, etc.). Compare the description of the work of "demons" in Apul. *De deo Socr.* 133: *per quas* (sc., *potestates*) *et desideria nostra et merita ad deos commeant . . . inter* (*terricolas*) *coelicolasque vectores hinc precum inde donorum . . .* etc.; and see on the multifarious functions given to angels, Daniélou, *op. cit.* in n. 422.

[430] The description compares closely with the Jewish concept of the angels ministering to the Great King. In this Oriental court-picture they were perhaps influenced by the Babylonian captivity; cf. Dan. 7.10 (quoted by Euseb. *H.E.* 1.2.24; 1 *Clem.*

34.5; Orig. *C.Cels.* 8.34, etc.): "Thousand thousands stood beside Him and ten thousand times ten thousand ministered to Him." The fearsome nod is also Homeric (and Vergilian): Hom. *Il.* 1.528; Verg. *Aen.* 9.106, 10.115.

[431] See n. 260 above.

[432] Plato does not, of course, use the word ἄγγελος, though that word later came to be used freely in its demonological sense by pagan writers of Greek; see W. Bousset, "Zur Dämonologie der späteren Antike," *Archiv. für Religionw.* 18 (1915) 134 ff., at 168 ff.

[433] The passages of the *Symposium* used in paraphrase are 195Ef., 202Df. The obelized phrase appears to be a corrupt explanatory gloss on love (*amor*). On the text see the discussion of B. Kytzler, "Notae Minucianae," *Traditio* 22 (1966) 419 ff., at 426 f. Relevant to this section of the *Symposium* is M. Detienne, "Sur la démonologie et l'ancien pythagorisme," *Rev. de l'hist. des relig.* 155 (1959) 17 ff., on the Pythagorean contribution to Plato's thought; Origen *C.Cels.* 4.39 also discusses the provenance of this myth of Eros (from Jewish tradition learnt during the visit to Egypt?). For the personification of *Cupido*, see Pease on Cic. *De nat. deor.* 2.61 (*Cupidinis*).

[434] This chapter purports to be a reply to 7.5 f.: proof from the sanctity of pagan shrines and the prophecies of their sooth-sayers. Shrines, Octavius claims, are not inhabited by *numina* but possessed by *daemones;* for this common notion, cf. Athenag. *Leg.* 23, 26; Just. *Apol.* 1.18; Tert. *Apol.* 21.31; Euseb *P.E.* 5.2.1, etc. M.F. does not explain clearly why the demons take up their residence in them; Origen suggests that they have been invoked by magic spells and incantations (*C.Cels.* 3.34, 7.64, 7.69) or enticed by the savor of sacrifices, by illicit pleasures and lawless men (*ibid.* 7.64); but sheer malignancy seems to be the most usual explanation (cf. §2 below).

The idea of *daemones* (but not with the connotation of *wicked* spirits) producing feats of divination was, of course, a respectable pagan outlook; cf. Celsus *ap.* Orig. *C.Cels.* 8.60; [Apul.] *Asclep.* 37; Apul. *De deo Socr.* 6.133 ff.; Plut. *De def. orac.* 13.417A.

[435] *Inspirantur.* If the reading is accurate, the literal meaning is "they are breathed into"; cf. 7.7: *pleni et mixti deo vates.*

[436] For these four major categories of divination, cf. Tibul. 2.5.11 ff.; cf. also the lists in Cic. *De nat. deor.* 2.163, 3.14; *De divin.* 1.11 f. For augury (birds) cf. Orig. *C.Cels.* 4.92; Tert. *Apol.*

35.12; for the entrails of victims, cf. Orig. *C.Cels.* 4.92; Tert. *Apol.* 35.12; for prophecy and oracles, cf. Just. *Apol.* 1.18; Herm. *Mand.* 11.3; Orig. *C.Cels.* 3.3, 3.24 f., 7.3 ff.; Athenag. *Leg.* 26. *Sortes,* or the drawing or shaking out of lots, i.e., small written tablets placed in an urn etc., were often associated with oracular sites (this method was also used for the allotment of some magistracies): the word is also applied to the random consultation of prophetic books (e.g., Sibylline); the *sortes* of the Temple of Fortuna at Praeneste were especially famous (Cic. *De divin.* 2.85 ff., and see Pease on Cic. *De divin.* 1.12 *sortium*). Consult, generally, DACL 4.1 (1920) *s.v.* Divination 1199 ff. (H. Leclercq); RAC *s.v.* Divinatio 1235 ff., esp. 1246 f. (P. Courcelle).

M.F., again, does not explain how, at least on occasion, these demons can effect true results—though that is why the topic was ostensibly introduced. Tert. *Apol.* 22.8 f. explains: the demons are winged creatures who can be everywhere in a moment and they thus make use of their present knowledge; they also exploit what they know of the future from their knowledge of the *dispositiones dei* as propounded by the prophets. Cf. Augustine's explanation of their powers, A. Mandouze, "Saint Augustin et la religion romaine," RechAug 1 (1958) 187 ff., at 211 ff.

[437] *Et falluntur et fallunt.* A. Beltrami, "Clemente Alessandrino nell'Ottavio di M. Minucio Felice," RFIC 48 (1920) 239 ff., at 256, attempted to find interdependence between Minucius Felix and Clement of Alexandria from this phrase, but such expressions are common; cf. Paul, 2 Tim. 3.13: *errantes et in errorem mittentes;* Arist. *Apol.* 16 (of pagans): "the rest of the peoples deceive and are deceived"; Phil. *De migr. Abrah.* 15.83 (of Magi): "they are cheated while they think they are cheating"; and generally, for the figure, P. Wendland, "Betrogene Betrüger," RhM 49 (1894) 309 f., and G. Williams, JRS 47 (1957) 243. Their self-deception means intransigence—and damnation.

[438] Such a catalogue of the havoc wrought by demons is common; of interest is the claim that demons cause not merely mental anguish—nightmares, madness (a widely diffused belief in antiquity)—but general physical maladies as well. The connection between curing the sick and casting out devils is traditionally close (cf. Luke 7.21, 9.1; Euseb. *H.E.* 1.13.6, letter of Abgar the Toparch to Christ; and generally, S. Eitrem, *Some Notes on the Demonololgy in the New Testament* [2nd. ed. Oslo 1966; Symb-Oslo Supp. 20] 35 ff., 66 f.). For this ascription of diseases (and

mania) to demons, Tat. *Or.* 16 ff.; Arnob. 1.48; Orig. *C.Cels.* 1.46, 1.67, 3.3, 3.24 f., 3.36; Tert. *Apol.* 22.4 ff., 37.9, *De an.* 46.12 f. (with Waszink's commentary); Lact. *Div. inst.* 2.14.14, etc.; cf. Diog. Laer. 8.32: Pythagoras believed the air was full of demons which sent dreams and "the signs of diseases and good health"; [Apul.] *Asclep.* 24: *statuas animatas sensu et spiritu plenas . . . imbecillitates hominibus facientes easque curantes.* Note the attribution of general material evils to demons in Orig. *C.Cels.* 8.31 (famines, droughts, crop failures, plagues, etc.).

[439] The notion that demons, being gross and gluttonous, were attracted by the smoke and odor of roasting meat and the blood of flesh meat—or that, if they were to remain in this gross air near the earth, they needed such food—was universal at this period: Just. *Apol.* 2.5; Tert. *Apol.* 22.6, 23.14; Orig. *C.Cels.* 3.29, 3.37, 4.32, 7.5, 8.60 ff.; Porphy. *De abst.* 2.42 etc. (their need for such nourishment is denied by Arnob. 7.3; Aug. *Cont. Faust.* 20.22 [CSEL 25.565]). For further passages, Christian and pagan, see G. Resch, *Das Aposteldecret* (TU n.f. 13.3; 1905) 155 ff.; J. Schümmer, *Die altchristliche Fastenpraxis* (Münster 1933) 23 ff.; RAC 2 *s.v.* Blut 459 ff. (J. H. Waszink). Note the primitive fear of spilling the chalice, the contents of which might be licked up by a *spiritus alienus:* R. H. Connolly, *The So-called Egyptian Church Order and Derived Documents* (Cambridge 1916) 106 n. 1. This general outlook is relevant to the Mosaic dietary regulations on meat attested to be in force in 30.6. The stench of such pagan animal sacrifices must have been unendurable, particularly in the summer months—hence a topic for derision, *Ad Diog.* 2.9, Arnob. 7.16. For the release of the demons' hold, see the passages cited above on diseases. The verb employed here, *constringo,* is used technically in medical language to describe *spasmus nervorum,* i.e., contractions and cramps (see TLL *s.v.* 4.543 f.).

[440] A rather obscure passage, the obscurity being enhanced by corruption in the reading. There seems to be a contrast and comparison intended between the *vates* of §1, who perform in temples haunted by demons, and these itinerant seers and wildly dancing prophetic priests who perform elsewhere. These, too, it is claimed, are victims of possession. In 7.6 the reference, from the context, seems to be to *vates* in the temples; now all types of *vates* are explained. The obscurity can best be accounted for by reference to Tert. *Apol.* 23.3, where it is ironically suggested that there is a different power at work in a demon in temples and

elsewhere, in a man who cuts his own genitals (in religious ritual) or his own throat.

The contrast, with the borrowing in phraseology (Tert. *loc. cit.: compar exitus furoris et una ratio est instigationis*) has been, therefore, imperfectly translated. Here the difference in manifestation appears to lie in the fact that prophecy is the result of "inspiration" in the first category, self-mutilation or the like (cf. 24.12) in the second. Cf. Lucan *Phars.* 5.172 f. on the contortions of the fanatic devotee.

[441] The first three examples of 7.3, artistically in reverse order.

[442] Appeal to the effectiveness of exorcism made in the name of the Christian God is a common motif in apology (e.g., Just. *Apol.* 2.6, *Dial.* 76, 85; Theoph. *Ad Autol.* 2.8; Tat. *Or.* 16; Orig. *C.Cels.* 1.6, 7.4, 7.67, 8.58; cf. Christ and Beelzebub, Matt. 12.24), but the emphasis here on the verbal confession of the demons who are being exorcized is less common; it does, however, appear in a developed form in Tert. *Apol.* 23.4 ff. (which is closely related to the present passage), *De an.* 57.5 ff. (with Waszink's nn.); cf. Cyp. *Ad Donat.* 5, *Ad Demetr.* 15; Lact. *Div. inst.* 2.15.3, 5.21.4 f., etc. Cyp. *Ep.* 69.15.2 warns, however, that the testimony of departing demons cannot always be trusted. The notions of "burning" and "torture" are traditional in such contexts (see the above passages and also J. Fontaine, "Démons et Sibylles: la peinture des possédés dans la poésie de Prudence," *Hommages à Jean Bayet* [Brussels 1964] 196 ff., at 198 nn. 1–3). For further discussion on the subject of exorcism, see S. Eitrem, *op. cit.* in n. 438; DACL 1.1 (1924) *s.v.* Adjuration 527 ff., 5.1 (1922) *s.v.* Exorcisme, Exorciste, 964 ff. (H. Leclercq), and F. J. Dölger, "Teufels Grossmutter," AC 3 (1932) 153 ff., esp. 164 ff. One recalls that about this time the Roman Church supported "exorcists, readers, and doorkeepers," who numbered 52 altogether (Euseb. *H.E.* 6.43.11).

[443] These "gods" (22.1, 22.3, 23.9 ff.) have been exposed as merely human beings; the argument that they are demons is formulated inconsistently with this exposure. For the devil asked for, and giving, his name ("Legion"), see Mark 5.9, Luke 8.30: the idea is that knowledge of a person's identity gives some hold over that person. See C. Bonner, "The Technique of Exorcism," HTR 36 (1943) 39 ff., at 44 ff.; cf. K. Preisendanz, *Pap. Gr. Mag.* 4.3038 ff.: "I adjure you, every demon spirit, to speak out whatever you are," and Peter to the daemoniac in the apocryphal *Acts*

of Peter 11 (James 315): "Show thyself unto all that stand here."
For further evidence, S. Eitrem, *op. cit.* in n. 438, 19, 70 ff.

⁴⁴⁴ For formulae of adjuration, see the articles in DACL cited
above in n. 442. The virtue of the name of Christ is frequently
attested for these purposes (Acts 16.18: *praecipio tibi in nomine
Iesu Christi exire ab ea;* Orig. *C.Cels.* 7.4, 8.58; Just. *Apol.* 2.6;
Tert. *Apol.* 23.15; so powerful that it is sometimes effective even
when pronounced by bad men: Orig. *C.Cels.* 1.6: cf. 2.49), and
it therefore occurred in pagan magic formulae (S. Eitrem, *op. cit.*
in n. 438, 8 n. 1, 16; P. Courcelle, "Propos antichrétiens rapportés
par saint Augustin," RechAug 1 (1958) 149 ff., at 154 ff., 174).
Other (more Jewish) formulations such as "The God of Israel,"
"The God of the Hebrews," were also in use especially among
non-Christians (Orig. *C.Cels.* 4.33 f., 1.22, 5.45); for pagan
examples see K. Preisendanz, *Pap. Gr. Mag.* 4.1230 ff., 12.287 f.,
13.815 f., 975 f. On this Jewish influence, see W. L. Knox, *St Paul
and the Church of the Gentiles* (Cambridge 1938) Note 2, 208
ff. M.F. seems to avoid deliberately mentioning Christ *nominatim.*

⁴⁴⁵ For such shudderings and convulsions, cf. Luke 9.39, Mark
1.26, 9.17 ff. For violent exits from the sufferer (to mark proof
of the demon's departure—or as a last spiteful act), see C. Bonner,
art. cit. in n. 443, at 47 ff.

⁴⁴⁶ *Prout . . . aut gratia curantis adspirat. Curantis* is normally
interpreted as referring to God; it might perhaps be better
referred to the exorcist (the effectiveness of the healing powers
depending, in part, on the sanctity of the agent). Cf. Cyprian
Ep. 69.12.2 on baptism of the sick by aspersion; full efficacy is
obtained *ubi plena et tota fide et dantis et sumentis accipitur.* It
remains a trifle doubtful whether *gratia* is here used precisely
as a Christian technical term, through the parallel with *fides* suggests that it may be (see Chr. Mohrmann, *Études* 1.117, 3.115 f.
[on *gratia*], 1.118 f. [on *fides*]). Boissier, however, declared (*La
fin du paganisme* 327): "La doctrine de la grâce non seulement
n'est pas mentionnée nulle part, mais elle semble même formelle-
ment contredite" (referring to 16.5 and "inborn ability"). Such
phrases as *inspirata patientia* (37.5) and *a quo (deo) et inspiratus
oravit* (40.3) militate against this extreme view; for a discussion
see Baylis 146 f.; and cf. Tert. *De an.* 57.5: *ille daemon . . . in-
stantia divinae gratiae victus id quod in vero est invitus confitetur*
(and see Waszink *ad loc.*).

⁴⁴⁷ For the elements of this phrase, cf. Tert. *Apol.* 27.6: *et quos*

de longinquo obpugnant, de proximo obsecrant, and *Apol.* 7.4: *in ipsis plurimum coetibus . . . nostris obprimimur.* By using here *coetus* M.F. avoids such unclassical "Christianisms" as *ecclesia, synodus,* etc.; cf. the studious gloss in Ammian. Marc. 15.7.7: *coetus in unam quaesitus eiusdem loci multorum (synodus ut appellant).* On this avoidance see Averil and Alan Cameron, "Christianity and Tradition in the Historiography of the Late Empire," CQ 14 (1964) 316 ff.

[448] For this motif of the *imperiti,* see n. 22.

[449] The concomitance of fear and hatred is a proverbial notion; cf. Ennius *ap.* Cic. *De off.* 2.7.23: *quem metuunt oderunt; quem quisque odit, periise expetit,* and for further examples see Otto *Sprichwörter* 252. For persecutions attributed, as frequently, to demons, cf. Just. *Apol.* 1.5, 14; *Apol.* 2.8, etc.; Orig. *C.Cels.* 4.32, 8.43; and esp. Tert. *Apol.* 27.4 ff.

[450] A nice rejoinder to 9.2 (on Christian "love"): *amant . . . paene antequam noverint.*

[451] To judge from the following context, *cognitos* may have rather a legal flavor here: hence the translation. For the idea of this sentence, cf. Tert. *Apol.* 1.3 ff.

[452] The theme of the demons as the source of persecutions—and of calumny—is now elaborated. There is an appeal to the personal experience of the earlier life of the convert—a common theme of apologetics (for examples see Intro. p. 24) and, therefore, of slightly dubious historical value; cf., too, the famous words of Tert. *Apol.* 18.4: *Haec et nos risimus aliquando. De vestris sumus. Fiunt, non nascuntur Christiani;* and Cyp. *Ad Donat.* 3, 4, 14. Here the first person plural is used either of Octavius alone, or of Octavius and Minucius Felix, or (as may be the case in §§3 ff.) of "we (erstwhile) pagans," generally.

[453] Probably referring to the charge of worshiping the head of an ass (9.3); but the word *monstrum* can also be used of any preternatural object. The parallels in §3 (*sacrilegos*), §5 (*inpietis sacris*) suggest, therefore, that the worship of the *sacerdotis . . . genitalia* (9.4) and *crucis ligna feralia* (9.4) may be intended as well.

[454] A similar claim is made in Tert. *Apol.* 7.5, Athenag. *Leg.* 35; confession (under torture) is, however, evidenced in Euseb. *H.E.* 5.1.14 (slaves of Christians at Lyons and Vienne) and Just. *Apol.* 2.12 (slaves, children, and women); cf. §4 below.

[455] This resembles closely Tert. *Apol.* 1.1: *in publico aut timet*

aut erubescit inquirere (cf. 31.1 below), and Tert. *Apol.* 1.12: *neminem pudet, neminem poenitet, nisi plane retro non fuisse.*

⁴⁵⁶ The Latin words *parricidium, parricida* cover the murder of any close relative (cf. 25.2, 31.8 where *parricidium* = fratricide, and see Pease on Cic. *De nat. deor.* 3.27 *familiari parricidio*) or, indeed, any particularly heinous crime. The context indicates that "infanticide" is intended here (as also in 30.2), for there is careful *variatio* in the presentation of the purported crimes of the Christians: in 28.2 they are expressed by noun and verb, in the order A,B,C (*monstra colerent, infantes vorarent, convivia incesta miscerent*), here by nouns in the order A,C,B (*sacrilegos, incestos, parricidas*), and in 28.5 by nouns and verbal participles in the order C,A,B (*incestis stupris, inpietis sacris, infantibus immolatis*). Tert. *Apol.* 2.4, 2.8 adds the charge of being a public enemy, *hostis publicus;* with his usual prudence Octavius avoids raising such a dangerous issue. M. Sordi, "L'Apologia del martire romano Apollonio come fonte dell'Apologeticum di Tertulliano e i rapporti fra Tertulliano e Minucio," *Riv. di stor. della chiesa in Italia* 18 (1964) 169 ff., at 184 f., unpersuasively sees in such an omission proof of the priority of M.F.

⁴⁵⁷ The construction is somewhat ambiguous: many take the first section of the period as referring to the Christians also, i.e., "when we used to undertake to defend and protect those so-called parricides etc., we thought they were entitled to no hearing." That is possible but gives less satisfactory sense; and cf. Lact. *Div. inst.* 5.1.2: *nam si sacrilegis, et proditoribus, et veneficiis potestas defendendi sui datur, nec praedamnari quemquam incognita causa licet non iniuste petere videmur ut . . . ;* Tert. *Apol.* 2.2: *quando nec liceat indefensos et inauditos omnino damnari.*

The martyrs are frequently depicted in their *Acta* as attempting to defend their religion (often in long-winded attempts) before the magistrates (Apollonius, Scillitan Martyrs, Justin, Pionius, etc.); they do not answer the immediate questions put to them but go into lengthy sermonizing on Christianity itself instead. The judge, after losing patience, is thus made to appear to condemn the Christian summarily, without a proper hearing. That is a somewhat misleading picture from the pagan point of view. "Tertullian's complaint that Christians were not allowed the ordinary forms of defence means not that the procedure was inquisitorial, but that the accused was only allowed to defend himself against the charge of Christianity; he was not allowed to defend Christianity itself any more than a murderer might defend murder" (A. N. Sherwin-White, "The Early Christians and Roman Law again," JTS n.s. 3 [1952] 199 ff., at 205). For trials of Christians by public acclaim (*epiboesis*) which might provide further grounds for this complaint, see J. Colin, *Les villes libres de l'Orient gréco-romain et l'envoi au supplice par acclamations populaires* (Brussels 1965) 126 ff.

[458] Much is made of this legal anomaly by Tert. *Apol.* 2.10 ff., as earlier by Just. *Apol.* 1.4; cf. Tert. *Ad Scap.* 4 on the illegality of torturing *confitentes;* Cyp. *Ad Demet.* 13. Likewise Origen *C.Cels.* 8.44 denies humanity was the motive of judges who put pressure on Christians to recant. However, the *Acta* (often unwittingly) reveal the reluctance of officials to pass sentence, and it is remarkable how frequently they gave a *locus poenitentiae* to accused Christians in an attempt to induce them to comply with official policy.

[459] Persecution "for the Name" appears constantly in Christian writings (e.g., Hermas *Vis.* 3.1.9, 3.2.1, *Sim.* 9.28.1; Athenag. *Leg.* 1; Just. *Apol.* 1.4,24, *Dial.* 96; Tert. *Apol.* 2.18 ff.), but how far this provides accurate testimony for the precise legal grounds of the Christian persecutions is a matter for considerable controversy. Much of the Christian phraseology may be based on the New Testament use of ὄνομα, *nomen,* e.g., 1 Peter 4.16, Phil. 2.9 f.; for this loaded notion of the Name, see Chr. Mohrmann, *Études* 3 (1965) 331 ff., at 344 ff. (= VC 8[1954] 154 ff.). And much may be due to Christian bias (for an example see W. Schmid, "The Christian Reinterpretation of the Rescript of Hadrian," *Maia* 7 [1955] 5 ff.). It is difficult, however, to dismiss lightly the considerable bulk of evidence that the Apologists produce so readily; they certainly believed–rightly or confusedly–that they were being punished for mere adherence to their *Nomen.* See n. 104 above; for recent discussion additional to the literature cited in that note, see P. Keresztes, "Law and Arbitrariness in the Persecution of the Christians and Justin's First Apology," VC 18 (1964) 204 ff.; A. Wlosok, "Der Rechtsgrundlagen der Christenverfolgungen der ersten zwei Jahrhunderte," *Gymn.* 66 (1959) 14 ff.; J. Zeiller, "Nouvelles remarques sur les persécutions contre les chrétiens aux deux premiers siècles," *Misc. Giov. Merc.* 5 (Rome 1946) 1 ff.

[460] These *imperiti* are those of 27.8, and see n. 22.

[461] For this explanation of Fama, see 9.3, of which this is a (textually difficult) confutation. On the text see B. Kytzler, "Notae Minucianae," *Traditio* 22 (1966) 419 ff., at 428 f. The sentence is designed to provide a transition from the subject of demons responsible for persecutions (a theme not sustained with notable vigor) to that of demons responsible for calumnies against Christians generally, but it fulfils its function somewhat awkwardly. M.F. does not mention other works of the *daemones*, e.g., heretical sects; cf. Euseb. *H.E.* 3.26.4–Simon Magus; *H.E.* 5.16.2 f.–Montanism.

[462] The cult of Epona, an equestrian goddess of Gallic religion (P. M. Duval, *Les dieux de la Gaule* [Paris 1957] 46 f.), became popular and Romanized with the growth of cavalry (for neat pictorial history of the progressive Romanization, see M. Pobé and J. Roubier, *The Art of Roman Gaul* [London 1961] plates 179–81). She is generally depicted sitting on asses or accompanied by them and was often to be found, in picture (Juv. *Sat.* 8.156 f.) or in image (Apul. *Met.* 3.27) form, adorning stables and protecting their inhabitants. See Roscher 1.1286–93. There is a similar rebuttal of the charge in Tert. *Apol.* 16.5, and (more closely) *Ad nat.* 1.11.6. As in these passages and in a parallel context in Joseph. *Contra Ap.* 2.81, the opportunity is seized for a general polemic against pagan theriolatry (Egyptian and otherwise) without which no early apology would be complete.

[463] Apparently a reference to cakes imprinted with a figure of an ass, symbol of the wicked Typhon (see nn. 287, 288 above). These would be offered to Isis, a portion burnt in her honor and the rest devoured by the worshiper. See Plut. *De Isid. et Osir.* 362F and J.-P. Waltzing, "*Asinos cum Iside devoratis* (Minucius Felix, 28.7)," *Musée belge* 13 (1909) 65–68. The argument is hardly impressive.

[464] For example, the cow was sacred to Isis (Hdt. 2.41; Athenag. *Leg.* 28; and cf. *Acta Apollon.* 18, AnalBoll 14 [1895] 289); the ram to Jupiter Ammon (see 22.6). There is a hint of an argument more fully elaborated in Tat. *Or.* 10: an ironical chapter on the indignities meted out by pagans to their pagan "gods": "Why do you plunder your god, why dishonor his handwork? Sheep you sacrifice and worship; the Bull (Taurus) is in the heavens, and you slaughter his likeness etc."

[465] Pan and the Satyrs, of course, for the goat-men (Hdt. 2.46); for lion-headed Frugiferus (Saturn), Arnob. 6.10; for Ialdabaoth,

Orig. *C.Cels.* 6.31; for lion-headed Mithraic representations of Cronos, F. Cumont, *Textes et monuments* 1.78, *Religions orientales* 28, pl. 1, fig. 1, etc. Contra Beaujeu, exclusively Egyptian deities do not seem to occur until the next section (*cum Aegyptiis*); cf. the mixed list in Cic. *De nat. deor.* 3.47 (*equos*). For the dog-(jackal-)headed Cynocephalus, or Anubis, see 22.1.

[466] Criticism of Egyptian theriolatry was a common theological topic; it formed part (especially in the Academic-Sceptic tradition) of the standard polemic against traditional religion (Cic. *De nat. deor.* 1.43, 1.82, 1.101; Sext. Emp. *Pyrrhon. hypotyp.* 3.219; Juv. *Sat.* 15.1 ff., etc.); it became part of Jewish apologetic (Joseph. *Contra Ap.* 1.225, 2.66, 2.81, 2.85 ff., 2.139; Aristeas *Ep.* 138, cf. Rom. 1.23), and thence (inexhaustibly) of Christian writing (Arist. *Apol.* 12; Theoph. *Ad Autol.* 1.10; Orig. *C.Cels.* 1.20, 1.52, 3.17 ff., 4.90, 5.27, 5.39, 5.51, 6.4, 6.80, 8.53; Just. *Apol.* 1.13; Arnob. 3.15; Clem. *Protr.* 2.39.4 ff.; Athenag. *Leg.* 1; Tert. *Apol.* 24.7; *Orac. Sibyl. fr.* 3 Geffcken, etc.). For further discussion and multitudinous references, see Pease on Cic. *De nat. deor.* 1.43 *Aegyptiorum.*

The cult of the sacred bull Apis provided one of the most celebrated of the bizarre Egyptian rituals; he was supposed to be the incarnation of Osiris, and was kept and fed (Fahy in ed. *ad loc.* mistakes the meaning here: there is no evidence that he was eaten [*pascitur*]) in a special court at Memphis (Hdt. 2.153). After a life span of twenty-five years he was drowned in a sacred fountain and mummified and buried with lavish mourning and expense. Egypt was then searched for another reincarnation recognized by special distinguishing marks. For *testimonia* see T. Hopfner, *Fontes historiae religionis Aegyptiacae* (Bonn 1922–24) 813 ff., and see Pease on Cic. *De nat. deor.* 1.82 (*Apim*).

[467] Snakes: in particular the asp, whose deadly bite was thought to confer deification (Arist. *Apol.* 12; Orig. *C.Cels.* 6.80; Athenag. *Leg.* 1; *Orac. Sibyl. fr.* 3 Geffcken *ap.* Theoph. *Ad Autol.* 2.36, and Pease on Cic. *De nat. deor.* 3.47 *aspidas*). Hence Cleopatra sought to assuage her "immortal longings" by its bite. For further *testimonia* see Hopfner, *op. cit.* 910 f.

Crocodiles: on the widespread crocodile worship, see esp. Hdt. 2.69; Pease on Cic. *De nat. deor.* 1.82, 3.47; and the *testimonia* in Hopfner, *op. cit.* 830 f.

Beasts: examples are the cat (Pease on Cic. *De nat. deor.* 1.82), the dog (*ibid.* 3.47), the wolf (*ibid.* 3.47), the "mongoose" (*Ich-neumenon; ibid.* 1.101), the beetle, the hippopotamus, the goat (*C.Cels.* 6.80), the monkey.

Birds: e.g., the ibis (Pease on Cic. *De nat. deor.* 1.82, 1.101), the hawk (*ibid.* 3.47), the swallow (21.3 above). Arist. *Apol.* 12 (Syr.) has also kite, vulture, eagle, crow, cormorant.

Fishes: on the sacred fishes of Egypt, see Hopfner, *op. cit.* 892; Pease on Cic. *De nat. deor.* 3.39 *piscem Syri,* 3.47 *pisces:* and especially F. J. Dölger, ΙΧΘΥΣ 2 (Münster 1922) 101 ff.

[468] A piece of common knowledge: Hdt. 2.65.5; Diod. 1.83.6; Pomp. Mela 1.9; Orig. *C.Cels.* 1.52; and Tert. *Apol.* 24.7.

[469] For onions avoided by Egyptians, see Pliny *N.H.* 2.16, 19.101; Aul. Gellius, *Noctes Atticae* 20.8.7; Plut. *De Isid. et Osir.* 8, 353E f., and see J. G. Griffiths, *Plutarch's De Iside et Osiride* (Univ. of Wales Press, 1970) 280 f.; Juv. *Sat.* 15.9 (with Mayor's lengthy note); Arist. *Apol.* 12; *Acta Apollon.* 21, AnalBoll 14 (1895) 289; Arnob. 7.16; Artemid. *Oneir.* 1.67, etc. See Hopfner, *op. cit.* 825, and Cook, *Zeus* 2.986 f. Various reasons were adduced, even in antiquity, for the prohibition, many claiming that the onion figured in fact among the Egyptian divinities. Relevant to the present expression is perhaps the story given by Plut. *op. cit.* that Dictys, nursling of Isis, was drowned in the Nile while gathering onions.

This example, with the following one of flatulence, is given by Orig. *C.Cels.* 5.35; Jerome *Comm. in Is.* 13.46 (ML 24.450): *ut taceam de formidoloso et horribili cepe et crepitu ventris inflati quae Pelusiaca religio est;* cf. also Theoph. *Ad Autol.* 1.10; [Clem.] *Hom.* 10.16.2; [Clem.] *Recog.* 5.20.3: *cepas et cloacas et strepitus ventris pro numinibus habendos.* The second illustration (flatulence) is not found in pagan authors and reads like a Christian parody of the superstitious confusion between physical wind and the metaphorical concept of spirit, a confusion common in antiquity. Hence yawning and sneezing, involving the loss of breath, were ominous activities; and such loss of breath is one of the very many reasons adduced for Pythagoras' ban on the notoriously flatulent (Diog. Laer. 8.24) broad beans. For discussion see A. Delatte, "Faba Pythagorae cognata," *Serta Leodensia* (Liège 1930) 33 ff.; T. H. D. Arie, "Pythagoras and Beans," *Oxf. Med. School Gazette* 11.2 (1959) 75–81.

H. Stern, *Le calendrier de 354: Étude sur son texte et ses*

326 NOTES ON PAGE 105

illustrations (Paris 1953) on Table, facing p. 116, n. 20, sees here a reference to the celebration of the Egyptian festival, the Pelusia, in Rome (unconvincing).

This tirade against animal worship can hardly have moved the general pagan reader; Arnobius 3.15 acknowledges that pagans laugh at the Egyptians giving their gods the bodies of dumb animals. But it was a traditional argument, and both the prevalence of foreign cults in Rome and the relationship of Caecilius with Serapis—carefully reserved for the final clause—made it a possible topic for counterattack. The apologist, as so often, is more interested in winning a verbal victory (despite the protestations of chaps. 14 and 15) than in scoring a genuine hit. G. Quispel, "A Jewish Source of Minucius Felix," VC 3 (1949) 113 ff., at 117 ff., investigates, rather speculatively, the source of the present passage. Axelson 76 ff. discusses the relationship with Tert. *Apol.* 16.13, 24.7.

[470] A reversal of the charge to be found in 9.4.

[471] *Apud quos sexus omnis membris omnibus prostat.* Hardly with Beaujeu ". . . des gens qui placent tous les organes sexuels avant tous les autres parties du corps," in view of Lact. *Div. inst.* 1.20.25: *libidinibus effrenatis omnem sexum et omnes corporis partes contaminantibus;* but *prosto* is apparently not used here in the technical sense of "prostitute," in view of *scortorum licentiae invident* below.

[472] I.e., *qui medios viros lambunt, libidinoso ore inguinibus inhaerescunt;* cf. Catul. 80.6; Mart. *Epig.* 2.61.2, 7.67.15, 11.61.5; Arnob. 2.42 f.

[473] A reference presumably to pederasty and the sexual abuse of slaves (against which there was legislation, e.g., Ulp. *Dig.* 1.6.2). Many suppose castration is referred to, but that, though possible (cf. Sen. *fr.* 34, Haase, *ap.* Aug. *De civ. Dei* 6.10), does not seem to be necessary.

To modern taste this passage seems inappropriately virulent and hardly calculated to win a sympathetic hearing for the Christian cause. But by the rules of forensic rhetoric, low-hitting polemic was quite in order (cf. 31.2); indeed, Lactantius *Div. inst.* 5.1.22 ff. complained of early Latin apologetics that there was not enough of this hard-punching stuff (cf. Intro. p. 19). One might compare Jerome's description of advocates in action (*In epist. ad Gal.* 1.2 [ML 26.365]): . . . *currebam ad tribunalia iudicum et disertissimos oratorum tanta inter se videbam acerbitate con-*

tendere, ut omissis saepe negotiis in proprias contumelias verte-
rentur et ioculari se invicem dente morderent. Of course, any
success that might be won from such a passage is only immediate,
for it has little or no bearing on Roman religion as such; these
aberrant practices merely have the flimsy rhetorical justification
of being considered (it is claimed) *quasi sacra* among such people.
However, a counterattack on pagan morals generally was by now
a fairly standard topic (Tat. *Or.* 28; Athenag. *Leg.* 34; Just. *Apol.*
1.27; cf. Rom. 1.26 ff.; for the relationship with Tert. *Apol.* 9.12,
see Axelson 78 f.) and passages contrasting the Christian and
pagan ways of life almost *de rigueur* (cf. 31.4 f., 35.5 f., 38.5 f.
below, and *Ad Diog.* 5 f.; Arist. *Apol.* 15 ff.; Just. *Apol.* 1.14 ff.;
Tert. *Apol.* 39, 44 f., etc.).

[474] A similar point made in Theoph. *Ad Autol.* 1.10 (on Cybele
and her devotees), in Cyp. *Ep.* 59.12.1 (on Novatianists), in
Euseb. *H.E.* 5.1.14 (Lyons and Vienne); cf. Ephes. 5.3: *fornicatio*
autem, et omnis immunditia, aut avaritia, nec nominentur in vobis,
sicut decet sanctos; and 30.6 below: *nobis homicidium nec videre*
fas nec audire.

[475] Now begins the reply to 9.4; as before, in the case of the
ass's head, the charge is denied and then made in turn against
paganism.

[476] A remarkable avoidance of any mention of the Incarnation
(cf. the coyness on this same topic in Arnob. 1.37 f. Indeed, so
anxious is M.F. to avoid admitting such a difficult doctrine that
he gives the appearance of denying it). The explanation is that
the humanity of Christ was a singularly embarrassing feature for
Christians in the Platonically-minded Empire; for Celsus He was
just another famous man (*ap.* Orig. *C.Cels.* 3.34). It was, accordingly, the superhuman qualities of Christ (as already in St Paul's
epistles), and hence the elaboration of the theological doctrine of
the Logos, that received stress. It is not surprising, therefore, that
M.F. also avoids any explanation of the redemptive mission of
Christ's death as a criminal: he would have had to establish
Christ's resurrection, an esoteric doctrine which he eschews
mentioning as well (as at 34.9 ff.); though he might have argued
more simply on the lines of Arnobius (1.40): the manner of death
does not affect the truth of someone's teachings. On M.F.'s
doctrinal poverty, see Intro. p. 30 and M. Mühl, "Zum Problem
der Christologie im 'Octavius' des Minucius Felix," RhM 111
(1968) 69 ff.

On the construing of the passage, see H. Wagenvoort, "Minuciana (ad Oct. 3,1; 29,2)," *Mélanges . . . Mohrmann* (Utrecht 1963) 66 ff., at 70 ff.

[477] For the folly of putting one's trust in man, cf. Just. *Dial.* 8 (Trypho of Christ), 2 Cor. 15.19: *si in hac vita tantum in Christo sperantes sumus, miserabiliores sumus omnibus hominibus.* M. Pellegrino, "Minucio Felice 29,3. Nec ille miserabilis," *Aevum* 21 (1947) 142 ff., argues for the retention of the MSS reading *nec ille miserabilis* ("not worth our pity"), comparing *inter alia* Jerem. 17.5: *maledictus homo qui confidit in homine;* this is a possible thesis, but *ne ille miserabilis* suits the context better.

[478] Beaujeu *ad loc.* takes this as a reference to the cult of the Pharaohs—long, of course, out of date, and the present passage accordingly assumed to be poorly adapted from an old source. The expression *hominem sibi quem colant eligunt* (notwithstanding the peculiar present tense) hardly suits such worship, however. The reference rather seems to be to a particular cult, still apparently current at this time, of the Egyptian village of Anabis, reported by Porph. *De abst.* 4.9: "In the village of Anabis they worship a man; there sacred offerings are made to him and burnt on the altars." The same phenomenon is reported by [Clem.] *Hom.* 6.23.1, who, like M.F., generalizes ("among the Egyptians even today").

For a discussion see G. Quispel, "A Jewish Source of Minucius Felix," *VC* 3 (1949) 113 ff., arguing (unpersuasively) for the priority of M.F. over Tert. *Ad nat.* 2.8.9 (on the cult of Serapis = Joseph) from this passage; also F. Ramorino, "Minucio Felice e Tertulliano: Nota biographico-cronologica," *Didaskaleion* 1 (1912) 125 ff., at 136 f., on M.F.'s use of literary commonplaces for his illustrations.

[479] Compare the points already made in 20.5 f., 24.1 f. (where see nn. 273, 351) on emperor worship. M.F. is again studiously general in his observations on this explosive topic—the charge of treason could readily be drawn from unguarded language; cf. Orig. *C.Cels.* 8.6 with equal care: ". . . would not worship the ruler of the Persians or of the Greeks or of the Egyptians or of any race whatever." By contrast see Tert. *Apol.* 28.2 ff. (on which see Axelson 79 f.).

[480] For the tutelary "genius" (τύχη) of the emperor, identified with his personal "daemon" (see n. 425 above, and L. R. Taylor, *The Divinity of the Roman Emperor* [Bryn Mawr 1931] 193),

cf. Orig. *C.Cels.* 8.6, 8.65; Tert. *Apol.* 32.2 f., 35.10. In these passages of Tertullian the identification is exploited more fully (hence an incidental argument for Tertullian's priority): to swear by the emperor's genius, it is argued, involves devil worship. Such an attitude must have caused considerable difficulty for Christians in everyday life; for such oaths, which began in official use under Domitian, are to be found in taxation proceedings (*Pap. Oxy.* 27.2472) and in the confirmation of the good quality of goods for sale (*Pap. Oxy.* 12.1445); see Frend, *Martyrdom and Persecution in the Early Church* 125 n. 94. They are also found in more official documents (cf. ILS 6088, 6089, the laws of Salpensa and Malaca; see M. P. Charlesworth, "Some Observations on the Ruler-Cult, Especially in Rome," HTR 28 [1935] 5 ff., at 33 f.). Polycarp is, accordingly, urged to swear by the genius of Caesar (Euseb. *H.E.* 4.15.18); so too Apollonius *Acta* 3 (AnalBoll 14 [1895] 287); Bishop Euctemon marked his apostasy by such an oath (*Acta Pionii* 18). Such an oath was indeed considered a mark of loyalty; cf. Epict. *Diss.* 4.1.14. Many early Christians, of course, avoided oaths entirely, e.g., Clem. *Strom.* 7.8.50.1 ff.; Euseb. *H.E.* 6.5.5; Tert. *De idol.* 17.3: *ne iuret quidem; Acta Apollon.* 6 (AnalBoll 14 [1895] 287), following Matt. 5.33 ff.

481 Notoriously, perjury by the gods was generally left to the gods themselves for punishment on the axiom *deorum iniurias dis curae* (Tac. *Ann.* 1.73.5); cf. *Cod. Iust.* 4.1.2: *iurisiurandi contempta religio satis deum ultorem habet* (Alexander Severus); but see Th. Mommsen, *Römisches Staatsrecht* 2 (Leipzig 1887) 810 for exceptional cases considered as *maiestas* and, therefore, punishable. On the other hand, perjury by the genius of the emperor might in law be a punishable offence (Tac. *Ann.* 3.66.2: *obiectantque violatum Augusti numen; Dig.* 12.2.13.6: *si quis iuraverit in re pecuniaria per genium principis . . . et peieraverit . . . imperator noster cum patre* (i.e., Septimius Severus and Caracalla) *rescripsit fustibus eum castigandum dimittere.* This same anomaly is exploited by Tert. *Apol.* 28.4: *citius denique apud vos per omnes deos quam per unum genium Caesaris peieratur* (cf. *Ad nat.* 1.10.33; Philos. *Vit. Apol.* 1.15.2: "[the governor] was clinging to the statues of the emperor, which were more dreaded at that time and more inviolable than the Zeus in Olympia"). G. Botti, "Postilla Minuciana," *Miscell. Stampini* (Turin 1921) 61 ff., unpersuasively tried to extract a Severan dating from this passage.

482 *Cruces etiam nec colimus nec optamus.* A rebuttal of the

charge of the cult of *crucis ligna feralia* in 9.4 (where see n. 120) and of adoring crosses in 12.4. The reply is hardly satisfactory: any direct mention of the cross of Christ (see on 9.4) is carefully avoided, and it is somewhat question-begging to reply merely that Christians do not worship crosses (in the plural)—a point emphasized by F. di Capua, "La croce e le croci nell'Ottavio di Minucio," *Rendic. Acad. Arch. Lett. e Bell. Art.* n.s. 26 (1951) 98 ff. Again there is the same (unconvincing) return of the charge to the pagan camp. Why M.F. has added *optamus* to the charge is not clear: it reads as if he were refuting an (unspoken) charge of "voluntary martyrdom" (cf. Tert. *Apol.* 50.1 ff.) or a misunderstood quotation (again unexpressed) of Matt. 16.24: *tollat crucem suam et sequatur me.*

It may be true that ". . . the observations on the sign of the cross which Minucius imprudently borrowed from other Apologists, are puerile and trifling" (Sir David Dalrymple, Translator's Preface xii), but they had a long and rich literary and liturgical history: among much generous reading on the topic, see F. J. Dölger, *Sphragis* (Paderborn 1911) esp. 179 ff.; H. Rahner, *Greek Myths and Christian Mystery* (London 1963) 46 ff., and his series of articles "Antenna crucis," ZkTh 65 (1941) 123 ff.; 66 (1942) 89 ff., 196 ff.; 67 (1943) 1 ff.; 75 (1953) 129 ff., 385 ff.; 79 (1957) 129 ff.; M. Sulzberger, "Le symbole de la croix et les monogrammes de Jésus chez les premiers chrétiens," *Byz.* 2 (1925–26) 337 ff.; and J. Daniélou, *Les symboles chrétiens primitifs* (Paris 1961).

[483] A (weak) point made with more specific detail (crude cult images of Pallas Attica and Ceres Pharia) by Tert. *Apol.* 16.6 ff., cf. *Ad nat.* 1.12.1 ff.

[484] Closely connected with (more expansive) versions in Tert. *Apol.* 16.8 and esp. *Ad nat.* 1.12.15 f. *Vexilla* also occurs in a similar, and celebrated, passage in Just. *Apol.* 1.55. These standards were apposite illustrations, as they were objects of military veneration; for examples see Tac. *Ann.* 1.39.7, 2.17.2: *propria legionum numina;* Suet. *Tib.* 48; ILS 2295: *dis militaribus, Genio, Virtuti, Aquilae sanc(tae) signisque leg. 1 Ital. Severianae. . . .* Oaths might be taken by them, Livy 26.48.12 (see F. J. Dölger, "Sacramentum militae," AC 2 [1930] 268 ff.); hence the horror of losing them (see 7.4), and their value in rallying mutineers (Tac. *Ann.* 1.18.3). See further on their cult R. O. Fink, A. S. Hoey, and W. F. Snyder, "The Feriale Duranum," YCS 7 (1940)

116 ff. We are close to Constantine's *labarum* (on which see G. Pitt-Rivers, *The Riddle of the "Labarum"* [London 1966]).

485 Trophies (see n. 388) also occur in Tert. *Apol.* 16.7, *Ad nat.* 1.12.14; Just. *Apol.* 1.55. The "appearance" of a figure of a man would be the captured helmet, shield, greaves, weapons, etc. of the conquered enemy hung up on the monument; for the classic description, see Verg. *Aen.* 11.5 ff. This is the nearest approach Octavius makes to the charge of 9.4. Note also Joseph. *Antiq.* 15.272 ff.: Herod's trophies gave offense; the leaders said they were "images of men" and Herod ordered them to be stripped to the bare wood. For the rich symbolism of the *tropaeum crucis*, frequent in later patristic writing, see H. Rahner, "Antenna crucis," ZkTh 75 (1953) 129 ff., at 145 ff.; Chr. Mohrmann, *Études* 3 (1965) 331 ff. (= VC 8 [1954] 154 ff.); for illustration on Christian sarcophagi, J. Vilette, "Origine et signification d'une scène symbolique chrétienne du IVᵉ siècle," *Revue archéologique* 26 (1946) 81 ff.

486 There appears to be here a vestigial remnant of the argument that the sign of the cross is a symbol of cosmic power, of the Logos which maintains the created world; see especially the concluding sentence of this section: *signo crucis . . . ratio naturalis innititur*. And on this cosmic cross, cf. Just. *Apol.* 1.55, 60; Firmic. Mat. *De error. profan.* 21.4, 27.3: *signum crucis caeli sustinet machinam et terrae fundamenta corroborat;* [Cyp.] *Carm. de pascha* [CSEL 3.305 ff.]; and see J. Daniélou, *Théologie du judéo-christianisme* (Paris 1958) 303 ff. The argument here, however, is not consistently sustained. (On the disjointedness of M.F.'s present discussion, see S. Colombo, "Tertulliano e Minucio Felice," *Didaskaleion* n.s. 3 [1925] 45 ff., at 51 ff.)

487 G. H. Rendall, in trans. *ad loc.*, remarks: "The Cross discerned in the mast and spread oars of a ship seems far fetched, but may be introduced as a touch of local colour." That is to ignore the long literary use of this imagery, on which see esp. H. Rahner, "Antenna crucis," ZkTh 75 (1953) 129 ff. ("Das Kreuz als Mastbaum und Antenne"); *idem, Greek Myths and Christian Mystery* (London 1963) 328 ff.; and for Jewish use, E. R. Goodenough, *Jewish Symbols in the Greco-Roman Period* 12 (New York 1965) 151 f. For this particular use of the symbol, cf. Tert. *Adv. Iud.* 10.7, *Adv. Marc.* 3.18.4; Just. *Apol.* 1.55; and cf. catacomb illustrations of boat with sail and oars, e.g., G. B. de Rossi, *La Roma sotterranea cristiana* 2 (1867) Tav. 39–40 fig. 27,

Tav. 49–50 fig. 26. For other Christian uses of this portmanteau symbol and illustrations, see G. Stuhlfauth, "Das Schiff als Symbol in der altchristliche Kunst," *Riv. arch. crist.* 19 (1942) 111 ff.; DACL 12 (1935) *s.v.* navire 1008 ff. (H. Leclercq); also K. Goldammer, "Navis ecclesiae. . . ," ZNTW 40 (1941) 76 ff.; *idem,* "Das Schiff der Kirche," *Th.Z.* 6 (1950) 232 ff.

[488] In Just. *Apol.* 1.55 there is the illustration of the plough; many think that M.F. may have, therefore, misinterpreted this passage. In Just. *Dial.* 88, however, Christ is declared to have made "plough and yokes" (or "crossbeams," ζυγά) by which He taught men "the symbols of righteousness." The ζυγά of Justin would correspond to the *iugum* here. See also J. Daniélou, "La charrue symbole de la croix (Irénée, *adv. Haer.* iv.34.4)," *Rech. de sc. rel.* 42 (1954) 193 ff., esp. 199 (he takes "plough" and "yokes" to be equivalent).

[489] Christians, of course (like the Jews before them, and most pagans of this period), generally stood for prayer with hands outstretched (the *orans* so frequently illustrated in the catacombs) facing the East (the attitude still liturgically surviving in the priest's stance during Mass). Kneeling was a penitential position (hence a posture generally forbidden on Sundays, DACL 4.1 [1920] *s.v.* Dimanche 959 f. [H. Dumaine]), much despised as undignified by pagans (Celsus *ap.* Orig. *C.Cels.* 6.15) and worthy of note among Christians (Euseb. *H.E.* 2.23.6: James the Just's hardened knees). The silhouette of the *orans* describing the figure of the Cross was heavily exploited by the early Christian writers: Just. *Apol.* 1.55; Tert. *Ad nat.* 1.12.7 (but not in the *Apology*), *De orat.* 14; Euseb. *H.E.* 5.1.41 (Blandina), *H.E.* 8.7.4 (martyr at Tyre). It was a symbolism which was particularly encouraged by the typology placed on Moses' outstretched arms during the battle with the Amalechites, Exod. 17.10 ff. (cf. *Ep. Barn.* 12.2 ff.; Just. *Dial.* 90; Tert. *Adv. Marc.* 3.18.6, *Adv. Iud.* 10.10, etc.).

Pura mente, "with purity of heart," may be merely an adverbial accompaniment somewhat gratuitously added to this picture of prayer; cf. Petron. *Satyricon* 44: *stolatae ibant nudis pedibus . . . mentibus puris;* 1 *Clem.* 29.1. Or it may possibly be instrumental; cf. Cic. *De nat. deor.* 2.71: *cultus autem deorum est optimus . . . ut eos semper pura, integra, incorrupta et mente et voce veneramur;* and cf. 32.2 below.

[490] The reply is to 9.5 of Caecilius' address; it parallels closely Tert. *Apol.* 8.2 ff., a lengthy chapter which has the same sort of

ad hominem argument as here. This section is a good illustration of the Roman forensic practice of using as many proofs as could be mustered: cf. Cic. *De nat. deor.* 3.8: *cum in foro diceres quam plurimis posses argumentis onerare iudicem.* . . .

⁴⁹¹ *Fundat, exhauriat.* Beaujeu translates "le répande jusqu'à la dernière goutte," but *drinking* is probably envisaged in view of *sitienter sanguinem lambunt* in 9.5.

⁴⁹² Cf. Tert. *Apol.* 8.5: *qui ista credis de homine, potes et facere.*

⁴⁹³ Abortion and the exposure (or strangulation—Tert. *Apol.* 9.7 has drowning) of infants was the subject of vigorous condemnation among Jewish and Christian writers. For Jews cf. Joseph. *Contra Ap.* 2.202; *Orac. Sibyll.* 2.281 ff., 3.765 (Geffcken); Philo *De spec. leg.* 3.108 ff.; among Christians, *Did.* 2.2 (where see the commentary of J. P. Audet 288 f.), 5.2; *Ep. Barn.* 19.5, 20.2; *Ad Diog.* 5.6; Athenag. *Leg.* 35; Just. *Apol.* 1.27; Orig. *C.Cels.* 8.55; Tert. *Apol.* 9.7 ff.; Hippol. *Philos.* 9.12.25 (GCS Hippolytus 3.250). At this period abortion could be a legal offense against the husband's rights (*Dig.* 47.11.4, 48.19.39), but the exposure of children (especially unwanted daughters, cf. *Oxy. Pap.* 4.744.9f.: "if you are delivered of a male child, let it live; if of a female, expose it") appears to have been not uncommon. Seneca allowed the drowning of deformed children (*Dial.* 3.15.2), though Musonius later condemned the practice generally, Stob. *Flor.* 3.74 f., 129 Meineke (and see A. C. van Geytenbeek, *Musonius Rufus and Greek Diatribe* [Assen 1963] 78 ff.). The question was the subject of much later legislation both by state (e.g., *Cod. Iust.* 8.52 *de infantibus expositis*) and Church (e.g., Counc. Elvira *can.* 63, Counc. Ancy. *can.* 21, see C. J. Hefele, *Histoire des conciles* 1.1 [Paris 1907] 256, 323 f.). Not to expose or abort was a *locus communis* for praise in the literary tradition: Tac. *Germ.* 19 (Germans); Tac. *Hist.* 5.5 (Jews); Dio 76.12.2 (Caledonians); Theopomp. *ap.* Athen. 12.517E (Etruscans). For further studies, see A. Cameron, "The Exposure of Children and Greek Ethics," *CR* 46 (1932) 105–14; F. J. Dölger, "Das Lebensrecht des ungeborenen Kindes und die Fruchtabtreibung in der Bewertung der heidnischen und christlichen Antike," *AC* 4 (1934) 1–61, esp. 23 ff.; *RAC* 1 (1950) *s.v.* Abtreibung 55–60 (J. H. Waszink); K. Hopkins, "Contraception in the Roman Empire," *Comparat. Stud. in Society and History* 8 (1965) 124 ff., esp. 136 ff.

⁴⁹⁴ Cf. the point made in 23.7 and see n. 335 there.

⁴⁹⁵ For Saturn's pedophagy see n. 296 above.

[496] Tearful victims would constitute a bad omen; cf. Macrob. *Sat.* 3.5.8 ff. Human sacrifices in honor of Saturn (the Phoenician Moloch) are widely attested, partly because they were an item in a series of stock instances (some occurring in 31.3 below) used in debating the question of the relativity of moral codes (on this see H. Chadwick, "Origen, Celsus, and the Stoa," JTS 48 [1947] 34 ff., at 35). Examples occur in [Plato] *Minos* 315B ff.; Varro *ap.* Aug. *De civ. Dei* 7.19; Arist. *Apol.* 9; Tert. *Scorp.* 7.6; Orig. *C.Cels.* 5.27; Arnob. 2.68; for Crete, Porphy. *De abst.* 2.56). Note the past imperfect tense *immolabantur:* just when human sacrifices ceased publicly in Africa is a matter for debate; the solution depends on the reading and interpretation of the corresponding passage in Tert. *Apol.* 9.2: *infantes penes Africam Saturno immolabantur palam usque ad proconsulatum Tiberii . . . teste militia patris nostri (Fuldensis), patriae nostrae (Parisinus).* Tertullian goes on to claim that the rites continued *in occulto.* (For a lucid discussion on the text, see T. D. Barnes, *Tertullian. A Historical and Literary Study* [Oxford 1971] 13 ff.) For discussion see J. Carcopino, *Aspects mystiques de la Rome païenne* (Paris 1942) 39 ff. (Rome et les immolations d'enfants) and "Survivances par substitution des sacrifices d'enfants dans l'Afrique romaine," *Rev. de l'hist. des relig.* 106 (1932) 592 ff.; J. Toutain, *Les cultes païens dans l'empire romain* 3 (Paris 1920) 78 ff.; and for a full coverage of the archeological and literary evidence on such ritual murders, see M. Leglay, *Saturne africain histoire* (Paris 1966) 314 ff.

[497] For the inhospitable custom of the inhabitants of the Tauric Chersonese, who sacrificed shipwrecked strangers to Artemis (on this goddess see 6.1, 23.5 above), see Clem. *Protr.* 2.3.42.3; Orig. *C.Cels.* 5.27; Athenag. *Leg.* 26; Juv. *Sat.* 15.116 and Mayor's n. *ad loc.*; Hyginus *Fab.* 120; and, of course, the subject of Eurip. *Iphig. in Tauris.* The same example in Tert. *Apol.* 9.5.

[498] Busiris was a legendary Egyptian king who slew foreigners in honor of Zeus in return for rain. He was killed by Hercules. See Hdt. 2.45; Ovid. *Ars. amat.* 1.647 ff.; Hyg. *Fab.* 31, 56; Tat. *Or.* 3; [Just.] *Or. ad Graec.* 3; Orig. *C.Cels.* 5.27, etc.

[499] *hospites:* a loaded word (hence the heavy translation), hospitality being a very necessary and highly valued virtue in antiquity generally. The early Christians were no exception and laid strong emphasis upon its practice. See *Did.* 11.4 ff. (and Audet's commentary 442 ff., 453 ff.); Herm. *Mand.* 8.10, *Sim.* 9.27.2;

Arist. *Apol.* 15; Just. *Apol.* 1.67; 1 *Clem.* 11, 12, 35; Euseb. *H.E.* 4.26.2 (Melito's tractate on the subject); and H. Chadwick, "Justification by Faith and Hospitality," *Stud. patr.* 4 (1961) = TU 79, 281 ff.

500 For Gauls and Mercury, see 6.1. The same example in Tert. *Apol.* 9.5 (for the relationship with Tertullian in this section, see Axelson 49 ff.), *Scorp.* 7.6. Mercury is presumably chosen, a little inaccurately, as the characteristic god of the Gauls: Teutates and Esus are specified in Lucan, *B.C.* 1.444 f. (where, however, the Schol. *ad loc.* [28 Endt] has *Teutates Mercurius sic* (sc., *a Gallis*) *dicitur*); Lact. *Div. inst.* 1.21.3; cf. Tac. *Ann.* 13.57.3: victorious Hermunduri sacrifice Chatti *Marti ac Mercurio;* see also Duval, *Les dieux de la Gaule* 19 ff., 67 ff. The Romans were shocked by the *dira immanitas* of the religion of the Gauls (e.g., Caesar *B.G.* 6.16.2 ff.; Petronius *ap.* Servius *ad* Verg. *Aen.* 3.57); Augustus, Tiberius, and Claudius all seem to have needed to attempt curtailment of their bloody rites (H. Last, "Rome and the Druids: A Note," JRS 39 [1949] 1 ff.) and they apparently survived, in ritual guise, in the use of prisoners who served as *trinqui* at their games, *veteri more et sacro ritu* (see J. H. Oliver and R. E. A. Palmer, "Minutes of an Act of the Roman Senate," *Hesp.* 24 [1955] 320 ff., esp. 324 ff.). On this topic see generally, F. Schwenn, *Die Menschenopfer bei der Griechen und Römern* (Religions. Vers. u. Vorarb. 15.3; Giessen 1915) 18 ff.

Cic. *De rep.* 3.9.15 has a similar list of these stock examples: *Quam multi, ut Tauri in Axino, ut rex Aegypti Busiris, ut Galli, ut Poeni, homines immolare et pium et dis immortalibus gratissimum esse duxerunt!* For discussion, with examples of other parallel catalogues, see Baylis 354 f.

501 This custom is notoriously attested during the panic of the dark days of the Second Punic War after the defeat at Cannae (216 B.C.), Livy 22.57.6. The victims were buried alive in the Forum Boarium. Was there similar sacrifice in 226 B.C. also (Plut. *Marcell.* 3.3; Oros. 4.13.3)? The last attestation of the custom was as late as 114 B.C. (Plut. *Q.R.* 83 = *Moralia* 283 ff.; Macrob. *Sat.* 1.10.5; Orosius 5.15.22; Livy *Per.* 63), and it was not until 97 B.C. that human sacrifice was formally abolished by the Roman Senate, Pliny *N.H.* 30.1.12; hence Pliny *N.H.* 28.12 (writing under Vespasian, 69–79 A.D.) declared (with exaggeration) that they were rites which *etiam nostra aetas vidit.* For discussion, J. S. Reid, "Human Sacrifices at Rome and Other Notes

on Roman Religion," JRS 2 (1912) 34 ff.; A. W. Lintott, *Violence in Republican Rome* (Oxford 1968) 39.

⁵⁰² On Jupiter Latiaris see n. 314 above. Beaujeu annotates: "la tradition d'un sacrifice humain, uniquement chez des auteurs chrétiens." That is to ignore Porphy. *De abst.* 2.56, who, like Lact. *Div. inst.* 1.21.3 (*etiamnunc*), declares that the sacrifice takes place in Rome "even today" (ἔτι καὶ νῦν); H. J. Rose, "De Iove Latiari," *Mnem.* n.s. 55 (1927) 273–79, plausibly argues that the story is the result of confusion with the gladiatorial games held in honor of Jupiter Latiaris on the *Feriae Latinae;* cf. Tert. *Apol.* 9.5: *Iuppiter quidam quem ludis suis humano sanguine proluunt. Sed bestiarii, inquitis. Hoc opinor minus quam hominis?"; Scorp.* 7.6:*et Latio ad hodiernum Iovi media in urbe humanus sanguis ingustatur.* See also Roscher 2.690 ff.

⁵⁰³ Cf. Tert. *Apol.* 9.9. This story is reported by Sall. *Cat.* 22.1: *humani corporis sanguinem vino permixtum* (cf., with variants, Plut. *Cic.* 10.3; Dio 37.30.3); for a discussion see n. 121 above and F. J. Dölger, "Sacramentum infanticidii," AC 4 (1934) 188 ff., at 207 ff.

⁵⁰⁴ For the rites of Bellona, see 24.12 above and n. 377.

⁵⁰⁵ This particular cure for epilepsy (*morbus comitialis*, so called because an attack of the "sacred disease" at the *comitia*, public assemblies, involved their suspension) is mentioned by Tert. *Apol.* 9.10; Pliny (along with suitable expressions of abhorrence) *N.H.* 28.4 (cf. *N.H.* 26.8, cure of elephantiasis in Egypt); Cels. *De medic.* 3.23; Aretaeus 1.312 (Kühn) *Corp. med. Graec.* 2.2.154 (who dryly remarks that he has met no one who can verify as to its effectiveness). Fresh blood flowing from the wounds of recently killed gladiators was considered to be the most efficacious. Scribonius Largus 17 gives a similar prescription: *item ex iecinore gladiatoris iugulati particulam aliquam novies datam consumant.*

⁵⁰⁶ The same bizarre argument is voiced (more gruesomely) by Tert. *Apol.* 9.11; cf. Athenag. *Resur.* 4 (the question of fish, birds, beasts who have preyed on men and then been eaten by men).

⁵⁰⁷ A reference to Christian avoidance of gladiatorial shows, and apparently the stage productions as well (cf. 37.12, but for *audire* cf. also 29.1). A similar point is made in the rejection of the charge of cannibalism by Athenag. *Leg.* 35; Theoph. *Ad Autol.* 3.15; cf. Tert. *De spect.* 19 f. Octavius here is made to score a neat point, horror of bloodthirsty gladiatorial games being

a commonplace amongst educated and cultivated Greeks and Romans; for abundant evidence see L. Robert, *Les gladiateurs dans l'Orient grec* (Paris 1940) 239 ff., and C. P. Jones, *Plutarch and Rome* (Oxford 1971) 123. For further discussion on Christians and *spectacula*, see 12.5 above and 37.11 below. C. J. Cadoux, *The Early Christian Attitude to War* (London 1919) 128, wrongly cites this passage as testimony of Christian pacificism.

[508] This point was made by Biblis during the persecution at Lyons and Vienne (Euseb. *H.E.* 5.1.26: "How would such men eat children when they are not allowed to eat the blood of even irrational animals?"), as it is by Tert. *Apol.* 9.13, and cf. Clem *Paed.* 3.3.25.2. How extensively the dietary regulations of the Pentateuch were interpreted literally during this period is far from clear. There was certainly a school which allegorized—or rejected—the ordinances: *Ep. Barn.* 10; *Ad Diog.* 4.1; Arist. *Apol.* 14 (Syr.); in *Did.* 6.3 abstention is a counsel of perfection; cf. Just. *Dial.* 47, who debates whether Christians who also observe the Law of Moses shall be saved; Euseb. *H.E.* 1.4.8. On the other hand, Tertullian at least, with his characteristic scorn of the allegory school, comes out strongly in favor of a literal interpretation, *De monog.* 5.3, *Adv. Marc.* 2.18.2 ff. See R. P. C. Hanson, "Notes on Tertullian's Interpretation of Scripture," JTS n.s. 12 (1961) 273 ff.; for strong Judaic attitudes in the African Church, see also W. H. C. Frend, "The *seniores laici* and the Origins of the Church in North Africa," JTS n.s. 12 (1961) 280 ff., at 283 f., and G. Quispel, "The Discussion of Judaic Christianity," VC 22 (1968) 81 ff., at 93. Tertullian's story, *Apol.* 9.14, that Christians in time of persecution were tested with blood sausages, *botulos . . . cruore distensos*, which by their religion were forbidden to them, sounds much too circumstantial to be an invention and indicates that abstention was fairly widespread. Orig. *C.Cels.* 8.29 f. (emphasizing blood as the daemon's food, see n. 439 above) confirms this impression. Does Lucian *De mort. Pereg.* 16 also refer to food laws in force among Christians? All this meant, of course, that many Christians would have to organize their own meat services or use the kosher shops (see n. 159 above).

By Augustine's day the ordinance of Acts 15.2 *ut abstineatis ab sanguine* might, controversially, be interpreted as an injunction to refrain from homicide (so too Ambrosiaster *In ep. ad Gal.* 2.2

[ML 17.346]), and Augustine goes on to say that the few who observe the law literally in his day are laughed at (*Contra Faust.* 32.13 f. [CSEL 25.771 ff.]).

For fuller discussion see G. Resch, *Das Apostledecret nach seiner ausserkanonischer Textgestalt,* TU n.f. 13.3 (1905) *passim;* J. R. Porter, "The 'Apostolic Decree' and Paul's Second Visit to Jerusalem," JTS 47 (1946) 169–74; S. Stein, "The Dietary Laws in Rabbinic and Patristic Literature," *Stud. patr.* 2 (1957) = TU 64, 141–54; R. E. Taylor, "Attitudes of the Fathers towards Practices of the Jewish Christians," *Stud. patr.* 4 (1961) = TU 79, 504 ff.; and for the influence of the Judeo-Christian movement on this question, M. Simon, *Verus Israel* (Paris 1948) 388 ff., and, more generally, J. Daniélou, *Théologie du judéo-christianisme* (Paris 1958) esp. chap. 1.

509 The charge occurs in 9.6 f. For a literary analysis of the imagery, tone, and color of 31.1–7, see J. Fontaine, *Aspects et problèmes de la prose d'art latine au IIIe siècle: La genèse de styles latins chrétiens* (Turin 1968) 111 ff.

510 The explanation of 27.8, 28.6, and see n. 449.

511 On Fronto see n. 123. On the notorious license granted the orator in Roman forensic practice, cf. Titus Castricius *ap.* Aul. Gellius, *Noctes Atticae* 1.6.4: *rhetori concessum est, sententiis uti falsis, audacibus, versutis, subdolis, captiosis, si veri modo similes sint et possint movendos hominum animos qualicumque astu inrepere;* Cic. *De orat.* 1.221: *orator autem omnia haec quae putantur in communi vitae consuetudine mala ac molesta et fugienda, multo maiora et acerbiora verbis facit.* For Fronto's oratory see the praises of M. Aurel., Fronto Naber 28 f.

512 This and the following examples provided standard illustrations in discussions on the variations in the moral code (see n. 496 above); cf. Hdt. 3.31; Orig. *C.Cels.* 5.27 (mothers, daughters), 6.80 (mothers, daughters); Tat. *Or.* 28 (mothers); Lucian *De sacrif.* 5 (sister); Tert. *Apol.* 9.16: *Persas cum suis matribus misceri Ctesias refert* (on which see Axelson 66 f., 85; the passage cannot be decisive for the priority of Tertullian, as is sometimes claimed).

513 In Egypt, uterine brothers and sisters might marry, as was the practice among the Pharaohs; cf. *Diod.* 1.27.1 (the precedent established by Isis and Osiris); Theoc. *Id.* 17.131 ff. (defending the incest of Ptolemy II by the example of Zeus). In Athens half-brothers and sisters with the same father might wed, Plut.

Cimon 4 ff.; Sen. *Apocol.* 8.2: *Athenis dimidium licet, Alexandriae totum;* cf. Joseph. *Contra Ap.* 2.275.

514 Tert. *Apol.* 9.16 cites the story of Oedipus and the Macedonians laughing at Oedipus' chagrin at discovering his incest. The traditions (*memoria*) of Rome contained such stories as the incest of Claudius with his niece Agrippina (Tac. *Ann.* 12.5), that of Nero with his mother, the same Agrippina (Tac. *Ann.* 14.2), that of Domitian with his niece Julia (Suet. *Dom.* 22), and so on.

515 A favorite topic of apologetic, Jupiter being presumably in mind (intercourse with Rhea his mother, Juno his sister, Proserpine his daughter); cf. Orig. *C.Cels.* 1.17, 1.25, 4.48 (daughter); Tat. *Or.* 8 (daughter); Theoph. *Ad Autol.* 3.3 (sister); Athenag. *Leg.* 20 (mother, daughter), 32 (mother, daughter, sister); Arnob. 4.24 (sister), 5.22 (mother, daughter), and, generally, Arist. *Apol.* 8 (Syr.) (mothers, daughters, sisters); Tert. *Apol.* 9.16: *proinde incesti qui magis quam quos ipse Iuppiter docuit?; Apol.* 14.3 (sister).

516 M.F. leaves unexplained that such foundlings were often exploited for prostitution (Just. *Apol.* 1.27, in a closely parallel passage). The same bizarre risks of incest through promiscuity are emphasized in Tert. *Apol.* 9.17 f., *Ad nat.* 1.16.10; Clem. *Paed.* 3.3.21.2 ff.; Lact. *Div. inst.* 6.20.22 ff. On the exposure of children, see n. 493 above.

517 I.e., you are re-enacting the stories of tragedy (e.g., cf. Oedipus); cf. Clem. *Paed.* 3.3.21.5.

518 Note that M.F. appears to condemn second marriages. There certainly was a school of thought which took such a rigorist line both among the orthodox (Athenag. *Leg.* 33; Theoph. *Ad Autol.* 3.13; Just. *Apol.* 1.15 [or does this refer to remarriage after divorce?]) and the heterodox (e.g., Novatianists, Montanists, Tert. *De monog.;* Epiph. *Adv. haer.* 48.9 [MG 41.869]). Hermas *Mand.* 4.4.1 f. allows remarriage (with reluctance), so too Clem. *Strom.* 3.1.4.3, 3.12.82.3 f. The charge of Hippolytus that Pope Callistus was the first to allow digamists to hold clerical office implies at the least that it was possible for the laity to be such (see J. J. I. von Döllinger, *Hippolytus und Kallistus oder die römische Kirche in der ersten Hälfte des dritten Jahrhunderts* [Edinburgh 1876] 129 ff.), but the implicit tone of disapproval continued (e.g., Jerom. *Ep.* 123.5 f., widows twice married excluded from Church alms; Ambrosiaster *In 1 Cor.* 7.40 [ML

17.225]: . . . *primae nuptiae sub benedictione Dei celebrantur sublimiter: secundae autem etiam in praesenti carent gloria*. And note the stress in Christian inscriptions on being married once, e.g., ILCV 4318 A.5 *mihi uno marito*, ILCV 1003 (the *Protogamia* inscription from Carthage); W. M. Calder, "Early Christian Epitaphs from Phrygia," *Anatol. Stud.* 5 [1955] 25 ff., at 31). For the early Church teachings on remarriage, see J. P. Arendzen, "Ante-Nicene Interpretations of the Sayings on Divorce," JTS 20 (1919) 230 ff.; G. H. Joyce, *Christian Marriage* (2nd ed. London 1948) 584 ff. (esp. on the more severe Eastern tradition); J. MacRory, *The New Testament and Divorce* (Dublin 1934) 65 ff. The social implications of this attitude in a world of high mortality must have been considerable; see M. K. Hopkins, "The Age of Roman Girls at Marriage," *Population Studies* 18 (1965) 309 ff. For pagan disapproval of second marriages, cf. Plut. *Quaest. Rom.* 105.289A f. It was a traditional Roman sentiment; cf. the stress on *univirae* for religious ceremonial (24.11 above), and the frequency with which pagan sepulchral inscriptions also approvingly refer to women as *univirae* (cf. Prop. 4.11.36: *in lapide hoc uni nupta fuisse legar*). For evidence see G. Williams, "Some Aspects of Roman Marriage Ceremonies and Ideals," JRS 48 (1958) 16 ff., at 23 f.; H. Funke, "Univira. Ein Beispiel heidnischer Geschichtsapologetik," JAC 8/9 (1965/66) 183 ff.

Note the stress on procreation; intercourse for the begetting of children only was stressed in the Christian as well as the Judaic and Stoic traditions; cf. Clem. *Strom.* 2.18.88.4, 2.7.58.2, 3.12.82.3; *Cons. apost.* 6.28.3; Athenag. *Leg.* 33; Just. *Apol.* 1.29; Orig. *Hom. in Gen.* 3.6 (GCS Origen 6.47); Joseph. *Contra Ap.* 2.199, 2.202; Musonius Rufus, in C. E. Lutz. "Musonius Rufus, the Roman Socrates," YCS 10 (1947) 3 ff., at 86. Octavius was also appealing to the deep-rooted Roman sentiment of marriage *liberorum quaerundorum causa;* see G. W. Williams, *Tradition and Originality in Roman Poetry* (Oxford 1968) 370 ff.

[519] Christian virginity is much vaunted among the Apologists, cf. Orig. *C.Cels.* 1.26, 7.48; Athenag. *Leg.* 33; Just. *Apol.* 1.15; Tert. *Apol.* 9.19 f. (on *senes pueri;* see Axelson 86 f.). The widely read *Acts of Paul and Thecla* 12 (James *Apoc. N.T.* 275) even taught that only virgins will be resurrected. The independent evidence of Galen is celebrated: "For their contempt of death and its sequel is patent to us every day and likewise their restraint in cohabitation. For they include not only men but also women

who refrain from cohabiting all through their lives; and they also number individuals who in self-discipline and self-control in matters of food and drink and in their keen pursuit of justice have attained a pitch not inferior to that of genuine philosophers" (R. Walzer, *Galen on Jews and Christians* [Oxford 1949] 15, and, for a useful discussion, 65 ff.).

520 This section purports to be a reply to 8.4. Octavius avoids offering any explanation for the refusal to engage in the offices of public life. See n. 111 above.

521 The charge of conspiracy (reading *factiosi*) was first suggested by Caecilius in 8.3: *inlicitae . . . factionis*, on which see n. 104 above, but that charge was not elaborated, as it is in Tertullian's *Apology*. The phrase *unum bonum sapimus* may echo Holy Writ, e.g., Rom. 15.5:*idipsum sapere*, Phil. 2.2: *ut idem sapistis eamdem charitatem habentes, unanimes, idipsum sentientes*. On M.F. and the Bible generally, note the discussion by D. Plooy, "Minucius Felix een Modernist?" *Theol. Stud.* 32 (1914) 30 ff.

522 Cf. Tert. *Apol.* 39.21: *hoc sumus congregati quod et dispersi, hoc universi quod et singuli;* the phrase seems to be added here somewhat awkwardly and argues for the priority of Tertullian (so R. Heinze, *Tertullians Apologeticum* [Leipzig 1910] 452 n. 1).

523 For the phrase *aut erubescitis aut timetis* cf. 28.2: *ut christianus reus nec erubesceret nec timeret*. The parallel suggests that a public hearing in law may be intended; this is explicitly so in the corresponding passage in Tert. *Apol.* 1.1 and thus lends some support to the theory that Tertullian is prior (so J. van Wageningen, "Minucius Felix et Tertullianus," *Mnem.* 51 [1923] 223 ff., at 226 f.; unconvincingly criticized by G. Hinnisdaels, "Minucius Felix est-il antérieur à Tertullien," *Musée belge* 28 [1924] 25 ff., at 30 f. See also Axelson 87 f.).

524 This charge is to be found in 9.1: *fecundius nequiora proveniunt.*

525 This argument from expansion (which was to have a long history) is heavily exploited by Origen, e.g., *C.Cels.* 1.47, *De princip.* 4.1 f. (GCS Origen 5.292 ff.), *Hom. in Luc.* 7 (GCS Origen 9.46); see H. Chadwick, "The Evidences of Christianity in the Apologetic of Origen," *Stud. patr.* 2 = TU 64 (1957) 331 ff., at 335 ff. It is formulated, with more caution, in Tert. *Apol.* 1.6 ff. Cf. also Cyp. *Ep.* 55.24.3.

[526] On this question see n. 115 above. There is no word here in defense or otherwise of the sign of the cross and other ritual gestures, as might have been expected.

[527] The charge is in 9.2; the defense as in Tert. *Apol.* 36.4, 37.1: *quem habemus odisse?, Ad Scap.* 1.3; Athenag. *Leg.* 11; *Did.* 1.3, 2.7, etc.

[528] On the Christian use of *frater* and *soror*, see n. 21 above. Stoic doctrine, too, of course, insisted on the brotherhood of man, e.g. Sen. *Ep.* 95.52 ff.: *natura nos cognatos edidit;* cf. Tert. *Apol.* 39.7 ff.: *fratres autem etiam vestri sumus, iure naturae matris unius.*

[529] Phrases (*consortes fidei, spei coheredes*) that appear to be ultimately derivative from Scripture: Tit. 3.7: *heredes simus secundum spem vitae aeternae;* Rom. 8.17: *coheredes autem Christi;* 1 Peter 3.7: *coheredibus gratiae vitae.* M.F. avoids noting, however, the partnership with Christ in these associations.

[530] This point appears to be merely a hyperbolic rhetorical flourish, with perhaps a reference to Roman legend (Romulus and Remus, see 25.2) or to mythology (Eteocles and Polynices, see 18.6; cf. Tert. *Apol.* 39.10). Some have wanted to see here, however, a specific historical allusion—to the murder of Geta by his brother Caracalla in 212 A.D.—but that is quite unnecessary, and out of character with M.F.'s (seemingly studious) avoidance of contemporary illustrations and references.

[531] The accusation of 10.2, and see nn. 113, 127 above. Observe that Octavius denies *templa* and *arae*, terms closely associated with pagan ritual and worship—they do not exclude *coetus, ecclesiae* etc., and *altaria.* The lines of the present argument, however, with their traditional motifs (the paramount value of spiritual sacrifice and worship), do give the misleading impression that the Christian community engaged in no liturgical action at all.

[532] On the question of iconography in the early Church, see n. 129 above. The likeness of man and God was a commonplace of both paganism and Christianity: for the pagan theme (much emphasized in the Platonic and Stoic traditions), see Plat. *Rep.* 6.501B and the many passages cited by Pease at Cic. *De nat. deor.* 1.90: *cur maluerit Epicurus;* cf. Cic. *ibid.* 1.103; for the Christian emphasis on the point, based essentially, of course, on Gen. 1.26 f., see Col. 3.10 and James 3.9; 1 *Clem.* 33.4; *Ep. Barn.* 5.5, 6.12; Tat. *Or.* 15; Just. [*Cohort.*] 34; Theoph. *Ad Autol.* 1.4, 2.18; Orig. *C.Cels.* 4.30, 6.63, 8.49. See also A. Altmann, "*Homo Imago*

Dei in Jewish and Christian Theology," *Journ. of Religion* 48 (1968) 235 ff.

[533] For the question, Cic. *De nat. deor.* 1.103: *quod eius* (sc., *dei) est domicilium, quae sedes, qui locus.* . . . For the thought see Acts 17.24 f., 28 f.; Cic. *De repub.* 3.9.14; Tac. *Germ.* 9.3. It is usual to go on and say (1) the world is in fact a temple of God—see 1 Tim. 2.8: *orare in omni loco;* Clem. *Strom.* 5.11.76.2; Orig. *C.Cels.* 7.44; Just. *Dial.* 22 quoting Isai. 66.1: *coelum sedes mea, terra autem scabellum pedum meorum;* or (2) that man is in fact a temple of God (a widely diffused notion—see 1 Cor. 3.16; 2 Cor. 6.16); cf. 1 Peter 2.5; John 2.19, 2.21; *Ep. Barn.* 4.11, 6.15; Tat. *Or.* 15; Clem. *Protr.* 11.117.4; Orig. *C.Cels.* 4.26, 6.63, 8.18 f. The ideas occur frequently in Stoicism, e.g., Sen. *Benef.* 7.7.3— the only worthy temple of God is the universe; and see the *testimonia* collected by V. Carlier, "Minucius Félix et Sénèque," *Musée belge* 1 (1897) 258 ff., at 267 f.; P. Courcelle, "Virgile et l'immanence divine chez Minucius Felix," *Mullus* (Münster 1964) 34 ff., and "Parietes faciunt christianos?" *Mélanges d'archéologie, d'épigraphie et d'histoire offerts à Jérôme Carcopino* (Paris 1966) 241 ff., at 244 ff.; Spanneut, *op. cit.* 263 f.

[534] A point also made, with characteristic prolixity, by Arnob. 6.3.

[535] Sen. *fr.* 123 Haase, is close (*ap.* Lact. *Div. inst.* 6.25.3): *non templa illi congestis in altitudinem saxis exstruenda sunt; in suo cuique consecrandus est pectore.* (For other parallels from Seneca, see F.-X. Burger, *Minucius Felix und Seneca* [Munich 1904] 27 ff.) The notion, now to be developed, that spiritual sacrifices make the most acceptable offerings, had a long history: it is traceable back to the pre-Socratic period (e.g., to Heraclitus, who questioned the value of animal sacrifices, and Empedocles), and the contemporary Hermetic movement proscribed not only bloody sacrifices but even offerings of honey, wine, incense (see *Corp. Hermet.* ed. Nock-Festugière 1.31, 13.18 f., and nn. *ad loc.*). Note, too, the similar views of Apollonius of Tyana (*ap.* Euseb. *Demons. evan.* 3.3.105cf.), Numenius of Apamea (*ap.* Euseb. *P.E.* 11.22), and esp. Porphy. *De abst.* 2.34. For further evidence see Pease on Cic. *De nat. deor.* 2.71; M. H. Shepherd, "The Early Apologists and Christian Worship," *Journ. of Rel.* 18 (1938) 60 ff., at 65; O. Casel, "Die Λογικὴ Θυσία der antiken Mystik in christlich-liturgischer Umdeutung," *Jahrb. für Liturgiewiss.* 4 (1924) 37 ff., and Pellegrino *ad loc.*

[536] The notion that the universe existed *hominum causa* was by no means an exclusively Christian viewpoint (cf. 36.5 below); it was particularly stressed in the Stoic tradition (evidence in Cic. *De nat. deor.* 1.23, 2.37, 2.133, 2.154 ff.: it is traceable to Chrysippus, who even observed that bugs are useful to us because they prevent us from sleeping too much! *S.V.F.* 2.1163; see Pohlenz 1.81 ff.). This anthropocentric attitude is attacked by Celsus (and defended by Origen) Orig. *C.Cels.* 4.23, 4.74 ff. On the theme cf. Arist. *Apol.* 1 (Syr.); Just. *Apol.* 1.10, *Apol.* 2.4 f.; Just. *Resur.* 7; Tat. *Or.* 4; Herm. *Mand.* 12.4.2; Athenag. *Resur.* 12. Arnob. 2.37 ff., on the other hand, denies the necessity of man in the scheme of creation.

For the (commonplace) idea of the absurdity of giving to the Giver, see Tat. *Or.* 4; Athenag. *Leg.* 13; Orig. *C.Cels.* 7.65; Arnob. 6.3, etc. For pagan defense that such offerings, though perhaps unnecessary, serve to manifest men's zeal, see Celsus *ap.* Orig. *C.Cels.* 8.21; that they avert destruction from the gods, Dio Chrys. *Or.* 48.15.

[537] Note esp. Cic. *De nat. deor.* 2.71: *cultus autem deorum est optumus idemque castissimus atque sanctissimus plenissimusque pietatis, ut eos semper pura, integra, incorrupta et mente et voce veneremur;* Sen. *fr.* 123 Haase (*ap.* Lact. *Div. inst.* 6.25.3): . . . *non immolationibus et sanguine multo colendum . . . sed mente pura, bono honestoque proposito;* Herm. *Sim.* 5.3.6 ff.; Just. *Apol.* 1.10,13, *Dial.* 22, 117; Athenag. *Leg.* 13; Tert. *Apol.* 30.5; Arnob. 4.30, etc.

[538] The objection is in 10.5; the question of the invisibility of God has already been discussed in 18.8.

[539] The argument has been elaborated in 17.3 ff. Cf. Rom. 1.20; *Corp. Hermet.* ed. Nock-Festugière 11.22, 14.3; Theoph. *Ad Autol.* 1.4 f.; Orig. *C.Cels.* 7.37 and esp. Xen. *Mem.* 4.3.13 f. (which also has the following illustrations from wind and sun; and see n. 257 above). The phrase *cum serenat* ("in the clear sky") appears to be added somewhat unusually as an afterthought and is left undeveloped: can M.F. have been thinking of Hor. *Od.* 1.34 (*parcus deorum cultor*) on thunder in the clear sky, (cf. Lucan *B.C.* 1.530: *fulgura fallaci micuerunt crebra sereno;* Verg. *Aen.* 8.528 f.), or is he simply referring to the canopy of heaven bedecked with sun, moon, and stars? The latter interpretation is to be preferred; the Christian does not need the usual signs of thunder etc. to recognize the presence of God.

[510] This illustration from the analogy of the sun has a rich literary history: Plato's use in *Phaed.* 99d f.; *Legg.* 897d is celebrated (in *Repub.* 516b, 532a he does, however, consider looking directly at the sun); cf. Xen. *Mem.* 4.3.14; *Ep. Barn.* 5.10; Theoph. *Ad Autol.* 1.5, 2.36 quoting *Orac. Sibyl. fr.* 1 (Geffcken, with his notes *ad loc.*).

[541] Note the much-used comparison of the sun with God: to the passages in the previous note add, e.g., Plat. *Repub.* 508b; Celsus *ap.* Orig. *C.Cels.* 7.45; Clem. *Protr.* 6.71.3; Just. *Dial.* 128; Athenag. *Leg.* 10; Theoph. *Ad Autol.* 2.15; Tert. *Apol.* 21.12; Cyp. *Ep.* 37.2.1; and see Pease on Cic. *De nat. deor.* 1.31. Did its exploitation help to spread the rumor that the sun was in fact the Christians' God (Tert. *Apol.* 16.9 ff.)? One of the most splendid passages on the rich Christos-Helios theme is to be found in Melito *fr.* 8, Goodspeed (περὶ λουτροῦ). For a full treatment, see the monumental work of F. J. Dölger, *Sol Salutis*[2] (Münster 1925), adding his "Sonne und Sonnenstrahl als Gleichnis in der Logostheologie des christlichen Altertums," AC 1 (1929) 271 ff.; also H. Rahner, *Greek Myths and Christian Mystery* (London 1963) 89 ff.; DACL 15.2 (1953) *s.v.* Soleil 1577 ff. (H. Leclercq).

[542] *oculis carnalibus.* On the Christian use of *carnalis*, see n. 226; for the implied comparison with *oculis animi*, see n. 3; and for the theme, cf. Cic. *De nat. deor.* 1.105; Orig. *C.Cels.* 7.33; Theoph. *Ad Autol.* 1.3, 2.36; Just. *Dial.* 3, 127; Tert. *Apol.* 17.2, etc.

[543] *vivificaris:* another "Christianism" and the most widely used of the series of apparently Christian formations in *-ificare* (*sanctificare, beatificare, justificare, glorificare*, etc.). See Mohrmann *Études* 2.125 in praise of the word's vigor.

[544] The criticism of 10.5. There has been a reply to the charge concerning the material world in 18.3.

[545] The ubiquity and omniscience of God are stressed together by, *inter alios*, Theoph. *Ad Autol.* 2.3; Just. *Dial.* 127; Orig. *C.Cels.* 7.34; in defense of the MSS reading *deo cognita, plena sint* (involving an unexpected zeugma), see P. A. C. Vega, "Notas criticas e la edición Hanstein del Octavio de M.F.," *Relig. y cult.* 17 (1932) 411 ff., at 416. For the (strongly Stoic) tradition of God permeating matter, see SVF 1.159 (Zeno), 2.441 (Chrysippus); Sen. *Ep.* 65.23 f.; Pohlenz 1.409, 416; and C. Tibiletti, "Sulla fonte di un noto motivo dell'*Ad Diognetum* (c. vi)," GIF 16 (1963) 262 ff.

[546] A frequently iterated Stoic thought, e.g., Sen. *Ep.* 41.1: *prope est a te Deus, intus est;* 120.14: . . . *supra quam nihil est nisi mens dei, ex quo pars et in hoc pectus mortale defluxit;* Epict. 2.8.11 f.; and cf. n. 549 below.

[547] *Nusquam eius claritudo violatur.* This analogy with the sun spreading its rays everywhere (cf. Sen. *Ep.* 41.5) but remaining undiminished and undefiled by what it shines upon is to be found in a wide variety of texts; cf. Orig. *C.Cels.* 6.73; Tert. *De spect.* 20.2; Diog. Laer. 6.63; Aug. *De civ. Dei* 9.16, etc. For further references see J. E. B. Mayor, "The Sun's Rays Shining Undefiled on Filth," CR 11 (1897) 449, and A. Olivar, "*Sol intaminatus,*" *Analect. sacr. Tarracon.* 25 (1952) 209 ff., 29 (1956) 20 f. A parallel analogy of light from fire (Athenag. *Leg.* 24) or torches lit from fire (Just. *Dial.* 61, 128; Tat. *Or.* 5; cf. Philo. *Gig.* 25) is also frequently employed.

[548] God's knowledge of the secrets of the heart is not only sound biblical theology (Acts 1.24; Rom. 8.27; 1 Cor. 14.25) much emphasized in the patristic tradition (see Ign. *Eph.* 15.3; Polyc. *Phil.* 4.3; Athenag. *Leg.* 31; Orig. *C.Cels.* 7.51; Cyp. *Ep.* 10.5.1) but also a commonplace of paganism (see Xen. *Mem.* 1.4.14; Diog. Laer. 1.36 [Thales]; cf. Val. Max. 7.2.E.8; Plut. *De superst.* 166D; Sen. *Ep.* 41.2: *sacer intra nos spiritus sedet, malorum bonorumque nostrorum observator et custos;* 83.1: *interest animus nostris et cogitationibus mediis intervenit*) and of magic (see Preisendanz, *Pap. mag. Gr.* 1.175 ff.; cf. [Clem.] *Recog.* 2.50, where power to read the heart figures as a standing test of miraculous ability).

[549] *cum illo, ut prope dixerim, vivimus.* Cf. Acts 17.28: *in ipso enim vivimus et movemur et sumus;* Eph. 3.17; 1 Cor. 3.16, 6.19; 2 Cor. 6.16; Luke 17.21; Ign. *Eph.* 15.3; Herm. *Mand.* 7.5, etc. Of course, close to Stoic doctrine, cf. n. 546 above.

[550] This remark has been frequently taken out of context and used as evidence for the growing number of Christians (e.g., Baylis 225; and recently, Frend, *Martyrdom and Persecution in the Early Church* 331). The artificial paragraphing is at fault, giving the mistaken impression that a new point is being dealt with; but, in fact, we have here the final argument that God is capable of looking after the whole of mankind qua individuals. The first person plural refers to the human race generally.

[551] For the analogy see 18.4 and n. 215. The singleness of the household is underlined by Sen. *Benef.* 7.1.7; cf. Tert. *De pudic.*

7.11: *totus hic mundus una omnium domus est;* Cyp. *Demet.* 19: *intra unam domum boni et mali interim continemur;* Pont. *Vit. Cyp.* 11: *christiano totus hic mundus una domus est* (on parallels in the *Octavius* with Pontius' *Vita*, see J. Martin, "Die Vita et Passio Cypriani," *Historisches Jahrb. der Görresgesellschaft,* 1919, 674 ff., at 680). Cf. Sen. *Ep.* 95.47: *non quaerit ministros Deus. Quidni? Ipse humano generi ministrat, ubique et omnibus praesto est.*

[553] See 32.9 and n. 549 above.

[554] The objection of 10.4 (where see nn. 133, 134) is now dealt with. Octavius draws on some of the most obvious points of the very considerable body of *Adversus Judaeos* literature written in the early Church: on this literature see A. B. Hulen, "The 'Dialogues with the Jews' as Sources for the Early Jewish Argument against Christianity," *Journ. Bib. Lit.* 51 (1932) 58 ff.; A. L. Williams, *Adversus Judaeos* (Cambridge 1935); and M. Simon, *Verus Israel* (Paris 1948) 166 ff. (Direct literary evidence for Jewish attacks and rejoinders is curiously scanty.) The attitude towards the Jews is standard; the reasonably sympathetic treatment given to that race in, e.g., Arist. *Apol.* is exceptional in the Christian apologetic tradition (heavily emphasized by G. C. O'Ceallaigh, "Marcianus Aristides, on the Worship of God," HTR 51 [1958] 227 ff.).

[555] There may be a slight lacuna in the text here. For discussion, B. Kytzler, "Notae Minucianae," *Traditio* 22 (1966) 419 ff., at 429 ff.

[556] Octavius has carefully denied a necessary connection between a nation's religious piety and its prosperity in chap. 25. He now, however, reverts to that hardy commonplace, for which see n. 82, and consult in particular K. Büchner, "Drei Beobachtungen zu Minucius Felix," *Hermes* 82 (1954) 231 ff., at 234 ff. (comparing especially Sall. *Cat.* 53.3). The historical allusion appears to be to Exod. 14 (the passage through the Red Sea) rather than to Jos. 10.11 ff. as suggested by Waltzing: there the details do not all apply.

[557] *scripta eorum relege:* a studiously vague reference to Jewish literature (i.e. the Bible). The only other possible references in the *Octavius* to the Bible are in 34.5: *de divinis praedicationibus prophetarum,* and 35.1: *de oraculis prophetarum,* which are even more vague. On the significance of such reticence, see Intro. p. 24 ff. and cf. Arnob. 3.12.

[558] The MSS read "or if you would rather Roman authors, get hold of the works of Flavius Josephus (I omit ancient writers) or those of Antonius Julianus," but the order is usually (but possibly unnecessarily) transposed on the grounds that Josephus was both a Jew and a Greek and Aramaic writer (he was, however, a Roman citizen). See W. A. Baehrens, PhW 44 (1924) 735 f.; E. Norden, "Josephus und Tacitus über Jesus Christus und eine messianische Prophetie," *Kleine Schriften zum klassischen Altertum* (Berlin 1966) 241 ff., esp. 272 ff.

Josephus, born 37 A.D. and author of the *Jewish Antiquities*, the *Jewish War*, the *Contra Apionem*, etc., is frequently cited and exploited by the Christian Apologists (e.g., Theoph. *Ad Autol.* 3.20 ff.; [Just] *Cohort.* 9, 10, 13; Orig. *C.Cels.* 1.16, 4.11; Tert. *Apol.* 19.6, etc.). See R. J. H. Shutt, *Studies in Josephus* (London 1961), and G. A. Williamson, *The World of Josephus* (London 1964). On the Latin Josephus, see F. Blatt, *The Latin Josephus* 1 (Copenhagen 1958) 12 ff.

This Antonius Julianus (PIR² A 843) is something of a literary enigma: there was a procurator of Judaea at the time of the war in A.D. 70 of that name (PIR² A 846: Joseph. *Bell. Jud.* 6.238). He has been frequently, and not unreasonably, identified with the authority which M.F. cites. It will be observed that he thus apparently gives a rather Hebraic interpretation of Jewish history —but the Roman historians were prone to correlate decline in morals with decline in empire; he might, however, be referring to a reportage of what the Jews themselves said on the vagaries and vicissitudes of their own history (cf. *Orac. Sibyl.* 4.115 ff.— the disaster of 70, the Jews claimed, was due to the folly of certain Jews themselves). Many have (perhaps unwisely) conjectured further that because of the casual nature of the reference in M.F. (Ant. Jul. was, therefore, a reasonably well-known authority) the writings of Antonius Julianus were an important source for Tacitus' *Histories;* see H. Bardon, *La littérature latine inconnue* 2 (Paris 1956) 205 f. and works there cited; A. M. A. Hospers-Jansen, *Tacitus over de Joden, Hist. 5.2–13* (Groningen 1949) 172 ff. (with a summary in English, 202 ff.); and for a possible fragment embedded in Sulp. Sev. *Chron.* 2.30.6 f., see H. Montefiore, "Sulpicius Severus and Titus' Council of War," *Hist.* 11 (1962) 156–70.

Besides Octavius' authority, we know of another literary Antonius Julianus, a rhetorician and a Roman contemporary of

Aulus Gellius, frequently mentioned by the latter (*Noctes Atticae* 1.4.1 ff., 9.1.2 ff., 9.15.1 ff., 15.1.1 ff., etc., and PIR² A 844). But there is no information to lead us to presume that he ever wrote on the Jews (see Bardon, *op. cit.* 2.192 f.).

For all we know, however, there may be three distinct persons called Antonius Julianus. That is the cautious attitude adopted by the authors of PIR² (A 843, 4, 6), and the conclusion of E. Hertlein, "Antonius Julianus, ein römischer Geschichtschreiber?" *Philol.* 77 (1921) 174 ff.

⁵⁵⁹ In 10.5.

⁵⁶⁰ *disciplina.* For a discussion of the significance of this word, and for references to other discussions, see P. G. van der Nat, "Tertulliana II," VC 18 (1964) 129 ff., at 134 ff. The image of (military) desertion to designate moral failure is common, e.g., Tert. *Scorp.* 4.4 f.; Cyp. *Ep.* 30.6.3, and cf. chaps. 35.6, 36.8, 37.3 below.

⁵⁶¹ See 11.1 for the objection and nn. 137–8 for the Christian doctrine.

⁵⁶² Note the theme dissociating oneself from, and associating one's opponent with, common ignorance; for this manoeuvre see n. 22 above. Octavius proceeds to appeal to the support of three (a rhetorically proper number) philosophical schools: Stoic, Epicurean, and Platonic. The rhythm of the passage suggests that Beaujeu *ad loc.* is probably incorrect in declaring that M.F. distinguishes "entre l'annonce biblique d'un incendie soudain et l'hypothèse stoïcienne d'un assèchement progressif, développée dans le § suivant." To draw any such distinction was hardly to his purpose. The defective text is discussed by E. Heikel, "Adversaria in Minucii Felicis Octavium," *Eranos* 2 (1923) 27 ff., and K. Abel, "Minucius Felix: Octavius: Das Textproblem," RhM 110 (1967) 248 ff., at 277 ff; some reference to dessication seems to be the most appropriate addition.

⁵⁶³ For these philosophical commonplaces, see 24.3 and n. 352.

⁵⁶⁴ *Stoicis constans opinio est.* It certainly was a much publicized view in the Stoic tradition that the world was a sort of cosmic *perpetuum mobile*, subject to a periodic cycle of floods and conflagrations, *exugrosis* and *ekpurosis*, a new cosmos emerging similar to the present one after each cataclysm. But it was not by any means a universal view (as here claimed) of Stoicism: Zeno of Tarsus (SVF 3.209 no. 5) and Diogenes of Babylon (Philo *De aet. mund.* 76 f.) were sceptical, Panaetius (Cic. *De nat. deor.*

2.118; Philo. *loc. cit.*) was inclined to doubt, Boethus of Sidon (Philo *loc. cit.*) abandoned the doctrine. Indeed, by the mid-second century it had generally been dropped; see A. H. Armstrong, *An Introduction to Ancient Philosophy* (2nd ed. London 1949) 122 ff. (on the doctrine), 142 f. (on its history); Pohlenz 1.79 f., 2.45 ff. The uncertain and much emended text, closely related to Cic. *De nat. deor.* 2.118, 3.37, may be misleading here; it reads very clumsily.

For the appeal to the Stoic theory (often including criticism of differences from the Christian doctrine of the final conflagration), cf. Orig. *C.Cels.* 4.67 f., 5.20, 6.71, 8.72; Athenag. *Leg.* 19, 22; Just. *Apol.* 1.20, *Apol.* 2.7; Arnob. 2.9; and (emphasizing the Christian view of the uniqueness of the occasion) Tat. *Or.* 6, 25. Other passages cited by Spanneut 92 f., 358 f.

[565] The balance and equilibrium in nature (emphasized in the Stoic world-picture) was destroyed by the gradual exhaustion of moisture which provided the nourishment of the heavenly bodies. For the idea of their nourishment derived ultimately from salt and fresh waters, see Cic. *De nat. deor.* 2.40: *cum sol igneus sit Oceanique alatur umoribus,* and Pease's nn. *ad loc.,* 2.83, 2.118, 3.37; for the notion of progressive dessication, Pease on Cic. *De nat. deor.* 2.118 (*umore consumpto*).

[566] E.g., Lucr. 5.380 ff. with Bailey's nn. *ad loc.*

[567] A (rather inaccurate) reference to Plat. *Tim.* 22C (where among the innumerable ways men have been and will be destroyed, flood and fire are singled out). Clem. *Strom.* 5.1.9.5 ff. quotes the passage for the same purpose, but with explanatory comment. Arnob. 1.8 also refers to Plato's "dread floods and world-wide conflagrations"; Orig. *C.Cels.* 4.40 uses the passage in discussing the Deluge.

[568] The famous passages of Plat. *Tim.* 32C, 41A-B, the precise interpretation of which was much disputed by later Platonists: was the world, though eternal, dependent upon God, or was it merely eternal by the will of God? See PW 5A 1 (1934) *s.v.* Taurus 63–66 (K. Praechter). These *Timaeus* passages were much exploited by Christian writers, e.g., Athenag. *Leg.* 6; Clem. *Strom.* 5.14.102.1; Just. *Dial.* 5; [Just.] *Cohort.* 23.

[569] Octavius seems careful not to attribute to Plato any adherence to the Christian dogma of *creatio ex nihilo,* a line of thought alien to the classical philosophical mind. For discussions on this difference, see R. Walzer, *Galen on Jews and Christians*

(Oxford 1949) 26 ff.; A. A. T. Ehrhardt, *The Framework of the N.T. Stories* (Manchester 1964) 200 ff.; H. Chadwick, *Early Christian Thought and the Classical Tradition* (Oxford 1966) 46 ff.

⁵⁷⁰ This argument from priority and plagiarism is certainly a very standard one of the Jewish and Christian apologetic tradition, but one wonders what a pagan reader, unacquainted with this line of thought, would have made of the extremely elliptical (and totally unsubstantiated) formulation of the argument here. Tert. *Apol.* 46.18 ff. has, on the other hand, an open and coherent discussion on the same subject (there are stylistic parallels in *Apol.* 46.18, 47.3, 47.14); this points towards the priority of Tertullian; cf. J. van Wageningen, "Minucius Felix et Tertullianus," *Mnem.* 51 (1923) 223 ff., at 227 f.; Axelson 94. For the general argument, cf. Athenag. *Leg.* 24; Theop. *Ad Autol.* 2.37; Tat. *Or.* 40; Just. *Apol.* 1.44; Hermias *Irris.* 7; Tert. *De an.* 2.3 ff. (and Waszink's nn. on 2.4); Orig. *C.Cels.* 4.36, 6.7, 6.19, 6.47; for Clement see A. Beltrami, "Clemente Alessandrino nell'Ottavio di M. Minucio Felice," RFIC 48 (1920) 239 ff., at 254: examples, *Strom.* 1.17. 87.1 f., 6.7.57.2 f.; and see, generally, Intro. p. 15, and RAC *s.v.* Erfinder II, 1247 ff. (K. Thraede). Of course, two could easily play at the same game, and Celsus. *ap.* Orig. *C.Cels.* 4.11 accuses Christians of plagiarizing the doctrine of periodic conflagrations and floods. M.F.'s only concession to the considerable divergences between these pagan philosophical views on some cataclysmic conflagration and the Christian eschatological doctrine seems to be found in the assertion that these philosophers are reproducing only *interpolata veritas*, garbled truth. To underline not dissimilarities but similarities was his intention. The extremely vague phraseology seems deliberate (see 33.4 above and n. 557 and 35.1 below).

⁵⁷¹ The topic of 11.2 ff. (on the resurrection) is now broached. It was fairly standard apologetic practice to appeal to the doctrine of metempsychosis, or transmigration of the soul, as evidence of pagan philosophical belief in the survival of at least the soul after death; e.g., [Just.] *Cohort.* 27 (Plato); Just. *Resur. fr.* 10 (Plato and Pythagoras); Theoph. *Ad Autol.* 3.7 (Plato and Pythagoras censured for this teaching of theirs); Athenag. *Leg.* 36 (Plato and Pythagoras); Arnob. 2.13 (Plato); Tert. *Apol.* 48.1 (Pythagoras); Tert. *De an.* 28.1 (Plato and Pythagoras); Hermias *Irris.* 2 (strong criticism of the pagan doctrine), and so on. Pythagoras (on

whom see n. 243) notoriously traced his own soul's descent; it
included a sojourn in a peacock (see O. Skutsch, "Notes on
Metempsychosis," CP 54 [1959] 114 ff.; Tert. *De an.* 33.8 and
Waszink's n. *ad loc.*). He is not always credited with being the
pioneer of this doctrine in Greek philosophy; his teacher Phere-
cydes is sometimes made the originator: Cic. *Tusc. disp.* 1.38;
Tat. *Or.* 25; cf. Tert. *De an.* 28.4. For Plato's exposition of his
doctrine, see, e.g., *Phaed.* 81E ff.; *Repub.* 620D, *Tim.* 42C.
Celsus accused the Christians (*C.Cels.* 7.32) of deriving their
teaching from the doctrine of metempsychosis; cf. n. 570 above.

[572] Some later Platonists added plants (e.g., Plotinus *Enn.* 3.4.2)
as well, though in fact the majority of Neoplatonists rejected or
allegorized animal reincarnation (e.g., Porphyry *ap.* Aug. *De civ.
Dei* 10.30); see Chadwick, *Early Christian Thought and the
Classical Tradition* 167 n. 85. Some of the Church Fathers were
charged with teaching the transmigration of souls, e.g., Clement
of Alexandria (doubtfully, see Chadwick, *op. cit.* 49) and Origen,
who was, of course, especially suspect for his adventurous specula-
tions on the soul (Chadwick 114, 150 f.; observe the criticism of
the doctrine of transmigration in *C.Cels.* 3.75, 4.83). Note Irenaeus
Adv. haer. 1.25.4 (MG 7.682 f.): Carpocratians added a belief in
metempsychosis to their enormities.

[573] *mimi convicio digna ista sententia est.* This provides perhaps
the most persuasive single instance for the priority of Tertullian
(the reading of P. *mimico vitio = mimi convicio* causes no difficulty; false divisions in the MS are by no means infrequent: see,
for a list, J.-P. Waltzing, "Le codex Parisinus 1661," *Musée belge*
11 [1907] 319 ff., at 320). For Tert. *Apol.* 48.1 has *nominatim* and
in paraphrase the source apparently referred to: *si qui philosophus
adfirmet, ut ait Laberius de sententia Pythagorae, hominem fieri
ex mulo, colubram ex muliere. . . .* See Axelson 94 ff. and M.
Bonaria, *Romani mimi* (Rome 1965) 43 and 108 f. This Laberius
was a *mimographus* of the late Republic (for *testimonia* see M.
Bonaria, *Mimorum Romanorum fragmenta,* fasc. 11 [Genoa
1956] nos. 338–54; he omits, however, these references in Tert.
and M.F.–and consult F. Giancotti, *Mimo e gnome: Studi su
Decimo Laberio e Publilio Siro* [Florence 1967] 43 ff.), quoted or
referred to by both Aulus Gellius (frequently, e.g., *Noctes Atticae*
8.15, 10.17.2 ff.; 17.14.1) and Fronto, Naber 19, 62, 156. Fragments
of Laberius confirm his philosophical interests: they refer to
Democritus (*Restio* 72 ff.), the Cynics (*Compitalia* 36) and again

NOTES ON PAGES 115–116

to Pythagoras (*Cancer* 17); he was not alone in these interests—for other references in Roman drama to the afterlife, see P. R. Coleman-Norton, "Philosophical Aspects of Early Roman Drama," CP 31 (1936) 320 ff., at 328 f. Pythagorean views (especially their vegetarianism) came in for much banter also in the earlier Middle and New Comedy of the Greek stage (see, generally, T. B. L. Webster, *Studies in Later Greek Comedy* [Manchester 1953] 50 ff. esp. 53, 110 ff.). Note, too, the burlesque made of the connected descent of Pythagoras to Hades by Hermippus of Smyrna *ap.* Diog. Laer. 8.41. It was a fit subject for comedy, Schol. *ad* Soph. *Electra* 62.

[574] The punch line is rephrased from 19.15; and cf. 34.5. Octavius now apparently dismisses the question of the survival of the *soul* after death—pagan philosophers agree with this doctrine up to a point. The following sections are concerned with the much more controversial issue, the resurrection of the body. Many have failed to observe the switch in subject matter in §9 and have, accordingly, but not unreasonably, credited M.F. with a belief in the corporeality and mortality of the soul (e.g., G. E. McCracken, *Arnobius of Sicca: The Case against the Pagans* [ACW 7; London 1949] 315 n. 106; W. Reeves in his translation [London 1717] 29 f. hotly defends M.F. against such a charge, emphasizing the *ad hominem* nature of his present arguments). The doctrine of the soul was certainly by no means settled at this stage, and many of the Apologists are incautious in some of their formulations (e.g., Theoph. *Ad Autol.* 1.7, Tat. *Or.* 13, Just. *Dial.* 5 f. all imply the soul may be susceptible of death; cf. Arnob. 2.14 ff., and Euseb. *H.E.* 6.37 [Origen's refutation of the heresy of the temporary death of the soul]): on these variable opinions, see F. Refoulé, "Immortalité de l'âme et résurrection de la chair," *Rev. de l'hist. des relig.* 163 (1963) 11–52; DTC 1A (1903) Ame 111: doctrines des trois premiers siècles 977–1001 (J. Bainvel). The language of M.F. suffers from a similar lack of precision, especially in the use of the ambiguous *nihil*.

[575] This argument from the omnipotence of God is frequently appealed to by the Apologists in defending the doctrine of the bodily resurrection. For a collection of references, see H. Chadwick, "Origen, Celsus and the Resurrection of the Body," HTR 41 (1948) 83 ff., at 84 ff. Unqualified formulations of the argument (for which the Stoics came under heavy fire, Cic. *De nat. deor.* 3.92) caused Origen much embarrassment (*C.Cels.* 5.14,

5.23). The present passage bears a very close resemblance to Tert. *Apol.* 48.5 f. (specifically on the body; see, on the relationship, R. Heinze, PhW 45 [1925] 956 ff., at 960 ff., and Axelson 110 ff.). The odd subsidiary argument of the ease of repeating a task which has been done before is repeated in Tert. *De resur. mort.* 11.10.

[576] M.F. now seems to qualify the bald "nothingness" in which, following Tertullian, he has left man's body between death and resurrection: his *elementa* are, in fact, preserved by God; cf. Just. *Resur.* 6 (with the additional analogy of jeweller and the pieces of a mosaic); Tat. *Or.* 6; Athenag. *Resur.* 2 ff. For other references on this argument, see Chadwick, *art. cit.* in previous n., at 88 ff. The assimilation of these *elementa* into other bodies exercised much ingenuity (Athenag. *Resur.* 4; Tat. *Or.* 6; Tert. *De resur. mort.* 4.3 ff.; a difficulty exploited by Porphyry *fr.* 94 Harnack). The formulation of Tat. *Or.* 6 (and Athenag. *Resur.* 8) is very close, on the interpretation of which see G. F. Hawthorne, "Tatian and His Discourse to the Greeks," HTR 57 (1964) 161 ff., at 173 f., against R. M. Grant, "The Heresy of Tatian," JTS 5 (1954) 62 ff., at 65. The rhetorical catalogue of ways in which the body may be dispersed matches that of 11.4 (on which see n. 144 and my article "The Date of the Oration of Tatian," HTR 60 [1967] 123 f.).—One wonders whether the pagan reader would have felt satisfied that the queries raised by Caecilius in 11.7 had all been really answered.

[577] On the Christian custom of burial, see n. 143. Note the careful appeal to antique usage for justification, a rhetorically effective, if incomplete, explanation of the Christian practice. On the antiquity of inhumation among the Romans see Pliny *N.H.* 7.187: *ipsum cremare apud Romanos non fuit veteris instituti; terra condebantur;* but in fact, as early as the Laws of the Twelve Tables, incineration was allowed (*Tab.* X. *Legg.* 1,2,10,11). Note also the (?)contemporary prize rhetorical composition by the pagan orator Apollonius of Athens against incineration, Philos. *Vit. Soph.* 2.20.601 f.

[578] The poetic appeal to the testimony of nature for the pattern of the resurrection to come was a favorite theme on this topic; cf. 1 *Clem.* 24 (day, night, seeds); Theoph. *Ad Autol.* 1.13 (seasons, days, seeds, fruits, trees, moon, the recovery of the sick), 2.14 f. (moon, seeds); Tert. *De resur. mort.* 12 (day, stars, moon, seasons), *Apol.* 48.7 f. (light and darkness, stars, seasons, fruit,

seeds), etc. The allegory of the seeds is of course Pauline (1 Cor. 15.35–38), though the idea was proverbial (cf. Lucr. 1.263 f.: *nec ullam / rem gigni (natura) patitur, nisi morte adiuta aliena*. Octavius here uses the Christianism *resurrectio*, one of the very few in the *Dialogue*.

[579] Augustine criticizes this rhetorically effective (but superficial) analogy of the renewed life of spring, *Serm.* 361.11 (ML 39.1604): *sed potest mihi aliquis dicere minus diligenter inspiciens mutationes instaurationesque rerum: illa folia putruerunt, nova nascuntur*. For a variation on this analogy, cf. Herm. *Sim.* 3.3: Just as the trees in winter . . . are alike, so are the righteous and the sinners . . . in this world etc.; *Sim.* 4.2: These trees which are budding are the righteous . . . for the world to come is summer for the righteous, winter for sinners. Observe that *in saeculo* ("in this world"), repeated in the following section, seems to have acquired something of its Christian sense ("in this material world").

[580] This appears to be a reply to 11.8, Caecilius' appeal for a substantiating example of the bodily resurrection. Octavius, significantly and predictably, eschews citing that central event of Christianity, the historical fact of Christ's resurrection.

[581] This observation is normally introduced as part of a supporting argument for the moral necessity of the resurrection; it is necessary in order to ensure the fair distribution of justice (cf. Tert. *Apol.* 48.4, *De resur. mort.* 34.1 ff.; Just. *Apol.* 1.18; Athenag. *Resur.* 2, 18, 20 ff.). This argument, however, M.F. does not formulate directly, but he employs instead the observation to form a transition to the allied topic of hell, which follows. The phrase *nihil se esse post mortem*, implying, from the context, complete annihilation, shows how careless (and thus misleading) was the phraseology of §9 *nihil esse post obitum*, where such total annihilation is denied.

[582] Freedom of will and action is insisted upon, relentlessly, by the Apologists: Orig. *C.Cels.* 4.3, 4.70, 5.21; Theoph. *Ad Autol.* 2.27; Just. *Apol.* 1.28, 43, *Apol.* 2.7, *Dial.* 141; Tat. *Or.* 7; Arnob. 2.64, etc. See below chap. 36.1 f., above 11.6 (for a denial); for further references, W. Telfer, "AUTEXOUSIA," JTS n.s. 8 (1957) 123 ff.; Spanneut 235–41.

[583] The patience of God (cf. 2 Peter 3.9) involving justice slow but sure ("the mills of God") was a proverbial pagan notion: Sext. Emp. *adv. Math.* 1.287; Livy 3.56.7; Eurip. *Bacchae*

883 (with other references in the notes of E. R. Dodds [Oxford 1944] *ad loc.*); Tibull. 1.9.4; Hor. *Od.* 3.2.31 f.; Plutarch's treatise on the topic *de sera numinis vindicta* (esp. 549D f.); Dionysius *fr.* 5 (Nauck) quoted by Theoph. *Ad Autol.* 2.37; Orig. *C.Cels.* 8.40, etc.

584 The question to be discussed, the *poena sempiterna*, has been raised in 11.5. For the appeal to poets etc., see nn. 228, 230. Arnob. 2.14 quotes Plat. *Phaed.* 112A ff. (cf. Just. *Apol.* 1.8; Athenag. *Leg.* 12); Theoph. *Ad Autol.* 2.37 quotes Aeschylus, Pindar, Euripides, Archilochus, Dionysius, Simonides, Sophocles on the subject: in *Ad Autol.* 1.14 he observes the derivative nature of the teaching of the "poets and philosophers" on the subject, as does Tert. *Apol.* 47.12 ff. See further E. Norden, "Zu Minucius Felix 35.1," *Kleine Schriften zum klassischen Altertum* (Berlin 1966) 216 f.; P. Courcelle, "Les pères de l'église devant les enfers virgiliens," *Archiv. d'hist. doct. et litt. du moyen âge* 22 (1955) 5 ff., at 25, and *idem*, "Interprétations néo-platonisantes du livre vi de l'Énéide," *Fondation Hardt: Entretiens sur l'antiquité classique* 3 (1955) 95 ff., at 102 ff.

585 That is, Pyriphlegethon, the fiery stream of Hades (the other two waterways being Acheron and Cocytus). According to Verg. *Aen.* 6.439 (*metri gratia?*) it is the Styx which makes nine encircling courses (*novies Styx interfusa coercet*); contrast Plat. *Phaed.* 113A f. See A. Setaioli, "Noviens Styx interfusa," *Atene e Roma* 14 (1969) 9 ff., esp. 14. For early Greek descriptions of hell, see M. P. Nilsson, *Greek Popular Religion* (New York 1940) 116 ff.; on the river of fire used for punishment, Cumont, *Lux perpetua* 452 f.; and for an exhaustive study of the relationship between Christian doctrine and classical views of Hades, A. Dieterich, *Nekyia: Beiträge zur Erklärung der neuentdekten Petrusapokalypse* (Leipzig 1893) *passim*, esp. 163 ff.

586 *et daemonum indiciis et de oraculis prophetarum cognita.* Such a statement appears to presuppose a theory, as in Theoph. *Ad Autol.* 2.5 f., that pagan poets are usually inspired by demons (on the unexplained demons' sources of information, see n. 436). Holden and Waltzing, however, *ad loc.*, see here an allusion to information divulged under stress of exorcism (cf. chap. 27.5 ff.), but that seems to be an inappropriate source of knowledge for *pagan* poets etc. (Exorcism is a possible allusion, perhaps, if one construes "learnt [according to the evidence of demons] even from the oracles of the prophets.") A hendiadys, "the evi-

dence of demons supplied in the oracles of prophets" (cf. 26.5 f.), might also be possible, but to construe as such seems strained here.

587 A vague phrase: it is possible that such information as *Orac. Sibyl.* 2.294 ff. (so Dieterich, *op. cit.* 160) or *Orac. Sibyl. fr.* 3 Geffcken (quoted by Theoph. *Ad Autol.* 2.36) is intended. Or M.F. may be elliptically alluding to Scripture (cf. the language of 34.5) and the plagiarism by pagans and/or demons of the doctrine of hell which it contains (as in Theoph. *Ad Autol.* 1.14; Tert. *Apol.* 47.14). See Axelson 96 f. on this (unsatisfactorily borrowed, or at least constructed) passage. The interpretation "which they have learnt from the information of demons and we have learnt from the oracles of the prophets" (i.e., Scripture) is hardly possible.

588 Not all Christians insisted on the eternity of the fires of punishment: they were purifying and, therefore, not everlasting according to Orig. *De princ. fr.* 25 (GCS Origen 5.182 f.), cf. *C.Cels.* 5.16; cf. Gregory of Nyssa (MG 44.1313A).

589 E.g., Hom. *Il.* 14.271, *Od.* 5.185 f.; Verg. *Aen.* 6.323 f. and esp. 9.104 ff. (echoed here): *dixerat: idque ratum Stygii per flumina fratris, / per pice torrentes atraque voragine ripas/ annuit.*

590 Why Jupiter qua demon (27.5 ff.) is prescient and so foredoomed is left unexplained. The punishment of his *cultores* (i.e., pagans) is elaborated below (§§4ff.). Tert. *Apol.* 23.14 is more satisfactory on this point (Axelson 97). For the doctrine of the punishment of demons, cf. Just. *Apol.* 1.18; Tat. *Or.* 14, etc.

591 *ignis sapiens.* Sir David Dalrymple, Translator's Preface xii, remarks that this "is a phrase altogether extravagant"; it was, however, a philosophical cliché (esp. Stoic.); see Aug. *De civ. Dei* 8.5: *Stoici ignem . . . et viventem et sapientem et mundi fabricatorem . . . putaverunt;* and Cic. *De nat. deor.* 2.40 f. for a brief exposé of the role the Stoics assigned to "fire"; cf. Plotinus *Ennead.* 4.7.4 πῦρ νοερόν; the phrase was freely used by Christians, e.g., Clem. *Strom.* 7.6.34.4 πῦρ . . . φρόνιμον, *Prot.* 4.53.3 πῦρ σωφρονοῦν; Orig. *Hom. in Ezech.* 1.3 (GCS Origen 8.324): *ignis iste . . . sapiens;* Tert. *Scorp.* 3: *sapiens ignis,* thus giving philosophical tone to their doctrines. For further parallels, V. Bulhart, "Ignis sapiens," SE 13 (1962) 60 f., and W. C. van Unnik, "The *Wise Fire* in a Gnostic Eschatological Vision," *Kyriakon: Festschrift Johannes Quasten* (Münster 1970) 277–288.

592 Such punishment matches that of the eagle and Prometheus' unconsumed liver, or the vulture and that of Tityrus (which

Lact. *Div. inst.* 7.21.5 adduces for comparison), in pagan mythology. The explanatory analogies which follow also appear (in
expanded and clearer form) in Tert. *Apol.* 48.14 f., but there the
(nonconsuming) thunderbolt and the (unspent) volcanic flames
figure as examples (rather than analogies) of the mysterious fires
of eternity. (For a discussion, Axelson 112 ff.; this is a passage
which argues for the priority of Tertullian.)

593 Tert. *Apol.* 48.14 has more specifically *et qui de caelo tangi-
tur, salvus est, ut nullo iam igni decinerescat,* i.e., a person struck
by lightning cannot be turned to ashes. Behind this fanciful idea
lies the common attitude that lightning implies a visitation from
God (cf. Aesculapius in chap. 22.7); hence the body of the person so struck was thought to remain incorruptible, dogs and
birds of prey dare not touch it (Plut. *Quaes. conv.* 4.2.3, 665D)
and no attempt may be made to have it cremated; some thought,
however, that it ought to be buried in the place just where the
lightning struck it, e.g., Pliny *N.H.* 2.54.145: *hominem ita exani-
matum cremari fas non est, condi terra religio tradidit;* [Quint.]
Decl. 274: (*Tyrannus fulminatus*) *quo quis fulmine ictus fuerit,
eodem sepeliatur* (120.24 f. Ritter); others thought that, being
incorruptible, it should be left unburied (Plut., *op. cit.* 4.2.3.665C).
See also E. Rohde, *Psyche*8 (London 1925) *Ap.* 1, 581 f.; H.
Usener, "Keraunos," RhM 60 (1905) 1 ff., at 8 ff.

594 On Aetna in eruption, see *Aetna, passim;* on Vesuvius the
locus classicus is Pliny *Epp.* 6.16, 6.20. Attempts to find here an
allusion to the eruption of Vesuvius of 203 A.D. are clearly nugatory (Dio 76.2); Dio 66.21 f. attests to its continuous volcanic
activity. On inexhaustible volcanoes cf. Tert. *De paenit.* 12.3:
*dissiliunt superbissimi montes ignis intrinsecus feti et–quod nobis
iudicii perpetuitatem probat–cum dissiliant, cum devorentur,
numquam tamen finiuntur.* A similar description of *quidam
notissimi Siciliae montes* in Aug. *De civ. Dei* 21.4; and cf. *Acta
Pionii* 4 (Ruinart 190) on the same subject of hell: *conferte
quoque Lyciae et diversarum insularum ignem ex infimis terrae
visceribus effluentem* etc.

595 Sc., as the fires of the thunderbolts.

596 Sc., as the fires of the volcanoes.

597 Octavius has now to justify eternal bliss predicted for
Christians *ut bonis,* eternal punishment for the rest of mankind
ut iniustis, as was the objection raised in 11.5. The reply has two
points: (a) ignorance of God is sufficient grounds for such pun-

ishment, but (b) anyway, Christians are so much morally superior
to the rest of mankind.

The notion of the wickedness of not acknowledging God was
touched upon in 17.2, where see n. 202 for parallels; and see also
on the theme E. Norden, *Agnostos Theos* (Leipzig 1913) 73 ff.;
RAC 1 (1950) *s.v.* Agnoia (Agnosia) 186–88 (L. Cerfaux). The
assumption that ignorance is culpable and implies moral turpitude
is, of course, thoroughly Platonic; cf. n. 22, Plat. *Theaetet.* 176C:
"For knowledge of this [the perfection of God] is wisdom and
true virtue, ignorance of it is stupidity and manifest wickedness";
Corp. Hermet. ed. Nock-Festugière 11.21: "the supreme evil is
ignorance of the divine" (a natural commonplace in Gnostic
writings). For the punishment of such ignorance, cf. Rom. 1.20
f.; 2 Thess. 1.8: *in flamma ignis dantis vindictam iis qui non
noverunt Deum;* Just. *Apol.* 1.19; Arist. *Apol.* 17; Clem. *Protrep.*
10.89.3 ff.; Tert. *De paenit.* 5.4: *cum etiam ignorantes dominum
nulla exceptio tueatur a poena.*

⁵⁹⁸ This clause *quamvis in nonnullis disciplina nostra minor est*
is vague and ambiguous in the extreme, and has accordingly enticed a bewildering variety of interpretations (e.g., "in some cases
our training falls short of yours"; "though our way of life is
regarded by many as inferior"; "though we have not so many
laws nor so many judges to restrain us"), but the context clearly
demands the admission that even second-grade Christians live
more virtuously than pagans; as Heraldus (in ed. 1613) paraphrased: *id est, quamvis nostrorum nonnulli disciplinam nostram
minus curiose observant.* For such a point, cf. Orig. *C.Cels.* 3.30;
Cyp. *Ep.* 54.3.1: *etsi videntur in ecclesia esse zizania;* and for the
language, cf. Tert. *Apol.* 46.17: *sed dicet aliquis etiam de nostris
excedere quosdam a regula disciplinae.*

On the (frequent) *topos* contrasting Christian and pagan morals,
cf. 28.10 f., 31.4 f., 38.5 f. and nn. *ad loca.*

⁵⁹⁹ Cf. 31.5 above and Tert. *Apol.* 46.11: *christianus uxori suae
soli masculus nascitur* (for the relationship with Tert. in this and
the following section, see Axelson 114 f.); Clem. *Paed.* 2.10.83.1
ff.

⁶⁰⁰ By no means, however, an exclusively Christian notion (but
cf. Matt. 5.28; Just. *Apol.* 1.15; Theoph. *Ad Autol.* 3.13; Athenag.
Leg. 31,32,33, etc.); the idea of the wickedness of thoughts as
well as their manifestation in action is implied in Sayings attributed
to Pittacus by Aelius Theon, *Rhet. Gr.* 2.97.203 (Spengel), to

Thales by Valerius Maximus 7.2.E.8, to the orator Pytheas by
Ael. *V.H.* 14.28: "not only he who has done wrong is wicked,
but also he who has planned to do wrong"; cf. Sen. *Dial.* 2.7.4:
*omnia scelera etiam ante effectum operis, quantum culpae satis
est, perfecta sunt;* Apul. *Flor.* 20: *etiam cogitata scelera non
perfecta adhuc vindicantur, cruenta mente, pura manu;* Juv. *Sat.*
13.209 f.: *nam scelus intra se tacitum cogitat ullum, / facti crimen
habet* (and see Mayor's n. *ad. loc.* for further examples).

⁶⁰¹ Cf. Sen. *fr.* 14 Haase (*ap.* Lact. *Div. inst.* 6.24.16): *custos te
tuus* (= *conscientia*) *sequitur . . . haeret hic quo carere numquam potes . . . quid tibi prodest non habere conscium habenti
conscientiam;* Lucr. 3.1068 ff. on the theme that man cannot
escape from himself; Hor. *Ep.* 1.11.27: *caelum, non animum,
mutant qui trans mare currunt* etc.; and cf. the descriptions of
protecting "demons" referred to in nn. 425–26.

⁶⁰² Closely parallel in thought to Tert. *Apol.* 44.3: *de vestris
semper aestuat carcer . . . nemo illic christianus nisi plane tantum
christianus, aut si et aliud, iam non christianus.* For the notion that
bad Christians are not real Christians at all, cf. Just. *Apol.* 1.16,
Athenag. *Leg.* 2; Orig. *C.Cels.* 4.25; in Just. *Dial.* 35 they are
identified with heretics and schismatics. No chronological information may be safely drawn from this observation; the pointed
phrase could well have been made for literary effect, irrespective
of the contemporary facts of history, and we know that Christians, even under "good" (i.e., nonpersecuting) emperors, might
continue the sentences imposed upon them in another's reign (cf.
under Commodus: Hippol. *Philos.* 9.12.10 ff. [GCS Hippolytus
3.247 f.]).

⁶⁰³ Caecilius had raised the argument that Christians really
believe in fate but in a disguised form (11.5 f., where see nn. 147–
48), and that in their choice of Christianity they are not, therefore, free agents. The early Apologists are vigorous in their denial
of the role of an improvident Fate: Just. *Apol.* 1.43 f., *Apol.* 2.7;
Tat. *Or.* 7 ff.; Athenag. *Leg.* 24 f.; Orig. *C.Cels.* 2.20; Arnob.
7.10.

⁶⁰⁴ See n. 582 above.

⁶⁰⁵ For the etymological connexion (commonly) drawn between
fatum and *fari* ("destiny" . . . "to destine"), cf. Enn. *Scaen.* 59
(Vahlen): *Namque Apollo fatis fandis dementem invitam ciet;*
Varro *De ling. lat.* 6.52: *ab hoc* (sc., *fari*) *tempora quod tum
pueris constituant Parcae fando, dictum fatum et res fatales;* Serv.

ad Verg. *Aen.* 2.54, glossing *fata deum: hoc est "quae dii loquuntur";* Fronto, Naber 233: *Fata a fando appellata aiunt,* etc.

⁶⁰⁶ The solution presented here (a rather inadequate reply, it must be admitted, to the charge of "election") is based on the prescience of God (providence) of our natures (*materia*); it is basically one adopted by some Stoics, cf. Sen. *De provid.* 5.9: *non potest artifex mutare materiam,* and the discussion in Aulus Gellius, *Noctes Atticae* 7.1–2, esp. 7.2.6 ff.: *ingenia tamen ipsa mentium nostrarum proinde sunt fato obnoxia ut proprietas eorum et ipsa et qualitas* (from Chrysippus' *De providentia*); Orig. *C.Cels.* 2.20 *ad fin.* follows the same line (God's foreknowledge does not interfere with man's free will). The predispositions of our *materia* remain, however, unexplained: Origen felt constrained to fall back on the Platonic concept of pre-existing souls (*Comm. in Matt.* 15.35 and Plat. *Repub.* 617E ff.) to explain their diversity. For further evidence of Origen's explication of the problem, see J. G. Préaux, "A propos du 'De fato'(?) de Minucius Felix," *Latomus* 9 (1950) 395 ff.; his case that M.F. must be drawing on Origen is, however, uncompelling.

⁶⁰⁷ *in nobis non genitura plectitur, sed ingenii natura punitur.* Note the elaborate etymological figure difficult to translate without extreme artificiality. *Genitura* (syn. *nativitas, genesis*) seems to be used here in its technical sense of astral horoscope (see TLL *s.v.* ii A1). Astral fatalism was an almost inescapable topic on this theme *de fato,* particularly at a period when belief in (and fear of) the controlling powers of the seven planets was notably prevalent; cf. Orig. *ap.* Euseb. *P.E.* 6.11.1; Aul. Gellius, *Noctes Atticae* 14.1 (a *dissertatio* of Favorinus against the "Chaldaeans"), and see Mayor's lengthy note on Juv. *Sat.* 14.248. Note the related funerary inscriptions giving the exact life span (down to hours) and, therefore, the astrological span of the deceased (see J. Carcopino, *Aspects mystiques de la Rome païenne* [Paris 1942] 214, 224); and the (contemporary?) grand Severan palace, the Septizonium, orientated and designed so that the emperor sat in a cosmic hall among the planetary gods assuming the role of fate: H. P. L'Orange, *Apotheosis in Ancient Portraiture* (Oslo 1947) 83; PW 11A2 (1923) 1578–86 (Th. Dombart).

The "star of David" and "my hour has not yet come" caused embarrassment to the early Church in this connexion: *mathematici* claimed that Christ's birth and life had in fact depended on the stars: Tert. *De idol.* 9, on which see L. Koep, "Astrologia usque

ad Evangelium concessa (zu Tertullian, De idolatria 9)," *Mullus*,
1964, 198–208; and for evidence of the same problem in Augustine, P. Courcelle, "Propros antichrétiens rapportés par saint
Augustin," RechAug. 1 (1958) 149 ff., at 158 ff.

⁶⁰⁸ *Ac de fato satis, vel si pauca, pro tempore, disputaturi alias
et uberius et plenius.* To dismiss a topic in this way (particularly
a complex one) was standard literary procedure: Cic. *De divin.*
2.19 *sed tamen apud Stoicos de isto fato multa dicuntur, de quo
alias* is close; cf. Arnob. 7.12 (on fate); Lact. *De opif. Dei* 19.7
(on astral fatalism): *sed non est nunc locus de fato disserendi, hoc
dicere satis est;* Orig. *C.Cels.* 4.68 (on the cyclical repetition of
the world), cf. 2.24; Cic. *De nat. deor.* 1.12: *alio loco diligentius;*
1.19: *verum hoc alias,* where see Pease's n., etc. It does not seem
necessary to conclude, therefore, granted this literary convention,
that M.F. should ever have intended to realize his promise, especially as it makes a neat antithesis to Caecilius' *multa ad haec
subpetunt, ni festinet oratio* (11.5) in the section to which this is
the reply. On the putative treatise *De fato* attributed to M.F.,
see Intro. p. 5 and J. G. Préaux, "A propos du 'De fato'(?) de
M.F.," *Latomus* 9 (1950) 395–413. Tertullian did, however, write
a treatise on the same subject (no longer extant), which he
promised in *De an.* 20.5: *nos secundum fidem disserenda suo iam
vovimus titulo* (with Waszink's nn. ad loc.) For the language cf.
also Cyp. *Ep.* 56.30.1: *plura in commune conferre et uberius et
plenius . . . tractare poterimus.*

⁶⁰⁹ The topic was raised in 12.2 ff. (where see nn. 152–53), both
as a social reproach to the Christians and as a proof of the impotence of the Christians' God. Some reply has already been made
in 16.5: poverty really fits men for philosophical contemplation.
The essence of the present reply is that so-called poverty is beneficial and in fact not really an adversity at all, but a testing time
used by God. Note that Octavius does not deny that the majority
of Christians are *pauperes.* G. Quispel, "The Discussion of Judaic
Christianity," VC 22 (1968) 81 ff., at 93 (unpersuasively) sees
here a recollection of the name of *Ebionim*, "the poor."

⁶¹⁰ *Qui Deo dives est.* This phrase is also often interpreted "who
is wealthy in God's eyes," i.e., "who has his treasure in heaven"
(cf. Luke 12.21). For the phrase cf. Cyp. *De hab. virg.* 10: *quae
se divitem saeculo mavult esse quam Christo,* where the same
ambiguity subsists; but in Cyp. *De hab. virg.* 7 *quae Deo dives
est* is followed by *quae locuples in Christo est,* which ought per-

haps to dissolve the ambiguity. On the theme "lacking much but desiring nothing" see Aul. Gellius, *Noctes Atticae* 13.24; Tat. *Or.* 11.

611 A hardy commonplace; cf. Sen. *Ep.* 2.6: *non qui parum habet sed qui plus cupit, pauper est;* the allied theme, the more you have the more you want, is equally common (e.g., Sen. *Ep.* 74.4, 119.6; Aul. Gellius, *Noctes Atticae* 9.8; Ovid *Fasti* 1.212; Juv. *Sat.* 14.139: *crescit amor nummi, quantum ipsa pecunia crevit* (and Mayor's n.); see Otto *Sprichwörter s.v.* avarus, avaritia, *s.v.* pecunia.

612 Cf. Sen. *De provid.* 6.6: *nemo tam pauper vivit quam natus est;* on the many parallels with this treatise of Seneca in this section, see V. Carlier, "Minucius Félix et Sénèque," *Musée belge* 1 (1897) 258 ff., at 285 ff. Cf., too, on bringing nothing into this world, 1 Tim. 6.7, Job 1.21: *nudus egressus sum de utero matris meae, et nudus revertar illuc.*

613 Cf. [Sen.] *De rem. fort.* 10.1: *"Pauper sum." Nihil deest avibus. Pecora in diem vivunt.* Cf. Matt. 6.26 *volatilia caeli,* Luke 12.24 *corvos.* For the insistence on man's central place in the created world, see n. 536. The cento of aphoristic phrases here does not make for an immediately intelligible sequence of thought, but the general connection of ideas seems to be that providence does in fact supply creation's needs, especially those of man, who should be deemed wealthy according as his desires are satisfied. See Axelson 59 f. for the ingredients of this section.

614 For this paradox cf. Val. Max. 4.4 praef.: *omnia nimirum habet qui nihil concupiscit;* cf. Clem. *Strom.* 7.3.18.2: "being utterly rich in desiring nothing"; *Ad Diog.* 5.13: "they (i.e., the Christians) lack all things and possess all things in abundance."

615 For the common metaphor, cf. 16.1 (and n. 183), 16.3, and cf. Sen. *De provid.* 6.2: *Democritus divitias proiecit onus illas bonae mentis existimans;* Sen. *Ep.* 44.7: *per insidiosum iter vitae non tantum ferunt sarcinas sed trahunt,* etc.

616 See 12.2 ff.

617 A common metaphor on this topic; cf. Sen. *Ep.* 96.5: *atqui vivere, Lucili, militare est; De provid.* 4.12: *verberat nos et lacerat fortuna? Patiamur: non est saevitia, certamen est.* (A gymnastic metaphor is also common; cf. 2 *Clem.* 20.2; Clem. *Strom.* 7.12.72.6.) Use of the military analogy was particularly favored in Christian writings: on this particular point cf. *Ad Diog.* 6.9 f.;

Clem. *Strom.* 4.11.78.1 f.; and for its general currency, see chap. 37.2 and n. 622.

The explanation that follows (that infirmities are a source of individual moral strength) was common; see *Ad Diog.* 6.9; Orig. *C.Cels.* 6.44, 6.56; Cyp. *De bon. pat.* 17; cf. 2 Cor. 12.9: *virtus in infirmitate perficitur;* Sen. *De provid.* 2.2: *omnia adversa exercitationes putat (sapiens);* 4.6: *calamitas virtutis occasio est.* Euseb. *H.E.* 7.30.21 observes that God permits persecutions "for the sake of training and conversions" (for the latter purpose, cf. Lact. *Div. inst.* 5.22.18). M.F. has (deliberately?) no word of such esoteric notions as atonement for mankind's sin, etc. The passage has a noticeably Stoic tone as a result.

[618] This second major point—infirmities are purposeful, God's loving means of testing our characters—is equally common; cf. Sen. *De provid.* 2.6 f., 4.7: *hos itaque deus quos probat, quos amat, indurat, recognoscit, exercet;* Tert. *Apol.* 37.3: *pati in quo (divina secta) probatur; De fuga* 3.1; Orig. *C.Cels.* 8.31; Clem. *Strom.* 4.11.78.1 f. (see E. F. Osborn, *The Philosophy of Clement of Alexandria* [Cambridge 1957] 70 ff.); Cyp. *Ep.* 11.5.3, *De mort.* 16: *explorat iustitiam singulorum et mentes humani generis examinat.*

[619] A proverbial comparison, common in biblical literature (Prov. 17.3, Sap. 3.6, Job 23.10, Mal. 3.2–3, 1 Peter 1.7), patristic literature (Hermas *Vis.* 4.3.4; Orig. *C.Cels.* 6.44, 5.15, 8.56—and, of course, canonical for martyrdom protreptics, Orig. *Exhort. ad marty.* 24; Euseb. *H.E.* 4.15.37 [Polycarp]; cf. *Mart. Polyc.* 16.2; *Mart. Fructuosi* 7.2 [Ruinart 267]; Cyp. *Ep.* 6.2.1), as well as pagan literature (Sen. *De provid.* 5.10; and see Otto *Sprichwörter* 170 f.; M. C. Sutphen, "A Collection of Latin Proverbs," AJP 22 [1902] 142 [*s.v.* ignis 2] for further instances).

[620] The chapter opens with a purple passage in praise of the spectacle provided by the Christian martyr, thus making a neat foil to the description, at the close of the chapter, of the disgraceful and degrading spectacles provided by pagan stage and amphitheatre. The misery of the Christians' sufferings had been briefly alluded to in 12.4; Octavius retorts, emphasizing their nobility and glory: Christians are no *pallidi, trepidi, misericordia digni* (12.6). Much is merely touched-up Stoic philosophizing on the *sapiens* contending with the vicissitudes of adversity, and bears a close resemblance to Sen. *De provid.* 2.7 ff.; cf. Aul. Gellius, *Noctes Atticae* 12.5.3; Orig. *C.Cels.* 2.45 (on Peter and

the other apostles): ". . . they were counted worthy to be put
to shame for His name, even surpassing many stories told by the
Greeks about the courage and bravery of the philosophers"
(trans. H. Chadwick). Of course, protreptic and martyrdom
literature is full of parallel hortatory phrases and illustrations;
e.g. 1 Cor. 4.9; Tert. *Ad mart.* 1.2 ff.; Clem. *Protr.* 10.95.3 ff.;
Orig. *Exhort. ad mart.* 18, 22; and frequently in Cyp. *Epp.* (e.g.,
37.1.3, 38.1.2, 58.8.1, 60.2.4).

   [621] *Vicit enim qui, quod contendit, obtinuit:* an aphorism more
appositely in place, in a similar context, in Tert. *Apol.* 50.2:
victoria est autem pro quo certaveris obtinere, where the prize
sought is not left unexplained (*gloriam placendi Deo et praedam
vivendi in aeternum*)—an incidental argument for the priority of
Tertullian (Heinze, *Tertullians Apologeticum* 482 n. 1). For the
context of this passage, cf. A. W. Ziegler, "Entwicklungstenden-
zen der frühchristlichen Staatslehre," *Kyriakon: Festschrift
Johannes Quasten* (Münster 1970) 49.

   [622] Christians as soldiers of Christ (cf. 36.8 above) is a very per-
vasive concept in early patristic literature. The basic analysis of
this theme is still the famous study of A. von Harnack, *Militia
Christi: Die christliche Religion und der Soldatenstand in den
ersten drei Jahrhunderten* (Tübingen 1905). Later literature has
tended to emphasize the frequency of usage in other contemporary classical religious and philosophical movements (cf. F.
Cumont, *Textes et monuments figurés relatifs aux mystères de
Mithra* 1 [Brussels 1899] 317 n. 1—followers of Isis, Egyptian
Gnostics, Stoic *sapientes*, Mithraic devotees; F. J. Dölger, "Sacramentum militiae," *AC* 2 [1930] 268 ff. For illustrations see Ch.
Pietri, "Le serment du soldat chrétien. Les épisodes de la *militia
Christi* sur les sarcophages," *Mél. d'arch. et d'hist.* 74 [1962] 649
ff.). The currency of the notion may possibly have given rise
to the technical use of *paganus* in Christian writings (= "mere
civilian"?: a very controversial topic; see recently, E. Bickel,
"Pagani: Kaiseranbeter in den Laren-Kapellen der pagi urbani
im Rom Neros und des Apostels Petrus," *RhM* 97 (1954) 1 ff.;
Mohrmann *Études* 3.277 ff.). 1 *Clem.* 37.1 ff., Ign. *Polyc.* 6.2 are
good examples of sustained metaphors on this theme. For Christians living under the eye of God, see 32.9 above and cf. Cyp.
Ep. 10.4.4: *militate fortiter, dimicate constanter, scientes vos sub
oculis praesentis Domini dimicare.*

[623] Cf. 2 Tim. 2.5: *nam et qui certat in agone, non coronatur nisi legitime certaverit.*

[624] As the Stoic *sapiens* in Sen. *De provid.* 3.1: *potest enim miser dici, non potest esse.*

[625] C. Mucius Scaevola attempted to assassinate the Etruscan king Porsenna, but he struck down his secretary by mistake. To elicit information from Scaevola, the king ordered him to be surrounded by menacing flames, but Scaevola plunged his right hand into the blazing hearth of an altar to prove that Roman fighting men cannot be intimidated. Impressed by such courage, Porsenna let him go free. The incident is related by Livy 2.12.1 ff., where see Ogilvie's nn. (The burning of the right arm sounds, in fact, like punishment for a broken oath.) Scaevola was prominent among the standard examples of Roman heroism; cf. Mart. *Epig.* 1.21, 8.30, 10.25; Sen. *De provid.* 3.4 f. (along with Fabricius, Rutilius [cf. 5.12 above], Regulus [cf. 26.3, and below], Socrates and Cato); Tert. *Ad mart.* 4.4 ff. (along with Regulus, Heraclitus, Empedocles, Peregrinus, Dido, etc.), *Apol.* 50.5 f. (along with Empedocles, Regulus, Anaxarchus, etc., and emphasizing the foolhardiness and vainglory of the pagan *exempla*), etc. The choice of example may have been partly dictated by "the test of fire" theme, on which see F. J. Dölger, "Der Feuertod ohne die Liebe: Antike Selbstverbrennung und christlicher Martyrium-Enthusiasmus. Ein Beitrag zu 1 Korinther 13,3," AC 1 (1929) 254 ff.; J. Gagé, "Le livre sacré et l'épreuve de feu," *Mullus*, 1964, 130 ff.; cf. the behavior of the Christian martyrs at Antioch, Euseb. *H.E.* 8.12.2: some put their right hands into the very fire sooner than touch the accursed sacrifice.

[626] For Regulus see n. 412. Manius Aquilius (cos. 101 B.C.), partisan and legate of Marius, was captured by Mithridates in 88 B.C. Mithridates poured molten gold down his throat to rebuke Roman venality; see Appian *De bell. Mithrid.* 21; Pliny *N.H.* 33.48; PW 2.1 (1895) 324–26 Aquilius no. 11 (E. Klebs). Arnob. 1.40 compares with Christ Aquilius and Regulus (as well as Pythagoras, Socrates, Trebonius).

Of the many articles on *exempla* literature, note M. L. Carlson, "Pagan Examples of Fortitude in the Latin Christian Apologists," CP 43 (1948) 93 ff.; H. W. Litchfield, "National *exempla virtutis* in Roman Literature," HSCP 25 (1914) 1 ff.; R. Helm, "Valerius Maximus, Seneca und die 'Exemplasammlung,'" *Hermes* 74 (1939) 130 ff.

[627] See n. 446; there is an incidental retort to 12.4 *ubi deus ille, qui subvenire . . . viventibus non potest?* Prime example at this period of such *patientia* would be *Passio ss. Felic. et Perpet.* 15; cf. *Ad Diog.* 7.9 (on Christian steadfastness and Christian expansion): "these things do not seem to be the works of man; these things are a miracle of God; these things are the proof of His coming."

[628] The wicked prospering and the righteous suffering was standard discussion material of disputes on providence (cf. Sext. Emp. *P.H.* 1.32; Philo. *De prov.* 2.13 [Aucher]; Orig. *C.Cels.* 3.38; 2 *Clem.* 20.1 f.; and chap. 5.11 f. above). For the present proverbial image, cf. Juv. *Sat.* 10.105 ff.: *numerosa parabat / excelsae turris tabulata, unde altior esset casus* (of Sejanus); Livy 30.30.23: *quanto altius elatus est, eo foedius conruit;* and see Otto *Sprichwörter s.v.* altus (xlii and 17).

[629] For *coronae* see nn. 25, 161; for this present usage, Mayor on Juv. *Sat.* 13.63: *coronata agna,* and cf. Tert. *De cor.* 10.9: *ipsae hostiae et arae, ipsi ministri ac sacerdotes eorum coronantur.*

[630] . . . *ut ingenium eorum perditae mentis licentiae potestatis libere nundinentur.* The precise construing of this passage has caused much divergence of opinion. Others translate variously, and not always intelligibly, e.g., "that the unrestricted exercise of power might make a market of their spirit to the unbridled licence that is characteristic of a ruined soul" (Wallis), "that by a reckless use of power they may freely market the character of their wicked minds" (Arbesmann), "that the dissoluteness of power may have unchecked traffic in their abandoned character" (Fahy), "that their profligate favourites may take advantage of them at pleasure" (Dalrymple), etc.

[631] A passage of uncertain punctuation; for a recent (but unconvincing) discussion, see F. Scheidweiler, "Zu Minucius Felix," *Hermes* 82 (1954) 489 ff., at 491 f. To translate *cum mors sit* (with Waltzing, Halm, van Wageningen, etc.) as "since ignorance of God is death" seems unduly strained in the context. For the general idea, cf. Prudent. *Cath.* 1.25 f.: *Hic somnus ad tempus datus / est forma mortis perpetis.* This passage seems designed to refute the charge that Christians have no real enjoy- ment of life (e.g., 12.6); there is further refutation in the next chapter (38.4).

[632] There follows a series of characteristically Stoic points customarily made when characterizing the *sapiens* and depicting his *vita beata;* worldly goods and fortunes, power and prestige are

to him affairs of complete indifference: virtue alone matters. For the standard litany on this type, see Pohlenz 1.261 ff., and cf. esp. Apul. *De deo Socr.* 23.175; for the Christianization of this model figure, note esp. Clem. *Strom.* 2.21.129.1 ff. (Christ as the realization of the ideal *sapiens* of Stoic aspiration) and see the evidence gathered by W. Völker, *Der wahre Gnostiker nach Clemens Alexandrinus* (Berlin 1952) 507 ff.; P. Wilpert, RAC 1 (1950) *s.v.* Autarkie 1039–50; Spanneut 243 ff. There is a passage similar to this section of the *Octavius* in Cyp. *Ad Donat.* 3 (ML 4.199 f.), but it hardly constitutes an "emprunt probable" (*contra* Beaujeu, Intro. lxix).

⁶³³ A proverbial notion ascribed to Laberius *ap.* Sen. *Dial* 4.11.4: *necesse est multos timeat quem multi timet,* to Publil. Syr. *ap.* Macrob. *Sat.* 2.7.4. Other instances are cited by Otto *Sprichwörter* 349 *s.v.* Timere.

⁶³⁴ For the image see n. 615 above. On *viaticum* in Christian usage, note the study of G. Grabka, "Christian Viaticum: A Study of Its Cultural Background," *Traditio* 9 (1953) 1 ff.

⁶³⁵ I.e., *fasces,* bundles of rods carried by a Roman magistrate's attendants ("lictors") and symbolic of the powers of authority and coercion invested in his office. This is the final reply to the Christians' rejection of such public offices (see 8.4, 32.6).

⁶³⁶ On this point cf. 16.5, 17.2, 31.8 and nn. *ad loca;* Sen. *Benef.* 3.18 (virtue embraces all, freedmen, slaves, and kings), *Benef.* 3.28.1: *eadem omnibus principia eademque origo; nemo altero nobilior, nisi cui rectius ingenium et artibus bonis aptius; Ep.* 47.10: *vis tu cogitare istum, quem servum tuum vocas, ex isdem seminibus ortum;* Cyp. *Ad Demetr.* 8: *eadem sors nascendi, condicio una moriendi.*

⁶³⁷ The abstention of Christians from such public events had been criticized in 12.5, on which see n. 158.

⁶³⁸ The idolatrous connexions are denounced by Tert. *De spect.* 5 ff.; [Cyp.] *De spect.* 4; Tert. *Apol.* 38.4: *aeque spectaculis vestris in tantum renuntiamus in quantum originibus eorum quas scimus de superstitione conceptas;* Lact. *Div. inst.* 6.20.34 ff.

⁶³⁹ The intense rivalry and fanatical rioting aroused among the circus factions, the supporters of the rival chariot teams of the blues, the greens, the reds, and the whites, is liberally described and castigated by Juv. *Sat.* 11.193 ff., with other references supplied in Mayor's commentary, esp. Pliny *Ep.* 9.6; [Cyp.] *De spect.* 5; Tert. *De spect.* 9.5, 16.1 ff.

[640] *Homicidium* has already been denounced in 30.6, where see n. 507 for parallels.

[641] For the *furor* of the theatrical audiences, see Tert. *De spect.* 16; for the notorious *turpitudo* of the theatrical productions, see Tert. *Apol.* 38.4, *De spect.* 17; [Cyp.] *De spect.* 3; Cyp. *Ad Donat.* 8; Theoph. *Ad Autol.* 3.15; Tat. *Or.* 22. Actors were not admitted into the Church (implied in Tert. *De idol.* 5.2 f. and especially Cyp. *Ep.* 2) and were vehemently condemned by the ecclesiastical authorities; see DACL 11.1 (1933) *s.v.* mime 1203–5 (H. Leclercq).

[642] "Actor of farce" = *mimus* (who performed with dialogue); "effeminate pantomime" = *enervis histrio*. The effeminacy of actors was notorious, and they might act women's parts or depict unnatural vices as well; see Arnob. 7.33; Tat. *Or.* 22; Tert. *De spect.* 17, 23.6; cf. Cyp. *Ep.* 2, *Ad Donat.* 8 (ML 4.211) *evirantur mares;* Tert. *Apol.* 15.3 on the (frequently) castrated *histrio* (*corpus inpurum et ad istam artem effeminatione productum);* and see Mayor on Juv. *Sat.* 3.93 ff. The *histrio* mimed (with or without assistant chorus, music, etc.).

[643] This pointed remark, casting further into the pagans' camp the charge of blood lust (see chap. 30), seems scarcely in place in the sequence of thought just here.

[644] The charge of 12.5, on which see n. 159. Octavius does not reply directly to the Christians' avoidance of *convivia publica*, which had also been raised in that section. Origen *C.Cels.* 8.21 ff. amasses the arguments in reply, one of which was that Christians must avoid being partakers of the table of demons (the argument used here on sacrificial food and drink). The *locus classicus* for such an argument is, of course, 1 Cor. 10.18 ff.; Tert. *Apol.* 35.2 ff. emphasizes the moral dangers of such public festivities.

[645] A direct riposte to 12.5: *sic reformidatis deos quos negatis.*

[646] See n. 536 for this view of creation, and cf. 1 Tim. 4.4: *quia omnis creatura Dei bona est et nihil reiciendum quod cum gratiarum actione percipitur;* and contrast Tert. *De cult. fem.* 2.5.4: *quod nascitur opus dei est: ergo quod infingitur, diaboli negotium est.*

[647] The famous arguments of 1 Cor. 10.18 ff.: for a fuller statement along the same lines, see Orig. *C.Cels.* 8.24; Tert. *Apol.* 27.1 f., *De spect.* 13. For the demons and sacrifices, see n. 439.

[648] The question of the use of flowers and garlands had been raised in 12.6. Octavius replies only tangentially to the charge

of denying *odores* to the body; he merely emphasizes that Christians do use fragrant flowers—but not in an unnatural manner.

⁶⁴⁹ This same feeble jest is also to be found in Tert. *De cor.* 5.9 f., *Apol.* 42.6 (see Axelson 44); Clem. *Paed.* 2.8.63.4 ff. As so often, the basic reasons have been left unstated; for those see n. 161. A similar observation is also to be found in Lucian *Nigrin.* 32: those who delight in the odors of violets and roses should be crowned under the nose; he is citing Momus, a figure of fable. The notion may, therefore, have been traditional.

⁶⁵⁰ A further retort against cremation; see 11.4, 34.10. J. G. Préaux, "A propos d'un dilemme de Minucius Félix," *Latomus* 14 (1955) 262 ff., argues—unconvincingly—for the reading *fascem* ("bunch of flowers") to replace *facem* ("torch"). But the passage has obviously been composed, in part, as a rejoinder to 11.4 with *si sentiunt . . . si non sentiunt* there, matched by *aut* [*non*] *sentienti . . . aut non sentienti* here. (For further doubts on Préaux' article, see Beaujeu *ad loc.*) Reeves (in trans. 1717) interprets "a light before the dead" (on which custom see n. 161), but such a custom has not been mentioned hitherto and is less appropriate to the context. For the thought here, cf. Diog. Laer. 4.7.48 (Bion): "He used to condemn those who burnt men as if they had no feelings and burnt offerings (or lamps) to them as if they had." (Hardly "cauterized" [for "burnt offerings": παρακαόντων] as translated by R. D. Hicks, Loeb Classical Library 1.1925: that meaning is possible but does not suit the context; see L.S.J.⁹ *s.v.*); cf. *Gnom. Vat.* 20, ed. L. Sternbach, WSt 9 (1887) 175 ff., at 186 (Anacharsis observing the same paradoxical behavior, in similar terms).

⁶⁵¹ A highly favoured eschatological image; see 1 Pet. 5.4: *immarcescibilem gloriae coronam;* 1 Cor. 9.25: *coronam . . . incorruptam;* James 1.12: *coronam vitae;* Herm. *Sim.* 8.2.1, 8.3.6, etc.; and standard for descriptions of martyrs (e.g., Euseb. *H.E.* 1.5.36—Lyons and Vienne; *Act. Fructuosi* [Ruinart 267]: *o beati martyres . . . qui coronati sunt diademate et corona immarcescibili).* See, generally, J. Daniélou, *Les symboles chrétiens primitifs* (Paris 1961) 21 ff. Octavius has omitted to give any justification for the Christian practice of reserving *unguenta* for funerals exclusively (see 12.6 and n. 160).

⁶⁵² *Quieti, modesti . . . dei nostri liberalitate securi:* these phrases reply to 12.7: *pallidi, trepidi, misericordia digni sed nostrorum deorum;* cf., in praise of the πραΰς and the ἡσύχιος,

Herm. *Mand.* 11.8; *Ep. Barn.* 19.4; *Did.* 3.8; Ign. *Trall.* 4.2; Matt. 5.4; 1 Pet. 3.4: *quieti et modesti spiritus.*

653 Cf. Tert. *Apol.* 19.8 (Fuld.): *unde et spes nostra quam ridetis animatur.*

654 A direct reply to 12.6 *ita nec resurgitis miseri nec interim vivitis;* for the sentiment cf. 1 Thess. 4.13 ff., Arist, *Apol.* 15.

655 This peroration is intended to match that of Caecilius (chap. 13). Socrates (chap. 13.1, where see n. 165) appeared there, qua founder of the Academic *secta,* as *sapientiae principem;* he, therefore, appears here, in contrast, as *scurra Atticus,* a quotation of the judgment of Zeno *Epicureus* (see Cic. *De nat. deor.* 1.93 and Pease *ad loc.*).

The testimony of philosophy has been cited with great liberality by Octavius, and one of his major endeavors has been to establish a certain measure of fundamental agreement between Christian beliefs and pagan philosophical theories (in the manner of Justin and Athenagoras); and in the following chapter Octavius is in effect credited with having successfully routed pagan philosophers on their own ground. It comes, therefore, as a somewhat jarring surprise that Octavius should be made to conclude his speech with what appears to be an immoderately phrased antiphilosophical polemic (in the manner of Tatian, Theophilus, and Tertullian). But it should be observed that Octavius is primarily concerned with attacking the Academic school of philosophy, the characteristic hesitant scepticism of which was favorably invoked by Caecilius in chap. 13. The school of thought Octavius has appealed to most consistently has been the traditional archenemy of the Academy, the Stoa, and Octavius ends, by contrast with Caecilius, on a note of triumphantly positive discovery and resolute confidence. The literary effect is obvious and has dictated the tone.

It must be agreed, however, that Octavius tends to slip into a tirade against pagan philosophy *generally,* as he picks up one of the commonplace themes of the protreptic composition: the inconsistency between philosophic profession and teaching, and philosophic action and practice. It provided copybook material for the *refutatio* of one's opponents (see P. Hartlich, "De exhortationum a Graecis Romanisque scriptorum historia et indole," *Leipzig Stud.* 11 [1889] 302 f., 306 ff.); and by means of this standard literary material Christians are thus made to emerge (versus not merely Academic but pagan philosophers generally) as the only true and successful philosophers. He has completely vindicated the *sectae sinceritas* (40.2). In the phrasing of this material, the influence of a parallel passage in Tert. *Apol.* 46.10 ff. on the vices of all manner of philosophers, not merely Academic, seems to be palpable (see Axelson 23 f., 97 ff.).

G. L. Ellspermann, *The Attitude of the Early Christian Latin Writers towards Pagan Literature and Learning* (Washington, D.C. 1949) 18, observes of this passage that in it M.F. shows "the marks of a discerning man . . . like Lactantius and Augustine he would not condemn pagan religion in its entirety, but, at the same time, he is forced, as a Christian, to withhold praise of the philosophers at the inevitable point of departure from Christian truth." But one rather suspects that while an attack on false scepticism was appropriate as a preliminary to a Christian commitment, yet artistic balance and rhetorical procedures ultimately dictated the particular terms of attack.

[656] *viderit:* a very common term of dismissal; see Pease on Cic. *De nat. deor.* 1.19: *Cotta viderit.*

[657] *testimonio licet fallacissimi daemonis gloriosus.* This ought to reply to 13.2 and thus to be a reference to the *testimonium* of the Delphic oracle (inhabited by a demon, as expounded in 26.5 ff.). But the allusion has been frequently, and perhaps more naturally, taken to be to Socrates' familiar spirit, his *daemonium* (see 26.9), which figures in the passage of Tert. *Apol.* 46.5 that M.F. appears to be exploiting. In 26.9 the example of Socrates' attendant demon was cited without any note of criticism, though later (27.2) we were told generally of demons *et falluntur et fallunt;* hence it could be described as *fallacissimus* here.

[658] On Arcesilaus and Carneades, see n. 168 above.

[659] Pyrrhon (c. 360–c. 270 B.C., of Elis) did not occur in Caecilius' list (13.3): he was the founder of the non-Academic branch of the sceptical school of philosophy (Pyrrhonism); see PW 24 (1963) 89–106 (K. von Fritz), and note the discussion in Aul. Gellius, *Noctes Atticae* 11.5, on the basic differences between the two branches (esp. §8).

[660] The anecdote is recounted in 13.4.

[661] *philosophorum supercilia:* cf. Sen. *Ep.* 94.9: *quae ingenti supercilio philosophi iactant.* Instead of continuing to talk about Sceptic philosophers in particular, Octavius, by an unannounced transition, seems now to be discussing all (pagan) philosophers generally.

[662] For this catalogue of philosophers' hypocritical vices (a common theme), cf. Tat. *Or.* 25; Just. *Apol.* 1.4; Lucian *De mort. Pereg.* 24, *Cynic.* 18 f.; Sen. *Ep.* 29.5 f.; and for many other references and quotations, T. B. L. Webster, *Studies in Later Greek Comedy* (Manchester 1953) 50 ff. In Tert. *Apol.* 46.10 ff. these particular vices figure *inter alia* with examples: Socrates as corruptor of youth (46.10—paederasty being a very common charge against philosophers: see Pease on Cic. *De nat. deor.* 1.79: *concedentibus antiquis*), Speusippus (see n. 246) as adulterer (46.10), Pythagoras and Zeno as aspiring to tyranny (46.13), Pythagoras at Thurii (cf. Arnob. 1.40), Zeno at Priene (otherwise unattested). It was also a common charge that Plato taught his philosophy pupils to seek after tyranny; Platonic pupils who became tyrants included Chieron (of Pellene), Hermias (of Atarneus and Assos). For the charge with further details, see Athenaeus 11.508D ff. (and cf. chap. 19.14 and n. 259).

[663] *semper adversus sua vitia facundos.* Cf. Aul. Gellius, *Noctes Atticae* 13.8.5 (quoting his friend Macedo): *nihil enim fieri potest indignius neque intolerantius dicebat quam quod homines . . . operti barba et pallio . . . vitia facundissime accusarent intercutibus ipsi vitiis madentes;* Sen. *fr.* 18 Haase *ap.* Lact. *Div. inst.* 3.15.11: *plerique . . . philosophorum tales sunt, diserti in convicium suum;* Juv. *Sat.* 2.9 f., 20 f.

[664] *Nos non habitu sapientiam sed mente praeferimus, non eloquimur magna sed vivimus.* For the thought cf. 31.5 above; it was a cliché to observe that a philosophical cloak, unkempt hair, nails and beard, and philosopher's talk did not make a genuine philosopher (e.g., Sen. *Ep.* 5.1; there are many examples in patristic writings: see Spanneut 102 ff. for abundant references). Cyp. *De bon. pat.* 3: *nos . . . nec vestitu sapientiam sed veritate praeferimus . . . qui non loquimur magna sed vivimus,* is, however, so close in expression that it is prudent to conclude that one must be dependent on the other; of the 8 "emprunts sûrs" (of Cyprian from M.F.) listed by Beaujeu (lxix), this is the most palpable and persuasive. For the implications for setting a *terminus ante* for the composition of the Octavius (i.e., before the mid-third century), see Beaujeu lxii ff. See also E. W. Watson, "The Style and Language of St. Cyprian," *Studia biblica* 4 (1896) 189 ff., at 225 n. 1. The possibility that such phrases may come from a third source must remain, but under the present circumstances and given the scatter of other possible parallels throughout

Cyprian's works, it is a reasonable course to conclude that Cyprian had read and drawn from the *Octavius*.

⁶⁶⁵ A slight hint at the problem of the lateness of the appearance of Christianity: if it is the sole source of grace and truth, why so tardy? See the objections raised by Porphyry *ap*. Aug. *Ep*. 102.8 (CSEL 34.551) (= Harnack *fr*. 81) and note the replies to the objection in Arnob. 2.63, 2.74 f.; *Ad Diog*. 9; Orig. *C.Cels*. 4.7, 6.78.

⁶⁶⁶ *fruamur nostro bono*. K. Büchner, "Drei Beobachtungen zu Minucius Felix," *Hermes* 82 (1954) 231 ff., discusses the literary affinities of this passage. He compares Tac. *Dial*. 41: *bono saeculi sui quisque . . . utatur*, and from the comparison concludes (unnecessarily) that M.F. means here *fruamur nostro bono temporis*; cf. Sen. *Ep*. 26.2: *bono suo utatur*, where there is no such temporal connection.

⁶⁶⁷ *recti sententiam temperemus*. This is clearly intended to stand in contrast (as are also the following clauses) with the concluding remarks of Caecilius in 13.5. There Caecilius had, sceptically, remarked: *nec . . . temere et audaciter in alteram partem ferenda sententia est*. Therefore, the present passage seems best interpreted as "let us keep our verdict (unlike yours) on what is right within due bounds"; or as a more direct reply, "let us qualify the verdict you gave on what is right"—with the carefully reversed optatives immediately following.

⁶⁶⁸ For the *superstitio . . . religio* motif, see n. 10: the roles have been inverted from 13.5.

⁶⁶⁹ An echo from Vergil *Aen*. 2.1: *conticuere omnes, intentique ora tenebant*, describing the effect of Aeneas' narrative on his audience. For the silence cf. Plato *Phaedo* 84C; Varro *De re rust*. 1.49.1: *cum conticuisset nec interrogaretur. . . .* If the work is a complete literary fiction, such a retrospective judgment seems a trifle gauche and naïve, but cf. 1.5, 14.1 and 3 for similar judgments. And other (literary) dialogues have their interlocutors make parallel remarks; cf. Cic. *De orat*. 2.89.362; Tac. *Dial*. 24.1; Plato *Protag*. 328D; Lucian *Nigr*. 4, 38. For examples of the device in Augustine see J. J. O'Meara, "The Historicity of the Early Dialogues of Saint Augustine," VC 5 (1951) 150 ff. at 174 ff.

⁶⁷⁰ *et argumentis et exemplis et lectionum auctoritatibus*: standard categories of rhetorical demonstration. M.F. carefully underscores the methods that Octavius has endeavored to exploit in

order to carry conviction. They would appeal especially to the rhetorically trained.

[671] *facilius est sentire quam dicere.* J. G. Préaux (comparing Cyp. *Ad Donat.* 2: *Accipe quod sentitur antequam discitur*) in "A propos du 'De fato'(?) de Minucius Felix," *Latomus* 9 (1950) 394 ff., at 395 n. 1, and in "A propos d'un dilemme de Minucius Félix," *Latomus* 14 (1955) 262 ff., at 269–70 n. 3, suggests *discere* for *dicere*. But surely erroneously. M.F. is referring back to 19.14 and Plato's adage on the impossibility of making a public statement about God; Octavius has now done what Plato thought to be an impossibility.

[672] *malevolos isdem illis, quibus armantur, philosophorum telis retudisset:* another important underscoring of a major object of the *Octavius*—to tackle pagan philosophers on their own ground.

[673] Note the deliberate reference back to the opening chapter, a description of silent soliloquy.

[674] A final and important underlining of the major theses of the *Octavius:* (1) the establishment of a providential dispensation in the world; (2) the existence of the unique, benevolent, and all-powerful Christian God; (3) the refutation of the calumnies spread against the Christian *secta* (on which word see n. 32).

[675] Caecilius' adoption of Christianity seems more than a little perfunctory. But the way is now left open for further instruction in the technical dogma of Christianity in which the *Octavius* is so notably deficient. In fact, the saving clause may have been deliberately inserted as an admission that the present dialogue was not designed to present the full and complete truth; but this point cannot be pressed, as in making this remark M.F. is also following literary convention (see next note); cf. one of M.F.'s literary forebears, St. Paul, in Acts 17.32 ff.: when Paul finished speaking, some of his audience desired to hear more (*audiemus te de hoc iterum*) and as a result of further instruction some came to believe.

[676] To conclude a dialogue with the onset of evening and to suggest that the discussion will be continued at a later date was a standard procedure (called by Hirzel *Dialog* 1.534 a *deus ex machina*); cf. Tac. *Dial.* 42.1: *erant de quibus plura dici vellem nisi iam dies exactus . . . de iis rursus conferemus;* Cic. *De fin.* 4.80: *sed quoniam advesperascit . . . nunc quidem hactenus; verum hoc idem faciamus saepe;* Cic. *De nat. deor.* 3.94: *sed quoniam advesperascit, dabis nobis diem aliquem ut contra ista*

dicamus; Lucian *Anach.* 40 (with both adjournment and evening); so, too, [Clem.] *Hom.* 2.53.1; Cyp. *Ad Donat.* 16: *inclinante iam sole in vesperam;* cf. Tert. *Adv. Iud.* 1.1: *alternis vicibus contentioso fune uterque diem in vesperam traxerunt;* Aul. Gellius, *Noctes Atticae* 18.1.16: *sed cum iam prima fax noctis et densiores esse tenebrae coepissent . . . discessimus;* Macrob. *Sat.* 1.1: *nec discedentes a se nisi ad nocturnam quietem;* Sulp. Sev. *Dial.* 1.27.6: *iam solis occidui umbra prolixior monet. . . ;* 2.14.7 f.: *nox ipsa cogebat . . . cras reliqua dicemus;* see also W. Speyer, "Octavius, Der Dialog des Minucius Felix: Fiktion oder historische Wirklichkeit?" JAC 7 (1964) 45 ff., at 47 n. 15.

⁶⁷⁷ *de toto congruentes promptius requiremus.* The concluding words of Caecilius have appropriately a contrasting echo of his opening speech (4.4): *de toto integro mihi cum Octavius res est . . . ;* (4.5) *intentius disputare.* For the general idea, cf. Cyp. *Ep.* 73.3.2.

⁶⁷⁸ *laeti hilaresque discessimus.* A cheerful departure to end a discussion was again a *topos* of dialogue technique; cf. Tac. *Dial.* 42.2: *cum adrisissent, discessimus;* Cic. *De orat.* 1.62.265: *et cum surgeret, simul arridens. . . ;* Cic. *Acad. pr.* 2.148: *Tum ille ridens . . . ita sermone confecto Catulus remansit: nos ad naviculas nostras descendimus;* and cf. Cic. *De fin.* 4.80: *quae cum essent dicta, discessimus;* Cic. *De nat. deor.* 3.95: *Haec cum essent dicta, ita discessimus ut . . .* (and Pease *ad loc.*); Plat. *Phaedr.* 279b. It is unnecessary to conclude, with Beaujeu, that *laeti hilaresque* has been borrowed from Sen. *Ep.* 12.9; they are not an uncommon pair, cf. Juv. 15.41: *laetum hilaremque diem;* Cic. *Tusc.* 1.42.100: *vultu hilari atque laeto;* Columel. 4.27.1: *laetius et hilarius;* Auson. 5.7.1: *laetos hilaresque mores;* and again in Sen. *Ep.* 66.15: *hilaris et laeta.*

⁶⁷⁹ Throughout the *Octavius* M.F. seems to have been careful not to stress overmuch the basis of Christian faith as "belief" (*pistis*). For one bred on Greek philosophy that would be the lowest form of cognition, tantamount to a slur on the intelligence. M.F., by giving the rationale first and putting the belief last, rebuts the charge and criticism leveled so frequently against Christianity by, e.g., Lucian *Pereg.* 13 (Christian beliefs are unsupported by evidence); Galen (R. Walzer, *Galen on Jews and Christians* [Oxford 1949] 15: Christians have three cardinal virtues, courage, self-control, justice; but they lack the fourth, *phronēsis*); Celsus *ap.* Orig. *C.Cels.* 1.9 (some Christians say

"Do not ask questions, just believe"), 3.75, 6.11; Porphyry *Adv. christ. fr.* 1.17, 73 Harnack (protesting against an irrational and unexamined *pistis*); Julian (*ap.* Greg. Naz. *Or.* 4.102 [MG 35.637]: there is nothing in your philosophy beyond the one word "Believe!"). For further discussion see Walzer, *op. cit.* 48 ff.

INDEXES

1. OLD AND NEW TESTAMENT

2. AUTHORS

3. LATIN WORDS

4. GENERAL INDEX

abortion, 107, 333
Abraham, 159
Academy, Academics, 27, 28, 71, 124, 181, 182, 196, 241 f., 251, 268, 324, 371, 372
Acca Larentia, 97, 306
Acta of martyrs, 154, 321, 322; *Acta Apollonii*, 240, 258, 298, 323, 325, 329; *Justini*, 155, 213; *Fructuosi*, 364; *Perpetuae et Felicitatis*, 195, 367; *Pionii*, 237, 329, 358; *Polycarpi*, 204, 212, 225, 232, 261, 364; *Acts of John*, 284; *of Paul and Thecla*, 340; *of Peter*, 319
Actaeon, 285
actors, Christian attitudes towards, 369
Adauctus, 36
Admetus, 90
Adonis, 238
Aemilian, 35
Aemilianus, Fulvius, 151
Aeneas, 90
aerarium Saturni, 293
Aesculapius, 59, 89, 191, 210, 279, 284, 285, 287
Aethiopia, 192
Aetna, Mt., 117, 282, 358
Africa, Africans, 7, 43, 92, 99, 108, 135, 153, 161, 163, 166, 178, 180, 278, 292, 295, 307, 309, 334
agape, 208, 215, 221
Agnes, 155
Agrippina, 339
Albula, river, 305
Alcmaeon of Croton, 267
Alexamenos, 155, 217 f., 220
Alexander Severus, 40 f., 43, 157–159, 226, 329
Alexander the Great, 87, 159, 250, 275, 277 f.

Alexander the Phrygian, 162
Alexandria, 276
Allia, 61, 200 f.
altars, no Christian, 66, 111, 225 f., 342
Amalthea, 283
Amasis, 298
Ambrosius, 41
Ammon, 277, 278
Amphiaraus, 99, 309
Anabis, 328
Anacharsis, 370
Anatolius of Alexandria, 162
Anaxagoras, 83, 267
Anaxarchus, 366
Anaximander, 266
Anaximenes, 83, 266 f.
Ancyra, Council of, 333
angels, 100, 311 f., 314; Gnostic angelology, 217
anger, attributed to gods, 196
Anthologia Palatina, 210
Antias, 306
Antiochus Epiphanes, 217
antiquity, attitudes towards, 13–16, 21, 60, 116, 140, 142, 189 f., 195, 273, 288, 351, 354
Antisthenes, 83, 268
Antonius Julianus, 114, 348 f.
Antonius Severianus, 35, 151
Anubis, 174, 281, 324
Aphrodite, 192, 210
Apion, 223
Apis, 105, 324
Apocalypse of St. Peter, 228
Apollinaris of Laodicea, Elder and Younger, 20, 144
Apollo, 87, 89, 90, 99, 184, 210, 238, 276, 284, 310
Apollonius, senator, 34, 35, 150, 151, 321

405

philosophy, pagan, Christian attitudes towards, 31, 85, 179 f., 240, 265, 273, 371–373
Picumnus, 305
Picus, 97, 305
Pilumnus, 97, 305
Pionius, 237, 321
Pittacus, 242, 359
Pius, Pope, 163
plough, symbol of, 107, 332
Pluto, 276, 279, 282
poetry, attitude towards, 69, 234, 263 f., 287 f.
Polla Argentaria, 223
Pollux, 197, 198
Polycarp, 160, 224, 329
Polynices, 259, 342
Pompey, 260
Pontian, Pope, 46
Poppaea Sabina, 40, 157
Porsenna, 366
Poseidon, 211, 283, 300
Posidonius, Posidonian, 252, 254, 260, 261, 269
Potone, 268
poverty, Christian, 69, 119, 234 f., 247 f., 362
prayer, formulae of, 202; stance during, 332
Procne, 274
Proculus, 39, 156
Proculus, Julius, 92, 294 f.
Prodicus, 87, 247, 275–277
Prometheus, 357
promiscuity, charges of, 64, 65, 105, 109, 339
Prosenes, 39 f.
Prosperine, 282, 300, 339
prostitution, 105, 216, 301, 306, 307, 326, 339
Protagoras, 62, 204, 205, 268
Protesilaus, 69, 234
Protogonus, 185
providence, providentia, 28–30, 58, 80, 85, 125, 149, 187, 188, 228, 233, 253–258, 261, 308, 361, 367, 375
Ptha, 278
Ptolemy, 338
public office, Christians in, 211, 212
Pyriphlegethon, 356

Pyrrhon, 124, 372
Pyrrhus, 99, 310
Pythagoras, Pythagorean, 83, 115, 159, 218, 234, 267, 312, 315, 317, 325, 351 f., 353, 366, 373
Pytheas, 360

Quadratus, 152

Regulus, M. Atilius, 99, 308, 366
Remus, 259, 260, 300, 342
resurrection, 30, 68 f., 115 f., 230 f., 233 f., 351 f., 353 f.
Rhampsinitus, 234
Rhea, 283, 339
rhetoric, deceptiveness of, 245
Rome, 6, 24, 25, 31, 39, 44, 46, 47, 52, 61, 70, 88, 97, 157, 163, 166, 178, 192–194, 197, 227, 236, 271, 302, 304, 326
Romulus, 92, 96, 97, 259, 260, 294 f., 300, 302 f., 305, 306, 308, 342
Rufius Albinus, 142
Rumor, 216, 323
Rutilius Rufus, 58, 188, 366

Sabines, rape of, 303
sacrifices, human, 108, 334–336; spiritual, 111, 343
Sages, seven, 82, 265 f.
Salii, 98, 300
Sardinia, 40
Sarpedon, 90
Saturn, 89, 91, 92, 102, 108, 191, 282, 285, 291–294, 305, 323, 333, 334
Satyrs, 323
Scapula, 39, 153
scepticism, 71, 181 f., 196, 204, 324, 372
Scillitan Martyrs, 321
Scylla, 86, 274
seasons, and their crops, 78, 253 f.; argument from, 253 f.
Senate, Christians in, 33, 35–38
Sentinum, 199
Septimius Severus, 38, 39, 42, 159, 203, 206, 329
Septizonium, 361
Serapis, 53, 87, 102, 105, 174, 175, 279, 326, 328